Analysis and Synthesis of Speech

Speech Research 11

Editors

Vincent J. van Heuven
Louis C. W. Pols

Mouton de Gruyter
Berlin · New York

Analysis and Synthesis of Speech

Strategic Research towards High-Quality Text-to-Speech Generation

Edited by

Vincent J. van Heuven
Louis C. W. Pols

Mouton de Gruyter
Berlin · New York 1993

Mouton de Gruyter (formerly Mouton, The Hague)
is a division of Walter de Gruyter & Co., Berlin.

⊗ Printed on acid-free paper which falls within the guidelines of the ANSI to ensure permanence and durability.

Library of Congress Cataloging-in-Publication Data

Analysis and synthesis of speech ; strategic research towards high-quality text-to-speech generation / edited by Vincent J. van Heuven, Louis C. W. Pols.
p. cm.
Includes bibliographical references and index.
ISBN 3-11-013588-4 (acid-free paper)
1. Speech processing systems. 2. Speech synthesis. I. Heuven. Vincent van. II. Pols, Louis C. W., 1941–
TK7882.S65A55 1993
006.4′54–dc20 93-1487
CIP

Die Deutsche Bibliothek – Cataloging-in-Publication Data

Analysis and synthesis of speech : strategic research towards high quality text to speech generation / ed. by Vincent J. van Heuven ; Louis C. W. Pols. – Berlin ; New York : Mouton de Gruyter, 1993
(Speech research ; 11)
ISBN 3-11-013588-4
NE: Heuven, Vincent J. van [Hrsg.]; GT

Camera-ready copy prepared by Holland Academic Typesetting, The Hague.
Printing: Ratzlow-Druck, Berlin.
Binding: Dieter Mikolai, Berlin.
Printed in Germany.

Contents

List of figures IX

List of tables XIII

Preface XVII

Antonie Cohen and Sieb G. Nooteboom
A five year research program "Analysis and Synthesis of Speech" 1

1. Input characteristics

Irena Petrič and Huub van den Bergh
Text features affecting listening performance in one way speech communication 13

Yvonne van Holsteijn
TextScan: A preprocessing module for automatic text-to-speech conversion 27

2. Linguistic aspects

Johan M. Lammens
Multiple paths to the lexicon 45

Josée S. Heemskerk and Vincent J. van Heuven
MORPA: A morpheme lexicon based morphological parser 67

Anneke M. Nunn and Vincent J. van Heuven
MORPHON: Lexicon-based text-to-phoneme conversion and phonological rules 87

Jeroen Reizevoort and Vincent J. van Heuven
Pattern-driven morphological decomposition 101

Hugo Quené and René Kager
Prosodic sentence analysis without parsing 115

Arthur Dirksen and Hugo Quené
Prosodic analysis: The next generation 131

3. Building blocks for speech synthesis

Rob Drullman and René Collier
Speech synthesis with accented and unaccented diphones 147

Henk Loman and Louis Boves
Development of rule based analysis for text-to-speech 157

4. Acoustic-phonetic data and synthesis rules

Rob J. J. H. van Son and Louis C. W. Pols
How does speaking rate influence vowel formant track parameters? 171

Louis F. M. ten Bosch
From data to rules: A background survey 193

Ellen van Zanten, Laurens Damen and Els van Houten
Collecting data for a speech database 207

5. Prosody

Wieke Eefting and Sieb G. Nooteboom
Accentuation, information value and word duration: Effects on speech production, naturalness and sentence processing 225

Jacques M. B. Terken
Human and synthetic intonation: A case study 241

Willy Jongenburger and Vincent J. van Heuven
Sandhi processes in natural and synthetic speech 261

6. Signal analysis

Berry Eggen and Sieb G. Nooteboom
Speech quality and speaker characteristics 279

Johan de Veth, Wim van Golstein Brouwers and Louis Boves
Robust ARMA analysis for speech research 289

7. Implementations and evaluation

René J. H. Deliège
A stand-alone text-to-speech system 309

Hugo C. van Leeuwen and Enrico te Lindert
Speech Maker: A flexible framework for constructing text-to-speech systems 317

Renée van Bezooijen and Louis C. W. Pols
Evaluation of text-to-speech conversion for Dutch 339

Appendix 1. Institutes and individuals participating in ASSP 361

Appendix 2. Publications by SPIN-funded researchers 365

References 383

Name index 407

Subject index 413

List of Figures

Petrič—van den Bergh
1. Mean percentages of correctly answered comprehension questions 20
2. Mean percentages of correctly recalled propositions of the whole text (whole text) and of the gist of the text (gist) 20
3. Mean rating (on a 10-point scale) of comprehensibility and suitability of texts for the general public 21

Lammens
1. Overall structure of a lexicon-based grapheme-to-phoneme conversion system 46
2. Percentage of newspaper text covered by a variable size lemma lexicon 54
3. Percentage of newspaper text covered by a variable size high-frequency wordform lexicon 55
4. Maximum and average chain length in a simulation study with the hashing algorithm 59

Heemskerk—van Heuven
1. Global functional architecture of MORPA 70
2. Summary of the test results 83

Nunn—van Heuven
1. The derivation of the surface pronunciation by MORPON 92
2. The lexical model 94

Quené—Kager
1. Three levels of sentence prosody 116
2. Alternative method for deriving the prosodic sentence structure (PSS) directly from an input sentence 120

Dirksen—Quené
1. Illustrations of the focus-accent relation 135
2. Metrical trees for (1a) and (1b) 138
3. Metrical trees for (2a) and (2b) 138
4. Syntax-to-prosody mapping of (5a) 139
5. Syntax-to-prosody mapping of (5b) 139

Drullman—Collier
1. Mean F_1-F_2 values of accented and unaccented vowels in diphones 154

van Son—Pols
1. Median values of F_1 and F_2 frequencies for 7 vowels 177
2. Example of Legendre polynomials and their use in modeling functions 184
3. Vowel space constructed by plotting mean second order Legendre polynomial coefficient values for F_2 against mean values for F_1 187

ten Bosch
1. Stylization of a diphone 197

van Zanten—Damen—van Houten
1. The structure of the database 209
2. Orthography of an example sentence 211
3. Acoustic signal and labeled segments of an example sentence . 213
4a. Examples of glottal stop present in our transcription as well as in the Jongenburger—van Heuven (1991) transcription 217
4b. Examples of glottal stop not present in our transcription, but added by the labeler; present in the Jongenburger—van Heuven (1991) transcription 217
5a. Example of "fast attack" following silent pause (%); transcribed as glottal stop by Jongenburger—van Heuven (1991); not present in our transcription and labeling 218
5b. Example of "smooth" vowel onset 218

Eefting—Nooteboom
1. Average duration (in ms) per phoneme as a function of word length in number of phonemes 228
2. Percentage differences in word duration in three comparisons . . 232
3. Percentage differences in duration of individual segments of one-syllable words 233
4. Percentage differences in duration of separate syllables of three-syllable words 234
5. Percentage differences in duration of separate segments of three-syllable words 236

Eggen—Nooteboom
1a. Results articulation test: mean percentage of phonemes correctly identified 282
1b. Results MASIT: Q measure in dB 282
2. Simplified speech-production model 283
3. Quality judgments of four speech versions 285

de Veth—van Golstein Brouwers—Boves
1. Poles and zeros may mask each other's spectral characteristics . 291
2. According to the robustness assumption the excitation signal is a statistical mixture of GWN and some outliers 292
3. Inverse filter results 299
4. Estimated frequency of pole 1, 2, 3 and 4 and zero 1 for /l/, followed by one of 12 Dutch vowels 303

Deliège
1. Possible applications 311
2. Text-to-speech conversion 312
3. Hardware block diagram 315
4. The text-to-speech board 316

van Leeuwen—te Lindert
1. Example of how the word *partijvoorzitterschap* is represented in Speech Maker 319
2. Example of most important streams in grid when all analysis modules have operated 321
3. General architecture of Spraakmaker 323
4. Simplified flow chart of module WORD 328

van Bezooijen—Pols
1. Mean percentages correct word identification (CVC+VCCV) for four versions of diphone synthesis and two versions of allophone synthesis 346

List of Tables

Petrič—van den Bergh
1. Standardized regression coefficients for combination of five text features on performance 22

van Holsteijn
1. Number of sentences, number of expressions, % of anomalous expressions, and % of anomalous expressions that have to be sent to the expander 38
2a. Percentage of avoidable sentence-level segmentation errors, expression-level segmentation errors, labeling errors, and expansion errors 39
2b. Percentage of unavoidable sentence-level segmentation errors, expression-level segmentation errors, labeling errors, and expansion errors 39

Lammens
1. Comparison of rule-based and lexicon-based grapheme-to-phoneme conversion systems 50
2. Correctness of decomposition 60
3. Processing speed (in words of input text) 62

Nunn—van Heuven
1. Percentage of words that receive a correct phoneme transcription 98

Reizevoort—van Heuven
1. Performance of pattern-driven morphological decomposition . . 113

Drullman—Collier
1. Relative spread in F_1 and F_2 of vowels in accented and unaccented diphones 155

Loman—Boves
1. Subset of the default specifications for the sound /l/ 166

van Son—Pols
1. Number of vowel pairs matched for normal versus fast rate ... 175
2. Median values for formant frequencies (Hz) 178
3. Percentage of pairs for which the fast rate realization has a higher formant target value than its normal-rate counterpart 178
4. As table 3, but only vowels uttered in *VC context are used 180
5. Mean percentage of formant track variance around the mean formant frequency 185
6. Mean values of Legendre polynomial coefficients for the first three orders 186
7. Linear correlation coefficients between Legendre coefficient values of corresponding vowel realizations uttered at fast and at normal speaking rate 189
8. Linear correlation coefficients between Legendre coefficient values and duration of vowel realizations 189

ten Bosch
1. A matrix representation of a speech database 201

van Zanten—Damen—van Houten
1. Frequencies of glottal stop transcription and labeling (54 files) 215
2. Frequencies of glottal stop transcription and labeling (27 files) 215
3. Frequencies of silent pause transcription and labeling (54 files) 219
4. Frequencies of silent pause transcription and labeling divided into three durational categories (54 files) 220
5. Frequency of inter-word silent pause transcription and labeling (54 files) 221

Eefting—Nooteboom
1. Average scale values and standard deviations 237
2. Mean reaction times 239

Terken

1. Mean onset (bfr) and offset (efr) frequencies for baselines (in Hz), baseline resets (in semitones), and corresponding standard deviations 247
2. Means, standard deviations and number of observations for offset frequencies (in Hz) preceding prosodic boundaries (efr), onset frequencies (in Hz) following the boundaries (bfr), and resulting declination resets (in semitones) as a function of the type of syntactic boundary 249
3. Rejection rate of synthetic intonation configuration over final two accents 253
4. Distribution of $\overset{*}{R}$ $\overset{*}{F}$ and other configurations in the *human* version for the last two accents 253
5. Number of phrases in which *human* and *test* version have the same or different types of boundary markers, and the number and percentage of rejections of the *test* realization 255
6. Distribution of different types of melodic boundary markers as a function of syntactic structure in the human version 256

Jongenburger—van Heuven

1. Frequency of potential and actual application of 32 sandhi rules in text corpus 263
2. Glottal stop distribution as a function of three dichotomous linguistic variables 267
3. Subjects' preferences for each sandhi rule and application of sandhi rules in natural PB speech 269

de Veth—van Golstein Brouwers—Boves

1. Four different families of techniques for speech signal analysis 294

Preface

In the period between 1985 and 1990 the speech research community in the Netherlands joined forces in an attempt to drastically improve the quality of text-to-speech conversion for languages in general, and for Dutch in particular. In this attempt the phonetics research groups at the Universities in Utrecht, Amsterdam, Nijmegen and Leiden, as well as the Institute for Perception Research (IPO) at Eindhoven and the Dutch PTT Telecom at Leidschendam, agreed to collaborate closely in what was called strategic speech research. The research was to remain fundamental but with an open mind towards applications. The regular budgets of the partner institutes were supplemented with a relatively large five-year subsidy granted by the Stimulation Project Information technology Netherlands (SPIN) which operated under the jurisdiction of the Ministry of Economic Affairs and the Ministry of Education and Science.

The ensuing research program, called "Analysis and Synthesis of Speech" (ASSP), involved some 50 researchers in the field, and was coordinated by Antonie Cohen, professor of Phonetics at Utrecht University, from its inception until the end of 1987. As of January 1988 Sieb Nooteboom succeeded Cohen both as the professor of Phonetics at Utrecht and as the ASSP program coordinator. We have asked the program coordinators to write the introductory chapter (1) to this volume, outlining the history of the program, its overall scientific objectives, the organizational superstructure, and the internal logic of the ASSP program.

At the start of the ASSP program the partner institutes agreed to share their speech software, both existing and to be developed. To improve efficiency and to facilitate software exchange all the partner laboratories standardized at that time their computer platforms to Digital VAX/VMS.

The actual work in the ASSP program was carried out by some 25, mostly junior, speech researchers who worked on a temporary basis under the supervision and guidance of a similar number of tenured researchers employed by the partner institutes. Each researcher worked on a single project, typically for a four year period, sometimes on a shorter project, or two shorter projects in succession.

The present book includes a chapter for each of the projects that were run within the ASSP program, written by the temporary researchers themselves, in a number of cases co-authored by supervisors or other individuals who were not themselves on the SPIN pay-roll.

Our strategic research effort concentrated on the development of a laboratory system for text-to-speech conversion with a highly modular structure. The system served as an experimental tool in which specific modules could be exchanged or rearranged, so as to determine the optimal architecture of a reading machine under different practical constraints. The ASSP program often considered parallel ways of solving the same problem. To give just one example, several ways of converting ASCII text to a phonemic transcription were developed: (i) straightforward lookup in a word dictionary that contained both orthographic and phonemic information, (ii) fast morphological decomposition using a pattern recognition technique followed by lexical lookup in a morpheme dictionary, (iii) slow but thorough morphological decomposition followed by lexical lookup, and (iv) text-to-phoneme conversion without any form of lexical lookup. The laboratory system allows the user to convert text-to-phonemes (and ultimately to speech) via any predetermined route through the modules. One module can be applied to the exclusion of others so as to determine which module provides superior performance. Alternatively, modules can be cascaded so that problems that cannot be solved by an earlier module can be dealt with by a later module.

It was decided early on in the ASSP program that our text-to-speech conversion system should model the behavior of one single talker, the designated talker. To this purpose a number of experienced broadcasters were screened for suitability by a panel of listeners. The speaker who was finally selected, then provided all the recordings from which the inventory of synthesis building blocks was derived; he also provided the speech materials for the rule extraction for intonation, temporal organization, Sandhi processes, and so on.

The chapters in this book following the introduction are presented in a non-arbitrary order. We have taken our organizational cue from the process of text-to-speech conversion itself, and roughly follow the serial ordering of processes that are part of a reading machine.

Part I: Input characteristics

(2) The first part of the book deals with the problem of text properties that make texts suitable for being converted to speech for listening purposes. As such, it presents an aspect of input requirements on a (psycho-)linguistic, pragmatic basis.

(3) On a much lower, concrete level, texts have to be scanned for special symbols and abbreviations, and where necessary expanded, before they are handed over to the grapheme-to-phoneme conversion rules. This is a basic and overall requirement for any text-to-speech conversion system that had not been met by any earlier system for Dutch.

Part II: Linguistic aspects

(4) Early in the ASSP program a project was carried out to establish the optimal size, access method, and internal structure of a word dictionary for use in a text-to-speech system. A survey of this work is presented in this chapter.

(5) In the next chapter the morphological parser MORPA (and the accompanying exhaustive morpheme lexicon) is presented. The parser takes as its input any Dutch word, be it monomorphemic or complex, and produces an array of possible morphological decompositions ordered from most to least likely, using both absolute linguistic rules as well as probabilistic heuristics.

(6) Following this, the program MORPHON is discussed. This module takes the abstract phonemic representations as input which are stored for each morpheme in the morpheme dictionary. An overview of the postlexical phonological rules that convert the lexical representations into pronounceable strings including proper sandhi and stress placement, concludes this chapter.

(7) As a faster (though less thorough) alternative to (5), the program PADMAN considers the feasibility of using a pattern matching technique for the purpose of morphological decomposition. The pattern matching technique concerned was successfully applied earlier to the problem of computer hyphenation.

(8) Our next chapter deals with the linguistic interface above the word level. It examines the possibility of deriving prosodic markers, i.e., the position of intonation boundaries and accents, without deep syntactic parsing and without the need for a complete morpheme dictionary.

(9) As a sequel to the work in chapter 8, an alternative program is presented that does derive prosodic markers by performing a deeper syntactic analysis using as its input the lattice of lexical categories proposed by e.g. MORPA for successive text words in the linear array of the sentence.

Part III: Building blocks for speech synthesis

The third part of this volume addresses the problem of finding suitable building blocks for speech synthesis.

(10) This chapter studies the question whether the quality and intelligibility of diphone synthesis can be improved when the diphone inventory is extended with a set of spectrally and temporally reduced units.

(11) The final chapter in this part reports on a project that aimed to improve the segmental quality of allophone synthesis for Dutch, and emphasizes the methodological aspects of such work.

Part IV: Acoustic-phonetic data and synthesis rules

This part involves work of a fundamental nature. Although the results may contribute towards better text-to-speech generation, the work has not evolved to a point where concrete implementations in our laboratory system were feasible.

(12) This is a study on the effects of speaking rate and accentuation on the spectral dynamics of vowels in continuous prose, set up to generate rules for automatic adaptation of spectral targets and trajectories as function of speaking rate and accent. A method for automatic stylization of formant tracks was developed as part of the research strategy.

(13) The next chapter considers the possibilities of automatically extracting CV and VC coarticulation rules for our allophone synthesis system from a complete inventory of diphones.

(14) This contribution discusses work on setting up a segmented and labeled speech database for the study of temporal regularities in the speech of our model talker. The paper focuses on the hierarchical structure of the database and on the reliability of the segmentation process.

Part V: Prosody

The prosodic studies included in this book address the question to what extent the quality of text-to-speech systems can be improved by having them mimic the more fine-grained prosodic detail (including Sandhi phenomena) of natural speech produced by an accomplished talker.

(15) This chapter examines the differential contribution of pitch accent placement and duration adjustments at the word and phrase level to the optimal encoding of the focus distribution of a sentence, i.e., the division of the sentence into parts that are communicatively important and those that are not.

(16) The next chapter reports on a detailed study carried out to enhance the intonation module of our text-to-speech system. Rules were extracted and perceptually tested that aimed at a livelier and more natural type of intonation than was used hitherto.

(17) Our text-to-speech system contains some 30 optional phonological rules that can be used to mimic within and between speaker differences in speaking style. This chapter gives a formal characterization of our model speaker's behavior in terms of his sandhi rule preferences, based on a detailed analysis of a corpus of continuous prose.

Part VI: Signal analysis

This part of our research effort was geared towards improving the naturalness of synthetic speech by developing more adequate methods for estimating source and filter parameters from natural speech.

(18) Chapter 18 concentrates on the development of a glottal-excited LPC-synthesizer which retains perceptually important speaker characteristics that are lost in ordinary LCP-synthesizers.

(19) The next chapter questions the validity of all-pole models of human speech production, and explores the possibility of valid and robust estimation of both spectral poles and zeros using ARMA-models.

Part VII: Implementations and evaluation

The final part of this volume is devoted to implementations in the shape of various laboratory systems, and to the assessment of the quality of the various systems and/or modules.

(20) In this chapter a description is offered of a compact, stand-alone text-to-speech system, called Typevoice, which was developed during the first half of the ASSP program by combining state-of-the-art diphone synthesis with an entirely rule-based text-to-phoneme converter.

(21) This chapter describes in considerable detail the technical and ideological background of SPEECHMAKER, the flexible framework for experimenting with the architecture of text-to-speech systems.

(22) The final chapter of this volume is an account of the ongoing evaluation study, made during and even after the program, of the quality of speech output of various competing systems and modules therein, developed both within and outside the ASSP research program.

In a number of appendices we have included a complete reports and publications list of the ASSP program (updated until the end of 1991), a list of researchers, projects, supervisors, members of the several advisory boards, and so on. Requests for ASSP-reports should be mailed to the following address:

Netherlands Speech Technology Foundation,
Trans 10,
3512 JK Utrecht
The Netherlands

Vincent J. van Heuven
Louis C. W. Pols

A five year research program "Analysis and Synthesis of Speech"

Antonie Cohen—Sieb G. Nooteboom

Abstract

This contribution is intended to reflect the managerial experiences of the two coordinators of the ASSP program. It can be seen as a self-evaluation of a research operation carried out on a nation-wide basis. As such it was an ambitious undertaking both in scope and in its intrinsic quality requirements, i.e. to raise the standard of Dutch speech technology with the emphasis on automatic text-to-speech conversion. The results of the actual research efforts are reported in subsequent chapters. We mainly report on the framework in which this research could come to fruition.

1. Introduction

This volume is intended to give colleagues in the field of speech technology an overall idea of the work involved in the research program Analysis and Synthesis of Speech (ASSP). This five-year program, covering the years 1985–1990, was sponsored by the Dutch government with a budget of DFl 6,000,000 and was carried out in six speech research groups in the Netherlands. The program involved some 25 full time research workers employed on a temporary basis, in addition to a number of permanent staff who spent part of their time on the program.

As such, the contributions to this volume will give an adequate impression of the work actually carried out and will therefore speak for themselves. Nevertheless, we feel it incumbent on ourselves, the successive research program coordinators, to give readers some background information on the organization and actual running of the program.

Below we will briefly deal with various aspects of the program in terms of subsequent events from its inception, its relation to the subsidizing body, its internal organizational structure and decision making in relation to the research tasks, and its attempts to meet the criteria set by the funding agency.

2. Prehistory

The run up to the actual research program was made in a personal contact of the present authors with the then directorate-general in charge of scientific planning of the Dutch Ministry of Science and Education. We were informed about a plan initiated by his department to devote a fairly large sum of money to subsidize work in the field of information technology as a stimulus for strategic research in a number of subfields that looked promising enough for further development with a view to their relevance for industry. Its main purpose was to subsidize university research which needed extra financial impulses in the field of information technology particularly with respect to put up with possible arrears in computing facilities. The overall amount made available, to be spent on a number of different national research programs, turned out to be ca. DFl 70,000,000. A temporary organization for the purpose was set up called SPIN (Stimulation Project Information Technology Netherlands) under the jurisdiction of two departments, the Ministry of Education and Science and the Ministry of Economic Affairs, in August 1985. We may refer to SPIN as the superstructure of ASSP.

From a small kernel of immediate collaborators we extended our efforts at the specific request of SPIN, so as to draw in as many interested research units all over the country as were likely to be interested. From the start, in drawing up our research proposal, this requirement has constituted an important objective in the program. The initial proposal was made by five research groups, viz. the Institute for Perception Research (IPO) in Eindhoven and the phonetics research groups of the universities of Amsterdam, Leiden, Nijmegen and Utrecht.

In December 1985, our research proposal was accepted and at the same time the Foundation for Speech Technology was established as a legal umbrella organization to expedite the otherwise complex operation of funding five (later six) individual participating research groups spread out over the country. Its domicile was the Arts Faculty of Utrecht University.

The main objectives of ASSP were the following:

(a) integration and coordination of extant fundamental and development-oriented speech research in the Netherlands;
(b) improvement of automatic text-to-speech conversion (TTS) for the Dutch language;
(c) development of laboratory systems for text-to-speech conversion;
(d) knowledge transfer to industry and a broader public.

We will revert to these research objectives towards the end of our survey. The proposal was supported by a detailed work plan involving quite a number of research projects in the areas of linguistic analysis, building blocks of speech synthesis, segmental and prosodic synthesis rules, signal analysis, building hardware and software systems, and evaluation. From the DFl 6,000,000 budget, 80 percent was to be spent on hiring personnel and 20 percent on buying equipment.

3. Superstructure

As for the superstructure of our program, we were mainly concerned with the directorate of SPIN, located on the premises of Delft Technical University, and with an advisory body, called Program Committee, made up of members with an interest and/or expertise in speech technology coming from either industry or university circles. The Program Committee was appointed by SPIN.

The main criteria upheld by SPIN for all the research programs to be subsidized were the quality of the research to be funded, the capability of the research program coordinator, and the overall chance of success of the chosen area of research in terms of its ability to clearly formulate problems and solve them.

As ASSP happened to constitute the very first program to be adopted by SPIN, we have greatly benefitted from this pioneer position to the effect that we had hardly any trammels of bureaucracy. We could ourselves largely determine the frequency and time of meetings in Delft which we strove to arrange so as to forestall actual problems that might otherwise crop up.

As for our relations with the Program Committee, as it was chaired by a benign and wise person and moreover highly efficient with an eye on the mainstream, we felt ourselves well served and protected against any wild changes of course due to perturbations from the outside world. We met with the Program Committee twice yearly, always at a different location, so as to combine a formal gathering with an on-site visit enabling local participants in the program to demonstrate their work.

The overall attitude of both SPIN and Program Committee was wholly supportive and liberal, on the one hand in keeping us on our toes, and on the other by making worthwhile suggestions in matters where we were undecided. Such was the case about changing the ratio between funds for personnel and for equipment where we had to try to fill gaps in computer facilities in some of the participating research groups. Such was also the case with respect to allowing us to spend money on visits of junior-researchers to international conferences.

A more far reaching principled decision was made about an intrinsically scientific problem. At the outset of our program, we had the intention of letting two different types of speech synthesis, diphone-based synthesis (see Drullman—Collier, this volume) and allophone-based synthesis (see Loman—Boves, this volume), run their separate courses for a period of two years after which a decision was to be made on persevering with only one. By the time this decision was to be made, we had second thoughts, since the two seemed to be capable of being converged (see ten Bosch, this volume). We were given the benefit of scientific doubt and we could continue our course the way we wanted.

4. Internal structure

From the moment the program was operative, we decided to appoint a Steering Committee to be filled in by members of the five participating research groups situated in the universities of Amsterdam, Leiden, Nijmegen and Utrecht, as well as IPO (Institute for Perception Research) Eindhoven, which is a joint venture of the Technical University and Philips Research. At a later stage, the PTT Research laboratory was represented by one of the university members who also acts as an advisor to this laboratory. All five members of the steering committee were senior researchers. The meetings of the Steering Committee were chaired by the program coordinator. These meetings were held on a monthly basis at Utrecht and prepared and seconded by a management assistant. The Steering Committee decided on starting and ending specific research projects, instituting thematic working groups, allocating personnel and equipment etc.

Already the first year the need was felt for a software expert whose main task it was to see to it that computer facilities were made to be compatible and computer programs were exchanged among the various research groups. He had no fixed abode and though structurally attached to the program coordinator, he led an itinerant existence.

From the beginning the need was felt to set up ad hoc working groups, each centered around a particular theme. These permitted us to include expert knowledge on a research topic from people who were not directly involved in ASSP and for that reason were not on the payroll of our program. The main purpose of setting up such thematic groups was to coordinate the research efforts of all those, often working at different laboratories, and to maximize the expertise distributed over the country. All meetings were always chaired by a member of the Steering Committee, under whose responsibility any particular theme rested. To give an idea of the field covered in this way, there was a rather extensive working group on *linguistic analysis,* covering grapheme to phoneme conversion, rules for lexical stress position, rule-based and morpheme lexicon-based morphological decomposition, and rules for sentence accents and speech pauses. There was a working group on *prosody,* including research on intonation, temporal patterning, and vowel reduction. There was also a working group on *building blocks of speech* and one on *signal analysis.* During the second half of the five year program there was a special task force for implementing results in a *laboratory system* for Dutch text-to-speech conversion. Typically, a number of researchers would take part in more than one working group.

As a whole, the total span of the ASSP-program covered a vast and diversified field of research efforts, involving people from different disciplines, and therefore a large amount of time was devoted to try to streamline their endeavors towards the same end. It turned out to be by no means easy to acclimatize such differently trained people as acoustic engineers, information specialists, phoneticians and linguists, so as to really make them work together. This was all the more so true at a later stage in the program, when one of the more tangible aims of ASSP was to be achieved, viz. the building of a laboratory system for direct TTS conversion, which resulted in SPEECHMAKER, a flexible framework for constructing text-to-speech systems.

By this time, roughly after the first half of the total running time of ASSP, a specialist from the field of computer science was attached to the program. As a general self felt criticism, we have to conclude that we were late in establishing the need for such an infusion.

Surveying the field of research activities, it can be said that the linguistic impact as compared to the acoustic-phonetic and signal processing contributions, was large. This can also be seen from the reports making up this volume. One particular project was devoted to the question which properties a text to be read aloud, either by human or machine, must have in order to be suitable to convey information to listeners. The background assumption was that texts written in order to be read visually are not necessarily suitable to be presented auditorily in spoken form (see further, Petrič—van den Bergh, this volume).

As will appear from the complete list of contributions reporting on the various subproblems making up the total ASSP-program, ours was indeed a very ambitious undertaking, which had to account for a thorough investigation of the whole field of TTS problems, both as a strategical reconnaissance of the field for future developments and with the express purpose of building an operational laboratory system. In other words, our set-up from the start was aimed to combine efforts in the field of basic research and applied work in constructing laboratory systems. With the overall strategic objective in mind, we opted for a parallel approach in which various competing techniques would run their course in order for us at a later stage to opt for the most successful or promising one. This applied intrinsically to the two highly diverse methods in dealing with the building blocks of synthetic speech which happened to have their own tradition and followers in different departments in the country. Our specific aim was to decide, after two years, whether to continue with diphones or with allophones. As pointed out above, this decision was not made at the time suggested, since on second thoughts we felt it desirable to make an effort to try and make the two competing systems converge, because either approach could learn from the findings made in the research accruing from the other one.

A similar two-pronged attack was envisaged to deal with the problem of morphological decomposition, in which the competing techniques involved both morphological parsing based on a morpheme-lexicon (see Heemskerk—van Heuven, this volume) and detection of morpheme boundaries based on a phonotactic pattern matching technique (see Reizevoort—van Heuven, this volume). In this case, rather early in the game it was decided to discontinue the rule-based pattern matching approach and to opt for the lexicon-based technique. In a later stage this was supplemented with a lexicon of whole words, each word with the necessary structural information.

Also in the field of actual implementation several roads leading to some highly diverse working systems were followed. In a way, the ASSP-program had a flying start in the circumstance that some development work had already been carried out at the start of the program. This has subsequently led to the more or less finished products of a speech aid for the vocally handicapped, viz. a simple system "Pocketvoice" with easy storage and retrieval of a limited number of speech messages, and an easily portable TTS system called "Typevoice" (Deliège—Speth-Lemmens—Waterham 1989). These two systems were further developed within ASSP. Yet a third system, Speechmaker, was the result of an initiative from within the program to act as a full-fledged optimum of the present state of the art anno 1990 of TTS conversion in the Netherlands, meant to be capable of competing with the best systems available internationally. Moreover, SPEECHMAKER, a modular experimental system, was meant to be a flexible tool for demonstration and further research and not an end product.

From the start, the need was felt for adequate assessment of the various approaches inherent in the ASSP set-up. This led to a special effort to monitor our results from the beginning until after the end of the program by means of evaluation studies involving listening experiments.

In the following section, we will discuss to what extent the program has met the requirements set by the funding agency.

5. Meeting the SPIN requirements

The whole undertaking constituting ASSP can be seen as an effort to accommodate the wishes entertained by government authorities in the Netherlands not to lag behind research in information technology abroad within the field of speech. To this end a number of requirements were stipulated which were to be the guidelines on which the program was to be based. At this juncture it is the proper place to reflect on the character and intensity of the way we have seen fit to implement our contractual undertakings. As such, these guidelines have certainly permeated and colored our efforts, not only in the actual research carried out, but even more particularly in terms of research management.

As for the first requirement, integration and coordination of basic and application oriented speech research in the Netherlands, it was imperative on us to draw in all workers active in the wide field of speech technology often working on their own and generally not directly involved or even interested in similar work carried out elsewhere. We feel safe to conclude that this requirement has constituted the raison d'être of the whole undertaking. A firm basis of cooperation and solidarity has been established among otherwise unconnected workers and research institutes. In a way, this was forced upon us by the funding authorities, but its actual achievement was secured thanks to the efforts of the Steering Committee. That this was not always plain sailing can be vouchsafed by us in our roles of coordinators in chairing its meetings. It was by no means easy whenever there were competing competences to decide where a particular research project was to be located with the added prestige involved in extending the research staff by one or more researchers on the payroll of SPIN. In this respect, as throughout the overall management of the program in affording good relations all round, both with the external fund raisers, the semi-external Program Committee and the internal research workers, distributed over five different university faculties, the golden rule of management was indeed "getting things done through people". Our experiences were that the further those we had to deal with were removed from the actual field of research, the easier it was to get their goodwill and participation. At close quarters with individual participants, much greater effort was needed to make them feel comfortable and aware of the joint undertaking ASSP presented. The services of the management assistant were of the greatest value, since it fell to his/her task to look after the needs of each contributor of the program from an administrative point of view. Such needs might involve the speedy drawing up of contracts and the regular installment of salaries and travelling expenses, and more in general the overall need to make sure that ASSP contractants felt really cared for. Not the least benefit of having an efficient assistant manager right from the start was the fact that it provided a solid basis for getting the confidence of the fund raising authorities.

The second objective to be reached was to bring Dutch speech research, especially where it is directed towards advanced TTS systems, well to the front in an international sphere. This objective was much harder to achieve, since we could not really foresee how the international scene would progress in five years' time. It is our impression that we have certainly made headway and have made up previous arrears not only quantitatively in terms of computer facilities and personnel, but also qualitatively in training a new generation of speech researchers and coming up with more sophisticated research methods and techniques. This certainly holds good for the high involvement of linguistic computerization, although we may have been less successful on the level of signal processing techniques which may have been under-exposed. As an acid test for the adequacy of the speech synthesis output, we had provided ourselves with a continuous assessment by way of listeners' judgments. Although both building block techniques used, diphone-based and allophone-based synthesis, showed improvement at the end of the program neither could really claim to have reached the stage of near naturalness (see van Bezooijen—Pols, this volume).

As for the third requirement, the design and construction of laboratory systems for the automatic conversion of text-to-speech in Dutch, the program has achieved more than foreseen at the outset. The following stand-alone systems have been made according to the original plans:

— A compact speech aid to be used by nonvocal people for the storage and retrieval of a limited number of economically coded speech messages.
— A portable diphone-based text-to-speech system to be used by nonvocal people. Instead of the pseudo-phonetic spelling foreseen as input in the original plans, normal unedited text can be used as input.
— A diphone-based text-to-speech system on an electronic board to be used with a personal computer.
— An allophone-based text-to-speech system on an electronic board, intended for vocally handicapped people and to be used with a personal computer.
— A portable system, based on an MS-DOS personal computer, as a semiautomatic aid in carrying out listening tests with synthetic speech. Responses are automatically processed.

In addition to these planned systems, the program has resulted in SPEECHMAKER, a rather extensive modular software laboratory system, meant to serve both as a demonstration system and as a research tool for further work in the domain of advanced text-to-speech systems. It has already shown its usefulness as a research tool. Also, SPEECHMAKER has been instrumental in achieving a high degree of integration of the specific projects in various research groups, and in stimulating an atmosphere of common purpose and enthusiasm among all researchers involved. SPEECHMAKER consists of a shell program controlling the communication between a number of functionally separate modules and a common hierarchically organized database. It has user-friendly tools for inputting and trying out new rules within each of the modules, and for accessing the data base. Modules are exchangeable with functionally equivalent other modules. (see further van Leeuwen—te Lindert, this volume).

With respect to the fourth criterion by which our efforts were to be measured, this constituted the task of transferring knowledge through the program to the general public and industry. This task does not come naturally to researchers used to the somewhat protected secluded environment of university departments in our country. Nevertheless, a firm attempt was made to meet this requirement much cherished by our fund raisers. In personal contacts made after the completion of ASSP, we learned that the SPIN directorate itself felt that it had perhaps not put enough effort in this undertaking. Nevertheless, we feel that we have done our level best to accommodate its wishes on this score, and we believe that in the eyes of the Program Committee we have certainly not shirked our duties in this respect. Again, it was mostly the task of the management of ASSP to see to it that this task was fulfilled. We regularly organized so-called speech days, once a year, and on a smaller basis the site visits of the bi-annual meetings of the Program Committee afforded a welcome chance of demonstrating work in progress. For insiders there was a regular opportunity to get to know about ASSP work in specially designed workshops on various research topics.

As we were the first regular program initiated by SPIN, we were not in advance obliged to draw in the interests of various industries by way of their commitment in terms of sponsoring fees, a requirement SPIN set for all later programs. In setting up a research proposal for the continuation of our program as ASSP-2, we are at present engaged in an effort to get such a specific commitment from interested industrial firms through sponsoring. At this moment, a number of firms have expressed their willingness to undertake such a commitment.

In the course of our program, we were able to secure a contract with Digital Equipment Corporation (DEC), which was largely responsible for the computer facilities in hardware, partly made available on attractive terms due to a contract with the firm's External Research Program. Contracts were also concluded with scientific organizations, viz. INL, the Institute for Dutch lexicology at Leiden, and CELEX, the Center for Lexical databases at Nijmegen. Halfway through the program the Foundation for Speech Technology was given a DFl 2,700,000 subsidy by the Ministry of Science and Education to set up the Speech Processing Expertise Center "SPEX", providing the infrastructure for acoustic-phonetic databases for speech research. SPEX is located in the Dutch PTT Research plant at Leidschendam. The Foundation for Speech Technology presently also takes part in a nation-wide project ELK, carrying out a large scale feasibility study on the possibility of supplying blind people daily with a wireless transmitted digital version of a newspaper, to be made audible via a Program Committee-controlled text-to-speech system on an electronic board. One of the text-to-speech systems used was developed in ASSP (see Deliège, this volume).

6. Conclusion

We are convinced that the scientific results of our program have a significant contribution to make. Due to the normal delays in publication, most of these results are yet to become public. Results are or will become available in several ways. There are some 40 intermediate and final unpublished research reports, some 125 publications published during the course of the program, some 25 publications submitted for publication, and 5 doctoral dissertations have been finished and defended, and several more will be completed in the near future. A list of reports and publications stemming from ASSP is added at the end of this volume.

Acknowledgments

Hereby, we would like to express our gratitude to Ir. H. P. Struch and Ir. J. W. Vasbinder of SPIN and Dr. W. Eefting, who was the first ASSP management assistant, for their cooperation in recovering some aspects of the early days of ASSP.

Part I

Input characteristics

Text features affecting listening performance in one way speech communication

Irena Petrič—Huub van den Bergh

Abstract

The suitability of news texts for being listened to, i.e., their suitability for being used as input to a text-to-speech system, was tested. It was established that "reading" texts cannot be presented auditorily without some loss in performance. A set of five text features was obtained which can predict performance when listening to news texts.

1. Introduction

Text-to-speech systems (TTS) are becoming more and more advanced. Consequently, it is necessary for researchers to ask questions which do not concern the system itself, but are relevant for its future functioning. In contrast to the majority of chapters in this book, which deal with different modules of the actual TTS system, this chapter deals with the applications of a TTS system. After presenting some general remarks about different applications of TTS systems, we report on research concerning one particular aspect of TTS applications, namely the suitability of input texts, which is one of the factors that contribute to the successful functioning of TTS applications.

Let us start by pointing out several possible applications of a text-to-speech system. Some of them already exist, and some will exist in the near future. Roughly, they can be divided into the following groups:

I. *Auditory databases*: information that is stored in a computer and can be retrieved whenever necessary. The information is presented auditorily. Examples of this group of applications are different specialized databases (e.g. medical databases), spoken dictionaries, and encyclopedias.

II. *Auditory instructions*: stored instructions which can be used in situations where hands and eyes are needed to perform a task. These are usually instructions about the use, assembly, or maintenance of equipment. An example of auditory instructions is the help-function in computer software.

III. *Information-lines*: the auditory equivalent of newspapers. Users are provided with current information in spoken form. Usually the information-lines can be consulted through the telephone. Examples of information lines are factory news-lines, newspaper-lines for the visually handicapped, news on airplane arrivals and departures, weather forecasts, etc.

In this paper we concentrate on the information-lines. In order to make this group of applications effective and successful, we have to make sure that the users can access the information they need as quickly and as accurately as possible. This can be achieved in different ways:

I. by making the instructions that lead to the stored information (usually a menu structure) as logical and as clear as possible, so that a user can get through them quickly and without making any mistakes,
II. by making the information (i.e. the input texts, the actual information users want to obtain from the information-line) suitable for auditory presentation, so that the users/listeners can understand and remember it easily,
III. by improving the quality of the text-to-speech system.

Here we deal only with the second aspect of improving the effectiveness of the TTS applications, namely the suitability of the input texts. The question we try to answer in this paper is: how should a text be written so that it is suitable for listening, i.e., easily understood and remembered? This question can be rephrased by making it more specific: what text features affect listening performance (i.e. performance resulting from listening to texts)?

1.1. Reading texts versus listening texts

Different TTS applications require different types of input text. However, all these texts have two things in common: they contain factual, objective information, and they are usually written in order to be read, i.e. for a reader. When these "reading" texts are used as input for TTS applications, they are used as "listening" texts, i.e., they are read aloud and presented to an audience of listeners. There are some basic differences in the processes of reading and listening, which should be taken into account when considering using "reading" texts for listening.

One of the disadvantages of listening is that the speech signal proceeds linearly in time, so that a listener cannot stop for a moment or go back ("rewind" the signal). In contrast, a reader can. Moreover, a listener cannot control the rate at which speech proceeds. A reader, on the other hand, can control his own reading rate. It can therefore be assumed that a text which is written in order to be read, probably does not take into account the disadvantages a listener has in comparison with a reader. Therefore, it could be expected that "reading" texts are not necessarily suitable for listening, as they do not take into account the disadvantages a listener has in comparison to a reader. They could possibly be too "difficult" for a listener to understand and remember.

This prediction was tested in an experiment in which the same reading texts were presented to a group of readers and a group of listeners. Retention of the texts was measured. Performance after listening to the texts was much poorer than after reading the same texts. Moreover, an interaction was found between the factors systematically varied in this experiment (length of text and degree of abstractness of text content) and mode of presentation. This means that the same characteristics of texts did not influence performance after listening in the same way as after reading.

This led us to the conclusion that texts which are meant for reading cannot be used as listening texts without some loss in performance. Also, readers and listeners seem to react differently to the same characteristics of texts. This observation makes it impossible to use readability formulae or prescriptions for better readability in order to improve the listenability of texts.[1] Results presented by Belson (in Gunter 1988) support this. Belson used the Flesch Index of Readability to predict comprehension of radio texts presenting the background to current news events. The index was a poor predictor of listening comprehension.

Obviously, reading texts have to be changed if they are to be suitable for (successful) listening. This conclusion brings us to the main question in the present study: Which text features influence listenability of texts? Finding an answer to this question may enable us to establish criteria for listenability and, in future formulate some advice for writing texts which are meant for listening.

It should be noted, however, that no general criteria for listenability of texts can be formed. Different TTS applications require different input texts. Listeners have different goals when listening to different texts. If a listener consults an auditory dictionary, for example, he usually wants to know the meaning of a certain word. Therefore, the whole paraphrase of that word's meaning in a dictionary is important for him. He will have to pay attention to all the information in a text in order to access the meaning of a word.

If, on the other hand, he consults the information-line about the arrivals and departures of the planes, he is only interested in one simple piece of information that is relevant for his purposes. His listening strategy can be much more selective as he does not need to attend to all the information in a text.

The criteria for the listenability of texts, and consequently, advice for writing listenable texts, depend on the goals listeners have for certain texts.

In the following section the problem of text features which are possibly responsible for listenability of texts is dealt with.

2. Text features that influence listenability of texts

How should a text be written in order to be suitable for listening? More specifically, what text features influence listenability of texts? In order to obtain a set of suitable text features, the following approach was decided on. From what is already known from research about text features that can influence readability and listenability of texts, an initial set of text features was obtained. This set of features served as the basis for the analysis and the comparison of the existing "reading" and "listening" texts. Assuming that "listening" texts are actually more suitable for listening than "reading" texts (this assumption had to be tested first), the features in which they differ could be regarded as possibly influencing listenability of these texts.

In order to be able to make the comparison between "listening" and "reading" texts, texts had to be used which had both a reading and a listening variant. Once such texts were found, a comparison was made between the two variants of the same texts with respect to the features which were assumed to have an influence on listenability. Finally, the influence of the selected text features on the actual listening performance was tested in a perception experiment. In this experiment listening and reading variants of texts were presented to the audience of listeners and their performance after listening to these texts was measured. First, it was investigated whether the performance after listening to "listening" texts was actually better than after listening to "reading" texts. Then, the influence of the selected text features on the obtained results was investigated.

The different stages of this approach are discussed in more detail below. First, the choice of texts for the purposes of this study is discussed. Then, the selected text features are presented; these are the features that were tested for their influence on listenability of texts in the perception experiment. Next, the tasks used to measure listenability in the perception experiment are discussed. Finally, the results of the perception experiment are presented and conclusions are drawn.

2.1. The choice of texts — materials

News texts were chosen as material for the present study. News texts have a reading variant, i.e. the newspaper texts, and a listening variant, the radio texts. They are also suitable for several applications of a TTS system, like the spoken newspaper and the factory news-lines.

The material was obtained in the following way. Six short newspaper texts were selected from a leading Dutch morning paper. They were presented to the staff of the Dutch radio newsroom. Their task was to rewrite the newspaper texts into suitable radio texts. They were left free in their choice of changes.

2.2. The selection of text features

Taking into account the purposes of this study in connection with the TTS applications, several restrictions were put on the selection of the features that may influence listenability of texts. The nature of these restrictions was mainly pragmatic. First of all we wanted to limit ourselves to the features which are present in a text, i.e. descriptive, quantitative, text-internal features. These features also had to be content-independent, in view of generalization across texts with diverse subject matters. As the ultimate goal of the present study was to formulate some advice about writing suitable listening texts, editors of such texts should be able to handle the resulting prescriptions. Therefore, the selected features also had to be easy to deal with, i.e., they were not supposed to be obtained by complex analyses which are too difficult for a non-specialist to work with. Finally, the choice of a type of text could also restrict the features which can be used.

Ideally, psychological reality of the selected text features would also be required. This is necessary for the interpretation of the results from a psycholinguistic point of view, i.e., to explain why certain features do or do not influence listenability in terms of slowing down or interfering with the mechanism of text processing. Unfortunately, there is no explicit theoretical framework of auditory text processing. It is therefore not known what factors are important during the different stages of auditory text processing. The selected text features could, therefore, only be surface features which we suspected of having influence on subjects' performance, but probably only indirectly, via some unknown psychological features.

On the basis of what is known from the psycholinguistic literature on readability and listenability of texts (van Hauwermeiren 1975; van Dijk 1988; Wagenaar—Schreuder—Wijlhuizen 1987; Gunter 1988), and keeping in mind the restrictions described above, 11 text features were selected for the purposes of the present study. These were regarded as possible features influencing listenability of news texts. We were, of course, aware of the fact that several features correlated with other features from the selected set. It was therefore to be expected that not all selected features would be needed to predict performance after listening. However, all 11 features were included in the set of selected features because it was not always clear which feature or which operationalization was the most suitable in connection with auditory processing of texts.

The 11 text features can be divided into four groups according to the level of processing they operate at. These are the features at word-, phrase-, sentence- and text-level. The selected features can further be characterized as either belonging to the category "length" or, at the sentence- and text-level, the category "complexity". The division and operationalization of the selected features is given below.

Word-level word length:
—mean number of syllables per word in a text

Phrase-level phrase length:
— mean number of propositions per (nominal and prepositional) phrase in a text[2]

Sentence-level sentence length:
—mean number of words per sentence in a text
—mean number of syllables per sentence in a text
sentence complexity:
—percentage of complex sentences in a text
—percentage of passive sentences in a text

Text-level text length:
—number of words in a text
—number of syllables in a text
text complexity:[3]
—number of coherence units in a text
—mean number of propositions per coherence unit in a text
—percentage of coherence units directly linked to the theme unit of a text

The selected newspaper and radio texts were assigned numerical values for each of these 11 text features.

2.3. Tasks used to measure listenability of news texts

In order to be able to test the influence of the selected text features on listenability of news texts, a perception experiment was set up. In this experiment performance after listening to newspaper and radio texts was measured. Three tasks were used to measure performance: comprehension task, recall task, and rating the texts' comprehensibility and suitability for the general public. These three tasks measure three different aspects of listenability: comprehension, memory and personal opinions about texts.

In the comprehension task subjects had to give written answers to questions about the content of the texts. The questions were identical for the two variants of the text. The percentage of correctly answered questions was measured.

In the recall task subjects had to write down as much as they remembered from the texts they had heard. Two measures were used to measure recall: the percentage of correctly recalled propositions from the whole text and the percentage of correctly recalled propositions from the gist of the texts. The second measure was introduced in order to reduce the effect of the difference in length between the newspaper and radio texts. The gist of the text was identical for the two variants of the text.

For the rating of personal judgments about comprehensibility and suitability for the general public, a 10-point scale was used.

2.4. Results

Two questions had to be answered on the basis of the results of the perception experiment. Firstly, the question whether the performance after listening to the radio ("listening") texts was actually better than after listening to the newspaper ("reading") texts. Secondly, the influence of the selected text features on performance in the three tasks had to be established.

2.4.1. Listening to newspaper vs. radio texts

Performance after listening to the newspaper and the radio texts was compared first. We expected the radio texts to be more suitable for listening to than the newspaper texts, because they were written in order to be listened to. Therefore, listening performance with the radio texts should be better than with the newspaper texts.

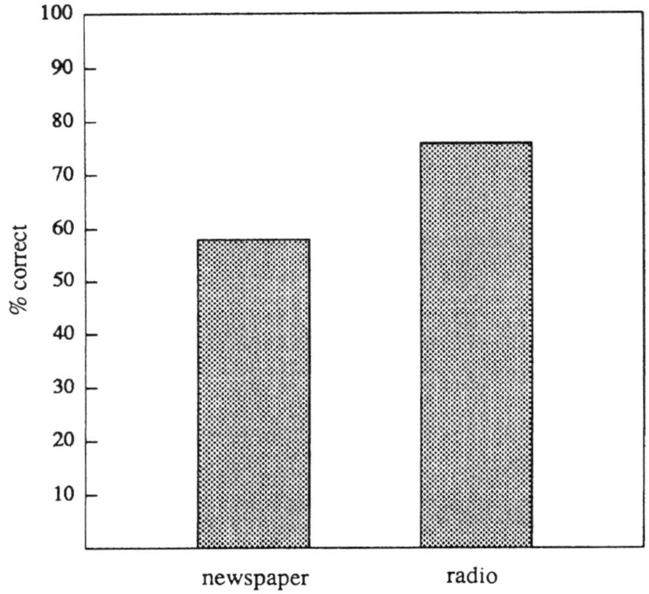

Figure 1. Mean percentages of correctly answered comprehension questions after listening to the newspaper and the radio texts

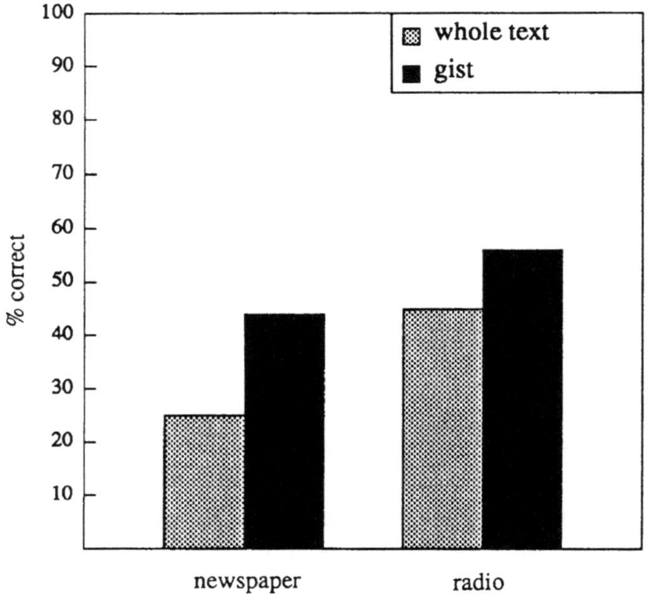

Figure 2. Mean percentages of correctly recalled propositions of the whole text (whole text) and of the gist of the text (gist) after listening to the newspaper and the radio texts

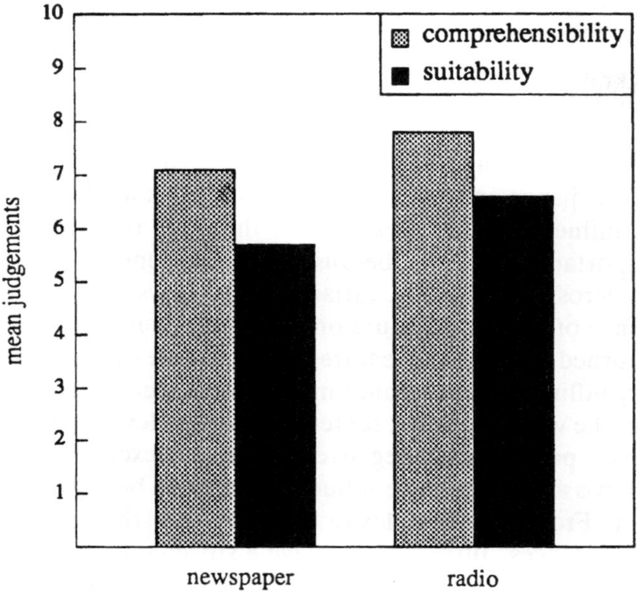

Figure 3. Mean rating (on a 10-point scale) on comprehensibility and suitability of texts for the general public after listening to the newspaper and the radio texts

Figures 1 through 3 give the mean performance in the comprehension test, the recall test and the mean personal judgments after listening to the newspaper and radio texts.

As can be observed in Figures 1 through 3 listening performance with radio texts is better than with newspaper texts. This difference in performance is significant for all three tasks. For the comprehension test the mean performance with the newspaper texts was 58 percent correctly answered questions, as opposed to 76 percent after listening to the radio texts. In the recall test subjects recalled 25 percent of the whole text and 44 percent of the gist of the text after listening to the newspaper texts. After listening to the radio texts they recalled 45 percent of the whole text and 56 percent of the gist of the text. The mean scores on subjects' ratings of comprehensibility were 7.1 for the newspaper texts and 7.8 for the radio texts. Mean rating of on suitability for the general public was 5.7 for the newspaper texts and 6.6 for the radio texts.

On the basis of these results it can be concluded that rewriting newspaper texts into radio texts paid off—the radio texts turned out to be more suitable for listening.

2.4.2. Influence of text features on listening performance

The main question in the present experiment was whether the selected text features influence listening performance with the newspaper and radio texts, and if so, to what extent. The following results were obtained.

Firstly, it was established that the influence of the selected text features was identical for the newspaper and the radio texts. This means that the selected texts features influence the two variants of the news texts in the same way. This is an important conclusion, because it permits generalization of the obtained effects across the different variants of the news texts.

Secondly, the influence of each text feature on performance in the three tasks was obtained. It turned out that the features which can be categorized into the length category influence performance most. This is true for all the levels of processing, i.e. the word-, phrase-, sentence- and text-level. All the length features influence performance negatively, with the exception of phrase length, which shows a small positive influence. This can be regarded as a redundancy effect. From the complexity features only the feature "percentage of passive sentences" turned out to have a strong influence on performance in the three tasks. The influence of this feature is negative, except on the judgments about suitability for the general public, where it has a positive influence on the scores.

The combined influence of several text features, where the inter-correlations among the features are taken into account, may yield a better prediction of listenability than the individual effect of any single text feature. In order to examine this possibility, multiple regression analysis was used to test different combinations of text features for their influence on performance. In selecting the combinations, two restrictions were imposed on a combination: all the levels of processing had to be represented (i.e word-, phrase-, sentence-, and text-level), and no high intercorrelations among the features in a combination were permitted.[4] The combination of five text features which could explain most variance in the data is given in Table 1.

We concluded that a combination of five text features: text length (measured in words), sentence length (measured in words), the percentage of passive sentences in a text, phrase length, and word length, is the best predictor of listening performance. The five text features explain approximately 65 percent of the variance in listenability scores.

It can be observed that four out of five features (text length, sentence length, percentage of passive sentences in a text, and word length) influence performance in all the tasks negatively. There are two exceptions: the feature "percentage of passive constructions" has a significant positive influence on judgments about suitability for the general public, and the

Table 1. Standardized regression coefficients for the combination of five text features on performance

TASK	TLW	SLW	PASS	PHL	WL
CT	-.185*	-.309*	-.292*	+.111*	-.117*
RT	-.202*	-.340*	-.154*	+.155*	+.070*
RG	-.091*	-.403*	-.333*	-.043	-.163*
JC	-.125*	-.279*	+.047	+.100*	-.102*
JS	-.120*	-.359*	+.125*	+.101*	-.136*

Note: CT = comprehension test, RT = recall of whole text, RG = gist of text, JC = judgments about comprehensibility, JS = suitability of texts. TLW = text length in words, SLW = sentence length in words, PASS = percentage of passive sentences in a text, PHL = phrase length, WL = word length). * = significant at 5 percent level.

feature "word length" has a significant, although relatively small positive influence on the recall of the whole text.

The fifth feature, "phrase length" (standing for the mean length of the nominal and prepositional phrases in a text), has an overall positive influence on performance after listening to the news texts.

2.5. Discussion

As already mentioned in the introduction, there were two reasons for conducting the present experiment. Firstly, in an earlier experiment it turned out that "reading" texts cannot be presented auditorily without loss in performance. This is not satisfactory in connection with the use of these texts as input for different TTS applications. Secondly, we assumed that text features influence performance after reading and after listening in a different way. Therefore, readability formulae are probably not suitable for predicting listenability of texts (see also Belson in Gunter 1988), and prescriptions for improving text readability cannot be used for improving listenability.

An extended set of text features was obtained. We hypothesized that these text features were possible factors influencing listening performance. In the present experiment these text features were tested for their actual influence on listenability of news texts. Newspaper ("reading") texts and radio ("listening") texts, which differed in terms of the selected text features, were presented to an audience of listeners. Comprehension, recall and personal ratings of the texts were determined. It was established that the listening performance with radio texts was significantly better than with newspaper texts. This means that it is useful to rewrite newspaper texts into radio texts—radio texts were obviously more suitable for listening than newspaper texts.

Furthermore, it was tested how strongly each of the selected text features influenced listening performance. Generally speaking it turned out that the features which indicate length (i.e. the amount of information) at different levels of processing, influenced the performance most. A combination of text features turned out to be a better predictor of performance than any single feature.

A combination of five text features was found which can explain the variation in the data best. These are the features "text length" (measured in words), "sentence length" (measured in words), "percentage of passive sentences in a text", "phrase length" (measured in propositions), and "word length" (measured in syllables). Four of the features (text length, sentence length, percentage of passive, and word length) have a negative influence on performance in the comprehension test, the recall test, and the personal judgments about the texts. Two exceptions can be observed (Table 1): the feature "percentage of passive sentences" has a significant positive influence on the judgments about suitability for the general public, and the feature "word length" has a significant positive influence on the recall of the whole text.

The first exception can be explained as follows. In the present experiment the subjects knew that they heard news items meant for radiobroadcasting. Regular news items can be characterized as formal texts, and passive constructions are one of the characteristics of formal style. The subjects, therefore, probably thought that the texts should be formal if they are to be suitable for their purpose, and consequently gave higher scores to texts which sounded more formal (i.e contained more passive constructions).

The positive influence of the feature "word length" on the recall of the whole text is small (+.070) but significant. We can think of the following explanation of this effect. In the texts used as material in the present experiment, long words (usually a part of the topic) were repeated several times. If a subject remembered the word he could use it several times in his recall of the whole text and thus increase the recall.

The feature "phrase length", which represents the mean length of the nominal and prepositional phrases in a text, has an overall positive influence on listening performance. This is not what one would expect on the basis of what we know about the processing of long nominal or prepositional phrases. However, the positive influence of this text feature can be explained. The length of the phrases was measured in propositions; this means that each complement to the head of the phrase forms a new proposition, and that long phrases contain more complements to the head. Performing the comprehension and the recall task obviously demands overall comprehension of the text, for which not all the details are required.

The complements in long nominal and prepositional phrases can be regarded as detail information which is not necessarily needed for the comprehension of the whole text. The positive influence of the feature "phrase length" could therefore be considered a redundancy effect in processing the whole text. We should, however, mention that this need not be a general effect of phrase length; very long phrases probably have the expected negative influence on processing of texts. There were, however, no very long phrases in the texts used in the present experiment.

The results of the present experiment can be used as an indication of the suitability of news texts for being listened to, i.e. to be used as input to the applications of a TTS system. They can be used in a formula-form as a predictor of listenability of news texts.

3. Concluding remarks

The study described in this chapter tested the suitability of news texts for being listened to, or, in the context of the text-to-speech research, their suitability to be used as input texts in applications of a text-to-speech system. These texts can be used as input in different applications belonging to the group of auditory information-lines. By making the input texts suitable for listening, so that the listeners/users of the information-line can understand and remember the information from texts easily, the information-lines will become more effective and successful.

Due to the lack of a theoretical framework for auditory text processing, the present study was of an explorative nature. The results obtained in the perception experiment, therefore, have to be treated as an indication of the influence of text features on listenability of texts.[5] Before they can get more prescriptive relevance, a phase of testing their predictive power by means of manipulation of the text features must be carried out. Also, a more systematic comparison between the predictions of listening and reading performance must be obtained. Only then can rules be formulated for writing news texts which are suitable for listening.

Acknowledgements

The authors wish to thank the supervisors of this project, S. G. Nooteboom and P. J. van den Hoven for their valuable comments during all the stages of the research.

Notes

1. Suitability of texts for being listened to is in the present study referred to as "listenability" of texts (analogous to the well known term "readability").
2. Propositions are defined on the basis of the propositional analysis by Kintsch—Van Dijk (1978).
3. The features that represent text complexity are obtained on the basis of the coherence analysis by van Wijk—Sanders (1987).
4. A value of a text feature can be perfectly predicted from the combination of two or more other features from the set.
5. A more detailed report on the experiment described in this paper can be found in Petrič (1991, 1992).

TextScan: A preprocessing module for automatic text-to-speech conversion

Yvonne van Holsteijn

Abstract

Automatic text-to-speech conversion requires some sort of preprocessing for two reasons: to perform a segmentation of the input text, and to convert anomalous symbol strings such as numerals and abbreviations into a lexical format. This paper describes a preprocessing module named TextScan. TextScan has been developed to serve as one of the components of a text-to-speech system for Dutch. Besides, due to its modular architecture, TextScan can also be used in other applications, such as parsing and automatic translation.

1. Introduction

An automatic text-to-speech (TTS) conversion system usually consists of a series of linguistic processing modules which convert unrestricted text into some phonemic representation from which speech output can be derived (Allen—Hunnicutt—Klatt 1987). Linguistic processing, however, can only be performed adequately after some form of text preprocessing has been carried out (Laver—McAllister—McAllister—Jack 1988; Laver—McAllister—McAllister 1989). There are two main reasons for this. Firstly, information on word and sentence boundaries is not simply available in a text, in whatever form it may be stored. The linguistic processing modules, however, apply to words and sentences. An essential task for a preprocessing module is therefore the detection of word and sentence boundaries, a process called segmentation. Secondly, we face the problem that unrestricted input text will contain many symbol strings such as numerals (*12, 12.45, 1,245*), abbreviations (*Prof., ft, m.p.h., N.Y.*), and acronyms (*BBC, DEC, UK*) which cannot be handled properly by the system's linguistic processing modules. These strings are often anomalous in their typographical or linguistic make-up, relative to the majority of more standard forms of text, such as words. Forms which do not conform to the system's limited notion of what constitutes a word, have to be converted into some recognizable format before any linguistic analysis can be applied properly.

At first sight, preprocessing of input texts for text-to-speech conversion may seem trivial. However, a closer look will show that this is not the case.

It is not always possible to mark word and sentence boundaries on the basis of form features such as spaces and punctuation characters. Not every period marks a sentence boundary: periods may also occur in several other functions elsewhere, for example, in abbreviations (*Dr.*), acronyms (*A.T.&T.*), and numerals (*12.45, 1.*). Correct segmentation requires a preprocessing module to distinguish periods used as end-of-sentence markers from periods ending anomalous forms. The hyphen also causes difficulties with respect to segmentation; it may be used for breaking off at the end of a line, in contraction (*16- to 19-year-olds*), as a phrasal structure marker, as a text delimiter, or in enumerations. It will have major implications for the overall phrasal structure of a sentence whether a hyphen refers to the word or the sentence level. Note that ambiguities caused by the multifunctional nature of punctuation characters, such as the hyphen, are partly due to the fact that, generally, computer character sets are very limited in size. In traditionally printed text, the length of a hyphen or dash usually denotes the function it performs.

The conversion of anomalous forms into a format suitable for linguistic analysis, a process called expansion, is not straightforward either. Strings which cannot be distinguished on the basis of orthography, frequently require different types of expansion. This is demonstrated by the all-digit string 14267, which may be an integer or, for example, a telephone number. Integers, however, always have to be pronounced as whole numbers, while telephone numbers require a digit-sequence interpretation.

2. TextScan

This paper describes a preprocessing module, named TextScan, which has been developed to serve as one of the components of a TTS system for Dutch (van Leeuwen—te Lindert, this volume). TextScan performs the following three consecutive tasks. First, an input text is divided into "textual units" and punctuation characters. A textual unit broadly corresponds to a word or an anomalous symbol string. Additionally, all possible end-of-sentence points are marked. After that, textual units are classified and provided with a label in order to obtain, through expansion, text suitable for linguistic analysis. Labeled textual units will be called expressions. Expressions are, for example, telephone numbers (*0800 525319*), years (*'92, 1991*), currency-strings (*$ 2.50, $ 7.4bn*), proper names (*Iraq*), and lexical items (*last-minute, taxpayer*), but also punctuation characters (*;*). Essentially, two expressions will carry different labels, that is, will belong to separate classes, if they need different types of expansion afterwards. Finally, anomalous expressions will be converted into a format suitable for subsequent linguistic analysis.

TextScan consists of two submodules. The first submodule deals with the segmentation and labeling of text (text analysis), while the second one involves the expansion of anomalous expressions. A major advantage of this modular approach is that essentially different functionalities are separated. As a consequence, the preprocessor is capable of producing different expansions for one particular group of expressions and still have information available about its segmentation and labeling. Another advantage of TextScan's modular architecture is that only the expansion submodule, rather than the entire preprocessor, will require modification for applications other than text-to-speech conversion, such as automatic parsing or translation.

In the next section the segmentation, labeling and expansion processes, briefly outlined above, will be described in detail. After that, TextScan's performance will be discussed, and finally, some concluding remarks on improvements and further research will be made.

3. Segmentation

3.1. General strategy

A natural first step in the segmentation of a text is the detection of "orthographic islands" (Laver et al. 1988). An orthographic island is any sequence of printable characters bounded by white space. In a relatively small number of cases, orthographic islands contain initial and/or final punctuation characters. These characters may either act as text or perform a punctuation function. Punctuation characters of the former type will be called *textual*. A textual punctuation character always belongs to the orthographic island it is part of, such as the period(s) in *Prof.*, *m.p.h.* and *12.30*. Punctuation characters which perform a punctuation function, on the other hand, such as a period denoting the end of a sentence, will be called *metatextual*. Metatextual punctuation characters are isolated and treated as separate units. Unfortunately, there are several punctuation characters which perform a dual role: they may occur both textually and metatextually.

In order to mark word and sentence boundaries, a distinction between textual and metatextual punctuation characters has to be made. The first step was to investigate which punctuation characters can occur both textually and metatextually. For these characters the environments in which they may occur were examined in terms of their relative position in the orthographic island (string initial or string final). This investigation led to the following generalizations:

I. Quote delimiters (‘ ’ ") and text delimiters (< ([{ / \ -) may occur metatextually in string initial position, while sentence terminators (. ! ?) and phrasal structure markers (, ; : -) never do. Quote delimiters and text delimiters always occur in pairs, so once a string-initial quote or text delimiter has been found, a string final equivalent must occur eventually.

II. Characters which can be either textual or metatextual in string-initial position are: the left and right single quotes, the double quote, and the left parenthesis.

III. Characters which can be either textual or metatextual in string-final position are: the period, the exclamation mark, the right single quote and the right parenthesis.

IV. Orthographic islands provided with both string-initial and stringfinal textual punctuation do not exist. In addition, if two or more punctuation characters occur at the boundary of an orthographic island, only one of them is textual. We came across one exception to this rule: an amount of money can be spelled as a digit string followed by a comma and one or two hyphens (e.g. 12,-), in which case both the comma and the hyphen(s) are textual.

On the basis of these generalizations, we have defined a large number of explicit validity constraints, such as: the question mark and colon in string-final position are always metatextual, string-medial punctuation characters are always textual, etc. Disambiguation of ambiguous punctuation characters, i.e. characters which may occur both textually and metatextually in the same position, requires additional information from the context. It is beyond the scope of this paper to discuss all ambiguous punctuation characters in detail. In the following section we will therefore only take a closer look at the strategy which has been applied to disambiguate the period, for ambiguities caused by the period form a major problem in segmentation (cf. Riley 1990).

3.2. Disambiguation of the period

Although the period may occur in acronyms, numerals, and in sequences of several periods indicating that a certain text fragment has been omitted (...), the real problem is to distinguish between the period used as an end-of-sentence marker and the period ending an abbreviation. Once a period has been detected, three possibilities must be taken into account. The period may denote the end of a sentence, the end of an abbreviation, or both.

Notice that in the latter case, formally two periods are expected: the first (textual) period to indicate that we are dealing with an abbreviation and the second (metatextual) period to denote the end of the sentence. In practice, unfortunately, only one period is used in this particular situation.

In order to decide whether we are dealing with a textual or a metatextual period, we examine the context in which the period occurs. First, we test whether the string to the left of the period (including the period itself) is an abbreviation. In order to do so, an abbreviation lexicon has been developed (Boef 1989). However, only when we cannot decide on the basis of orthography whether we are dealing with an abbreviation, a lexicon is search performed. Note that each time a string of lower-case letters is followed by a period, the abbreviation lexicon has to be consulted. Second, we test whether the right context of the period corresponds to the beginning of a new sentence. If a certain string happens to be an abbreviation, and it also occurs in sentence-final position, then the period is made textual and, in addition, a special end-of-sentence marker is inserted.

Unfortunately, the disambiguation of the period is not as straightforward as suggested so far. We have to cope with various orthographic patterns which incorrectly suggest that we are dealing with an abbreviation in sentence-final position, such as *Dr. Sagisaka* and *tel. 12345* (*telephone number 12345*). These examples show an abbreviation whose right context corresponds to the beginning of a new sentence, and according to the strategy described above, end-of-sentence markers would incorrectly be inserted. It is even more complicated, as *tel.* may also be a lexical item in sentence-final position (meaning: 'second'), in which case the period does perform a metatextual role.

3.3. Context features

To distinguish real from apparent end-of-sentence points, "context features" have been introduced. A context feature denotes for each abbreviation listed in the lexicon whether the abbreviation expects a proper name, a digit string, or neither of these two, to its right. The general idea is, that if it is known that an abbreviation expects a proper name or a digit string to its right, incorrect detection of end-of-sentence points can be avoided. This method works well, as long as these abbreviations do not occur (as abbreviations) in sentence-final position; normally they do not.

A significant problem occurs, however, when one particular orthographic pattern corresponds both to an abbreviation and a lexical item in sentence-final position, such as the string *tel.* If *tel.* is followed by a digit string, then it will always be interpreted as a mid-sentence abbreviation on the analogy of a telephone number, although it may be a lexical item in sentence-final position as well. However, if it cannot be decided on the basis of context features whether a certain period is textual or not, a situation we face when the string *tel.* is followed by a word with a capital initial letter, then the period is treated as a metatextual punctuation character by default. Making the period textual in this particular situation would lead (afterwards) to lexical items being labeled as abbreviations, and in our opinion, this would cause more severe errors in pronunciation than abbreviations labeled as lexical items.

Obviously, there are ambiguities which cannot be solved by a preprocessing module such as TextScan, which is entirely based on the identification and interpretation of form features. In some cases, disambiguation can only be achieved with help from syntactical and sometimes even semantic analysis. It should be said, however, that ambiguities with which a form-based preprocessing module cannot cope are relatively few.

After the segmentation procedure, the original input text has been converted into a sequence of spaces, metatextual punctuation characters, and textual units, that is, orthographic islands from which metatextual punctuation characters have been removed. Textual units broadly correspond to words (neutral strings made up of lowercase letters not violating the grapheme structure rules for Dutch) and anomalous symbol strings. In addition, all possible end-of-sentence points are marked, although the actual separation of sentences is performed only at a later stage.

4. Labeling

4.1. Introduction

The purpose of the labeling procedure is to classify and label anomalous textual units in order to obtain, via expansion, text suitable for linguistic analysis. The labeling algorithm performs a classification based on the expansion each textual unit requires afterwards. Before this expansion-based labeling can be described in more detail, however, some terminology has to be introduced.

A distinction is made between single textual units (*MPs, ft, 22nd, mid, 170, BBC1*) and compound textual units (*mid-1970s, 30-year-old, 2,000-ft, IRA's*). Compound textual units always contain two or more single units separated by a hyphen and/or an apostrophe (and sometimes a slash).

It occurs every so often, that correct expansion requires several textual units to be viewed as parts of larger expressions. This is illustrated by the expression *DFl 2,50 ($ 2.50)*. The fact that the single textual unit *2,50* denotes an amount of money follows exclusively from the presence of the preceding abbreviation. An expression, which has been defined as a sequence of one or more textual units relevant with regard to expansion, may therefore correspond either to a single or a compound textual unit, or to a sequence of two or more textual units. In the former case, the correct expansion of the unit in question can be derived from the orthography of the unit itself, while in the latter case, the correct expansion of the individual units can only be achieved by combining them into one larger expression. Accordingly, the labeling process can be defined as the conversion of textual units, metatextual punctuation characters, and spaces, into expressions.

The initial step in the development of the labeling algorithm was the analysis of a large corpus of text in order to draw up an inventory of the labels required. Approximately fifty labels, of which the large majority concern different types of digit-bearing expressions, are distinguished.

4.2. Ambiguous textual units

The major problem for a labeling algorithm is that a lot of textual units are ambiguous. A textual unit is viewed as ambiguous if it can be classified, according to its form, as a member of several classes. Proper names, for example, are marked by an initial capital letter. However, lexical items in sentence-initial position always begin with a capital letter, too. It is, of course, possible to check whether a string with an initial capital occurs in sentence-initial position or not. But even then, a labeling error may occur if the first word of the sentence happens to be a proper name. An unambiguous textual unit, on the other hand, is made up of a unique sequence of characters, which can always be distinguished from other units (for example, dates like *10-02-'66*).

Disambiguation of textual units is done by means of a layered labeling process. Essentially, single textual units are labeled first, resulting in a basic layer. Acronyms embedded in compound textual units, for example, and acronyms occurring separately, are labeled by the same pattern matching rule. Labeled single units of the basic layer are then combined into compound textual units, or into larger expressions if expansion requires such an operation. Obviously, it has to be known when and if two or more textual units have to be combined into one larger expression. This knowledge is, again, represented in the abbreviation lexicon by means of context features.

For segmentation purposes, it suffices to know that a specific abbreviation expects a proper name or a digit string to its right (see section 2.2).

However, correct labeling of a larger expression requires information on the type of digit string an abbreviation expects to its left or to its right. A currency-string, for example, should be combined with a currency symbol, a time-string with an abbreviation which denotes a time, etc. This more specific information has also been added to the abbreviation lexicon. An abbreviation is united with an adjacent digit string, only if the adjacent digit string corresponds to the digit string specified by the abbreviation's context feature. What counts as a proper digit string, i.e. telephone number, time string, etc., is defined by means of rules.

Context features were introduced to disambiguate single textual units such as the string *1982* in the expression *1982 ft*. The abbreviation indicates that the digit string *1982* is a whole number and certainly not a year. However, context features may also determine the correct expansion of an abbreviation, if the abbreviation has several different fully expanded forms. Often, one form may represent the singular as well as the plural form of a noun. The abbreviation *p.*, for example, may be expanded to *pages* or *page*, depending, among other things, on whether the digit string precedes or follows the abbreviation.

The preceding argumentation may suggest that larger expressions always consist of abbreviations in combination with digit strings. Although this is not always the case, it is (apart from some exceptions) the only type of larger expression defined in module TextScan due to the fact that abbreviations and digit strings can be recognized by form. That, for example, a digit string followed by the word *million* must be a whole number, is knowledge which has not been implemented, although it is possible and probably desirable in the future. A problem that must be solved first, however, is how to represent this type of knowledge in a form-based preprocessing module.

After the labeling procedure, the original input has now been converted into sentences, divided into expressions. The label of an expression indicates the type of expansion an expression requires.

5. Expansion

5.1. Rules or lexicons

Some anomalous expressions, such as abbreviations, have fully expanded forms which can only be specified individually by entry into a lexicon. For the large majority of anomalous expressions, however, we have a choice: the fully expanded form can be obtained either by applying rules depending on the expressions' orthographic form, or by specification in a lexicon. In our opinion, rule-based expansion is to be preferred to lexicon-based expansion due to the fact that a preprocessor has to deal with a huge variety of orthographic structures. This is the result of a lack of unambiguous rules concerning the use of punctuation characters, and the orthography of anomalous expressions (Renkema 1987; Horst 1990). The size of the various lexicons needed in a lexicon-based expander would be enormous, but more importantly, these lexicons are likely to be highly incomplete.

5.2. Alternative expanded forms

As a result of the expansion-based strategy applied in labeling, expansion itself becomes rather straightforward. The expansion of telephone numbers, years, currency-strings, etc., is more or less self-evident. However, there will always remain some ambiguous expressions, that is, expressions for which disambiguation on the basis of context fails. An example of such an expression is the string *2/4*, which may be a date (2nd of April), a fraction, a proportion, a division, or a range. Concerning ambiguous expressions in general, the most acceptable or neutral expansion, given the various possible contexts in which such an expression may occur, will be selected. This is not necessarily the alternative which causes the fewest errors; it may, for example, be the literal form (*two slash four* for the expression 2/4).

There may also exist several alternative fully expanded forms for one expression in one context. The year *1966*, for example, may be expanded to *nineteen sixty six* or to *nineteen hundred sixty and six*; the currency-string *$ 2.50* may be expanded to *two fifty* or to *two dollars fifty cents*. Often, one of the alternatives can be regarded as more formal or ceremonial than the other(s).

Another complicating factor with respect to expansion is that human readers may want to choose alternative fully expanded forms for one expression, depending on the purpose of the reading. The acronym *US*, for example, will probably be pronounced as a letter-name in casual speech. A professional news reader, however, usually reads aloud the fully expanded form of an acronym, while someone who is spelling a name and address over the telephone will most likely choose to pronounce everything in the literal form. It is obvious that different applications (reading machines for the blind, dictating machines) require different expansion-rule sets.

5.3. Expander output

The labeling process described in the previous section produces around fifty different labeled expressions. Eight of these expressions, viz. digit strings (always whole numbers), fractions, ordinal strings, proper names, acronyms, lexical items, metatextual punctuation characters and undefined symbols (for example, non-printable characters), are not sent to the expander. Instead, they are sent to TextScan's output level straightaway. Digit strings, fractions, ordinal strings, proper names, and acronyms are expanded at a later stage of the text-to-speech conversion process for several reasons, but primarily for reasons of efficiency: all expressions which have been converted into words within TextScan undergo morphological analysis. This is a time-consuming process, which should be avoided as much as possible; here we avoid it by not expanding those expressions which can easily be expanded later, as a result of very straight correspondence between orthography and pronunciation. Lexical items, metatextual punctuation characters, and undefined symbols are suitable for further analysis in their original form.

All other expressions are passed to the expander and converted into one of the eight TextScan output level expressions listed above. The currency-string *$ 2.50*, for example, is expanded to *d(2)*, *l(dollars)*, *d(50)*, *l(cents)*, where *l* stands for lexical item and *d* for digit string. These labels indicate the type of further processing that is required once TextScan has been applied.

6. Evaluation

6.1. Introduction

The number of anomalous strings in an input text for text-to-speech conversion depends on the type and subject of the text. If we confine ourselves to newspaper texts, then classified advertisements, film and theater listings, radio & television guides, and so on (henceforth referred to as telegraphic-style texts because of the cryptic and ungrammatical constructions), contain more anomalous strings than, for example, sports or business columns. Sports and business columns, in turn, are anomaly-rich compared to news items on the home and foreign news pages. Telegraphic-style texts are highly suitable for evaluating a preprocessing module, such as TextScan, for a relatively small amount of text will contain many anomalous strings. However, these texts differ so much from "standard" newspaper texts that it can be argued that they are not suitable to be read aloud and listened to, and necessitate an initial pre-editing or rewriting phase in order to make them suitable for text-to-speech conversion (Petrič—van den Bergh, this volume).

6.2. Material

The material that was used to evaluate TextScan consisted of a large set of short newspaper texts (press reports) released in June 1990 by the Dutch press-agency ANP. In total, the material consisted of 1,631 sentences, containing 26,657 expressions (metatextual punctuation included). The material was divided into three sets: a set of telegraphic-style texts (202 sentences, 2,570 expressions), a set of editorial newspaper texts, normally located on the home and foreign news pages (786 sentences, 13,699 expressions), and a set of editorial texts on sports (643 sentences, 10,388 expressions).

In order to evaluate module TextScan, we have to compare the current TextScan output with the maximum that can be achieved with a form-based preprocessing module. This maximum is defined as the maximum a preprocessor is able to achieve purely on the basis of form features, i.e., without help from any form of syntactical or semantic analysis. Consequently, TextScan may produce two types of errors. On the one hand, errors which cannot be avoided because TextScan is unable to benefit from linguistic analysis, and on the other, errors which can be avoided by improving the current module, either by changing the rules, or by the incorporation of other lexicons. For the present evaluation, the former type of errors will be referred to as unavoidable errors and the latter as avoidable errors. The number of avoidable errors is an indication of the improvements that can still be made within the limits of a form-based preprocessing module. The number of unavoidable errors is an indication of the necessity of integrating preprocessing with linguistic analysis.

Errors are also classified according to the stage at which they occur; during segmentation, labeling, or expansion. In addition, segmentation errors are divided into sentence-level errors and expression-level errors, while labeling and expansion errors always involve expressions. An example of an unavoidable (sentence-level segmentation) error is a missed end-of-sentence point caused by an unusual sentence ending in *Mr.*, and the next sentence starting with *Jones*. An example of an avoidable (labeling) error is a sentence-initial proper name labeled as lexical item; this could be avoided with the use of a proper name lexicon. It should be emphasized that an error is always counted only once, even if it leads to additional errors. A segmentation error on the sentence level usually involves a segmentation error on the expression level as well. In that case, only the sentence-level segmentation error is counted.

For each text type, the following figures were counted by hand: the number of sentences, the number of expressions, the number of anomalous expressions, and the number of anomalous expressions that have to be sent to the expander. These figures are summarized in Table 1. The percentage of anomalous expressions has been calculated over the total number of expressions, and the percentage of anomalous expressions that have to be sent to the expander has been calculated over the total number of anomalous expressions.

Table 1. Number of sentences, number of expressions, percentage of anomalous expressions, and % of anomalous expressions that have to be sent to the expander

	number of sentences	number of expressions	% anomalous expressions	% anomalous expressions to be expanded
editorial home/foreign	786	13,699	13.9	3.5
editorial sports	643	10,388	16.2	5.5
telegraphic style	202	2,570	47.9	21.8

The data in Table 1 show that TextScan has to deal with two to three anomalous expressions in each sentence in the case of editorial texts (home/foreign and sports). The telegraphic-style texts contain approximately six anomalous expressions per sentence. Note that the first word of each sentence is anomalous according to the definition of what counts as an anomalous string. For the editorial texts only 4.5 percent of the anomalous expressions have to be passed to the expansion module, which means that more than 95 percent of all anomalous expressions are proper names, acronyms, whole numbers, fractions, or ordinal numbers. A little less than a quarter of the anomalous expressions found in telegraphic-style texts have to be passed to the expansion module. These texts contain relatively many abbreviations and complex digit-bearing strings, such as times, dates, years etc.

6.3. Results

In Tables 2a and 2b, which show TextScan's error rates, the number of errors for each class is given as a percentage: sentence-level segmentation errors are given as a percentage of the total number of sentences, expression-level segmentation errors are given as a percentage of the total number of expressions, labeling errors are given as a percentage of the total number of anomalous expressions, and expansion errors are given as a percentage of the total number of expanded anomalous expressions.

Table 2a. Percentage of avoidable sentence-level segmentation errors, expression-level segmentation errors, labeling errors, and expansion errors

	% sentence-level segmentation errors	% expression-level segmentation errors	% labeling errors	% expansion errors
editorial home/foreign	0.4	<0.01	3.8	0.0
editorial sports	0.4	<0.01	4.0	0.0
telegraphic style	0.5	0.0	2.5	0.4

Table 2b. Percentage of unavoidable sentence-level segmentation errors, expression-level segmentation errors, labeling errors, and expansion errors

	% sentence-level segmentation errors	% expression-level segmentation errors	% labeling errors	% expansion errors
editorial home/foreign	0.1	<0.01	0.9	1.5
editorial sports	0.2	<0.01	0.3	0.0
telegraphic style	0.0	2.0	0.9	0.7

An important conclusion that can be drawn from the data in Tables 2a and 2b is that refinement of the current form-based preprocessing module will cause a larger overall improvement than help from syntactical or semantic analysis. If we take a closer look at the various stages of preprocessing, we may conclude that the segmentation algorithm works almost perfectly. Only the number of unavoidable expression-level segmentation errors is relatively high (2.0 percent). The vast majority of these errors concern textual units which contain two expressions instead of one.

The labeling algorithm is responsible for the majority of errors. Note that approximately 75 percent of all labeling errors are due to lexical items being mistaken for proper names and vice versa. A major improvement would therefore result from the incorporation of a proper name lexicon or a sophisticated rule set.

Note that the number of expansion errors is relatively low due to the approach followed in labeling. Let us assume that the expression *2/4* has been labeled as a fraction, and is eventually expanded as such. This will certainly not be the appropriate expansion in the phrase: *Date of next meeting: 2/4.* In fact, this is a labeling error, because the expansion in itself is correct once the expression has been labeled as a fraction. Incompleteness of several expansion rules was the cause of the very few avoidable expansion errors.

7. Conclusion

The evaluation results may suggest that module TextScan is nearly perfect. It should be emphasized, however, that the evaluation involved only a limited amount of text. In our opinion, the segmentation algorithm is very good indeed; however, the labeling and consequently the expansion algorithms still need further refinement, for other test material will certainly contain new and unexpected orthographic patterns. The present shortcomings of TextScan are that it does not identify roman numerals, foreign words, multi-word anomalies, like *de facto*, embedded sentences, acute, grave, and circumflex accents, diaeresis, and all sorts of fonts and styles, such as bold, underlined, italic, etc. Most of these features did not occur in our test material, but it is obvious that perfect speech output necessitates the identification of these features as well. It is not at all evident, once fonts and styles etc., can be identified, how these features should be realized in speech. Obviously, the most significant improvement of module TextScan would involve the identification (and "expansion") of proper names, either by rules or by means of a lexicon.

In general, it is not at all clear what type of output a preprocessing module has to produce. Clearly, a preprocessing module has to perform a segmentation of the input text, and furthermore, anomalous forms have to be converted into some recognizable format. Apart from these tasks, however, it is also possible to extract relevant linguistic information from orthography. Preprocessing can, for example, assist syntactic and prosodic analysis in grouping words (into noun phrases) and defining word categories (O'Shaughnessy 1990; Monaghan 1989). An intonation module would benefit from having first names and surnames combined into complex names which function, in turn, as noun groups. A similar argument applies to expressions such as *Van Gogh-exhibition*, which now constitutes two expressions.

It can be argued that extracting linguistic information from orthography is not a task a preprocessing module should perform, because preprocessing and linguistic analysis are two functionally different processes. We believe, however, that successful text-to-speech conversion can only be achieved by using all potential information available during the complete text-to-speech conversion process (Monaghan 1990b). At present, TextScan does not extract linguistic information from orthography because the subsequent linguistic modules, which were already in an advanced development stage when TextScan was designed, are unable to deal with input that also involves linguistic information.

Part II

Linguistic aspects

Multiple paths to the lexicon

Johan M. Lammens

Abstract

This chapter describes a research project that investigated the use of large lexicons as a primary source of lexical information for text-to-speech conversion systems, specifically for grapheme-to-phoneme conversion. A general outline for a lexicon-based grapheme-to-phoneme conversion system is presented. The optimal content and size of lexicons are considered, as well as the implementation of fast retrieval algorithms. Some results are presented in terms of correctness of transcription, conversion speed, and memory usage. We conclude with an evaluation of the developed system for lexical access, and a brief comparison with other methods of grapheme-to-phoneme conversion in the context of text-to-speech systems.

1. Problem definition

The research described in this paper set out with a number of goals related to the development of an orthographic/phonologic lexicon-based grapheme-to-phoneme conversion system:

— reducing the execution time for grapheme-to-phoneme conversion, relative to existing rule-based systems
— specification of the optimal content and size of the lexicon for this purpose
— implementation of fast retrieval procedures and data compression methods for the lexicon
— comparing lexicon-based systems with other approaches for grapheme-to-phoneme conversion

In the course of the project, the focus has shifted away from the problem of data compression, and some minor goals were added, viz. the implementation of a simple method for morphological decomposition of complex wordforms,[1] and the deduction of a phonemic representation and part of speech information for those wordforms after decomposition. With respect to these goals, it is interesting to compare the results described here with the results obtained using a fullblown morphological analyzer (see Heemskerk—van Heuven, this volume), and with the results obtained in a project that specifically studied morphological decomposition without a lexicon (see Reizevoort—van Heuven, this volume).

2. General system outline

A general structure for a lexicon-based grapheme-to-phoneme conversion system has been developed (Lammens 1987; Berendsen—Lammens—van Leeuwen 1989). This structure is usable in practical applications, while at the same time it facilitates the study of the behavior of the system, e.g. with different kinds of input text or different sizes and contents of lexicons. The general outline of the system is based on a description of a lexical component for a text-to-speech system by Carlson—Granström (1986). Figure 1 represents the overall system structure.

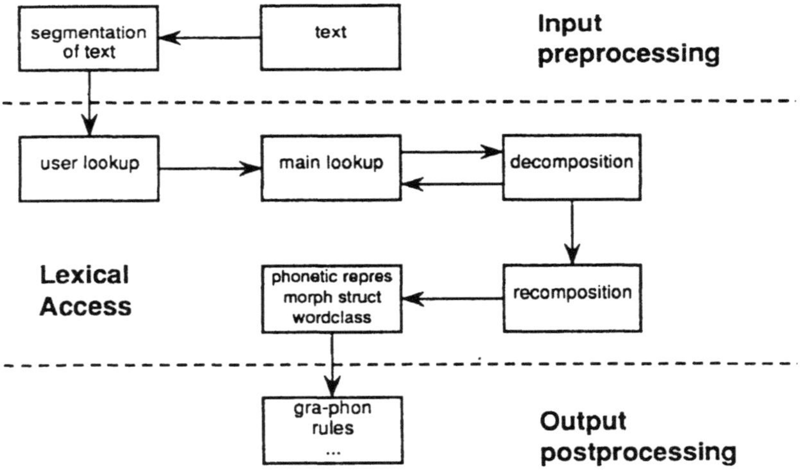

Figure 1. Overall structure of a lexicon-based grapheme-to-phoneme conversion system

The function of the complete system is to provide a phonemic transcription, part of speech information, and in some cases a representation of the morphological structure of wordforms, for as many words of the input text as possible. Completeness is not a goal, as a complete lexicon is both theoretically and practically impossible. Correctness and speed of transcription are the main goals. There are also provisions for storing and retrieving inherent accentuation and function word status (for use in prosodic analysis, cf. Kager—Quené 1987, this volume), and additional information in the user and main lexicon. As far as this project is concerned, the most interesting part of the system is the one labeled "Lexical Access" in Figure 1 (henceforth LA). The preceding and following parts, input preprocessing and output postprocessing, are outside of the scope of this project.

The function of the system for lexical access within a text-to-speech conversion system (TTS system) is to retrieve as much information as possible about as many words as possible, before any other processing takes place. The rationale is, of course, that it usually takes much less effort to look up some piece of information in a table than to compute it, in addition to the fact that some properties of words just cannot be computed. For example, some exceptions to grapheme-to-phoneme conversion rules always remain, no matter how refined the rules are (Berendsen et al. 1989). We will now discuss some aspects of the LA system in more detail.

2.1. User lookup

The User Lookup module is provided to allow the user to tailor the system to his/her own needs, and to store exceptions for other parts of the TTS system, including any of the other lexicons. User lexicon entries contain the following fields:

1. grapheme string: the representation of a word in normal orthography
2. phoneme string: the phonemic representation of the word, including primary and/or secondary stress markers
3. part of speech: a code indicating the part of speech of the word
4. function word value: a value indicating whether or not the word is a function word, and if so, what kind of function word
5. function word part of speech: a special part of speech value related to function word status
6. decomposition: a representation of the morphological structure of the word
7. other: a free format field that can be used for future expansion, or in general for any other information the user might want to store and retrieve in association with the word.

Of these seven fields, only the first three must always be present, as the system will always return at least these three kinds of lexical information for any word present in one of the lexicons. The other fields are optional. The function-word related fields (4 and 5) are provided for another analysis component of the TTS system as a whole, viz. the prosodic analysis component (Kager—Quené 1987, this volume). This prevents words from having to be looked up twice. The user lexicon is meant to be the most flexible and accessible one in the system. Its precedence over the main lexicon also makes it suitable for overriding the information stored in the main lexicon without physically affecting the latter.

2.2. Main lookup

This is the central lookup module of the LA system. Its lexicon is much bigger than the user lexicon, typically more than 10,000 entries, but contains the same kinds of data. The performance of the system is largely dependent on the size and content of this lexicon, as we will discuss below. The function of the main lookup module is rather simple: to retrieve the data that is stored for a word in normal orthographic (graphemic) form. As the main lexicon contains the same kinds of data about words as the user lexicon does, its function with respect to other parts of the TTS system is the same. The main difference is the number of entries stored, and the accessibility. The main lexicon is not meant to be altered by the user, as this may have rather unpredictable effects on the decomposition module (see below). If anything needs to be changed or added, it should be done in the user lexicon.

2.3. Decomposition

To maximize the use of stored lexical data, a simple module for decomposition of morphologically complex words has been added. The concept of morphological analysis in a TTS system has proved its usefulness before, cf. Allen—Hunnicutt—Klatt (1987), Carlson—Granström (1986), Daelemans (1987), Berendsen—Don (1987). This module is not meant as a computational model of Dutch morphology or as an exhaustive morphological analysis component, but rather as a relatively inexpensive way to increase the potential use of lexical data that is present anyhow. Again, completeness is not a goal, but correctness is. The rather pragmatical nature of this module may also be inferred from its place in the overall structure of the LA system (cf. Figure 1), viz. after the modules for user and main lookup. This has a double reason. The first is to make certain that no valuable time is wasted in trying to decompose a complex word that is already present in the user or main lexicon. The second reason is that this order circumvents many problems with ambiguous decompositions of complex words. The latter is a notorious problem for decomposition algorithms that always attempt a full decomposition of a word using a morpheme lexicon (cf. Allen et al. 1987; Heemskerk—van Heuven, this volume), as opposed to the wordform lexicon that is used in our system.

The decomposition and recomposition component draws on ideas from several sources, mainly in the framework of lexical morphology (e.g. Siegel 1974; van Beurden 1987) and is related to other research within the ASSP framework (Berendsen—Don 1987; Heemskerk—van Heuven, this volume; Reizevoort—van Heuven, this volume) and outside of the ASSP framework (Daelemans 1987). The LA system can be used in five distinct modes which differ in the number of words that can be transcribed, but also in the amount of resources that are required to do so. Briefly, in Mode 0 only the user lexicon is consulted, without any decomposition being attempted; in Mode 1 the user lexicon and the main lexicon are consulted, without decomposition; in Mode 2 the user lexicon and the main lexicon are consulted, and compounds are decomposed without spelling adjustments or affix processing; in Mode 3 the linking graphemes *s* and *e* are processed as well, as in *dood+s#kist* 'death#coffin' and *boer+e#jongens* 'farmer#boys' and in Mode 4, finally, compounds are split with full affix processing, as in *bekwaam+heid+s#proef* 'able+ness#test' or *be+lezen+heid* 'being well-read'. In these examples # represents a compound (word) boundary, and + represents an affix boundary.

After a wordform has been decomposed into its constituent morphemes,[2] it must be reassembled into a complete wordform. The recomposition routines return a string indicating the decomposition that was arrived at, a phonemic representation, and part of speech information for the complex wordform. Since the recomposed wordform is not present as a whole in any of the lexicons, this information has to be inferred from the data that has been retrieved for the morphemes making up the complex wordform.

The decomposition module uses a number of small specialized lexicons, containing e.g. affixes, strings that should not be decomposed, as well as some commonly occurring morphemes. Full details on the decomposition and recomposition algorithms can be found in Lammens (1989).

2.4. Interfacing with other components of a TTS system

The system for Lexical Access is not complete, in the sense that it does not cover all of the vocabulary of Dutch. Of course, this means that some of the input text will have to be processed by components outside of the LA system. For now, we will only consider grapheme-to-phoneme conversion, although the LA system may provide other kinds of data as well (see above). Possible candidates to interface our system to in order to obtain complete vocabulary coverage are a full morphological decomposition system (Heemskerk—van Heuven, this volume; Reizevoort—van Heuven, this volume) or a rule-based grapheme-to-phoneme conversion system (Berendsen—Langeweg—van Leeuwen 1986). Since full morphological decomposition systems are meant to be complete in their own right, we will not consider them any further. Rule-based grapheme-to-phoneme conversion systems such as the one mentioned above exhibit a number of differences as compared to our LA system, cf. Table 1.

Table 1. Comparison of rule-based and lexicon-based grapheme-to-phoneme conversion systems

Rule-based	Lexicon-based
— operates on letter basis	— operates on word basis
— in principle complete	— in principle not complete
— some degree of incorrectness	— in principle completely correct
— based on phonological principles	— based on pragmatic principles
— linguistically relevant	— not necessarily linguistically relevant
— often rather slow, due to the interpreter-like application of rules	— reasonably to very fast, due to application of fast storage and retrieval algorithms on word-level

From this comparison it is apparent that both kinds of system complement each other to a large extent. It is this complementary nature that allows them to be integrated in a natural and efficient way. Such a system, with the lexical part ordered before the rule part, combines the advantages of both approaches and results in a system that is correct, fast and flexible. The most difficult problem in creating such a system is striking a balance between the size of the lexicon and the size of the rule component. Though this must in part depend on the nature of the hardware the system is being used on, a few general principles can be given:

- the lexicon must contain all words that are not transcribed correctly by the rule component
- although it is theoretically possible to tune the rule system so that it covers only that part of the vocabulary that is not covered by the lexical component, it is wiser to design the rule component to be in principle

complete. In practice this will always leave some exceptions that are not handled correctly by the rule system.
— given the considerable difference in speed between both types of system, it is advisable to make the lexical component cover as much of the vocabulary as possible. We will come back to this issue when discussing the content of the lexicons below.

As mentioned before, the LA system has provisions for storing other types of data besides a phonemic representation (e.g. part of speech information, or specialized information for prosodic analysis). It should be seen as a central depository for all kinds of lexical information used by different components of the TTS system. From that function it follows that the LA system should be positioned as one of the first components in the TTS system (cf. van Leeuwen—te Lindert, this volume).

3. Content and size of the lexicons

This section provides a brief overview and motivation of the content of the different lexicons. Naturally, the content of the lexicons is of decisive importance to the performance of the complete system.

3.1. The user lexicon

As the name implies, the content of this lexicon is to be supplied by the user, so by default it is empty. The reasons for including certain entries in the user lexicon are diverse: one might want to expand the standard vocabulary by including technical terms, user-specific jargon etc; another important reason might be to correct errors in any of the other lexicons, or to customize pronunciation of certain words, etc.

3.2. The main lexicon

The main lexicon is a high-frequency wordform lexicon. It contains 12,116 wordforms with corresponding phonemic representations and part of speech information. It has been derived by merging a large wordform frequency list obtained from newspaper text (van den Broecke—Elstrodt—Aerts 1986) with a phonetically transcribed dictionary. That dictionary is in turn based on the "Woordenlijst der Nederlandse Taal", an official Dutch vocabulary list, and produced at CELEX Nijmegen.

There are several alternative choices for the content of a lexicon to be used in a TTS system, or in other language technology systems for that matter. The most straightforward kind of lexicon, also the one that requires the least processing effort to retrieve lexical data, is the kind of wordform lexicon that we are using here. The wordforms are stored as they are encountered in real-world texts like newspapers, with the corresponding lexical information. To find a word, one just looks it up in the list and retrieves the lexical information. A problem with wordform lexicons is that there is a considerable amount of redundancy. Plural nouns, for instance, are different from the singular form and thus will be stored as separate entries. Most, if not all, of the lexical information stored along with a plural and singular form of the same noun will be identical, not to mention the wordforms themselves of course, which might differ in as little as one letter (e.g. the plural morpheme *-s*). To make a sensible selection of wordforms to include from a very large set (in principle all possible wordforms of the target language, which means at least several hundreds of thousands, if not millions), the frequency criterion is often applied. One counts the number of times any wordform occurs in a particular corpus, and selects only the most frequently occurring ones. Note that different forms of the same word may have very different frequencies, and therefore may or may not occur together in the lexicon.

A slightly more abstract kind of lexicon is a lemma lexicon. This kind of lexicon contains only lemmata, i.e. words without inflection (the singular form for nouns, the infinitival form for verbs, non-inflected adjectival forms, etc.). This reduces redundancy as compared to a wordform lexicon, e.g. a noun will only be stored in the singular form. Accessing the lexical information in this kind of lexicon is more complicated however. To retrieve the lexical information for a word, it has to be reduced to its lemma form before it can be looked up. The lexical information that is retrieved in this way may have to be processed further. For instance, take a plural wordform for which one wants to retrieve the phonemic form. The wordform is lemmatized to the singular form, and the corresponding phonemic representation is retrieved. That representation has to be converted to a plural form, which may require some nontrivial processing. So a lemma lexicon will be smaller in size, but it will also require more processing than the corresponding wordform lexicon (assuming both cover the same set of wordforms).

A third, even more abstract, kind of lexicon is a morpheme lexicon. Here only the basic "building blocks" of words are stored. A complex noun like *headhunter*, for instance, will not be stored as a whole. Instead, the morphemes *head*, *hunt* and *-er* will be stored. Of course, this kind of lexicon is even less redundant than a lemma lexicon, but will require even more pre- and postprocessing. Retrieving the phonemic form for *headhunter* requires that the word be split into its constituent morphemes first, then those morphemes and their phonemic representations will be retrieved, and finally they have to be reassembled into a phonemic form for the complex word, which may be a complex task. One of the major problems of using a morpheme lexicon is decomposing words into their constituent morphemes. Numerous ambiguities arise, and complex (and processing-intensive) algorithms have to be devised to disambiguate them. Morpheme lexicons can theoretically be complete, and cover the entire vocabulary of a language with a relatively small number of entries (for standard non-regional Dutch this number is estimated to be about 17,000, cf. Heemskerk—van Heuven, this volume). So morpheme lexicons are the least redundant and the smallest in size, but require the most processing effort.

In the ASSP context, the use of a morpheme lexicon in a TTS system was being investigated elsewhere (Heemskerk—van Heuven, this volume), so the choice for our project was really limited to a wordform lexicon or a lemma lexicon. Both kinds of lexicons were available with phonemic transcriptions: a high-frequency wordform lexicon of about 12,000 wordforms, and a lemma lexicon of about 70,000 lemmas. Obviously the latter is much more complete in a lexical sense, but also substantially bigger in size. As the focus of our project has always been to achieve good performance (in terms of correctness and speed) with relatively simple means, the lemma lexicon approach has not been favored because of the extra computational effort involved. Considering that newspapers constitute a reasonably realistic source of lexical material for a real-world TTS system, I compared the percentage of newspaper text that could be covered by both types of lexicon, without any further processing. Figures 2 and 3 represent the findings.

To make a fair comparison possible, the varying lexicon sizes were obtained in both cases through frequency selection, so that a lexicon of size N always contained the N most frequent entries of the appropriate kind. It is apparent from the figures that the relation between lexicon size and percentage of text covered is essentially logarithmic, so that the first few thousand entries cover the bulk of the text, and the remaining several thousand entries cover only a small additional part. This is encouraging for a system like ours, because it means that relatively small lexicon sizes can cover very large percentages of input text. Although both curves have the same overall shape, the one for the wordform lexicon shows consistently higher percentages than the lemma lexicon, for equal lexicon size. Even when using the full size of the lemma lexicon (not shown in Figure 2), the maximum percentage of text covered is about 63, while the wordform lexicon reaches about 94 coverage with about 12,000 entries. Given that we

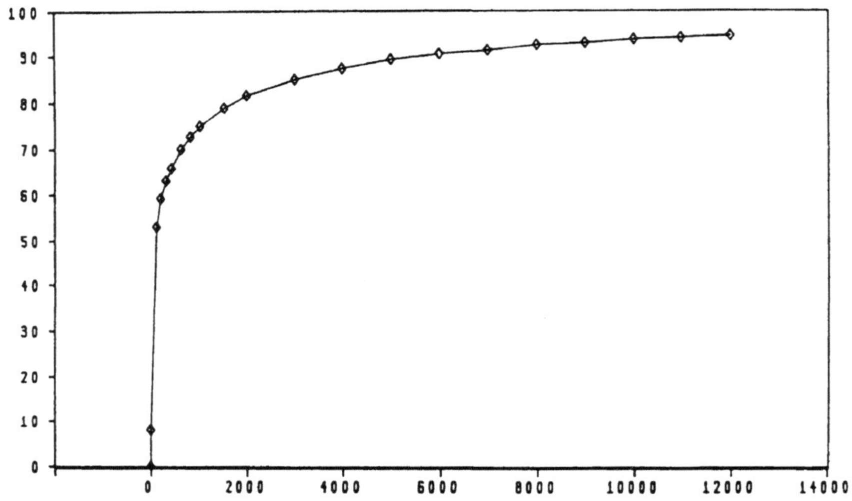

Figure 2. Percentage of newspaper text covered (Y axis) by a variable size lemma lexicon (X axis)

do not want to use a lemmatization routine, this clearly leaves the wordform lexicon as the right choice. Results discussed in this paper are all based on the use of this 12,000 entry wordform lexicon.

Although we have not considered memory space limitations in developing the system for Lexical Access, some recommendations can be made if they do apply. A theoretically interesting point to cut the curve in Figure 3.4 is the point of maximum curvature, which would be around a lexicon size of 1,200 entries. This point strikes a good balance between memory usage and effectiveness in terms of the percentage of text covered. As it turns out, the wordform lexicon is also a good database for a simple decomposition component that enhances the productivity of the stored lexical material considerably, without compromising efficiency for words that are stored as such.

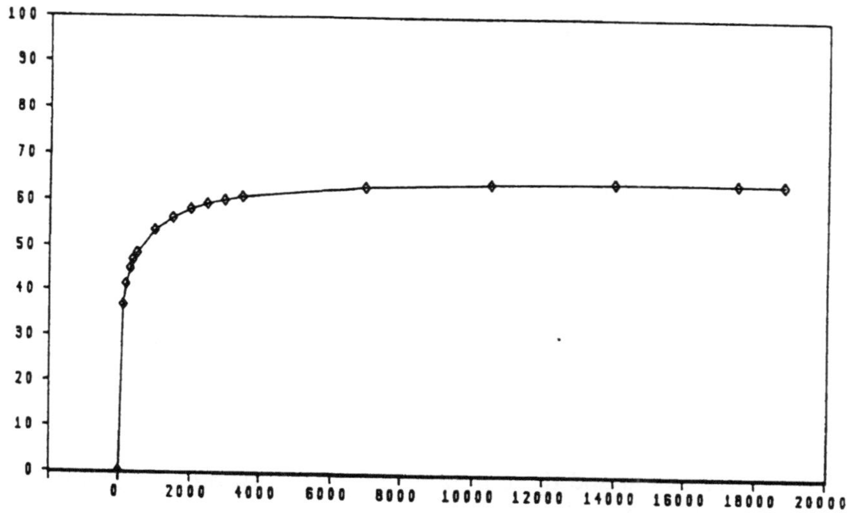

Figure 3. Percentage of newspaper text covered (Y axis) by a variable size high-frequency wordform lexicon (X axis)

4. Data structures and algorithms

4.1. Data structures

The main lexicon uses a simple linear array of pointers (*the primary table*), combined with a hashed access method (see below). To ensure proper functioning of the hashing algorithm, this array is prime-sized (and must always be). A pointer in the primary table may point to none, only one, or a chain of data records, each containing the lexical information associated with a word. This data structure is meant to contain a considerable number of lexicon entries, on the order of thousands to tens of thousands. The memory used by the primary table is constant, but the memory used by the data records is a function of the number of entries in the lexicon. Note that the entire data structure is kept in (virtual) memory. For larger lexicon sizes this is only possible when either a lot of physical memory or virtual memory is available. See the section on performance for a motivation of this approach. The actual lexicon entries are stored in a straightforward record of strings representation, with one field acting as the key for storage and retrieval, and the other fields acting as the data associated with the key.

The user lexicon uses a different data structure, viz. a trie (Knuth 1973). A trie is a special kind of binary tree that stores individual letters at its nodes, and words along paths in the tree. Some advantages of trie structures are: relatively high access speeds, automatic prefix compression, flexible storage and retrieval of entries, and its dynamic nature which makes the memory usage directly proportional to the length and number of words stored. Disadvantages of tries (in this form) are the rather large memory usage, as each letter of a word requires a separate node and two pointers for child nodes. Therefore the trie structures in the LA system are only used for relatively small lexicons. Again, this assumes the availability of a large physical memory or virtual memory capabilities. The trie data structures as implemented for the LA system use nodes consisting of records with a single character field and three pointer fields. Two of the pointers point to the node's child nodes (if any), and the third one points to the data record associated with a keyword whose path in the trie ends at the current node.

4.2. Algorithms

4.2.1. Description

We will limit our discussion to the hashing routines, since they are the most important factor in determining system performance. At the center of the hashing routines is the hash function that converts character strings (key strings) into a numeric value used for indexing the primary table array described above. The hash function I have been using is a variation on the well-known scheme that translates character values into a numeric representation and then uses that value modulo the size of the array as an array index (Knuth 1973; Horowitz—Sahni 1976; Snader 1987). This also reveals the reason for using a prime-sized primary table, since that ensures a maximum spread of key values over array indexes. The implemented hash function takes the first 28 characters of the key string (padded with null characters if it is not long enough), splits it into seven 4-byte (32 bit) words, and computes the exclusive-or (XOR) value of the seven words, seen as unsigned integers in binary representation. The resulting unsigned integer value modulo the size of the primary table gives us the index into that table.

The pointer stored at that table location points to the record containing the key and data strings, or to a chain of such records, one of which contains the key-data pair being searched. Chaining is used to resolve collisions that come about when two or more key strings are mapped onto the same primary table index. Chaining is not the only possibility to resolve collisions, but it turned out to be faster than alternatives like rehashing or linear search for the next available location.

4.2.2. Analysis

Time complexity. The theoretical goal for hash functions is to find a minimal perfect hash function (Haggard 1986). Here, *minimal* means that there are no empty places in the primary table after all entries are stored, and *perfect* means that there are no collisions (multiple key values being mapped onto the same primary table index). Stated more formally, a hash function is a function h whose domain W is the set of all key words, and whose co-domain (range) I is the set of all primary table indexes and a minimal perfect hash function is injective. Unfortunately minimal perfect hash functions are unattainable to date, at least for primary table sizes of more than a thousand or so (Haggard 1986).

To convert a key string into an array index, the implemented algorithm first pads the string with null characters if it is shorter than 28 characters, or truncates it to 28 characters if it is longer. Both padding and truncating are implemented using built-in functions of the VAX Pascal compiler, with no data available on algorithmic properties. After that, seven XOR operations are performed. We will assume a constant time t_{conv} for this step. Next, the primary table has to be indexed, for which we assume a constant time t_{tab}, or t_{init} for the first two steps together. The last step involves dereferencing a pointer and comparing a stored key to the one sought, for which we assign constant time t_{comp}.[3] The last step may have to be repeated when following a chain of items until the right one is found. For the sake of simplicity we ignore the delays that may occur due to page faults and virtual memory management. We further assume that memory accesses are equally distributed among all words, which is of course not true in reality, but this allows us to use average chain length in our computations. Average chain length is not easily predictable, as it depends in a complex way on the primary table size, the number of entries stored, and the graphemic structure of the keywords. A simulation with a fixed primary table size of 70,003 and a varying number of entries yielded the data presented in Figure 4. In this case the average chain length was about 1.5, and grew linearly with the number of entries. The relation could be described with the following regression equation: $L_{avg} = 1 + 7.14 * 10^{-6}N$, where l_{avg} is the average chain length, and N is the number of entries.

For a perfect hash function, the chain length would always be one. Ours is not perfect, but still rather close. It is expected that a primary table size of about the number of lexicon entries (but prime) will always result in similar values. Smaller sizes will result in a longer average chain length, and thus in poorer performance. Too large sizes, however, will result in an excessive amount of unused primary table entries and thus in a waste of memory space. In a general form, we can express the average chain length as $L_{avg} = 1 + cN$ ($c \ll 1$) which is linearly dependent on N, but grows very slowly. Summing up, we can characterize the time complexity for the retrieval of an item by the hashing routines as

(1) $$T_h = (1 + cN)t_{comp} + t_{init} + t_{div} \quad (c \ll 1)$$

where t_{div} is an additional constant for some diverse computations. This means that the search time is linearly dependent on N, the lexicon size, but only with a small factor. Using O-notation, we can write

(2) $$T_h = O(N)$$

Again, since c is very small, T_h is close to the theoretically optimal constant order, as illustrated in Figure 4.

The time complexity for the trie search routines evaluates to $O(L)$ where L is the length of the word being searched, as described in Lammens (1989). The worst-case time complexity for the morphological decomposition routines we use is exponential in the length of the word being decomposed, as described in Lammens (1989).

Space complexity. Given the data structures described in the previous section, the space complexity of the hashing algorithm can be described as $S_h = wN_p + c_a + N(L_k + c_s) + N(L_d + c_s) = N(L_k + L_d + 2c_s) + wN_p + c_a$, where N_p is the number of primary table entries, w is the machine word size (for pointers), L_k is the maximum key string length, L_d is the maximum data string length, N is the number of items stored, c_s is a constant for string storage overhead (usually for storing variable string length), and c_s is the overhead for array storage (the array descriptor). Clearly, the memory requirements are linearly dependent on N, since the size of the primary array N_p is constant. Filling in the values for the LA system on a VAX computer, this results in a total of 1.07 Mb, for a primary array size of 75,011 and 12,116 entries stored. Note that the primary array size is really too large for the actual number of lexical entries stored, but this value has been chosen to allow for larger lexicons if needed.

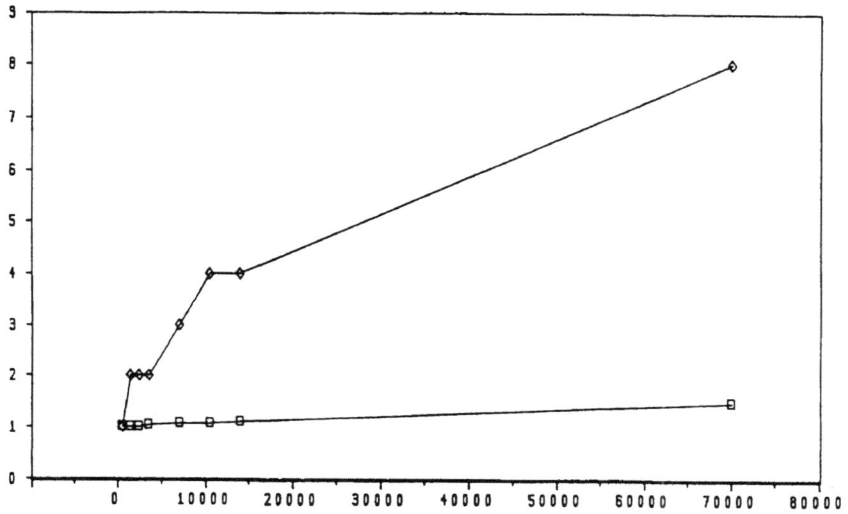

Figure 4. Maximum and average chain length (Y axis) in a simulation study with the hashing algorithm. The primary table size is fixed as 70,003, the number of lexicon entries ranges from 100 to 70,000 (X axis)

How minimal is our hashing algorithm? This question is hard to answer in general, but a simulation study with N_p = 70,003 and N = 70,038 showed that 38 percent of the primary array locations remained empty, which is clearly not minimal. The memory overhead due to the non-minimality of our algorithm is limited, however. If we let N_{pe} be the number of empty primary array locations, then it is given by wN_{pe}. In our case this evaluates to 103 kb which is only 3.75 percent of the total memory space of 2.7 Mb required to store all 70,038 entries (in an uncompressed format).

The memory space required for a trie structure is dependent on the degree of coinciding initial key segments (since they share partial paths in the trie). If we take the worst case, where there are no shared paths (which is not realistic), the trie contains one node per letter of each key string, and one data record for each key string. We can then express the size of the trie as $St = L_a(c + b + 3p) + N(L_d + c_s)$ where L_s is the average key string length, c is the space required to store one character (usually one byte), b is the size of a boolean variable (usually one byte, too), p is size of a pointer, N is the number of entries stored in the trie, L_d is the maximum data string length and c_s is a constant for string overhead as before. If we fill in the values for the LA system on a VAX computer, we get $S_t = 14L_a + 52N$ which is linearly dependent on L_a and N. It is also possible to store only key strings and no data in the trie, in which case the last term is reduced to 0.

5. Results

5.1. Correctness

If no decomposition is used, the system is in principle completely correct. That is, it is as correct as the database it uses (in our case, the high-frequency 12,000 wordform lexicon). Of course, some percentage of phonologically or syntactically ambiguous words remains for which our lexicon lists only one alternative. The other possibilities are not generated. Note that it is possible to include more than one representation for these words in the lexicon, however. Probably this is not advisable as it puts an extra disambiguation burden on other components of the TTS system.

Table 2 indicates the correctness of decompositions with a 53,375 complex word list as input, the usual 12,116 entry wordform lexicon, and other default lexicons:

Table 2. Correctness of decomposition

mode	%found	%wrong
1	2.35	0.00
2	34.77	0.00
3	41.12	0.00
4	42.45	0.24

Note: The test was performed on a 53,375 complex word list. The usual 12,116 wordform lexicon was used as the main lexicon (see text).

The first column shows the decomposition mode (see above), the second column shows the percentage of input words for which a solution was produced (either the word was found as a whole, or it was successfully decomposed), and the third column shows the percentage of wrong decompositions relative to the number of words in column two. The test data for these results consisted of a 53,375 entry complex word list, containing normal orthographic word representations and full decompositions of these words. The normal orthographic representations were fed to the LA system as input. To check a returned decomposition, it was compared to the one provided in the test list. For a decomposition to be considered correct, each returned morpheme boundary had to correspond to a boundary of the same kind and at the same place in the test lexicon's decomposition. Note that the system's answer may contain fewer boundaries than the test list's representation, and still be considered correct. This is of course a consequence of using a wordform lexicon rather than a morpheme lexicon. Full decompositions may be produced if wordforms in the lexicon are provided with decomposed representations as well.

We have repeatedly remarked that the system is not complete, which shows in the percentages of the second column, but insisted on correctness, which is reflected in the low error percentages of the third column. Note how the addition of the decomposition routines increases the percentage of complex words found from a mere 2.35 percent to a maximum of 42.45 percent, without changing the content of the lexicons used. Reizevoort—van Heuven (this volume) report a preliminary result of 96.0 percent correct (or 4.0 percent wrong) decompositions with his pattern approach. The results for our system on the same test corpus, for decomposition modes 3 and 4, are 34.79 percent found, 0.08 percent wrong, and 41.18 percent found, 1.44 percent wrong, respectively. No results are available for modes 1 and 2. No data is available on the performance of other systems on the same test corpus.

5.2. Speed

We will first consider the speed of the system in the lookup-only mode, modes 0 and 1. In these modes, speed is determined solely by the speed of the respective lookup algorithms (trie and hashing). A test in which all words of a piece of average newspaper text (about 70 Kb large) were fed to the system as input, using only main lookup with the hashing routines described above, resulted in a throughput of about 750 words per cpu second, on a multi-user μVAX 2000. There is no precise data available on the performance of the trie routines alone, but we may estimate it to 200 to 300 words per cpu second on the same system. Contrary to the hashing routines, the trie routines' performance is dependent on the length of the words being looked up.

Although this kind of performance will not be attained in a realistic setting, it indicates that the speed of the lookup routines is more than sufficient to keep the system running in real time, as shown below. I have already mentioned that the system speed is considerably reduced when decomposition is being used, due to the repeated lexicon accesses necessary for the decomposition of a single word. This is reflected in Table 3, which shows processing speeds for a list of 7,570 input words taken from different kinds of text (newspapers and stories). The drop in speed from mode 1 to the other modes is apparent.

Table 3. Processing speed (in words of input text)

system mode	words per cpu second
1	395.17
2	50.30
3	48.79
4	13.69

Mode 4 is again a lot slower than modes 3 and 4, due to repeated scanning of the affix lists. This mode can probably be speeded up considerably, but I have not looked into that. The data just given was measured in a realistic setting, with a fully configured system as described by the default setup file and lexicons provided (Lammens 1989). The figures also include the creation of an output file and some post-lookup computations that are not part of the LA system as such. Even in the slowest mode, the system still attains real time performance, and is always considerably faster than current implementations of the rule-based grapheme-to-phoneme conversion system of Berendsen et al. (1986), which would typically be around 2.5 words (average length 10 characters) per cpu second, on a VAX 8530 (which is considerably faster than our μVAX 2000).

Although the hashing routines' performance is reasonably close to the theoretically attainable maximum, the rest of the LA system is not really optimized for speed. Even with this partially optimized system, the goal of reducing grapheme-to-phoneme conversion speed with respect to existing rule-based systems is attained.

5.3. Memory usage

Memory usage is not optimized in our system. Although this was one of the initial goals, attention has shifted away from it in the course of the project's development. The reasons are twofold. On one hand, the development of memory technology makes memory efficiency a less important issue in software development altogether. On the other hand, developing and/or implementing data compression algorithms was deemed less important for a system like this one, which is to a large extent meant to test and evaluate the concept of using large lexicons in a TTS system. Together these considerations led to the implemented system philosophy, relying entirely on the virtual memory capabilities of the VAX/VMS system for memory management.

6. Conclusion

We will now evaluate the developed system for lexical access with regard to the objectives as formulated in the research proposal, which were summarized in section 1.

The execution time for grapheme-to-phoneme conversion is considerably reduced as compared to that of existing rule-based systems, by at least an order of magnitude. We were only able to compare execution times with the system of Berendsen et al. (1986), but in view of the speed of the hashing lookup routines, which account for the major part of lexicon accesses, and the trie routines, which account for a much smaller part, it is reasonable to assume that this system will be faster than a rule-based conversion system running on the same machine. However, when the additional (and optional) feature of decomposition of complex words is used, conversion speeds are reduced substantially. In providing this option, the system exceeds the original specifications. When decomposing words, more information besides a phonemic transcription is being produced. The LA system in general provides (or is able to provide) more than just a phonemic transcription for words. In this respect the original specifications are also exceeded.

The optimal form and size of the lexicon was determined to be a high-frequency wordform lexicon of about 12,000 entries. For smaller systems with severe memory limitations (or lack or virtual memory facilities) a size of a few thousand or even a few hundred words will already produce significant coverage of average (newspaper) text.

Fast retrieval procedures were implemented in the form of hashing and trie routines. Both techniques have been long known and described in the computer science literature. They have been adapted to our specific use, and combined in an elegant and transparent way.

Although experiments were performed with several kinds of data compression algorithms for the lexicons, none was implemented in the LA system. Data compression is considered to be of minor importance for a proof-of-concept system like ours.

Summarizing, the objectives as specified in the research proposal have been met and exceeded, except for one which came to be regarded as unimportant in the course of the project. If the system were to be further developed beyond its present state, the following topics might prove interesting enough to be looked into:

— quantification of the correctness of derived phonemic transcriptions and part of speech information for decomposed words
— other lexical databases might be tested and compared to the current 12,000 entry high-frequency lexicon
— the user lexicon might be provided with a long-term automatic update procedure when the LA system is coupled to a rule-based transcription system; words that have to be transcribed repeatedly by the rule system might automatically be included in the user lexicon, which will optimize system performance over a longer period of time.

Along the same lines, the user lexicon (or part of it) might be used as a short-term cache memory with respect to the rule-based system. In that case it would start out empty and quickly be filled with words that are not present in any of the lexicons. Caching is a well-known mechanism for improving the performance of memory systems, and the computer science literature provides ample algorithms (e.g. the popular least recently used or LRU cache replacement algorithm).

This project was also meant in part as a comparative study of different ways to tackle the grapheme-to-phoneme conversion problem in the context of text-to-speech conversion systems. As was argued above, the system for lexical access is not complete as such, and needs to be interfaced to another, probably rule-based, system (cf. Berendsen et al. 1989). In that respect the problem is really narrowed down to the choice between a rule-and-lexicon based and a morpheme lexicon based system. Although the final choice is probably in part a practical matter, I think the morpheme lexicon approach has a number of decided advantages. It has a sound language-theoretical base, and the feasibility of the approach has been demonstrated before (cf. Allen et al. 1987). All of this is equally true for the rule-base approach (cf. Carlson—Granström 1986; Berendsen et al. 1986; for a mixed lexicon-rules system cf. Daelemans 1987), but a morpheme lexicon system can provide much more information than a rule-based system can (morphological structure of words, part of speech and other kinds of syntactic data, even semantic information). A morpheme lexicon can also be made reasonably complete, both theoretically and practically, without requiring excessive storage capability. In my opinion, the morpheme lexicon approach must therefore be preferred, at least when taking possibilities for future development into account.

The system for lexical access as it stands is complete and ready to use in various kinds of experimental settings. I regard it as a versatile tool for storing and retrieving all sorts of lexically bound data.

Notes

1. I will use the term *wordform* to refer to words as they occur literally in a text, including inflection.
2. I am using the term *morpheme* in a rather loose sense here, as it refers to anything that is present in the main lexicon or the special-purpose decomposition lexicons.
3. This is a simplifying assumption, but since the length of the key has a practical upper bound, we can safely make it.

MORPA: A morpheme lexicon based morphological parser

Josée S. Heemskerk—Vincent J. van Heuven

Abstract

MORPA is a MORphological PArser developed at Leiden University for use in the text-to-speech conversion system for Dutch, SPRAAKMAKER. MORPA operates in three successive stages. First, it generates all possible segmentations of an input word into strings of stems and affixes. Secondly, it tests each segmentation for morpho-syntactic well-formedness while determining word class. Finally, all remaining analyses are ordered, with the most likely analysis in topmost position.

In this paper we shall outline the architecture of MORPA, which comprises a dictionary of 17,087 entries, a Categorial Grammar based parser, a module for level-ordered attachment of stems and affixes and a module for likelihood determination. The major problem that our system faces is ambiguity, i.e., the generation of alternative segmentations and word class assignments for one input word, many of which are ungrammatical or implausible. We shall discuss three kinds of strategy that have been combined in MORPA to deal with ambiguity. Firstly, the system filters out ungrammatical segmentations by means of linguistic knowledge. Secondly, the system orders the remaining analyses by means of frequency information. And finally, morphological information that is irrelevant for pronunciation determination is eliminated. In conclusion, we shall present illustrative performance data obtained from an evaluation run, involving a 3,077 word test corpus.

1. Introduction

The MORphological PArser that will be described, MORPA, has been developed as a component in a text-to-speech conversion system for Dutch. Since in Dutch there is no one-to-one correspondence between orthography and pronunciation, such a system has to contain an intelligent method for converting orthography into a phonetic transcription.

As far as the pronunciation of words is concerned, we cannot just list all Dutch words with their pronunciation in a dictionary, since the speakers of the language have the possibility to create new words and the vocabulary, as such, is indefinitely large. Nominal compounding, e.g., is a highly productive morphological process in Dutch. Moreover, new compounds are spelled without spaces or hyphens between their parts, as in (1):

(1)	a.	woord	'word'
	b.	woordgrens	'word boundary'
	c.	woordgrenssymbool	'word boundary symbol'

The alternative way to obtain the phonetic transcription is the phonological-rule approach. Dutch phonological rules are dependent in several ways on morphemic segmentation and word class assignment. For example, as shown in (2a), the graphemes *d* and *b* are pronounced voiceless when they occur stem-finally, but voiced when they occur stem-initially. As shown in (2b) stress in compounds differs from stress in monomorphemic words. In (2c) it is shown that stress in (predicatively used) adjectival compounds differs from stress in nominal compounds:

(2)	a.	hoofdagent	hoof[t] + agent	'police sergeant'
		loofdak	loof + [d]ak	'roof of foliage'
		krabijzer	kra[p] + ijzer	'scratch iron'
		slaboon	sla + [b]oon	'butter bean'
	b.	avonduur	ˈavond + uur	'evening hour'
		avontuur	avontˈuur	'adventure'
	c.	onecht	on + ˈecht, Adj	'unreal'
		onrecht	ˈon + recht, N	'injustice'

It will be clear from these examples that if the text-to-speech system is to produce high quality speech it must be provided with a module for morphological analysis that recovers morphemic segmentation and word class.

MORPA performs only part of the linguistic processing that is necessary to convert orthography into a phonetic representation. In the linguistic processing of the input text two aspects are of importance:

I. The morphological structure of words and the syntactic structure of sentences have to be obtained;
II. The morphological structure of words has to be interpreted in order to be able to assign a phoneme representation, syllabication and stress. The syntactic structure has to be interpreted in order to determine the place of accents and pauses.

Schematically,

sentence level

↑ ↓

word level

↑ ↓

orthography pronunciation

Within SPRAAKMAKER the distribution of tasks is as follows:

Orthography →	Word Level:	MORPA	
Word level ↔	Sentence Level:	PROS2	(cf. Dirksen—Quené, this volume)
Word Level →	Pronunciation:	MORPHON	(cf. Nunn—van Heuven, this volume)

MORPA provides word structure and word class. The word class is used by PROS2 in order to build syntactic structure and both word structure and class are used by MORPHON to determine syllabification, stress and phoneme transcription.

2. Architecture of MORPA

Within MORPA two kinds of modules are distinguished: the morphological modules for morphological analysis and the application modules that have been created with a view to implementation in the text-to-speech-system. Section 2.1 will describe the morphological modules; section 2.2 will describe the application modules.

2.1. Morphological modules

Figure 1 shows the structure in which the morphological modules operate. The module MORPA is the coordinating module that delegates the main tasks. Within module MORPA the morphological analysis of an input word is carried out in three successive stages. First, the word is segmented into a string of stems and affixes. This task is delegated to the SEGMENTATION module. In the second stage each segmentation is checked for its grammaticality by the PARSING module, and, if it is grammatically well-formed the word class and the likelihood of the analysis are determined. Finally, all remaining analyses are ordered on the basis of their likelihood. This task is not delegated but performed by module MORPA. Below we shall discuss each stage and go into the details of the module structure.

2.1.1. Segmentation module

The SEGMENTATION module divides the input word into all possible substrings. Each substring is submitted to the module MORPHEME which checks whether it is a Dutch morpheme or not. In order to find out whether a substring is a morpheme or not, the module MORPHEME uses (1) a LEXICON, which contains a large number of morphemes, (2) the module

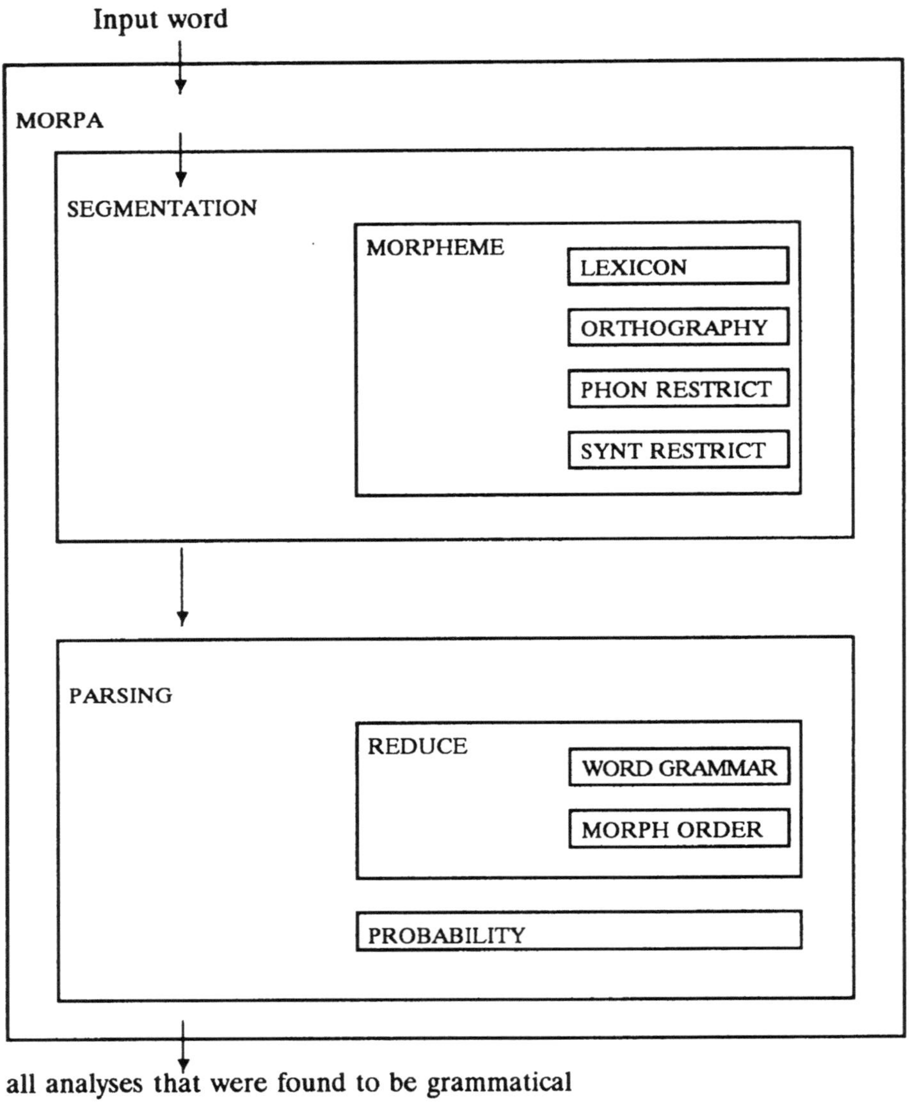

Figure 1. Global functional architecture of MORPA

ORTHOGRAPHY, which has knowledge of the orthographic rules that have to be taken into account, (3) the module PHON RESTRICT, which tests for some phonetic restrictions and (4) the module SYNT RESTRICT which tests for some preliminary syntactic restrictions. Each of the modules that are used by MORPHEME, are discussed in this section.

Our method for morphological analysis comprises a LEXICON. In this approach the word or word parts are recognized through dividing the word into substrings that correspond to entries in the lexicon.

Each entry in the lexicon contains the following fields of information:

I. *Orthographic form.* This form is the key to recognition. Since many morphological processes are highly productive, we cannot just list all Dutch words with their relevant information in a lexicon. We can, however, list all word formations that belong to closed classes, along with all simplex words and productive affixes, which are potential ingredients of newly formed words.[1] In that case the morphological parser only has to analyze words formed according to productive rules. The notion "potential ingredients of newly formed words" is a pragmatic operationalization of the theoretical notion "morpheme", which is traditionally defined as "the smallest meaningful part in word formation".

II. *Morpho-syntactic properties.* In this field the following syntactic categories are distinguished: N(oun), V(erb), Adj(ective), Adv(erb), Prep(osition), Det(erminer), Pro(noun), Q(uantifier), Conj(unction), Int(erjection) and P(roper)N(name). For the benefit of inflection (MORPA) and syntactic analysis (PROS2) some of these categories are subdivided on the basis of inflectional and selectional features. See (3) for some examples:

(3)	a.	[orth = *huis,* cat = n (n, *en,* c)]	'house'
	b.	[orth = *zeg,* cat = v (stem (h), [i (*te*), f (*dat*)]]	'say'
	c.	[orth = *ver,* cat = n (_, _, _) \v (stem (z), [ ])]	PREFIX

In (3) the orthographic form *huis* is morpho-syntactically specified as noun(neuter, plural: *en,* count_noun); *zeg* is specified as verb(stem(auxiliary: *heb* 'to have'), [infinitival_complement_with(*te* 'to'), finite_ complement_with(*dat* 'that')]. As we shall discuss in section 2.2. the complex categorial representation of the affixes, such as *ver,* comprises the word grammar implemented. From the set of word formation rules the improductive rules were excluded.

III. *Morphological classification.* This field classifies the morpheme for purpose of stress assignment. The labels comprise notions such as prefix, stem or suffix; native or non-native; stress attracting, stress neutral or stress bearing, etc. (See section 2.2. and Nunn—van Heuven, this volume, for motivation and application).

IV. *Phonological form.* Each lexical entry has been provided with an underlying pronunciation. After analysis by MORPA, MORPHON uses underlying pronunciation, morphological classification and word category to determine the surface pronunciation of complex words (cf. Nunn—van Heuven, this volume).

V. *Frequency information.* In order to be able to determine the likelihood of an analysis on the basis of the likelihood of the constituents each lexical entry is provided with frequency information, viz. the logarithm of the probability that the morpheme is member of its syntactic class. (See section 2.1.2. for a description of likelihood determination).

VI. *Morpho-phonological peculiarities.* Three optional fields contain codes that indicate (a) phonetic restrictions on the recognition of specific suffixes, (b) for some suffixes to trigger orthographic rules, (c) for some morphemes to be marked as exceptions to an orthographic rule. Below we shall discuss the orthographic rules and phonetic restrictions.

At present, the lexicon contains 17,087 entries: 12,264 simplex words, 468 affixes and 4,355 improductively formed complex words.

The ORTHOGRAPHY module takes into account that Dutch word stems, when inflected or used as the basis of a derivation, may undergo spelling changes. See e.g. the words in (4) that undergo (a) vowel degemination, (b) consonant gemination and (c) voicing of the stem-final *s* when pluralized:

(4)	a.	baan	banen	'jobs'
	b.	man	mannen	'men'
	c.	laars	laarzen	'boots'

When segmenting, MORPA has to undo the spelling changes in order to recover the stem from the plural and be able to access it in the lexicon. In the morpho-phonological field of the lexicon a number of suffixes are marked as potential triggers of spelling changes. Since these triggers always follow the stem that undergoes the spelling change, we decided to make our segmentation procedure operate from right to left: only if a potential trigger is found, does MORPA attempt to apply the spelling rules (in reversed direction) to the remainder of the input word. The spelling rules are embedded in our Prolog program; see for a more principled account of spelling changes in morphological parsing Koskenniemi (1983).

The module PHON RESTRICT tests whether there are phonological or phonetic restrictions on the recognition of the morpheme in a specific context, i.e., following a phonologically specified left neighbor. For instance, the agent suffix *-aar* is an allomorph of the suffix *-er* which only occurs when following a so called "schwa-stem", i.e. a stem ending in /-əl/, /-ən/ or /-ər/. Therefore, *-aar* is accepted in (5a) but rejected in (5b). The stem *werk* 'work' takes the suffix *-er* (5c):

(5)	a.	wandelaar	wand[əl] + aar	'walker'
	b.	werkaar	*werk + aar	
	c.	werker	werk + er	'worker'

This test is initiated by a special code in the lexical representation of the morpheme.

The module SYNT RESTRICT tests on some preliminary syntactic properties in order to prevent the parsing module from doing work of which we know beforehand that it will be in vain. The two main tests are:

I. Test on open class. Only morphemes that belong to open classes (N, V, Adj, Adv) and affix-categories are allowed as word parts. Morphemes that belong to closed classes are rejected beforehand.

II. Test on reduplication. In Dutch reduplication, i.e., the occurrence of a specific morpheme twice in succession, is not allowed. A morpheme that is recognized a second consecutive time is excluded.

To illustrate the effect of the segmentation procedure, its output for the noun *beneveling* 'intoxication' is shown in (6):[2]

(6)
a. be + neef + eling
b. be + neef + e + ling
c. be + nevel + ing
d. been + e + veel + ing
e. be + n + e + veel + ing
f. be + neef + eel + ing

The segmentation procedure analyses the input word into all possible strings of stems and affixes without any further grammatical knowledge. Thus, along with the plausible segmentation *be + nevel + ing*, (6c), several alternative segmentations are generated which violate grammatical and/or semantic restrictions. So, in order to filter out the ungrammatical segmentations and determine the word class of the grammatical ones, each segmentation must be checked for its grammaticality. Therefore each segmentation is submitted to the PARSING module that contains a categorial parser (which may be viewed as a word grammar)[3] and rejects every segmentation that is not in accordance with the rules of Dutch morphology. This categorial parser is discussed in the next subsection.

2.1.2. The parsing module

In the PARSING module all the segmentations that are generated by the SEGMENTATION module are tested for their morpho-syntactic well-formedness. Of each grammatical segmentation word class and likelihood are determined.

A segmentation is found to be well-formed if the string of constituents can be reduced to one constituent. Therefore the PARSING module recursively submits two constituents to the module REDUCE, which will try to reduce them to one. Two constituents can be reduced if the combination is in accordance with the rules for Dutch word formation. These rules are applied by the modules WORD GRAMMAR and MORPH ORDER. If a reduction has succeeded, the syntactic class of the new constituent is derived and the PARSING module will activate the module PROBABILITY in order to determine the likelihood of the constituent. In this section we will discuss the modules WORD GRAMMAR, MORPH ORDER and PROBABILITY.

Our word grammar is designed according to the principles of Categorial Grammar (cf. Moortgat 1987). As a consequence all relevant morpho-syntactic information is represented in the lexicon while the syntax, which is implemented in the module WORD GRAMMAR, merely consists of three simple reduction laws.

In our lexicon, all affixes are assigned a complex category. That is, prefixes have been assigned a category of type X/Y, which means that they take a stem of category X on their right-hand side to yield a word of category Y. For instance, the prefix *be-* with category N/V demands a nominal stem to the right to form a verb. Likewise, suffixes of category X\Y look for a stem of category X on their left-hand side to combine to a word of category Y. Thus, the suffix *-ing*, V\N, demands a verbal stem to the left to form a noun. Two adjacent stems XY may, according to the Right Hand Head Rule, be combined into a word of category Y.[4]

The reduction laws are iteratively applied to adjacent categories in a strictly bottom-up fashion. An analysis fails as soon as a string of categories cannot be reduced to one single category.

The examples in (7) illustrate how iterative categorial reduction results in a successful parse. The structures show the derivation and determination of the output category of (6c).

(7) a.

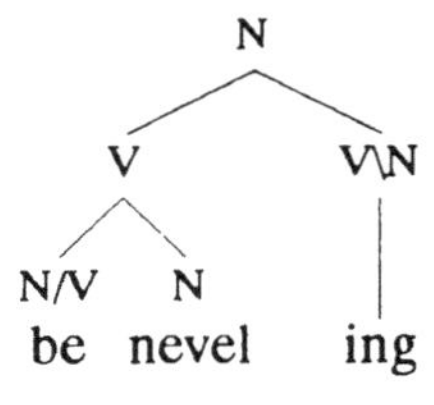

b.

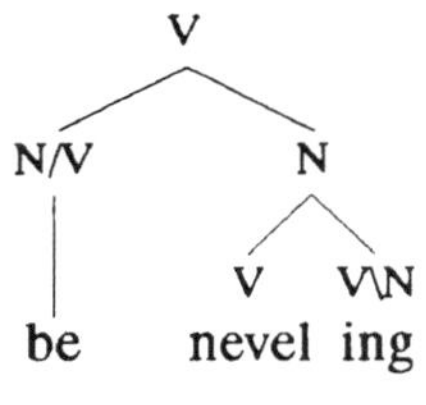

The ambiguity in (7) is due to the fact that the morpheme *nevel* has more than one lexical category and as a consequence can be reduced in more than one way, resulting in an incorrect word class assignment in (7b).

Obviously, the word grammar is not restrictive enough. In order to be capable of excluding analyses like (7b), the parser is supplemented with a component for attachment ordering. This module imposes an ordering on the attachment of affixes and stems which restricts the type of stem that an affix or stem may attach to.

The module for attachment ordering, MORPH ORDER, is inspired by Lexical Morphology and by one lexical theory for Dutch in particular (cf. van Beurden 1987). The model implemented is an extension of van Beurden's model in a way which is consistent with its basic assumptions.[5]

According to this theory the Dutch vocabulary can be divided into four levels, as in (8), which may be viewed as possible successive stages in word formation. The first level, or lexical level, comprises our lexicon of simplex words, affixes and irregular formations. This level also contains all (borrowed) Romance words. The elements of this lexical level may be successively developed on the second level on which V(erbal)-morphology takes place; the third level on which A(djectival)-morphology takes place and the fourth level on which N(ominal)-morphology takes place. Each of these levels preserves the possibility for suffixation, compounding and prefixation. On the levels for V-morphology and A-morphology each of these processes may take place only once. We assume that only the processes on the N-morphology level are recursive, i.e., may take place more than once. (cf. Heemskerk 1989 for more detail).

(8)

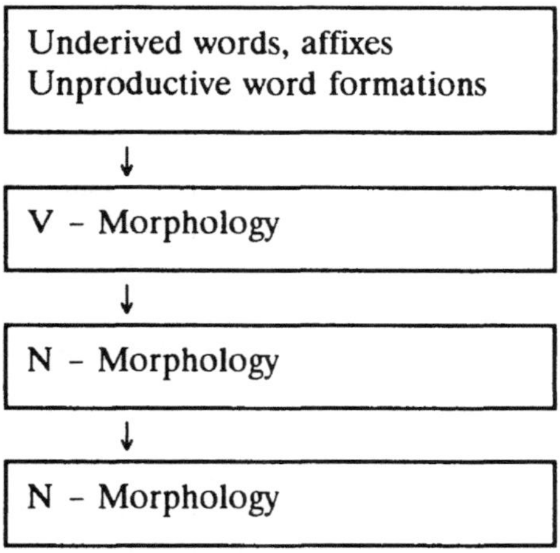

With respect to the word *onverdraagzaamheid* 'intolerance' in (9) the model correctly predicts that verbal prefixation precedes adjectival suffixation and prefixation, which, in turn, precedes nominal suffixation:

(9) $[\,[\,\text{on}_{pref}\ [\,[\,\text{ver}_{pref}\,\text{draag}_{stem}\ {}_{V}]\ \text{zaam}_{suf\ Adj}]\ {}_{Adj}]\ \text{heid}_{suf\ N}]$

This level module rules out the analysis in (7b): the nominal suffix *-ing* may not be attached before the verbal prefix *be-*. Therefore the word cannot be analyzed as a verb.

At this point, we return to the example of (6). Of the six alternative segmentations, four (10a-d) are accepted by the categorial component. The assigned word classes are given in (10i). The level module rejects (10b) and (10d) and the verbal derivation of (10ci), as shown in (10ii):

(10)	a.	be + neef + eling	i) N	ii) N
	b.	be + neef + e + ling	N	—
	c.	be + nevel + ing	N V	N
	d.	be + neef + eel + ing	N	—

This leaves us with two analyses; the first of which (10aii) is implausible; the second of which (10cii) is correct.

Clearly, the ultimate handling of the remaining ambiguity demands recourse to semantics and world knowledge. For pragmatic reasons, however, we explored several different strategies for ordering analyses in terms of plausibility, aiming at a system that generates the best analysis first. If the correct analysis is not generated in first position, as in (10), the word may receive a wrong pronunciation.

The ordering of the analyses in (6) and (10) is imposed by two preliminary criteria: firstly, in our right-to-left segmentation procedure priority is given to the longest morpheme in the dictionary that matches the input, an idea that has been suggested by several authors for various languages (cf. Allen—Hunnicutt—Klatt 1987; Daelemans 1987). Secondly, whenever an affix has alternative category assignments, the one with the highest lexical frequency is tried first. As we can conclude from (10) these criteria do not always succeed in selecting the best analysis out of the set. Therefore, we improved the ordering strategies by employing both lexical and text frequencies of morphemes, categories and category transitions. The heuristic strategy which is implemented in the module PROBABILITY, orders the competing analyses along a scale of plausibility and replaces the criteria mentioned above. We shall describe the ordering strategy below.

Suppose that MORPA proposes the analysis in (11) for a word that is the concatenation of the morphemes m1, m2 and m3:

(11)

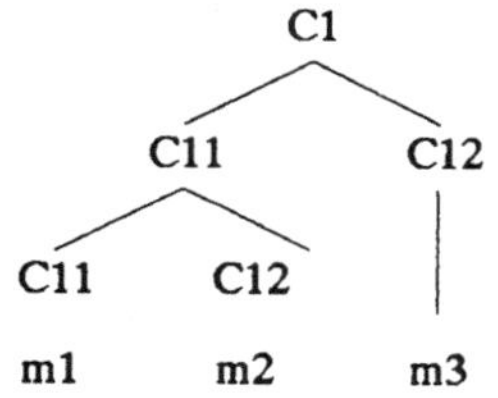

In order to determine the probability of (11) we need the following information:

I. The probability that the word belongs to the syntactic category C1 that MORPA proposes. In formula:

$$p(WCn) = \frac{\#(WCn)}{\#(W)}$$

Where:

W	=	the set of words;
WCn	=	the subset of words from W that are of category Cn;
p(WCn)	=	the probability that a random word in W is of category Cn;
#(WCn)	=	the number of words in WCn;
#(W)	=	the number of words in W.

II. The probability that a word has the hierarchical structure that MORPA proposes. We consider a hierarchical structure to be a series of transitions from mother to daughter categories. In (11) the mother category C1 branches into the left-hand daughter category C1 and the right-hand daughter category C2. These daughters are called C11 and C12 to indicate that they originate from mother category C1. Daughter category C11, in turn, branches into the daughter categories C1 and C2 and these categories are called C111 and C112 to indicate that they originate from C11.

In order to determine the probability of this structure we do not take into account the position of every category in the structure. Rather, we consider the transitions C1 → C11, C12 and C11 → C111, C112 to be identical, i.e., embeddedness is not taken into account.[6] The probability of the structure is the product of the probabilities of the separate transitions. In formula the probability of a transition Cn → Cn1, Cn2:

$$p(TCnCn1Cn2) = \frac{\#(TCnCn1Cn2)}{\#(TCn)}$$

Where:

T	= the set of mother-daughter category transitions;
TCn	= the subset of transitions from T with mother category Cn;
TCnCn1Cn2	= the subset of transitions from TCn, with left-hand daughter category Cn1 and right-hand daughter category Cn2;
p(TCnCn1Cn2)	= the probability that a random transition of TCn is Cn → Cn1, Cn2;
#(TCnCn1Cn2)	= the number of transitions that are in TCnCn1Cn2;
#(TCn)	= the number of transitions that are in TCn;

III. The probability that a word contains the morphemes that MORPA proposes. In (11) the analysis comprises the morphemes m1 of category C(11)1, m2 of category C(11)2 and m3 of category C(1)2.
The probability that an analysis contains m1, m2 and m3 is the product of all the individual morpheme probabilities. In order to determine the probability of a morpheme its position (leftmost, rightmost, middle) in the analysis is not taken into consideration.[5] In formula:

$$p(m \mid MCn) = \frac{\#(m \mid MCn)}{\#(MCn)}$$

Where:

M	= the set of morphemes;
MCn	= the subset of morphemes from M that are of category Cn;
p(m|MCn)	= the probability that a random morpheme from MCn is m;
#(m|MCn)	= the number of morphemes m in MCn;
#(MCn)	= the number of morphemes in MCn.

Then, the probability of an analysis is the product of the probabilities of the syntactic category, the structure and the morphemes. For instance, the probability of (11) is:

p([C1 [C11 [C111, m1],[C112, m2]], [C12, m3]]) =
p(C1) * (syntactic category)
p(C1,[C11,C12]) * p(C11,[C111,C112]) * (transitions)
p(m1|C111) * p(m2|C112) * p(m3|C12) (morphemes)

The set of words W on which our determination is based is the CELEX-database that contains approx. 123,000 Dutch stems provided with syntactic information, a morphological decomposition and token frequency information (cf. van der Wouden 1988). The frequency information is based on a 44 million words corpus. The morphological decomposition and frequency information were used to extract mother-daughter category frequencies and morpheme frequencies. The syntactic category and frequency information were used to extract word category frequencies.

From our database we simultaneously collected lexical (type) frequencies and usage (token) frequencies. Lexical frequencies are extracted from a dictionary and usage frequencies are extracted from a text corpus. Therefore, the module PROBABILITY exists in two versions: the version that is based on lexical frequencies is used for tests on dictionary samples in which every word is analyzed by MORPA once; the version that is based on usage frequencies is used for tests on text samples in which every word is analyzed by MORPA as many times as it occurs in the text.

In conclusion let us return to the example *beneveling* of (10). After determination of the likelihood of the remaining analyses (10a) and (10c) by the module PROBABILITY the correct analysis (10cii) *be + nevel + ing* is correctly ordered in topmost position:

(12) a. *be + nevel + ing* , N
b. *be + neef + eling*, N

In section 3 we shall give performance data which are based on a test sample containing 3,077 test words.

2.2. The application modules

Several modules have been created for the purpose of implementing MORPA in a text-to-speech system. These modules take care of the communication of the morphological parser with external modules that precede or follow MORPA within the text-to-speech system. Here we shall describe the interfaces to TEXT-SCAN, the preceding module and MORPHON, one of the following modules.

TEXT-SCAN is a module that preprocesses text in order to make text containing symbols, abbreviations, acronyms, proper names, etc. suitable for linguistic analysis. For this purpose the input text is segmented into sentences, and words or phrases are labeled. Each label refers to the status of the segment, e.g., *acronym, proper name, punctuation, abbreviation, number,* etc. (cf. van Holsteijn, this volume). MORPA is unable to analyze non-lexical items such as numbers, acronyms and proper names, because they belong to very large classes of which complete storage in the morpheme lexicon is impossible. Therefore, MORPA will only be presented text segments that are labeled "lexical item". Then, words containing acronyms (13a), numbers (13b) or proper names (13c) are problematical because they have to be analyzed by MORPA, but contain elements that MORPA is not able to recognize.

(13) a. HTS-er, CAO-overleg
b. 18-jarige, begroting-1991
c. Madonna-rage, Gorbatchov's

In order to be able to analyze them properly, TEXT-SCAN labels each part of these words and assigns the label "lexical item" to the whole word:

(14) CAO-overleg ⟶
lexical(acronym(*CAO*), punctuation(-), lexical(*overleg*))

In this way, MORPA is able to interpret the various TEXT-SCAN labels and act on them. In order to deal with the non-lexical items they are added to a temporary lexicon to which the morphological modules of MORPA have access. In this lexicon the non-lexical items have a default specification: acronyms are specified as noun, digits as numeral and proper names as proper names. The only thing the temporary lexicon cannot provide is a phonological form. A module following MORPA provides for it (cf. te Lindert—van Leeuwen, this volume).

MORPHON is the module that contains phonological rules that derive a pronunciation representation (cf. Nunn—van Heuven, this volume). As we have seen in section 1, phonological rules are dependent in several ways on morphemic segmentation and word class assignment. Therefore MORPA must precede MORPHON. The output of MORPA, however, contains some information that is irrelevant to pronunciation determination. These overspecifications are eliminated since they give rise to unnecessary ambiguity, which reduces the chance for the correct analysis to end up in topmost position and, as a consequence, for the word to receive its correct pronunciation.

To some extent the categorial labeling of morphemes is redundant. It appears that for correct assignment of pronunciation, the morphological classification, i.e., prefix-, stem- or suffixhood of the morphemes, is more crucial than categorial classification. For instance, in (15) the verbal stem *verwerk* 'to process' has been assigned two analyses:

(15) a. $[_V [_{N/V}$ *ver*], $[_N$ *werk*]]
b. $[_V [_{V/V}$ *ver*], $[_V$ *werk*]]

Although the analyses in (15) differ in the labeling of the morphemes, both receive the same, correct, pronunciation /vər-ˈwɛrk/. This does not hold for the analyses in (16):

(16) a. $[_{V}\ [_{Adj}\ \textit{ver}],\ [_{V}\ \textit{spring}]]$
b. $[_{V}\ [_{V/V}\ \textit{ver}],\ [_{V}\ \textit{spring}]]$

According to (16a) the word, meaning 'do the long jump', is pronounced /ˈvɛr-sprɪŋ/, whereas (16b), meaning 'change suddenly', is pronounced /vərˈsprɪŋ/. This difference in pronunciation arises from the fact that in (16a) *ver* 'far' is a stem, and as a consequence the word a compound, whereas in (16b) *ver* is a prefix and the word a derivation.

There is also a measure of overspecification in the hierarchical morphological structure that reflects the derivation. It may play a role in compound stress assignment, but its effect is marginal. Moreover, hierarchical structure can only be used for stress assignment on the condition that MORPA presents the correct structure. In practice, however, MORPA offers more than one structure and for choosing the right structure semantics has to be taken into account. Consider e.g. the analyses of the word *paardenfokkerij*. The analysis in (17a) is pronounced with primary stress on the last syllable and corresponds to the meaning of 'horse-breeding'; the analysis under (17b) is pronounced with primary stress on the first syllable and could be said to correspond to the meaning of 'stud-farm'. MORPA generates both analyses, but will not be able to choose between them for other reasons than likelihood. Also on the basis of likelihood, MORPHON will assume that the left-branching analysis (17a) is correct:

(17) a. $[_{N}\ [[_{N}\ \textit{paarden}],\ [_{V}\ \textit{fok}]],\ [_{V\backslash N}\ \textit{erij}]\ ]$
b. $[_{N}\ [_{N}\ \textit{paarden}],\ [[_{V}\ \textit{fok}],\ [_{V\backslash N}\ \textit{erij}]]\ ]$

Morphemic segmentation and overall category are relevant information. Consider, e.g., the word *balletje* in (18). The analysis in (18a) corresponds to the meaning 'ball + DIM(imutive)' and is pronounced /ˈbɑl-lə-tjə/; the analysis in (18b) means 'ballet + DIM' and is pronounced /bɑl-ˈlɛt-jə/. Here, the difference in pronunciation is due to different segmentations:

(18) a. $[_{N}\ [_{N}\ \textit{bal}],\ [_{N\backslash N}\ \textit{etje}]]$
b. $[_{N}\ [_{N}\ \textit{ballet}],\ [_{N\backslash N}\ \textit{je}]]$

The word *apetrots* in (19) is also ambiguous in pronunciation: the analysis under (19a) corresponds to the meaning 'pride of a monkey' and is pronounced /ˈa:-pə-trɔts/; the analysis under (19b) means 'proud as a monkey' and is pronounced /a:-pə-ˈtrɔts/. Here, the difference in stress is due to different overall category:

(19) a. [$_{N}$ [[$_{N}$ *aap*], [$_{N\backslash Nlnk}$ *e*]], [$_{N}$ *trots*]]
b. [$_{Adj}$ [[$_{N}$ *aap*], [$_{N\backslash Nlnk}$ *e*]], [$_{Adj}$ *trots*]]

Consequently, the output of the morphological modules undergoes two (ordered) operations in order to yield an output that contains only information that is relevant to pronunciation:

I. *label-conversion*, i.e., each lexical category label is replaced by a label that is in the lexical representation of the morpheme and that reflects the morphological classification of the morpheme. For purpose of the determination of the pronunciation this notion "morphological class" is enriched with distinctions such as native/non-native, stress-neutral/-stress-attracting/stress-bearing etc.[7]

II. *linearization*, i.e., all alternatives which have the same segmentation (i.e., string of labeled morphemes) as well as the same overall category are collapsed into one linear representation. Thus, (15a) and (15b) are collapsed into (20a) and (17a) and (17b) are collapsed into (20c) as they contain unnecessary, redundant information. The analyses of (16), (17) and (18), which do not contain irrelevant information, are still distinguished in (20b), (20d), and (20e):

(20) a. [$_{V}$ [$_{pref}$ *ver*], [$_{stem}$ *werk*]]
b. [$_{V}$ [$_{stem}$ *ver*], [$_{stem}$ *spring*]]
[$_{V}$ [$_{pref}$ *ver*], [$_{stem}$ *spring*]]
c. [$_{N}$ [$_{stem}$ *paarden*], [$_{stem}$ *fok*], [$_{suf}$ *erij*]]
d. [$_{N}$ [$_{stem}$ *bal*], [$_{suf}$ *etje*]]
[$_{N}$ [$_{stem}$ *ballet*], [$_{suf}$ *je*]]
e. [$_{N}$ [$_{stem}$ *aap*], [$_{link}$ *e*], [$_{stem}$ *trots*]]
[$_{Adj}$ [$_{stem}$ *aap*], [$_{link}$ *e*], [$_{stem}$ *trots*]]

Through converting output that contains hierarchical structures and categorial labels to linear structures and morpheme classification labels much unnecessary ambiguity is eliminated.

3. The performance of MORPA

In order to evaluate the performance of our system in the state described above and with output as described in section 2.2., a lexical test was run on a dictionary sample of 3,077 words, taken from texts of the so called "PB corpus" (cf. Bringmann 1990). Figure 2 shows the test results.

As is shown in Figure 2, MORPA assigns no analysis at all to 3 percent of the test words. Ninety-six percent of the test words were assigned a correct analysis, but for 52 percent of the test words the correct analysis was among alternatives; the average number of analyses for the whole test being 2.0. For 48 percent of the test words the correct analysis was generated as the most likely member of a set of alternatives. To 44 percent of the sample MORPA assigned a single, correct analysis. In sum, 92 percent of the test words received a correct analysis that is generated in first place.

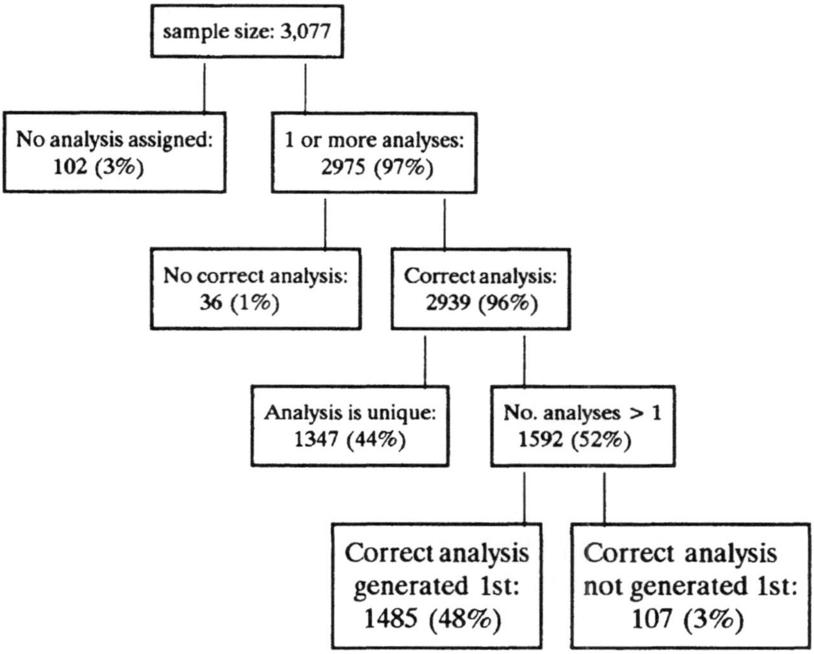

Figure 2. Summary of the test results; all percentages are expressed relative to N = 3,077.[8]

At the time that MORPA was only provided with a segmentation module and a parsing module that only consisted of the module WORD GRAMMAR the correct analysis was generated as the first or only alternative for 79 percent of the test words (cf. Baart—Heemskerk 1988). After addition of the module MORPH ORDER this percentage had risen to 85 percent (cf. Heemskerk 1989). In these stages MORPA contained the preliminary criteria that imposed an order on the set of alternative analyses. The eventual rise to 92 percent is due to the substitution of the module PROBABILITY for the preliminary ordering criteria.

As to the relevance for word level pronunciation, it was established that 82 percent of the errors made by MORPA led to an incorrect pronunciation representation (cf. Nunn—van Heuven, this volume).

4. Conclusions

For high quality text-to-speech conversion in Dutch a module for morphological analysis is needed. The morpheme lexicon approach is a principled one, but a major problem that it faces is ambiguity. In this chapter we have shown that within MORPA the ambiguity problem is largely reduced or sidestepped: MORPA has a success rate of 92 percent. In the first place ambiguity was reduced by implementing a word grammar and limiting the analysis to productive word formations. Next, ambiguity was reduced by implementing a module that defines the order in which morphemes may be attached to stems. Ambiguity was further reduced through eliminating information that is irrelevant for pronunciation. Finally, an heuristic strategy was implemented that orders the set of remaining alternatives along a probability scale.

Acknowledgements

This project was carried out by the first author, under the supervision of Joan Baart and the second author. The morpheme lexicon was compiled with the assistance of Marjan Grootveld, Brit van Ooijen, Jenny Doetjes, and Cecile Davis. Programming assistance came from Maarten Hijzelendoorn, Pieter Toussaint, and Jos Pacilly.

Louis ten Bosch' help on the construction of the probability module is gratefully acknowledged.

Finally, we thank all participants of the theme group "Linguistic Analysis" for their patient help, recommendations, support and fine cooperation during the project.

Notes

1. Because we assume word formation to be word based, our lexicon does not contain roots.
2. This example only shows a small number of segmentations. With increasing lexicon size and decreasing average length of the lexical elements, the number of alternative segmentations

for an input word grows. A combinatorial explosion can be the result, causing hundreds of segmentations to be generated.

3. Note that here "word grammar" is used in the sense of "a set of word formation rules", and is not to be confused with Richard Hudson's "word grammar".
4. The rules for prefixation and suffixation are functional application laws. The law for compounding is not a categorial law; it is the implementation of the Right Hand Head Rule (cf. Trommelen—Zonneveld 1986).
5. Because we are mainly interested in the morphological aspects of the proposed level model, we shall leave the phonological claims for what they are.
6. The position of a transition or morpheme is not taken into account for two reasons: (a) the determination of dependent probabilities would result in very large tables; (b) every structure that is not in the corpus W would receive a probability $p = 0$ with the result that newly created words are always ordered in last position.
7. For the sake of clarity, these labels are not mentioned in the examples.
8. Because the percentages are rounded off they do not add up to 100 percent.

MORPHON: Lexicon-based text-to-phoneme conversion and phonological rules

Anneke M. Nunn—Vincent J. van Heuven

Abstract

In this contribution MORPHON is outlined. This module provides the text-to-speech system with phonological rules. It will be argued that such rules are needed because the pronunciation of a sentence does not consist of the concatenation of the pronunciation of the constituting morphemes, but the pronunciation of morphemes is modified in certain contexts. These rules can only apply properly if exceptions can be listed in a lexicon, and if rules can refer to morphological and morpho-syntactic information. Therefore a lexicon-based approach to text-to-phoneme transcription conversion was chosen. Finally, the pronunciation accuracy of MORPHON is compared with that of two rule based text-to-phoneme transcription systems.

1. Introduction

An important step in text-to-speech conversion is the generation of the correct pronunciation representation on the basis of the input text. This requires a mechanism to convert spelled words of the input sentence into a phoneme representation. We will argue that these phoneme representations should be entered in a morpheme lexicon rather than be derived by rule.

Let us first note that the pronunciation of a sentence does not consist of the concatenation of the pronunciation of the individual words since the pronunciation of those words can be modified in certain contexts. As an example, consider the pronunciation of the sentences (1) and (2):

(1) a. De onderzoeker vond de verschillen significant.
b. The researcher found the differences significant.
c. də ʔɔn-dər-ˈzuˑ-kər ˈvɔnt də vər-ˈsχɪ-lən sɪχ-niˑ-fiˑ-ˈkɑnt

(2) a. De onderzoeker vond een significant verschil.
b. The researcher found a significant difference.
c. də ʔɔn-dər-ˈzuˑ-kər ˈvɔnt ən ˈsɪχ-niˑ-fiˑ-kɑnt fər-ˈsχɪl

One pronounces the first consonant of *verschillen* as a voiced [v] in (1) but in (2) it is changed to a voiceless [f] under the influence of the voiceless final obstruent of the preceding word. The word *significant* is spoken with final stress in (1) but in (2) the stress may be shifted to the first syllable due to a clash with the stressed syllable in *verschil.*

Generative phonology has provided us with rules that account for these processes. The formalization of such phonological rules on the word level has been the main object of this project, sentence prosody is accounted for in another module (cf. Dirksen—Quené, this volume). The name of the resulting rule set is MORPHON (it has MORphemes as its input and supplies them with their surface PHONeme representation). In this contribution we give a brief description of MORPHON, for a more detailed account, see Nunn (1991).

The organization of this contribution is as follows: In section 2 and 3 we will discuss the two stages of the derivation of the pronunciation, viz. spelling to underlying phoneme transcription and underlying to surface phoneme transcription conversion in more detail. In section 4 the role of the syntactic category of words for the proper application of the rules is discussed, and section 5 gives a comparison of MORPA-cum-MORPHON with two existing text-to-phoneme representation conversion modules for Dutch.

2. From spelling to underlying phoneme representation

Phoneme transcriptions can not be derived directly from orthographic input, for there is no one-to-one mapping between graphemes and phonemes in Dutch (Wester 1985; Berendsen—Langeweg—van Leeuwen 1986). Therefore phoneme transcriptions must be derived by one of the following two methods.

The first method consists in the application of a set of rules that map graphemes or grapheme combinations to phonemes. We will refer to this method as rule-based conversion. The second method consists of looking up the pronunciation of words in a lexicon (lexicon-based conversion). In MITalk, an English text-to-speech system (cf. Allen—Hunnicutt—Klatt 1987) the lexicon-based method was chosen, because a lexicon is needed anyway. The lexicon is necessary to analyze words for the purpose of pronunciation as grapheme-to-phoneme conversion rules do not work across morpheme boundaries, and to account for numerous exceptions to grapheme-to-phoneme conversion rules. Therefore it is elegant to use this lexicon for letter-to-sound conversion as well.

The same argument can be made for Dutch: grapheme-to-phoneme conversion rules do not work across morpheme boundaries in Dutch either. This has even more consequences in Dutch, as compounds are written as one word. For instance, the rule that turns the grapheme sequence *sch* into the phonemes [sχ] should not work in a compound like *afdelingschef* 'departmental chief' because that would yield the incorrect pronunciation [ɑfde:lɪŋsχɛf] instead of [ɑfde:lɪŋʃɛf]. As in English, there are many exceptions to Dutch grapheme-to-phoneme conversion rules and some exceptions involve highly frequent words.

Moreover, just like letter-to-sound conversion rules, phonological rules as discussed above both are sensitive to morphological boundaries and subject to numerous exceptions as well. To illustrate the sensitivity of phonological rules to morphological boundaries, consider the following two words:

maandag	[ma:n#dɑχ]	'monday'
maandabonnement	[ma:nt#ɑbɔnəmɛnt]	'monthly subscription'

Both words begin with the string *maand* but the /d/ is changed into [t] in the second word, where it is the final consonant of the first morpheme and not in the first word where it is the first consonant of the second morpheme. This can be explained as follows: the rule that affects the /d/, final devoicing, is sensitive to syllable structure and syllabification is sensitive to morphological structure of a word: compound boundaries are also syllable boundaries.

The main source of exceptions for languages such as Dutch is (word) stress assignment. As noted by, for instance, Langeweg (1988) and Kager (1989), Dutch word stress is only predictable to a certain extent (from syllable weight). According to Langeweg, in ninety percent of the monomorphemic words the stress can be accounted for by rules, the remaining ten percent show idiosyncratic behavior. For instance, words consisting of three open syllables regularly have penultimate stress but two deviating stress patterns occur, namely antepenultimate stress and final stress:[1]

[ko:-ˈlo:-ni·]	'colony'
[ˈko:-li·-bri·]	'hummingbird'
[pro:-zo:-ˈdi·]	'prosody'

Therefore a lexicon is necessary and we will use it for text-to-phoneme transcription conversion. In section 5 we will present an important advantage of this approach.

The lexicon cannot contain all words of a language, because new words are created every day. Therefore within the ASSP-project a lexicon was chosen that contains all morphemes, that is monomorphemic words and affixes, of Dutch (cf. Heemskerk—van Heuven, this volume). In order to look up their pronunciation, derived words must be decomposed into their constituent parts. This requires morphological analysis. For this reason

MORPA, a morphological parser, was developed (cf. Heemskerk—van Heuven, this volume). MORPA analyzes all words that are created by productive processes. Words formed by improductive processes are listed in the lexicon.

The lexical representation of each morpheme contains among other things the orthographic form, phoneme transcription (pron), and classification (cls) of the morphemes, and the category (cat) of the resulting word. The phoneme representation in the lexicon consists of the phonemic form of the morpheme supplemented with word stress and syllable structure. For instance, the representation of the word *monument* 'id.' is given in (3):

(3) *monument*, [[pron,ˌmo:-ny·-ˈmɛnt], [cat,noun], [cls,stem]]

By choosing the lexicon-based approach, we can be sure that phonological rules generally operate on correctly analyzed words and exceptions can be treated efficiently. For instance, the irregular stress patterns of the words *ˈkolibrie* and *prosoˈdie* do not have to be derived because word stress is in the lexicon. Idiosyncratic stress behavior of nonnative derived words is not problematic either. If a syllable is exceptionally stressed it is usually in the suffix, so this stress pattern can either be noted in the lexical representation of the suffix, or accounted for by a special suffix label that triggers a specific stress rule. For example, the suffix *-ologie* in *methodologie* 'methodology' which has irregular final stress, has the representation /o:-lo:-ˈɣi·/.

As in MITalk, grapheme-to-phoneme conversion rules are still used for words that MORPA fails to analyze, or words that should not be analyzed by MORPA such as proper names, acronyms, and digits (cf. van Leeuwen—te Lindert, this volume).

3. From underlying to surface phoneme representation

In this section we will discuss which rules are needed to convert the phoneme representation found in the lexicon into the surface phoneme representation that is the input for synthesis modules. Subsequently we will present the formalization and organization of these rules.

3.1. Division of labor between lexical representation and rule set

At first sight it would be easiest to enter the surface representation of each morpheme in the lexicon. However, this is not possible since some phonological processes work across morpheme boundaries, as was illustrated in (2). An example of such a process is progressive voicing assimilation:

/zɑk/ 'pocket'	⇒	[zɑk] in	[lo:n#zɑk]	'pay packet'
			[ɪn##zɑ-kən]	'in pockets'
		[sɑk] in	[hø:p#sɑk]	'hip pocket'
			[ɔp##sɑk]	'in one's pocket'

Another reason why a morpheme can receive more than one surface pronunciation, is that one or more processes that can be applied to it, are optional and depend on factors such as style, tempo etc. An example of a optional rule is n-deletion, that is illustrated below:

lopen	'to walk'	⇒	[lo:-pə]	(n-deletion applied)	or:
		⇒	[lo:-pən]	(n-deletion not applied)	

In generative phonology such variation is accounted for by choosing a sufficiently abstract form and deriving all surface variants from it by rule:

hø:p#zɑk	lo:n#zɑk		lo:-pən	lo:-pən	
s	–	assimilation		Ø	n-deletion
høp#sɑk	lo:n#zɑk		lo:-pən	lo:-pə	

We have adopted this approach for the derivation of surface forms in MORPHON.

However, in generative phonology processes that are both morpheme internal and obligatory are formalized by rules as well, because all regularities are expressed by rules rather than in the lexical representation. These rules will not be adopted by us, as it is more efficient to enter the effect of those processes in the lexical representation. For instance, word stress and syllable structure are entered in the lexicon. Subsequent modification of morphemes in context is accounted for by restressing and resyllabification rules. Therefore stress assignment and syllabification are lexical but restressing and resyllabification are part of our rule set.

In some cases resyllabification and restressing can be seen as reapplications of the rules for underived words to derived words. This holds for words derived with nonnative affixes, for instance the word *ˌkristalliˈseer* 'crystallize', that consists of the word *kristal* 'crystal' followed by the nonnative suffix *-iseer*, has exactly the same syllable structure and stress pattern as the comparable monomorphemic word *ˌexperiˈment* 'id.'. Consequently, rules for underived words must be part of MORPHON, although real underived words receive their stress pattern and syllable structure in the lexicon. Affixes must be classified as either native or nonnative. Nonnative affixes and roots are only syllabified and stressed after affixation has taken place. Some derivations are given below:

	underived stem	stem+nonnative affix	root+nonnative affix
input	krɪs-ˈtɑl	krɪs-ˈtɑl + iˑzeːr	ɑtmiˑniˑstr + aːtsiˑ
rules	-	ˌkrɪs-tɑ-liˑ-ˈzeːr	ˌɑt-miˑ-niˑ-ˈstraː-tsiˑ
	krɪs-ˈtɑl	ˌkrɪs-tɑ-liˑ-ˈzeˑr	ˌɑt-miˑ-niˑ-ˈstraː-tsiˑ

MORPHON therefore contains rules that work across morpheme boundaries as well as optional rules. The derivation of the surface pronunciation by MORPHON is illustrated in Figure 1:

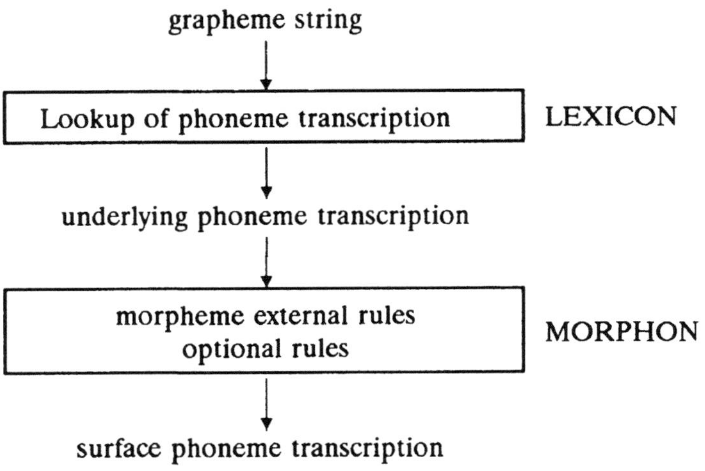

Figure 1. The derivation of the surface pronunciation by MORPHON

A subset of the phonological rules, i.e. the segmental rules (and only those that are phonologically motivated, not morpho-phonological rules) were investigated in the project FONWET (cf. Jongenburger—van Heuven, this volume). Rules that are optional or potentially redundant, are switched on or off in accordance with the findings of this project. Anticipating the findings of FONWET, all optional and potentially redundant rules were implemented. This makes MORPHON very flexible.

3.2. Formalization of the rules

MORPHON is formalized as a set of ordered rewrite rules of the form A ⇒ B / X _ Y, which means that A is converted to B in the right context X and left context Y (cf. Chomsky—Halle 1968). An example of a MORPHON rule, viz. progressive voicing assimilation, the rule that devoices the /v/ in (2), is given in (4):

(4) <-son, +cont, +voice> ⇒ <-voice> / <-son, +segm, -voice> _

The notation slightly differs from that of phonologists, because MORPHON was implemented with the rule compiler TooLiP (cf. van Leeuwen 1989a). The use of a compiler has the advantage that computational and linguistic knowledge are separated (cf. Berendsen—Langeweg— van Leeuwen 1986). On the other hand, a serious disadvantage of TooLip is that it can only handle a linear string of phonemes. This means that syllable boundaries must be represented as segments and stress is denoted by labels. An example of a stress rule is given in (5), viz. a rule assigning tertiary stress to a vowel before a consonant:

(5) vow ⇒ <3stress> / _ cons

3.3. Organization of the rule set

We already saw that some words composed with nonnative affixes undergo stress assignment and other rules as if they were underived. Native suffixes are stress neutral (cf. van Beurden 1987; Trommelen—Zonneveld 1989). This can be illustrated by the following examples: *-ist* and *-iseer* are nonnative suffixes that trigger restressing; *-heid*, *-loos*, and *-achtig* are native suffixes, which do not influence the stress pattern of the word to which they attach:

kristal	kristalliseer	kristalachtig
[krɪs'tɑl]	[krɪsɑli·'ze:r]	[krɪs'tɑlɑχtəχ]
'crystal'	'crystallize'	'crystalline'

Recent theories of morphology and phonology explain this phenomenon as follows: stress is applied to underived words and words derived with nonnative affixes before native affixes are attached. As word formation takes place in the lexicon, the same must hold for phonological rules and the model mentioned above is referred to as "lexical phonology and morphology". The word formation rules and the phonological rules that apply to its output are represented as levels in the lexicon. Rules that do not refer to internal structure apply outside the lexicon. The model is given in Figure 2.

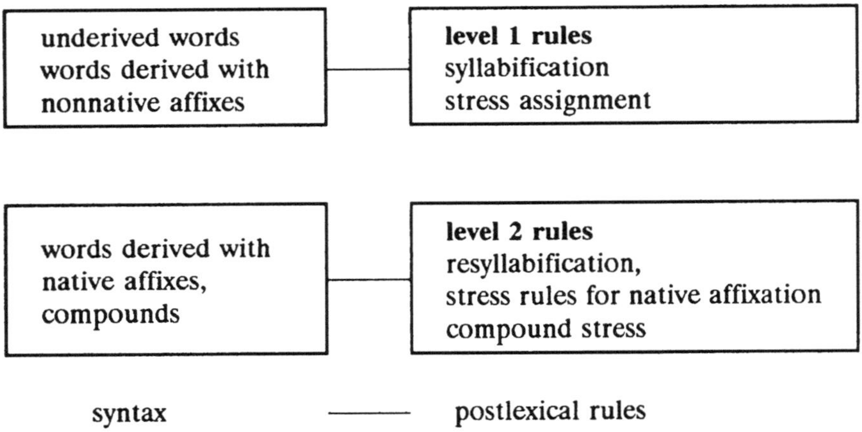

Figure 2. The lexical model

In the text-to-speech system that incorporates MORPHON, SPRAAKMAKER (cf. van Leeuwen—te Lindert, this volume), morphology and phonology are separate modules, so the difference between the two suffix types cannot be explained by the relative ordering of certain morphological processes and phonological rules. Therefore the older approach of Chomsky—Halle (1968) to this problem has to be chosen: native suffixes and nonnative suffixes get different morpheme boundaries and level 1 rules are blocked by native morpheme boundaries. The lexical model is used in MORPA, however, to reduce the number of possible analyses for each word by taking ordering restrictions that follow from this model into account (cf. Heemskerk 1989; Heemskerk—van Heuven, this volume).

The organization in levels was adopted as the organizational principle of MORPHON. MORPHON consists of the following three modules:

MORPHON_1 contains rules for words derived with nonnative affixes. The most important rules on this level are syllabification and stress assignment. These are linear versions of the non-linear rules by Kager (1989). An advantage of our stress rules is that secondary stresses, which are relevant to stress-dependent segmental rules and stress adjustment rules, are generated as a by-product of main stress assignment. MORPHON_1 also contains some morpho-lexical rules, e.g. velar softening, the rule that accounts for the alternation between [k] and [s] in words like *provoceer* [pro:vo:ˈse:r] 'provoke' and *provocatie* [pro:vo:ka:tsi·] 'provocation'.

MORPHON_2 contains rules for words derived with native affixes and for compounds. These rules account, for instance, for stress attraction in words composed with *-lijk* and *-ig*, and rhythmical rules for words composed with *-baar*, *-loosheid* and *her-* (cf. Langeweg 1988; Trommelen—Zonneveld 1989). Compound stress and stress adjustment are also ordered in this module. We will return to these rules in section 5.

MORPHON_3 contains rules that are not sensitive to the internal structure of words, such as sound adjustment rules like (voicing) assimilation and n-deletion. These rules are discussed in detail in Jongenburger—van Heuven (this volume).

To illustrate MORPHON, the derivation of sentence (2) is given below:

input:	də	˜ɔn-dər#ˈzu·k%ər	ˈvɔnd	ən	sɪχni·fi·C+ɑnt	vər#ˈsχɪl
MORFON_1		˜ɔn-dər-ˈzu·k%ər				–
velar softening					sɪχni·fi·kɑnt	
syllabification					sɪχ-ni·-fi·-kɑnt	
stress					ˌsɪχ-ni·-fi·-ˈkɑnt	
MORFON_2						
syllabification		˜ɔn-dər-ˈzu·-kər				
stress adjustment					ˈsɪχ-ni·-fi·-ˌkɑnt	
MORFON_3						
glottal stop		ʔ˜ɔn-dər-ˈzu·-kər				
final devoic.			ˈvɔnt			
assimilation						fər-ˈsχɪl
output:	də	ʔ˜ɔn-dər-ˈzu·-kər	ˈvɔnt	ən	ˈsɪχ-ni·-fi·-ˌkɑnt	fər-ˈsχɪl

4. The role of syntactic category

So far we have only illustrated the necessity of segmentation and morpheme classification for the derivation of the correct pronunciation (recall that syllabification is sensitive to morpheme boundaries, and that native and nonnative affixes behave differently with respect to stress assignment).

MORPA also provides morpho-syntactic information, viz. syntactic category. Some rules, notably stress rules, need this type of information. In this section we will discuss rules that could only be formulated because the category of words is known, viz. compound stress rules and stress adjustment. We will not give the precise formulation of these rules in MORPHON but concentrate on their effect.

In earlier linguistic interfaces for Dutch text-to-speech conversion such as GRAFON and FONPARS, primary stress is indiscriminately assigned to the leftmost member of any compound. However, the stress pattern of compounds depends on the syntactic category of the top node (cf. Langeweg 1988). If the compound is a noun or verb, stress is assigned to the left-hand member and if it is a adjective, adverb or preposition to the right-hand member. This is illustrated by the following compounds:

(6)	*noun or verb*		*adjective, adverbial, etc.*	
	ˈonrecht	'injustice'	onˈecht	'unreal'
	ˈkolenschop	'coal shovel'	bovenˈop	'on top of'

Syntactic category is not only crucial for the determination of compound stress in regular cases but also for some exceptions. Compounds that consist of a lexicalized phrase or contain a phrase exhibit a deviating stress pattern. In phrases stress is on the right-hand member in the cases that concern us here, even if the category of the resulting word is noun or verb (the elements between brackets are lexicalized phrases):

[rodeˈkruis]verpleegster	'red cross nurse'
[buitenˈboord]motor	'outboard motor'
[stadˈhuis]	'city hall'

This is accounted for by the Phrasal Stress Rule that stresses the right-hand element irrespective of word category. Some phrases can be distinguished formally, for instance, words that contain an inflected adjective like *rodeˈkruisverpleegster* are almost always phrases.

[gemeneˈbest]land	'commonwealth country'
[rondeˈtafel]conferentie	'round table conference'

Not all phrases can be identified this way. Therefore some highly frequent phrases (e.g. *stadhuis*) are listed in the lexicon.

Syntactic category is also important for rhythmic adjustment rules that reverse the prominence pattern laid down by word and compound stress rules (cf. Visch 1990). For instance, the primary and secondary stresses are interchanged in adjectives that are followed by a word that begins with a primary stressed syllable. This rule that is called stress shift, is illustrated in (7):

(7)	ˌrespec ˈtabel	ˈrespec ˌtabel ˈman	'respectable man'
	kon ˈtant	ˈkontant ˈgeld	'cash'
	ˌregio ˈnaal	ˈregio ˌnaal ˈdagblad	'regional newspaper'

Stress shift can not be formulated in rule-based convertors, because the rules cannot refer to the syntactic category of a word. However, since this rule is optional, this is not disastrous.

However, there is a similar rule, called stress retraction, that reverses prominence within adjectival compounds. This rule is obligatory when the whole compound is in focus (but not when *donkerblauw pak* 'deep blue suit' contrasts with *donkerbruin pak* 'dark brown suit'). The effect of this retraction is illustrated in (8):

(8)	ˌdonker ˈblauw	ˈdonker ˌblauw ˈpak	'deep blue (suit)'

We conclude that for the correct assignment of stress to compounds and lexicalized phrases, as well as for stress adjustment and stress retraction word category is crucial. This is yet another justification of our approach, as this type of morpho-syntactic information is made available by lexicon-based letter-to-sound conversion only.

5. Comparison with earlier grapheme-phoneme conversion systems

In section 2 and 4 we claimed that lack of morphological information such as segmentation, morpheme classification and syntactic category, may well lead to errors in grapheme-to-phoneme conversion and phonological rules. Therefore it is to be expected that MORPA-cum-MORPHON as a lexicon-based convertor has a better pronunciation accuracy than rule based-systems. The pronunciation accuracy of MORPA-cum-MORPHON was compared with that of two grapheme-to-phoneme conversion modules for Dutch that are currently available, namely GRAFON (Berendsen—Don—Langeweg 1986; van Leeuwen 1989a) and FONPARS (Kerkhoff—Wester—Boves 1984).

The test material consisted of isolated words in order to keep the test simple (although some MORPHON-rules have a larger scope, there are few rules that *only* work across word boundaries). This implies that the effect of PROS, the SPRAAKMAKER-module that takes care of, among other things, disambiguation of MORPA-analyses and phrasing (cf. Quené—Kager, this volume; Dirksen—Quené, this volume), and TEXTSCAN, the module that handles punctuation, abbreviations, etc. (cf. van Holsteijn, this volume), could not be included in the evaluation.

A test file was created that consisted of words from newspaper text, compounds and words with a very low frequency. The most frequent words were deleted, because MORPA-cum-MORPHON, when functioning in the text-to-speech system SPRAAKMAKER, will only convert words that are not found in HIFREQ, a dictionary of the 10,000 most frequent word forms (cf. Lammens, this volume). Of the remaining words of the three files the first 700 words were selected. Acronyms and words with punctuation marks such as hyphens and apostrophes, proper names and words with spelling errors were deleted, as MORPA-cum-MORPHON were not designed to handle these words. A file of 1,985 words remained. This test file was submitted to each of the three systems and the transcriptions of these systems were classified as correct or incorrect. A word is considered correct if it has a proper phoneme transcription, which means that all appropriate non-optional phonological rules have been applied. Furthermore, the words must have the correct syllable structure and stress pattern. The results of the comparison are given in Table 1:

Table 1. Percentage of words that receive a correct phoneme transcription

LEXICON BASED MORPA-cum-MORPHON	RULE BASED	
	GRAFON	FONPARS
78%	66%	60%

On the basis of the data in Table 1 the following observations can be made: MORPA-cum-MORPHON has a considerably better pronunciation accuracy than either GRAFON or FONPARS. This is a remarkably good result, given the fact that we are dealing with low frequency words. The difference in accuracy between the two rule-based systems is quite small, but GRAFON is to be preferred.

On the basis of the test results, we can also make some observations on MORPA-cum-MORPHON in its own right. Seventy-eight percent of the words are assigned a correct phoneme transcription. Sixteen percent of the errors could be traced back to the phonological module, the remaining errors are due to faulty morphological analysis. Of the errors made by MORPA 82 percent led to an incorrect pronunciation representation. As expected, segmentation errors almost always led to an incorrect phoneme transcription. Interestingly, category assignment errors also cause incorrect pronunciation, though less often. This bears out the importance of syntactic category information.

In order to see how MORPHON would perform when applied to perfectly analyzed words, the morphological analyses were corrected by hand, and again converted by MORPHON. MORPHON then provides correct phoneme transcriptions. For ninety-five percent of the words the remaining errors made by MORPHON have to do with stress assignment.

MORPA and MORPHON were still being developed at the time that this evaluation was performed (July/August 1990), for instance, MORPA did not yet contain the algorithm that selects the most plausible analysis from the list of alternatives on the basis of frequency information. The results would probably be even better if the evaluation were repeated now, since MORPA now provides the correct analysis for ninety-two percent of the words (cf. Heemskerk—van Heuven, this volume).

6. Conclusions

In this contribution we argued that the pronunciation representation should be derived from spelled input via the lexicon because this lexicon is needed anyway for exceptions and to provide grapheme-to-phoneme conversion rules with syntactic category. The phoneme representations in lexicon do not render phonological rules superfluous, because some processes are optional, potentially redundant, or sensitive to information outside the morpheme. The phonological rules benefit from the syntactic category now made available. Segmentation and morpheme type information are crucial for almost all rules, whereas word category information is relevant for compound stress and stress adjustment rules. Some other improvements of the phonological rules are independent of morphological information, for instance the translation of some properties of non-linear stress theories in linear rules. Finally, the problem of exceptions is solved by listing exceptional words in the lexicon. The results of a comparison of MORPA-cum-MORPHON with other text-to-phoneme transcription conversion systems proved that MORPA-cum-MORPHON has a considerably better pronunciation accuracy, but is considerably slower.

Notes

1. When relevant, syllable boundaries are indicated in the transcriptions by hyphens; primary stress is indicated by a superior vertical stroke, secondary stress by a inferior vertical stroke, and tertiary stress by a tilde. Affix boundaries are indicated by '%', word boundaries by '#'.

Pattern-driven morphological decomposition

Jeroen Reizevoort—Vincent J. van Heuven

Abstract

In this chapter we describe a technique for morphological decomposition which is based on a form of pattern recognition. This technique was then combined with insights gained in lexical morphology. This combination of technology and theory enables us to quickly split up words into morphemes and to generate the morphological information that is needed in high-quality text-to-speech (TTS) systems.

1. Morphology and text-to-speech systems

Dutch orthography uses 26 alphabetic signs to code about 50 speech sounds. Clearly, there can be no one-to-one relationship between spelling and pronunciation.

When converting text to speech, two methods can be distinguished: the lexicon-based method versus a method based on phonological rules.

The lexicon approach boils down to this: look up every text word in the lexicon and retrieve, quickly and simply, the correct sounds and stress pattern (further see Lammens, this volume). Obviously, this method will be error-prone since the vocabulary of Dutch can be extended indefinitely. Compound words will have to be split up into their constituent parts in order to look up their pronunciation.

The phonological approach generates the pronunciation of words through linguistic rules. This approach fails for words such as *huidarts* /hʌyt$ɑrts/ 'skin doctor, dermatologist' versus *heldin* /hɛl$dɪn/ 'heroine' (further see Heemskerk—van Heuven, this volume). It then transpires that pronunciation is conditioned by morphological boundaries.

It follows from the above that, when no morphological component is available, only severely limited TTS-systems can be produced. A lexicon-based system could accommodate a restricted vocabulary only, whilst the phonological rules could handle only monomorphemic words and complex words with stress-neutral affixes. However, morphological decomposition can help the lexicon-based method by allowing the look-up of word constituents. On the other hand, morphology may help phonology by indicating morpheme boundaries, which may be crucial for deriving the proper pronunciation.

2. The influence of morphology on pronunciation

As we shall expound below, the influence of morphology on pronunciation is mediated by the phonological and syntactic structure of a text utterance.

2.1. Morphology and phonological structure

Morphology influences both the stress pattern of whole words and the pronunciation of individual letters. Each affix has a specific influence on the stress pattern of the base word.

(1)	ˈafval	(defection)	afˈvall+ig	(defective)
	kampiˈoen	(champion)	kampiˈoen+schap	(championship)

These examples show that suffixation with *-ig* changes the position of the stress whilst the suffix *-schap* does not affect the stress pattern of the base word. Moreover, de-stressing a syllable generally triggers reduction of the vowel.

The effect of morphological structure on the pronunciation of individual words is demonstrated by the following examples:

(2)	spelling		pronunciation
	huid#arts	(skin doctor)	hʌyt$ɑrts
	held+in	(heroine)	hɛl$dɪn

The first word, a compound of the nouns *huid* 'skin' and *arts* 'doctor' contains an internal word boundary #. This boundary triggers devoicing of the word-final /d/ of the morpheme *huid*, just as would happen if this word were pronounced in isolation. The second word is a derivation of the noun *held* 'hero' using the female suffix *-in*. The morpheme boundary + is invisible to the syllabification rules of Dutch, so that *d* is parsed as the onset of the second syllable, and remains voiced accordingly. *Heldin* is thus pronounced as if it were a monomorphemic word such as *kade* /ka:də/ 'quay'.

2.2. Morphology and syntax

When determining the syntactic characteristics of complex words we may use the RIGHTHAND HEAD RULE (RHR) as defined by Williams (1981: 5). This rule predicts that the rightmost part of a derivation or compound determines (among other things) the syntactic category of the complex word. This proves valid for Dutch as well:

(3)	a. diep$_A$ deep	b. de zee$_N$ the sea	c. de diepzee$_N$ the deepsea
	vind$_V$ find	plaats$_N$ place	de vindplaats$_N$ the finding place
	de naam the name	het woord the word	het naamword the nameword (i.e. noun)
	de bal the ball	het spel the game	het balspel the ballgame

(after Trommelen—Zonneveld 1986: 149)

The examples in (3) show that, whatever the syntactic category of the first element of the compound (a), the properties of the second part (b), i.e. syntactic category and choice of article, determine the properties of the compounds (c).

3. Methods of morphological decomposition

Automatic morphological decomposition is generally achieved by using a lexicon, rules, or a combination of both. We shall now discuss some properties of lexicon-based versus rule-based systems. The properties discussed provide the background against which the third method of morphological decomposition, the pattern-based approach, will be sketched later.

3.1. The rule-based approach

A rule-based system for morphological decomposition employs linguistic, often phonological, rules, such as

(4)	e,n $\Rightarrow$	%,e,n	/ voc, cons$_0$ – <-segm>	ben%en kop%en slap%en
	e $\Rightarrow$	e,#	/ voc, cons – cons,voc	eike#boom

(Berendsen—Don 1987)

The advantages of such systems are that linguistic insights can be tested, and that — in principle — all possible words in the language can be analyzed.

A disadvantage of such methods is that the rule system may grow quite complex, which slows down execution time. The interactions among the many rules tend to become untractable, which makes the introduction of changes to the system a hazardous affair.

3.2. The lexicon-based approach

The lexicon approach uses an exhaustive morpheme lexicon. Polymorphemic words are split up by checking which concatenations of morphemes may cover the entire word.

The advantages of this method are that all possible words can be decomposed, since all morphemes are contained in the lexicon, and that information on syntactic category can be obtained through morpheme combination rules. A disadvantage of this type of system is that it tends to generate multiple analyses for one word form. Additional precautions, typically in the form of (ad hoc) rules, will then have to be taken in order to restrict the number of competing analyses (see Heemskerk—van Heuven, this volume).

3.3. Is there a superior method?

It seems impossible to prefer one method over the other. The ultimate choice depends on the objective of the decomposition. Relevant criteria may be speed, linguistic insight, precision, flexibility, and versatility.

A problem that faces any method, are ambiguities of the type *kwart#slagen* 'quarter beats' versus *kwarts#lagen* 'quartz layers' and *'balletje* 'little ball' versus *bal'letje* 'little ballet'. Other problems reside in spelling and typing errors, foreign words and technical vocabulary.

4. The pattern technology

4.1. Patterns and hyphenation

The pattern approach was introduced by Liang (1983) as a solution to the problem of computer hyphenation at line breaks. Liang aimed for a hyphenation algorithm that was fast, error-free, easy to adapt, memory-independent, and non language-specific.

Liang assumed that there can be no complete lexicon for any language containing all the correct hyphenation positions for all the words, and that even an approximation to such a database would be too demanding in terms of memory space and look-up time. A rule-based system, on the other hand, would always be language-specific, and hard, if not impossible, to get error-free.

In a way Liang then opted for the best of both worlds: his pattern technology combines features of the lexicon-based and the rule-based approaches.

4.1.1. Generating patterns

The algorithm that generates the hyphenation positions is as follows:

1. Compile a dictionary with only correct hyphenations.
2. Determine for each word in this dictionary how it would be hyphenated with the present set of patterns.
3. If the word is correctly hyphenated with the present set, do nothing.
4. Else: store as many characters around the word's hyphenation position until a unique pattern is obtained that contains the correct hyphen position.

Patterns are strings of alphanumeric characters that describe the environment for hyphen insertion. The length of a pattern depends on the generality of the hyphenation rule that is captured by it. Typically, short and general patterns are generated first, and patterns grow longer as the words they apply to are more exceptional. In order to obtain an error-free set of hyphenation patterns the maximal length of the patterns will have to be such that any exception to the general patterns can still be characterized by a pattern. Patterns will, however, always be optimally compact since only those characters around a hyphen position are stored that are necessary to uniquely define it. The effectivity of a pattern, expressed as the number of words that can be hyphenated by it, will be inversely proportional to its length.

For example, it is generally possible to hyphenate words immediately before the Dutch character string *heid* (*ijdel-heid* 'vanity', *dom-heid* 'stupidity', etc.). Therefore a short pattern will be generated for this suffix. The word *afscheid* 'farewell' is an exception to this pattern, and will have to be covered by a longer pattern.

Patterns are generated in tiers. An odd-numbered tier generates patterns that indicate hyphenation positions, the subsequent even-numbered tier determines which words are incorrectly hyphenated by the earlier patterns, and then generates patterns that indicate illegal hyphen positions. For each pattern that is generated at a specific tier, the number of successful hyphenations is counted, as well as the number of errors. These counts are made going through the entire dictionary, after which the system decides whether a pattern makes a sufficient contribution to warrant permanent incorporation.

4.1.2. Using the patterns

After patterns have been generated for the entire dictionary, these can be used to hyphenate words. For a given text word the program selects the patterns that are applicable. On the basis of the patterns selected the text word is hyphenated. An example is:

```
(5)      input: s c h o l e n g e m e e n s c h a p
                      o1l e n3
           p           3l e n g
           a                2n g e
           t                  1g e m
           t                     1m e e
           r                        e e2n1s
           e                          e n3s c
           n                            2n 1s c
           s                                    h2a p
                                                 4a p
        output  s c h o3l e2n3g e1m e e2n3s c h4a p

                s c h o-l e n-g e-m e e n-s c h a p
```

The example shows that the following patterns match the word *scholengemeenschap* 'comprehensive school': *o1len3*, *3leng*, *2nge*, *1gem*, *1mee*, *ee2n1s*, *en3sc*, *2n1sc*, *h2ap*, *4ap*. Here odd numbers within a pattern are imperative (i.e., hyphenation is mandatory in this position) whereas even numbers are prohibitive (i.e., under no circumstances may a word be hyphenated in this position). In case of overlapping patterns the highest valued (odd-numbered) pattern takes precedence. In (5) above the correct hyphenation of *scholengemeenschap* is listed under output. Whenever multiple values occur in a column between individual characters, the highest value percolates to the final result. All odd-numbered values are then taken as hyphenation positions.

4.2. Results with pattern hyphenation

The success of Liang's pattern technology, in terms of speed, accuracy, flexibility, compactness and language independence, has been demonstrated by test results for English by Liang himself, as well as for Dutch by Aerts (1986). The latter program is currently commercially used in the printing industry.

The flexibility of the pattern approach is apparent in many ways. Firstly, the method clearly works independently of any specific language. Secondly, words that are incorrectly hyphenated can be added to the dictionary, so that — after generating an updated set of patterns — these, too, will be correctly hyphenated. Crucially, the pattern technology is flexible enough to allow us to extend its applicability to other processes:

(6) The effectiveness of pattern matching suggests that this paradigm may be useful in other applications as well. Indeed more general pattern matching systems and related notions of productions systems and augmented transition networks (ATNs) are often used in artificial intelligence applications, especially natural language processing. While AI programs try to understand sentences by analyzing word patterns, we try to hyphenate words by analyzing letter patterns. (Liang 1983: 42)

4.3. Patterns and morphology

Linguistic rules underlie syllabification, hyphenation, as well as morphological decomposition. The word *rules* points to the existence of regularities, and regularities can be expressed in terms of patterns. Such patterns can be traced in a dictionary that contains word-internal morpheme boundaries, using a pattern generator of the type discussed in section 4.1.1. This would yield a method of morphological decomposition that allows us to combine the advantages of the rule-based approach (section 3.1) with those of the lexicon-based approach (section 3.2). The resulting patterns are global enough to function as rules, while, on the other hand, they may be detailed enough to correctly deal with exceptions.

The advantages of the pattern approach, as opposed to the rule-based approach, are greater speed and flexibility. Particularly, exceptions and subregularities will be processed appreciably faster. The advantages over morphological decomposition with a full-fledged morpheme lexicon are greater speed and conciseness. Processing is faster since only a single solution is sought through a single search beam. As for conciseness, we may expect the number of patterns to be smaller than the number of morphemes in the language, and the patterns generated to be shorter than the morphemes. This is caused by the fact that patterns incorporate the graphotactic constraints that are operative in any given orthography.

As we have stated above, neither the pattern approach, nor the lexicon-based and rule-based methods, can handle semantic ambiguities. Yet, it will never be the case that the pattern generator will end up oscillating between two possible decompositions; the mere fact that there is a maximum pattern length, will prevent this from happening. Only one out of many possible decompositions will be chosen.

5. The theory, lexical morphology

5.1. Introduction

The goal of the PADMAN project (PAttern Driven Morphological ANalysis) was to design and test a module for morphological decomposition based on Liang's pattern approach.

The original hyphenation algorithm, as described in section 4.1.1, cannot be used for morphological decomposition just like that. For hyphenation purposes it is sufficient to just indicate where hyphens must be inserted. There is, in other words, only one type of boundary. As we have demonstrated earlier on, the pronunciation of complex words depends, among other things, on the type of morpheme boundary that separates the constituents within the word. In order to exploit morphology in a sensible way for text-to-speech purposes, we will therefore have to be able to insert several types of boundary. When generating the patterns, we need not only indicate where boundaries are to be inserted but also what kind of boundaries.

The word list that forms the basis for generating the patterns, will have to contain boundaries that are motivated by a morphological theory that accurately predicts the pronunciation of complex Dutch words. The most complete morphological theory for Dutch is LEXICAL MORPHOLOGY (see Heemskerk—van Heuven, this volume). This theory has been adopted for PADMAN. The next three sections sketch the theory.

5.2. The creation of lexical morphology

The influence of morphology on phonology is widely known and was first extensively commented on by Chomsky—Halle (1968) in *The sound pattern of English* (henceforth SPE). Chomsky—Halle distinguish two types of morpheme boundary in English, with different effects on the pronunciation, specifically on the stress pattern, of polymorphemic words for each type: stress neutral (#) versus stress sensitive (+) boundaries.

This binary split of affixes in SPE prompted Siegel (1974) to devise a model in which stress rules operate in the morphological component, i.e., within the lexicon, rather than in the phonological component: Lexical Morphology was born.

Siegel observed that, in English, +-suffixes never occur closer to the word edge than #-suffixes. She then proposed that these suffixes each attach on their own level, and to formulate specific phonological rules for each of these morphological levels separately. These phonological rules operate cyclically, but only within their own level. As a consequence, morphology has (limited) access to phonological rules. This allows us to explain a number of morphological processes (see, e.g., van Beurden 1986: 13).

5.3. Lexical morphology and Dutch

Van Beurden (1986) shows that lexical morphology can also be used for Dutch, if more than two levels are distinguished (see section 5.3.2). Unlike English, native Dutch suffixes come in three types: they can be stress neutral, stress attracting, or stress bearing. We shall now discuss some of the consequences of the theory of lexical morphology for the assignment of stress (section 5.3.1) and the combinatory possibilities of Dutch morphemes (section 5.3.2).

5.4. Stress assignment

For the purpose of stress assignment four types of suffix have to be distinguished in Dutch:

(7)	a.	Nonnative/Roman	*sport*	'sport'	*sport-'ief*	'sportive'
	b.	Stress bearing	*held*	'hero'	*held-'in*	'heroine'
	c.	Stress neutral	*vrolijk*	'cheerful'	*vrolijk-'he id*	'cheerfulness'
	d.	Stress attracting	*vijand*	'enemy'	*vij'and-ig*	'enemical'

In terms of stress assignment, nonnative or Roman suffixes behave as if the derived word were monomorphemic. This is because such suffixes end in a superheavy syllable, i.e., typically contain three or more segments in the rime part (cf. Kager 1989; Neijt—van Heuven 1992). Monomorphemic words ending in a superheavy syllable, are invariably stressed on that syllable. If we consider words with nonnative suffixes to be morphologically simplex, we correctly predict main stress on the suffix.

The three remaining types of suffix are of Germanic origin. Stress bearing suffixes are *-ˈin*, *-ˈes*, and *-ˈij*. Stress attracting suffixes shift the main stress to the nearest non-schwa syllable before the suffix (*ˈ-ig*, *ˈ-(e)lijk*, *ˈ-isch*). Stress neutral suffixes, as the name suggests, leave the stress pattern of the base word unaffected (*-schap*, *-heid*, *-dom*). All inflections fall in this latter category as well.

There are four prefixes that generally leave the stress pattern of the base word unaltered: *be-*, *ge-*, *ont-*, and *ver-*. All other prefixes, such as *aarts- oer-*, and *over-*, behave as the leftmost part of a compound, and are generally considered to be words rather than prefixes (cf. Langeweg 1988). Words with Roman prefixes are best considered as morphologically simplex, at least as far as stress assignment is concerned.

5.5. Morphotactic constraints

Derivation of complex words through affixation is bound to morphotactic restrictions. It is not the case that any affix can be attached to any morpheme. Van Beurden (1987) discusses the ordering relationships among the various affixation processes. Diagram (8) below summarizes van Beurden's conclusions (see also Heemskerk—van Heuven, this volume):

(8)	Underived words/ Romance derivations	⇒	main stress rule (generalization: words referring to human beings take the article *de*
	V-derivation	⇒	V-level phonology
	A-derivation	⇒	main stress on first (full) vowel before suffix
	N-derivation	⇒	N-level phonology

First, stress is assigned to morphologically simplex words and to words with nonnative affixes. In the next stage verbs are allowed to be derived; since at this stage only simplex words are available, it follows that verbs can only be derived from simplex words. Adjective formation takes place after the generation of verbs, and may therefore be derived by either attaching a stress attracting suffix to a simplex base form, or by attaching a stress attracting suffix to a derived verb. Derived nouns can never be the base for the derivation of an adjective. Finally, nouns can be derived from any type of word, be it simplex or complex, including derived nouns.

6. Linguistic theory and language technology in practice

6.1. Implementing the theory

Lexical morphology distinguishes between various levels of morpheme attachment, and — as a consequence — various types of morpheme boundary (see above). Since this organization in terms of levels is largely based on stress behavior, it is highly appropriate for use in text-to-speech (TTS) systems. The morphemic information that is being used in PADMAN is inspired by lexical morphology. In PADMAN nine types of boundary are distinguished:

(9)	*Germanic*	*Roman*	*Other*
	Stress neutral prefix	Prefix	Compound boundary
	Stress neutral suffix	Suffix	Binding grapheme
	Stress attracting suffix		Improductive
	Stress bearing suffix		

Any morpheme combination can now be characterized using these types of boundary. By marking the words in the training lexicon not only for position of morpheme boundaries, but also for type of boundary (with an integer between one and nine), the theory of lexical morphology is implicitly incorporated into the patterns. When the resulting patterns are applied to the task of automatically segmenting words into morphemes, information on boundary type comes available as a bonus. With the aid of this information the phonological component of the TTS system is in a position to determine the correct pronunciation of any Dutch word.

6.2. Implementation

6.2.1. Adaptation of the original algorithm

A closer study of the hyphenation pattern generator developed by Aerts (1986) revealed that this program had to be adapted substantially in order to produce the desired patterns needed for morphological decomposition. The original program has no provision for hyphenating words immediately after the first or immediately before the final letter, since this is highly unusual in the printing industry. There are, however, several single-letter morphemes in Dutch, which have to be followed or preceded by a morpheme boundary, e.g., *a-sociaal* 'non social', *tafel-s* 'tables'. The program was adapted so as to allow single-letter morphemes in word-marginal position. Further adaptations were made in order to allow the program to recognize information on boundary type.

6.2.2. Building a training lexicon

The pattern approach crucially depends on the availability of a correctly segmented word list on the basis of which the segmentation patterns can be generated, i.e., a training lexicon. The NWO/SURF Expertise Centre for Lexical Data (CELEX, Nijmegen) supplied us with a computer readable corpus containing 123,093 morphologically segmented Dutch words. Information on type of boundary, in terms of the nine types distinguished above, was added to the corpus automatically.

6.2.3. Generating the patterns

In order to test the feasibility of the pattern approach as a means of morphological decomposition, we decided to first generate patterns for compound words and for derivations with native affixes. For this purpose a subcorpus was extracted from the CELEX word list containing 64,096 morphologically segmented words. Patterns were then generated in six tiers with a maximum length of five characters. The algorithm produced 6,482 patterns, which were able to detect 82.4 percent of the morpheme boundaries. This list of patterns could be stored in 50 kbytes of memory, whereas the source lexicon occupied 1,015 kbytes. This was a highly encouraging result.

We discovered that the source lexicon contained many inconsistencies. Such inconsistencies, e.g. *aanrecht-kast* 'sink-cupboard' versus *aan-recht-keuken* 'sink-kitchen', force the generation of additional patterns, or yield errors when the maximum string length in too short to capture the correct pattern. We expected that elimination of inconsistencies would reduce the size of the pattern inventory, reduce the maximum pattern length, and improve the percentage of correct decompositions.

After manual correction of the training lexicon, decomposition performance was much improved, indeed. Patterns were generated on eight tiers, and performance was as indicated in Table 1:

Table 1. Performance of pattern-driven morphological decomposition

Tier	Pattern length	Total number of patterns	Cumulative percent correct
1	1-2	209	29.6
2	1-2	210	29.8
3	2-3	1274	56.5
4	2-3	1294	56.5
5	3-4	6102	82.4
6	3-5	6253	82.4
7	4-6	11385	95.9
8	4-7	11979	96.0

The memory size of the pattern inventory had grown to 105 kbytes; the size of the training lexicon has remained unchanged (1,015 kbytes). Notice that at tier 6 percent correct decompositions was the same as in the case of the uncorrected training lexicon, but with a reduction in pattern inventory of 229. Unfortunately, there was no time to do an extensive error analysis of the remaining incorrect segmentations, which in turn might have allowed us to further fine-tune the pattern inventory. Also, a proper evaluation of the pattern approach can only be obtained when the training lexicon is also includes productive non-native and inflectional morphology. In spite of these caveats, however, we consider this first exploration of the possibilities of the pattern approach to morphological decomposition highly encouraging.

Prosodic sentence analysis without exhaustive parsing

Hugo Quené—René Kager

Abstract

Suprasegmental phenomena in synthetic speech should reflect the linguistic structure of the input text. An algorithm is described which establishes the prosodic sentence structure (PSS). This can be achieved without exhaustive syntactic parsing, using a dictionary of 550 function words. Subsequently, phrase and accent locations are derived from the PSS; accentuation is also affected by some semantic and contextual information. Some exemplary rules for labeling, prosodic domain construction and accentuation are discussed. Comparison of the resulting sentence prosody with natural speech suggests that more detailed syntactic analysis may be necessary. Most of the accentuation errors are caused by semantic, pragmatic and contextual factors. These can only partly be imitated, since the relations between linguistic representations and real-world knowledge are not yet fully understood.

1. Introduction

Our ultimate aim, when listening to speech (be it synthetic or natural), is to understand the message it conveys. Usually, this boils down to comprehension of the semantic content of an utterance. This task is considerably easier, if the speech utterance contains adequate prosodic cues with regard to its semantic and pragmatic content (e.g. Collier—'t Hart, 1975; Wingfield 1975; Nooteboom—Brokx—de Rooij 1978; Cutler 1982; Cutler—Clifton 1984; Nooteboom 1985; Nooteboom—Kruyt 1987). Using suprasegmental cues, the listener can extract the linguistic structure of the message. Pauses, for example, divide the continuous speech signal into (linguistically) coherent word groups or chunks of acoustic-phonetic information. Hence, adequate pauses increase the intelligibility of the speech signal (Scharpff—van Heuven 1988). Likewise, *accentuation* guides a listener's attention to the words which are considered important by the speaker, and which are acoustically most reliable.

These perceptual functions of sentence prosody become even more important when the speech signal is less redundant, providing fewer segmental cues to the intended speech sounds, words, and meaning. Since the output of a text-to-speech conversion system lacks the normal degree of acoustic-phonetic redundancy, suprasegmental cues may significantly improve its perception and comprehension. Text-to-speech systems should aim at optimizing sentence prosody, in order to compensate for their reduced overall speech quality.

In the production of natural speech, various suprasegmental phenomena depend on the abstract linguistic notions *phrasing* and *accent*: F_0 movements (Collier—'t Hart 1975; Cooper—Sorensen 1977), location and duration of silent intervals (Goldman-Eisler 1972), segmental durations (Klatt 1975, 1976), intensity pattern (Lehiste 1970), coarticulation and sandhi (Cooper—Paccia-Cooper 1980) and vowel reduction (Koopmans-van Beinum 1980). All these suprasegmental phenomena can (in theory) be derived from the "abstract prosody". Considering the perceptual interest of adequate prosody, a high-quality text-to-speech system should attempt to establish both *phrasing* and *accentuation* and to convert these into adequate suprasegmental properties of the synthetic speech signal.

In natural speech, the (abstract) phrasing and accentuation are assumed to be related to the linguistic structure of an utterance. According to nonlinear phonological theory, abstract sentence prosody does not depend directly on the syntactic surface structure, but rather on the related *prosodic sentence structure* (Nespor—Vogel 1982, 1986; Gee—Grosjean 1983; Selkirk 1984, 1986). In addition, abstract accentuation is also affected by (a) the *thematic* structure, which specifies the semantic constituents functioning as Predicate, Argument and Modifier (Gussenhoven 1984), as well as by (b) the *focus* structure, which relates the syntactic constituents to be emphasized with specific accents (Ladd 1987; Baart 1987).

Extending this line of thought, we assume that accentuation and phrasing can both be derived from the prosodic sentence structure, provided that thematic structure and focus information are taken into account. To illustrate matters, our view of the various levels of sentence prosody is represented in Figure 1.

linguistic:	prosodic structure, thematic structure, focus structure
abstract prosody:	phrasing, accentuation
phonetic prosody:	segmental durations, pausing, F_0 movements, intensity, vowel reduction, coarticulation, sandhi, etc.

Figure 1. Three levels of sentence prosody

The aim of the present project is to investigate whether "abstract prosody" can be derived automatically for text-to-speech conversion. To this end, we have developed an experimental algorithm (Pros). First, a hybrid prosodic sentence structure is established (hence PSS). Subsequently, accentuation and phrasing are derived from this PSS, while contextual, thematic and rhythmic information is also taken into account. The output of the PROS component is converted to suprasegmental parameters by other components: silence segments are inserted in the phoneme string, segmental durations are adjusted, and an F_0 contour is calculated (te Lindert—Doedens—van Leeuwen 1989; Terken—Collier 1989; van Leeuwen—te Lindert, this volume).

The algorithm presented in this chapter is the latest member of a steadily growing family of similar algorithms (Kulas—Rühl 1985; Allen—Hunnicutt—Klatt 1987; Ladd 1987; Monaghan 1990a, 1990b, 1990c; Quazza—Varese—Vivalda 1989; O'Shaughnessy 1989; Carlson—Granström—Hunnicutt 1989; Bailly 1989; Hirschberg 1990; Bachenko—Fitzpatrick 1990). All these algorithms acknowledge that suprasegmental phenomena cannot be derived from syntactic information alone; non-syntactic information also plays an important role in determining sentence prosody (e.g. phrase length, reference to "given" vs. "new" concepts). Since syntactic factors can be "overruled" by non-syntactic factors, an exhaustive syntactic analysis is generally superfluous. In spite of these similarities, however, our method differs in several respects from those mentioned above (apart from the language for which it was developed). These differences mostly stem from our distinction between three separate tasks in generating sentence prosody, viz. (a) derivation of sentence structure, (b) derivation of abstract phrasing and accentuation, (c) generation of suprasegmental parameters.

This three-step approach offers many advantages over other methods, where two or more of these tasks are combined. Firstly, it seems to be a better approximation of human speech production. The suprasegmental phenomena associated with phrasing and accentuation (pausing, intonation, segment duration, etc.) are obviously intertwined. Hence, both phrasing and accentuation are likely to be derived from the same sentence representation. This representation should combine syntactic, semantic and rhythmic relations; the adjusted PSS matches these requirements—as opposed to syntactic surface structure (e.g. Quazza et al. 1989), Tone Group structure (e.g. Ladd 1987) or phrase structure. Secondly, the PSS may also be used to control other suprasegmental phenomena in the resulting speech signal, such as those indicated in Figure 1. Thirdly, there will be no conflicting suprasegmental cues in the resulting synthetic speech: all cues indicate the same abstract prosody and linguistic structure. This makes the sentence structure relatively easy to retrieve.

2. Prosodic sentence structure

From many languages, it is known that sandhi phenomena have their own specific domains of application, not necessarily identical to syntactic constituents. Among others, Nespor—Vogel (1982, 1986) and Selkirk (1984, 1986) have made proposals as to the mapping between syntactic constituents and *prosodic domains.* Two prosodic domains employed in this sense are the phonological phrase (Phi) and the intonational phrase (Int). These domains are part of a hierarchical tree structure, viz. the prosodic sentence structure. In their definition, the distinction between content words and function words plays a crucial role. The main semantic load of a sentence is carried by its *content words* (hence CWs: nouns, verbs, adjectives and adverbs; note that these are extendable word classes). *Function words* (FWs) express the relations between the content words, while they have hardly any independent meaning (prepositions, conjunctions, complementizers, copula, etc; fixed word classes).

In languages such as English and Dutch, the *Phi* domain (phonological phrase) is built around a lexical head, i.e., the content word which is the head of a syntactic constituent. This *prosodic head* plays an important role in accentuation. The Phi domain includes this head, its preceding specifiers, as well as all preceding FWs.

The next higher prosodic constituent is the *Int* domain (intonational phrase), constructed by grouping adjacent Phi domains. Hence, a whole Phi domain is always contained within a single Int domain. In addition, however, important syntactic breaks are also respected; each syntactic constituent which is attached to any S-node (in the syntactic surface structure) establishes a separate Int domain. Consequently, (a) displaced syntactic constituents, (b) most subordinate clauses, and (c) parentheticals, are all separate Int domains.

In the following example, the Phi and Int domains are illustrated in a flat representation (where '##' indicates an Int-boundary, and '#' a Phi-boundary). Note that prosodic domains do not necessarily correspond to syntactic constituents.

(1) ## Kasyapa's great war elephant # turned aside
to avoid # a patch # of marshy ground

(2) ## De computer # spreekt # tot de bemanning ## op de betweterige # en begrijpende toon ## die we kennen # uit de zachte sector ##
'## the computer # speaks # to the crew ## in the pedantic # and understanding tone ## which we know # from the soft sector ##'

Prosodic domains tend to be of equal length as much as possible, and their length increases in faster speech. To account for these effects, separate rules restructure the prosodic domains (by merging and dividing them).

3. Automatic prosodic analysis

According to the linguistic theory described above, the prosodic sentence structure is initially derived from the syntactic (surface) sentence structure. Hence, syntactic parsing is necessary for any text-to-speech system performing prosodic analysis. For two reasons, however, this linguistically motivated method is not applicable to *automatic* prosodic sentence analysis. Firstly, there is no algorithm for syntactic analysis available with satisfactory performance (speed, accuracy, hardware requirements, Dutch language). In fact, it may be doubted whether any parser could perform satisfactorily, when confronted with ambiguous sentences like the following:

(3) a. I (have mown) (the lawn with the flowers).
b. *I (have mown) (the lawn) (with the flowers).

(4) a. Het was (ondanks de luchtverversing) (door de tv-lampen
it was in-spite-of the air-conditioning because-of the TV-lights
snikheet).
suffocatingly-hot
b. *Het was (ondanks de luchtverversing door de tv-lampen)
it was in-spite-of the air-conditioning by-means-of the TV-lights
(snikheet)
suffocatingly-hot

Solving this type of thematic ambiguity (with solutions yielding different prosody) requires a semantic and pragmatic analysis; the parser must "know" that one cannot use flowers to mow a lawn, and that TV lights produce heat rather than fresh air. Again, no system exists for this type of sentence analysis.

Secondly, syntactic information is insufficient for establishing sentence prosody. Syntactic factors may be overruled by non-syntactic factors (e.g. phrase length, reference to "given" or "new" concepts): some results of the syntactic analysis are subsequently discarded. Hence, an exhaustive syntactic analysis seems to be superfluous.

For these reasons, we have chosen to derive a correct PSS directly, using the minimum amount of syntactic information as input. Shortcomings of the correct *syntactic* sentence structure, or even its absence, need not detract from the adequacy of the resulting prosody, as long as a correct *prosodic* sentence structure underlies the latter. This follows from our assumption that prosody can be derived correctly from the PSS (as explained in section 1). The present project aims at (a) establishing the PSS from incomplete syntactic information; (b) deriving abstract sentence prosody (phrasing and accentuation) from the resulting PSS. This approach is illustrated in Figure 2 below.

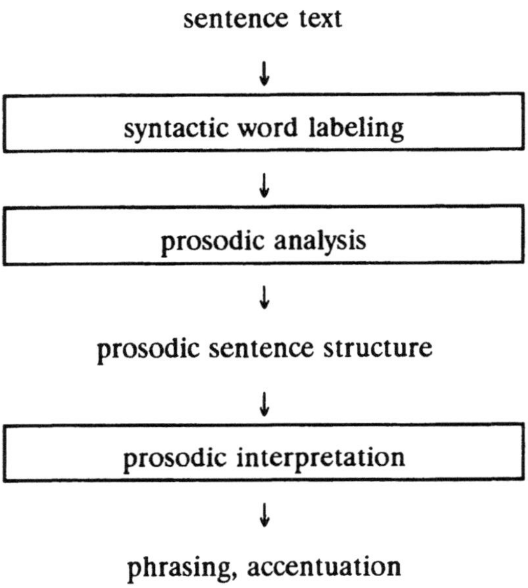

Figure 2. Alternative method for deriving the prosodic sentence structure (PSS) directly from an input sentence

In order to achieve the *first* aim, two types of syntactic information are indispensable. Firstly, lexical heads must be identified, since prosodic domains are constructed around these. To this end, word classification as CW or FW is sufficient. In theory, each last CW preceding an FW (or sentence boundary) constitutes a lexical/prosodic head. The CW-or-FW status of a word (hence "prosodic label") is determined by means of lexical lookup, in a dictionary containing all Dutch FWs (554 types). In addition, the dictionary contains another 300 CWs which behave anomalously for one reason or another. For all words, the syntactic word class is also specified. This syntactic labeling serves two purposes: it is used for (a) determining the syntactic labels of the words not found in the dictionary, and (b) the construction of prosodic domains, as explained below. (More details on this dictionary are given by Quené—Kager 1990, 1992).

Secondly, syntactic phrasing must be known, since it is relevant for prosodic domains. For example, the main verb (or verb group) in a sentence must be identified (cf. O'Shaughnessy 1989). This word (group) establishes a predicate constituent, corresponding to a separate Phi domain (Gee—Grosjean 1983). In Dutch, as in English, this Phi domain may separate the subject and object arguments of the predicate. Likewise, subordinate clauses must be identified, because they usually establish separate Int domains (see section 2). However, an exhaustive syntactic analysis appears to be superfluous for establishing prosodic domains: it is not necessary to determine the structural relations between the words in a sentence. Returning to (1), for example, it is not necessary to decide which is the internal structure of the subject NP:

(1) a. (Kasyapa's (great (war elephant)))
b. (Kasyapa's ((great war) elephant))
c. ((Kasyapa's (great war)) elephant)

Instead, it suffices to determine that these four CWs together establish a single constituent, which in turn establishes a separate Phi domain. This information can be derived from the sequence of syntactic word classes (the colon indicates a sub-classification):

(1)	Kasyapa's	great	war	elephant	#	turned	aside	...
	N	A	N	N	#	V:Infl	A	...

The words *elephant* and *turned* must belong to separate syntactic constituents, as a noun cannot be a specifier to an inflected verb. Since both words are lexical heads of syntactic constituents, they cannot both belong to the same Phi domain. Consequently, a Phi boundary must separate these two words. In more general terms, syntactic constituency is derived from restrictions on possible sequences of syntactic labels within a syntactic constituent. If constraints on the possible label sequences are violated, then we may assume a syntactic boundary. Not all syntactic boundaries, however, are equally important for the PSS. For the purposes of sentence prosody, it generally suffices to demarcate those syntactic constituents which are respected by prosodic domains, while ignoring other syntactic structures. It should be noted, however, that this resulting PSS is an *approximation* of the theoretical PSS, since not all relevant syntactic information is available for the prosodic analysis.

Because the algorithm demarcates prosodic domains on the basis of both the CW/FW distinction and syntactic word labels, it can deal with a large variety of input text types. For its development, a large corpus of newspaper articles was used (approx. 450,000 word tokens). Its CW:FW ratio is roughly 1:1 (46:54). Although the analysis rules (described in more detail below) were primarily based on observations regarding this corpus, they also apply to other types of input text. If an input text would contain predominantly FWs, then the rules based on syntactic label sequences ensure correct demarcation of prosodic domains (5a); if no syntactic labels could be determined, then prosodic domains are derived from the CW/FW distinction (5b). Only in this latter case are problems to be expected, if subsequent unlabeled words are all classified as CW (5c).

(5) a. van al wie er toen was ## is hij het geweest ## die ...
V\FW ## V\FW V\FW ## Comp\FW
of all who there then was ## is he (it) been ## who ...
b. de aan mijn broer verkochte ## zeer gevaarlijke auto
?\CW ## ?\FW
the to my brother sold ## very dangerous car
c. de onlangs dubbel verkochte (##) uiterst gevaarlijke auto
?\CW ?\CW ?\CW ?\CW ?\CW
the recently doubly sold (##) extremely dangerous car

In order to achieve its second aim, viz. derivation of phrasing and accentuation from the PSS, additional information is again indispensable. As regards phrasing, boundaries of Int domains are simply converted into pause locations. As regards accentuation, however, matters are considerably more complex. This prosodic phenomenon is known to be influenced by three types of additional information, which our algorithm should also take into account. The first factor is the discourse context of a sentence, specifically the distinction between "given" and "new" concepts (Fuchs 1984). A phrase is unaccented if the speaker assumes its content already known by the listener ("given"). Usually, only domains introducing new information are accented, as demonstrated below (accent indicated by capitals):

(6) a. he came # by CAR
b. his car # was BLUE

Secondly, thematic relations between prosodic domains also play an important role (Gussenhoven 1984; Baart 1987). Predicates are usually left unaccented; they receive accent only if their argument(s) are unaccented or if they are not adjacent to their argument(s). Thirdly, rhythmic factors affect accentuation: speakers prefer some alternation between accented and unaccented words. If multiple adjacent accents should occur, then one of the accents is removed or shifted to a different word (Kager—Visch 1988; Visch 1990).

In summary, then, the algorithm starts by providing the words constituting the sentence with a syntactic label. Subsequently, the PSS is derived from both the orthographic input sentence (text string), and from the syntactic labeling of its constituent words. Finally, (abstract) phrase boundaries and accents are derived from the PSS, as well as from additional information.

4. Some typical examples

4.1. Syntactic disambiguation

In the algorithm's representation, words can have multiple syntactic labels. These can be copied from the dictionary, output by the morphological analysis (Heemskerk—van Heuven, this volume), or generated by rule (on the basis of string features, e.g. affixes). Prior to the demarcation of prosodic domains, these syntactic label ambiguities must be resolved. As explained in section 3 above, this is done on the basis of restrictions on label sequences: linguistically motivated disambiguation can only be achieved when taking account of the context.

This selection of the appropriate syntactic label is often based on linguistic constraints on word sequences: for example, an inflected verb may not be preceded by an article (since the article label of the first word comes from the dictionary, the verb label of the second word should be discarded). In addition, several rules employ statistical constraints: for example, prepositions are usually followed by nouns, rather than by verbs. Such probabilistic observations are based on our analyses of the newspaper text corpus. Although these rules filter out many incorrect labels (7a), they may occasionally introduce errors (7b):

(7) a. Vogels broeden **in nesten.**
birds breed in nests
b. Hij wil zich daar **in mengen.**
he wants (to) himself there in mingle

In addition, orthographic conventions guide the selection of syntactic labels: strings containing a hyphen are compound nouns; strings containing digits are numerals; words starting with a capital (not sentence-initial) are proper names; long words (over 13 characters) are probably nouns (e.g. *wapenhandelaren* 'weapon-traders') rather than verbs (although the latter are possible, e.g. *herprogrammeren* 'reprogram').

4.2. Separate Int's for sub-clauses

As explained in section 2 above, each sub-clause constitutes a separate Int domain. To produce such domains, several rules in the algorithm insert an Int boundary between two adjacent words which cannot both belong to the same clause (as may be deduced from their syntactic and prosodic labels). Note that Dutch is an SOV language, where the inflected verb takes the final position in subordinate clauses, and the second position in main clauses. Some generalizations in our rules for Dutch do not apply to English, since that is an SVO language (cf. glosses (8-10)).

Rule (8) demarcates the end of a subordinate clause (with final verb). Rules demarcating the beginning of a subordinate clause are exemplified by (9). Two juxtaposed main clauses are demarcated by rule (10); it is determined from the right-hand context of the conjunctive whether it links two clauses (and not two other constituents).

(8) Ø ⇒ IntBound / <VERB:INFL> ___ <VERB:INFL>
— omdat het geen haast **had ## deed** ik het later
because it no hurry had ## did I it later
— de fresco's die hij **schilderde ## zien** er nog fris uit
the frescoes which he painted ## look (there) still fresh (out)

(9) Ø ⇒ IntBound / <VERB:PART> ___ <NOT <VERB>>
— hij is erin **geslaagd ## om** dit goed weer te geven
he has (in-it) succeeded ## this correctly to represent
— hij heeft **beloofd ## morgen** te komen
he has promised ## tomorrow to come

(10) Ø ⇒ IntBound / ___ <CONJ> {<VERB:INFL>}
{<FW>}
— hij raapte een steen op **## maar aarzelde** om die weg te gooien
he picked up a stone ## but hesitated it away to throw
— Thero excuseerde zichzelf **## en hij** verliet de kamer
Thero excused himself ## and he left the room

4.3. Phi demarcation

As explained in section 2 above, Phi domains are strictly enclosed within Int domains. Our algorithm produces this hierarchy by first demarcating Int domains; subsequently, Phi domains are demarcated within these Int domains. (This procedure deviates from the theoretical construction of prosodic domains, e.g. Nespor—Vogel 1986.) Analogously to Int domain demarcation, a Phi boundary is inserted between two adjacent words which cannot both belong to the same domain. The most important of these rules (11) uses the fact that the prosodic head of a Phi is typically its rightmost CW. FWs always belong to the prosodic head on their right-hand side, i.e. to the right-hand Phi domain. Hence, a Phi boundary is assumed between a CW (which is the prosodic head of the left-hand Phi domain) and a following FW (which is a specifier for the right-hand prosodic head):

(11) Ø ⇒ PhiBound / <CW> ___ <FW>
— she **prunes # the** red **roses # in** her garden

Of course, this requires additional rules for Phi domains whose prosodic head is not a CW, but rule (11) correctly identifies the majority of Phi domains.

4.4. Verb accentuation

Predicates are accented, if a sentence modifier intervenes between the verb (group) and its arguments, or if all of the arguments are unaccented (not in focus)—or simply absent (cf. section 3). The verb accentuation rules work on single CW verbs, as well as on longer sequences of verbs, of which the first CW is accented. In addition, they work on complex verbs, of which the stem and particle can occur separately. Stem and particle occur together only in participles (12a), where the two parts should be written as a single word. But in infinitive constructions, the infinitive marker *te* can be interposed (12b), whereas in inflected forms in Dutch, the inflected stem in second position in main clause may be far away from the particle in "original" clause-final position, as in (12c). Nevertheless, it is always the particle that is accented, even if the stem is far away (12b,c):

(12) a. Ik **heb #** mijn MOEDER # VANDAAG # **OPGEBELD.**
I've # my mother # today # phoned
b. Ik heb GEPROBEERD # mijn MOEDER # VANDAAG # **OP te bellen.**
I've tried # my mother # today # to phone
c. Ik **belde #** haar # VANDAAG # **OP.**
I phoned # her # today # Ø

However, particles are often identical to prepositions (e.g. *op* in (12)), which makes their detection difficult. Some can be identified because they occur immediately before the infinitive marker *te* (12b); these are treated as the prosodic head of the predicate Phi domain. Others may be identified because they occur in clause-final position (12c), where "real" prepositions cannot occur. The rules discussed below also work on these "stranded" clause-final particles.

A verb (group) is accented if it follows an adverb (13a) or adverbial phrase (13b). An adverbial PP is detected through its initial preposition, which is seldom used within an $[NP\ PP]_{NP}$ complex (argument) (e.g. *ondanks* 'notwithstanding', *sinds* 'since'). The verb (group) itself must be followed by an Int (or sentence) boundary, since a clause-internal predicate would typically be followed by an (adjacent) argument.

(13) a. Hij heeft # het GAZON # **VANDAAG**$_{\mathrm{Adv}}$ # **GEMAAID.**
he has # the lawn # today # mown
b. Hij heeft # het GAZON # **ondanks** de REGEN # **GEMAAID.**
he has # the lawn # in-spite-of the rain # mown

If the predicate is accompanied by an un-accented argument, then the predicate (verb group) must be accented. Such arguments are indicated by pronominal FWs. In addition, deictic qualifiers (such as *dit, deze* 'this', *dergelijke, zulke* 'such') imply that the following term refers to "given" information. Any words following one of these cue words in the same Phi domain are de-accented, and an adjacent predicate receives integrative accent (14a). In cases with comparative adjectives, however, this qualifier takes the integrative accent, instead of the predicate (14b). Finally, the predicate is also accented if there is no argument at all.

(14) a. De ZEEHONDEN # hebben # **deze** lage temperaturen # **OVERLEEFD.**
the seals # have # these low temperatures # survived
b. Ze heeft # de **HOGERE** weg # **genomen.**
she has # the higher road # taken

5. Evaluation

5.1. Introduction

As explained in section 1, the algorithm described above aims at establishing the correct abstract sentence prosody (accentuation and phrasing). It is assumed that these aspects (or rather, their appropriate phonetic correlates) make synthetic speech more natural and intelligible. In order to evaluate whether our algorithm achieves this aim, two methods are possible.

First, its output can be evaluated from a perceptual viewpoint, viz. by investigating whether synthetic speech is sufficiently intelligible and adequate, if accents and pauses are derived automatically. Van Bezooijen (1989a) reported subjects' ratings on a 10-point adequacy scale of sentence prosody under four accentuation conditions: (a) derived automatically [mean 6.0], (b) same number of accents, distributed at random over CWs [mean 4.6], (c) subjects' preferred accentuation, as established earlier [mean 7.7], and (d) as produced by a human professional speaker [mean 7.4]. From these results, she concludes that the algorithm produces sufficiently adequate accentuation, although its output is still defective in several respects (see also van Bezooijen—Pols, this volume).

Secondly, we can compare the output accentuation and phrasing with those produced by a human speaker. Ideally, there should be no difference between the two. Even if we allow some variation, any differences found should not disturb the semantic and pragmatic equivalence between the natural and synthetic versions. This comparison is reported in the following section.

5.2. Comparison with natural prosody

The accentuation and phrasing produced by our algorithm was compared with natural speech on a word-by-word basis (a phrase-by-phrase comparison is reported by Quené—Dirksen 1990). A professional speaker, the designated talker of the ASSP program, read aloud several texts (10,766 words, of which 5,273 were CWs and 5,493 FWs, in 600 sentences, grouped into 43 texts). Recordings were transcribed with respect to accents and prosodic boundaries by the two authors (and occasionally, by a third transcriber). Subsequently, this transcription was compared with the phrasing and accentuation produced by our algorithm.

We must realize, however, that a difference in phrasing or accentuation between speaker and algorithm does not necessarily imply that the latter has been wrong. In fact, both versions may be equally acceptable, and roughly equivalent (15). All such discrepancies between equivalent versions were discarded.

(15) a. Een aantal ONDERZOEKERS meent overigens ## dat de VRAAG ## of passief meeroken SCHADELIJK is ## al LANG positief kan worden BEANTWOORD.

b. Een AANTAL onderzoekers MEENT overigens ## dat de vraag of PASSIEF MEEROKEN SCHADELIJK is ## al lang POSITIEF kan worden beantwoord.

a number (of) researchers thinks indeed ## that the question (##) whether passive smoking detrimental is ## already positively can be answered

The algorithm generated 86 percent of the naturally produced phrase boundaries (N=1,319), while 21 percent of its output *phrase boundaries* were incorrect. An error occurs in 5 percent of all word boundaries in the input sentences (N=10,167).

Of the naturally produced *accents* (N=4,173), 85 percent were also generated automatically, while 19 percent of the output accents were incorrect. It must be noted that the two error types are not independent here, since accents usually occur in a rhythmic pattern. Therefore, incorrect accentuation of one word corresponds to an incorrect non-accent on a neighboring word, as in the fragments *een aantal onderzoekers meent* and *al lang positief* in (15) above. The different accentuations of such fragments are not equivalent, since semantic prominence is guided towards different words.

The "human" and automatic accentuations are in agreement in 87 percent of all words in the input sentences (N=10,766). Since FWs are seldom accented, the agreement in their (non-)accentuation is considerably higher (viz. 94 percent; this class includes all particles) as compared to CWs (77 percent).

5.3. Error analysis

In a post-hoc analysis of the discrepancies (Quené—Kager 1992), both "misses" and "false alarms" in the PROS output were classified according to their origin (e.g. labeling, syntax, rhythmic, "given"/"new", etc.). Results show that most *phrasing* errors (73 percent) are caused by incorrect mapping from syntactic constituents to prosodic domains. Most often, subordinate clauses are incorrectly demarcated, as in (16):

(16) De strepen worden doorgesneden ## langs de deuren # om het instappen # te vergemakkelijken.
the strips are cut ## along the doors # in-order-to the getting-in # to facilitate

These are serious errors, since they result in "garden path" sentences: the prosody signals an incorrect linguistic structure. In addition, they may also propagate into subsequent accentuation errors.

Most errors in *accentuation* (69 percent) are caused by semantic, pragmatic and contextual factors. Any accentuation algorithm should decide which words convey "given" information, and adjust the accentuation accordingly (see section 4.4). Moreover, it should also decide which words are important, and then assign a contrastive accent on these words (or an integrative accent on its prosodic head). Our algorithm performs poorly on both of these tasks. Regarding the first task, this is primarily due tot the fact that its scope is limited to the single sentence, yielding errors such as (17):

(17) a. De OLIEVLEK # zal aan DUIZENDEN VOGELS # het LEVEN kosten.
the oil-slick # will of thousands [of] birds # the life cost
b. Er zijn al # TIENTALLEN **VOGELS** # DOOD AANGETROFFEN.
there are already # tens [dozens of] birds # dead found

The obvious remedy might be to widen this scope, e.g. by maintaining a buffer of content words (Silverman 1987) or root morphemes (Hirschberg 1990) across sentences, and resetting this buffer at paragraph boundaries. This strategy would avoid some errors, but co-references involving synonyms and paraphrases are likely to go undetected — even though these are more frequent than the former type.

Moreover, it has been observed that there is no perfect correspondence between the distinctions "given"/"new" and ±accent. Words conveying "new" information can be unaccented (18a), and (implicitly) "given" words can be accented (18b):

(18) a. de HERENIGING # **van de twee Duitslanden**
the reunion # of the two Germanies
b. **ZIJN** salaris # is VEEL hoger # dan het UWE
his salary # is much higher # than yours

In the latter case, contrastive accents are selected solely on pragmatic and contextual grounds. Such accents can be derived partly from statistical regularities and other heuristics (Monaghan 1990c). Yet, the majority of such errors cannot be solved without a better understanding of the complex relation between accentuation and our knowledge of the real world.

6. Conclusion

In the present chapter, it was argued that suprasegmental phenomena in synthetic speech should be derived, via abstract accentuation and phrasing, from an underlying linguistic sentence representation. We therefore attempted to establish the prosodic sentence structure (PSS; Nespor—Vogel 1982, 1986). This structure is based on a well-established phonological theory (supported by independent evidence from various languages), and predicts many prosodic phenomena. Yet, it does not require exhaustive syntactic analysis of the input sentence, which (even if required at all) is currently unavailable. The algorithm described in this chapter approximates the PSS on the basis of syntactic word labeling. Subsequently, phrasing and accentuation are derived from the PSS, while for accentuation some semantic and contextual information is also taken into account.

A large proportion of the errors in the resulting phrase boundaries could be solved by more exhaustive and more advanced syntactic analysis. Accentuation errors are mainly caused by contextual and pragmatic factors. It is in the nature of things, however, that such errors cannot be avoided in a principled way. At present, linguistic generalizations cannot include the real-world knowledge shared by speakers and listeners, which seems to be responsible for most of the variation in our use of prosodic patterns.

Prosodic analysis: The next generation

Arthur Dirksen—Hugo Quené

Abstract

In many text-to-speech systems, sentence prosody is derived by string-oriented rules, which are often rather ad hoc and linguistically unsound. By contrast, a system which employs a syntactic parser allows for highly general and computationally simple procedures defining the mapping between syntax and prosody. The program described in this paper, PROS2, is a first attempt towards a "next generation". First, the input sentence is parsed by applying phrase structure rules. Next, the syntactic representation is mapped onto a metrical tree, augmented with "focus" markers. The metrical tree provides an abstract characterization of accent and phrasing. While the program, at the time of writing, is still at the prototype stage, it holds considerable promise for further development and can be expanded in several directions.

1. Introduction

From an architectural point of view, text-to-speech systems are rooted in grapheme-to-phoneme conversion. Minimally, such a system takes as input an orthographic representation, which is converted by a process of derivation into a string of phonological segments (phonemes), from which speech is synthesized. In such a minimal system, all linguistic representations are strings and transformational rules are used to implement the derivation. Transformational rules of the type introduced by Chomsky—Halle (1968) have a long tradition in linear phonology, and they seem to provide a natural framework for implementing grapheme-to-phoneme conversion rules. One problem, however, is that encoding supra-segmental information in strings is rather awkward. To accommodate this problem, second-generation systems have replaced the notion of strings with the notion of streams (Hertz—Kadin—Karplus 1985; see also van Leeuwen—te Lindert, this volume). Using streams allows the developer to encode different types of information at different levels of representation, which are related to one another through synchronization.

The stream-oriented formalism is a vast improvement in that a more modular approach is feasible, while rules and data are encoded in an intuitive manner. A serious limitation, however, is that streams cannot encode recursive structures, at least, not in an insightful manner. Thus, if a syntactic tree is to be represented inside a text-to-speech system, then streams are of little help. Also, building syntactic structures for input strings is usually not done by transformational rules, whether stream-oriented or not, but by parsing the string using phrase-structure rules. Transformational rules apply deterministically, and (as a consequence) are intrinsically ordered. Grammar rules, on the other hand, are intrinsically unordered, and are (usually) interpreted non-deterministically. Another difference is that grammar rules are monotonic (or: incremental):they add information (i.e., by building hierarchical structure), but cannot delete or otherwise modify information.

We conclude that current architectures for text-to-speech systems do not lend themselves very well to syntactic processing. In our view, this is a historical accident: early systems simply ignored syntax, concentrating instead on grapheme-to-phoneme conversion (and, of course, speech synthesis). It is also unfortunate, in that rules for sentence prosody are necessarily crippled: these rules need syntactic information, but any information above the lexical level cannot be represented appropriately.

Making necessity a virtue, Quené—Kager (and many others) have stuck to using stream-oriented rules and have tried to do prosody without doing (too much) syntax. As indicated in their chapter (this volume), they have come a long way. However, while their program PROS is inspired by linguistic theory, it is not an implementation of any linguistic theory in a strict sense. Instead, PROS uses clever rules to mimic the output of more general rules. As a result, the relation between theory and implementation becomes rather murky: there is no way of verifying formally whether or not PROS does what it is designed to do. Instead, the program is evaluated as a black box, that is, it is asked whether or not it produces acceptable output.

Such an informal evaluation is useful, of course, but it is not sufficient. First, the notion of "acceptable output" is very hard to make operational, especially so in the case of sentence prosody, where there is a great deal of contextual variation. Second, in case of "errors", there are several possibilities: (a) the error is caused by a design error in the program; (b) the error reflects a flaw in the underlying theory; (c) the error reflects a phenomenon which is outside the scope of a theory. These different types of "error" are hard to tell apart, especially if the relation between theory and implementation is unclear (see Quené—Dirksen 1990). As a result, informal evaluation might suggest ad hoc modifications to a program, while in fact the underlying model is wrong or too limited in scope.

For these reasons, and others, we have decided to make virtue a necessity, and leave the domain of stream-oriented rules, so that a more direct and obvious relation between theory and implementation would become feasible. We have started developing a new generation of PROS (called PROS2), aiming at a direct implementation of one linguistic theory, in this case (a version of) focus-accent theory. The program implements a syntactic parser which uses phrase structure rules. The output of the parser, a representation of the syntactic surface structure of a sentence, is mapped onto a metrical tree, which together with a simple heuristic for "informational focus" directly characterizes accent and potential phrase boundaries.

The mapping from syntactic to metrical tree is defined in a highly general manner, which should work with different (types of) grammars in a similar manner. Also, we have reason to believe that our method should work for other languages as well.[1] The strict separation of syntax and prosody in our program, together with the explicitness of the underlying model, make a formal verification possible.

This paper is organized as follows. Section 2 rather informally illustrates the different ways of PROS and its successor, so that the reader can get a clear picture of what exactly is new here. Section 3 discusses focus-accent theory and how it has been implemented. We present our own version of the theory, which is in fact a generalization of Baart (1987).[2] Section 4 discusses how focus-accent theory may be extended in order to deal with intonational phrasing as well. Finally, section 5 deals with some remaining issues.

2. Deaccenting in PROS and PROS2

As indicated in section 1, the main difference between PROS2 and its predecessor is the way in which linguistic theory has been implemented. Whereas PROS2 aims at a direct implementation of focus-accent theory, PROS has no alternative but to simulate some of it, as the necessary data (syntactic structure) are not available. By way of illustration, this section discusses how the two programs deal with deaccenting. The example may not be fully representative of PROS' way of operating, but it is very illustrative. Consider the following paradigm:[3]

(1)	a.	ik	zag	een	MEISJE	
		I	saw	a	girl	
	b.	ik	ZAG		haar	
		I	saw		her	
(2)	a.	ik	zag	een	MEISJE	lopen
		I	saw	a	girl	walk
	b.	ik	zag		haar	LOPEN
		I	saw		her	walk

The pairs in (1) and (2) illustrate the general phenomenon of accent shifting from a word which is "deaccented" (as pronouns normally are) to an adjacent predicate. In (1), if *een meisje* is replaced with *her*, accent shifts to the left. In (2), on the other hand, accent shifts to the right.

As far as these sentences are concerned, there is no difference between the output representations of PROS and PROS2. However, the two programs arrive at their results in radically different ways.

PROS first marks all content words, except verbs, as [+Accent]. All function words are marked [-Accent]. Subsequent rules mark a verb [+Accent] if it adjacent to an object pronoun, [-Accent] otherwise. This takes care of the difference between (1a) and (1b). However, it is predicted that both *zag* 'saw' and *lopen* 'walk' in (2b) are accented, as both are adjacent to the object pronoun *haar* 'her'. This is fixed by lexically marking all forms of verbs which subcategorize for raised infinitivals as function words. But now there is no accent for *zag* 'saw' in (1b)! Fortunately, there is a catch-all rule saying that, if no element of a phrase is accented, a verb (if any) is marked [+Accent]. This is clever, of course, but also rather ad hoc and derivationally more complex than theory would lead us to expect.

In PROS2, the difference between (1) and (2) is analyzed as a difference in syntactic structure. In (1a) and (1b), the NP *een meisje/haar* 'a girl/her' is a sister of the verb *zag* 'saw', whereas in (2a) and (2b) the NP is a sister of the verb *lopen* 'walk'. In both cases, NP is an argument of the verb that it combines with, and, as a general rule, arguments "attract" accent (see section 3). However, if an element is deaccented, accent shifts to a sister node. In (1b), *zag* 'saw' is the lucky one, whereas in (2b) the accented sister is *lopen* 'walk'.

This account not only takes care of the contrast between (1) and (2), but applies quite generally. Each time two elements combine to form a larger syntactic constituent, one element is semantically an argument of the other element, and attracts accent — unless it is deaccented. Thus, PROS2 need not know the syntactic category of nodes in a tree, but only the way in which they combine. Hence, the syntax-to-prosody interface is, to a large degree, grammar- and even language-independent. Like its predecessor, PROS2 needs to know which elements are typically deaccented, and whether or not in a given domain there is any accent at all. The latter information is of a pragmatic nature (context-dependent), which is outside the scope of focus-accent theory as such. It is currently modeled by simple, and rather crude, heuristics.

3. Accent in PROS2

Focus-accent theory (Baart 1987; Gussenhoven 1984; Ladd 1980) aims to reconcile two approaches to accent: the semantic and the syntactic approach. The semantic approach (e.g. Bolinger 1972) assumes that a speaker will use accent to indicate which parts of his message are of special interest from a communicative point of view. In practical systems, this is often approximated by making a distinction between "content" words and "function" words. The former carry the informational content of a message, and thus are potential candidates for accent, while the latter, supposedly, provide "syntactic glue", which is not to be accented. The syntactic approach, on the other hand, originating from Chomsky—Halle (1968), abstracts away from informational content and assumes that accent is determined by syntactic constituency.

Focus-accent theory combines the two approaches by making a distinction between:

—*focus markers* indicating which parts of a structure are "interesting";
— a *metrical tree* associated with a syntactic structure, in which nodes are either *w(eak)* or *s(trong)* with respect to a sister node.

Focus markers come in two types: [+F] and [-F]. If a node X in a syntactic tree is marked [+F], this means that the corresponding information is focused upon, i.e. is of special interest. This information includes all the information which is contained in the daughters of X, that is, a compositional semantics is assumed. Also, information may be excepted from focus by being marked [-F].

Each [+F] marker corresponds with one accent, and metrical theory (Liberman—Prince 1977; Liberman 1978) specifies the relation between the two: for each [+F] node, follow a path crossing only *s*-nodes down to a terminal element, which is accented. For example, in the left-hand tree of Figure 1, the terminal element B is accented.

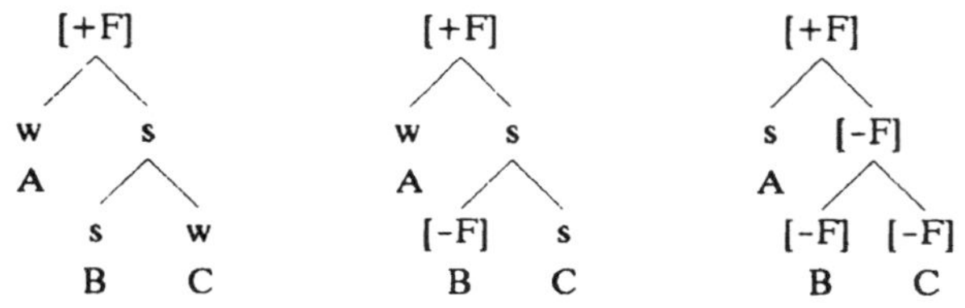

Figure 1. Illustrations of the focus-accent relation

Assuming that for each focus there is exactly one accent, then a -[F] node cannot be marked *s(trong)*. Otherwise, the [-F] marker cannot effectively block focus. Thus, a [-F] marker causes accent to shift to a sister node. This is illustrated by the middle tree of Figure 1, where C is accented. (The terminal node B, which is marked [-F], is also marked *w(eak)*. For typographical reasons, this redundant information is not shown). A special case arises when two sister nodes are marked [-F]. Since they cannot both be marked *w(eak)*, the directly dominating node becomes blocked for focus. As a result, accent shifts to a higher level in the tree. This is illustrated by the right-hand tree of Figure 1, where A is accented.

So, the metrical tree dynamically adapts to the distribution of focus as a result of the requirement that [-F] nodes cannot be marked *s(trong)*. These adaptations take as a starting point a "default" labeling, which reflects rather general properties of syntactic phrases. Baart (1987) distinguishes several grammatical relations, such as specification, complementation and adjunction, which determine the default metrical labeling associated with a phrase. However, we prefer an even more general approach, in which metrical labeling directly reflects the compositional semantics of an utterance.

Roughly, if two elements X and Y are combined to form a phrase Z, then either X or Y is a functor *f*, the other is an argument *a*, and Z evaluates to a function *f(a)*. We propose that, by default, functors are weak and arguments are strong.

Here, we need not know the exact details of compositional semantics. What we do need to know is how to apply the distinction between functors and arguments to a syntactic configuration. To this end, we introduce the following notation:[4] if two nodes X and Y combine, then (X/Y) or (Y\X) indicates that X is the functor and Y the argument. By using this notation, phrase-structure rules such as those in (3) are augmented to indicate functor/argument status of elements, yielding (4).

(3)	a.	S	⇒	NP VP	(4)	a.	S	⇒	(NP\VP)
	b.	NP	⇒	Det N		b.	NP	⇒	(Det/N)
	c.	VP	⇒	V NP PP		c.	VP	⇒	((V/NP)/PP)
	d.	VP	⇒	V NP		d.	VP	⇒	(V/NP)
	e.	PP	⇒	P NP		e.	PP	⇒	(P/NP)

In (4a), the backslash indicates that NP is an argument of VP. The forward slash in (4b) indicates that a Det(erminer) is a functor and that the head noun of an NP is its argument. A special case arises in (4c), which shows how the metrical system, which is binary, deals with multibranching structures: first V combines with an NP-argument (as in (4d)), forming a "virtual" VP category; on the next level up, the virtual VP combines with a PP argument to form the final VP. Finally, (4e) indicates that a P(reposition) is the functor of a PP, and the NP its argument.

Using rules such as those in (4), PROS2 assigns syntactic structure to sentences. Functor/argument status of nodes in the syntactic tree is used to assign default metrical labeling. Informational focus is modeled in the system by simple heuristic rules. Certain elements are lexically marked as being typically [-F] items. These elements include definite pronouns, prepositions and certain determiners (e.g. *the* but not *each*). Other elements are marked as typically [+F] (e.g. the determiner *each*), or are left unmarked for focus.

The mapping from syntax to prosody is defined by the following rules:

Metrical Labeling Rule
Given a structure of the following form:

Z ⇒ (X/Y)
or Z ⇒ (Y\X)

then:

a. If Y is focusable then Y is strong and X is weak, otherwise:
b. If X is focusable then X is strong and Y is weak, otherwise:
c. Z is blocked for focus.

Focus Rule
Each XP node which is focusable is accented.

Accent Rule
A node X is accented if:

a. X is strong and the node which immediately dominates X is accented, or
b. X is [+F].

In these rules, a node X counts as focusable unless X has been blocked for focus by being marked [-F]. The three cases of the metrical labeling rule implement the accent-shift phenomena illustrated in Figure 1. The focus rule ensures that each XP (each major syntactic phrase) contains at least one accent — unless it has been deaccented. The accent rule recursively defines what it means for a node to be accented.

The above rules account for the deaccenting phenomena discussed in section 2. The metrical trees assigned to the sentences in (1) and (2) are shown in Figures 2 and 3, respectively.

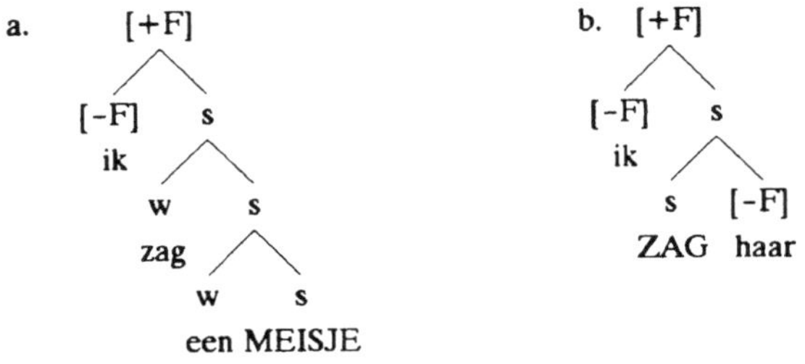

Figure 2. Metrical trees for (1a) and (1b)

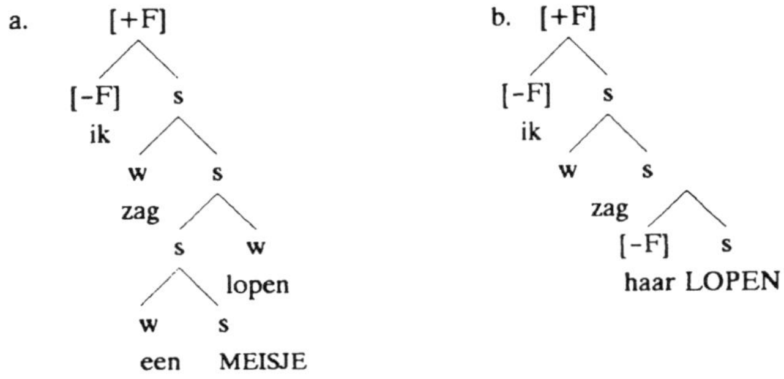

Figure 3. Metrical trees for (2a) and (2b)

Also, our rules account for data discussed by Gussenhoven (1984). Compare:

(5)	a.	Ik	heb	GISTEREN	die MAN	zien	lopen.
		I	have	yesterday	that man	seen	walk
	b.	Ik	heb	die MAN	GISTEREN	zien	LOPEN.
		I	have	that man	yesterday	seen	walk

Gussenhoven accounts for the contrast between (5a) and (5b) by assuming a rule which says that if an argument and a predicate (i.e. what is called a functor here) are adjacent, then the argument is accented; however, if an adverbial modifier intervenes, then both argument and predicate are accented. Baart (1987) also needs a special rule for this kind of data. However, in our system the contrast between (5a) and (5b) follows naturally. We assume that the verb phrase in these sentences (i.e. the part to the right of the auxiliary verb) is structured along the lines of the following set of phrase-structure rules:

(6) a. VP ⇒ (AdvP/VP)
b. VP ⇒ (NP\V) (*unmarked*)
c. VP ⇒ (NP\VP) (*marked*)
d. VP ⇒ V

According to (6a), adverbial modifiers (adjuncts) are functors that take as argument the category that they modify. We assume clustering of "raised" verbs into one V. The syntactic structure of (5a) is defined by the combination of (6a) and (6b), which, in our view, is the unmarked option. The syntactic structure of (5b) is defined by (6c), (6a) and (6d), in that order. The latter is a marked option.[5] The syntax-to-prosody mapping of these structures is shown in Figures 4 and 5. No special measures are needed to account for the difference between (5a) and (5b). In (5a), the verb cluster *zien lopen* is marked *w(eak)*, and, as it is not an XP, it is ignored by the focus rule. In (5b), on the other hand, the verb cluster is marked *s(trong)*, and the VP node which immediately dominates it is marked +[F] by the focus rule.

Figure 4. Syntax-to-prosody mapping of (5a)

Figure 5. Syntax-to-prosody mapping of (5b)

4. Phrasing in PROS2

It has often been observed that there is no one-to-one correspondence between syntactic constituents and prosodic phrases. Characteristic examples are (7a) and (7b), where phrase boundaries occur within NPs with a relative clause or PP complement.

(7) a. this is the CAT | that caught the RAT | that ate the CHEESE
b. there was a MAN | with a HAT

According to Selkirk (1984) and Nespor—Vogel (1986), prosodic structure is characterized by two types of phrases: I and Phi. Each utterance consists of one or more I-phrases, which are separate domains for intonation rules. Pauses occur at I-phrase boundaries. Each I-phrase consists of one or more Phi-phrases, which are separate domains for supra-segmental phonological rules (i.e. coarticulation and sandhi rules).

In PROS2, no principled distinction is made between I- and Phi-phrase boundaries. We assume one type of phrase boundary, which may or may not be realized by a pause (or by prepausal lengthening). In either case, a phrase boundary should block coarticulation and sandhi phenomena. Prosodic phrase boundaries are assigned by the following rule, which applies to the metrical tree:

Phrasing Rule
A phrase boundary occurs between A and B if:
a. A and B are sisters,
b. B is an XP, and
c. both A and B are accented.

According to this rule, no phrase boundaries occur in the sentences of (1) and (2), as in each of these sentences there is only one [+F] node, hence only one accent. In (5a), the phrasing rule applies once, whereas in (5b) two phrase boundaries are assigned. This is shown in (8a) and (9b). The phrasing rule also takes care of the phrase boundaries in (7a) and (7b).

(8) a. ik heb GISTEREN | die MAN zien lopen
b. ik heb die MAN | GISTEREN | zien LOPEN

Requirements a and b of the phrasing rule above express the fact that there is only a partial correspondence between syntactic and prosodic constituents, which is mediated by the (binary-branching) metrical tree. A phrase boundary may occur within a syntactic constituent on the condition that the right-hand node is a major phrase. Thus, a phrase boundary starts a new syntactic phrase, but it need not complete one. For example, in *a NICE MAN with a HAT*, it is predicted that no phrase boundary intervenes between *nice* and *man with a hat*, as the latter is not an XP. French liaison provides an interesting illustration of the XP-requirement. In French, an adjective phrase may either precede or follow the head noun of an NP. In the former case, there is liaison, in the latter case, liaison is blocked. Compare: *trois beaux enfants* with *les maisons italiennes* (Nespor—Vogel 1986:179).

Requirement c of the rule expresses a rather strong claim, saying that each prosodic phrase contains at least one accent. Thus, it is predicted that a deaccented phrase cannot incur a phrase boundary. For example, in (8b), deaccenting of *die man* 'that man' precludes the first phrase boundary. And indeed, a pause after *man* would seem rather infelicitous in that case. However, we are not fully confident that a similar correspondence holds between deaccenting and possibilities for coarticulation and sandhi.

The phrasing rule provides a first characterization of prosodic structure. Subsequent rules should determine whether or not a phrase boundary must be realized by phonetic means. Such rules must take into account both hierarchical prominence of phrase boundaries and phrase length (e.g. Gee—Grosjean 1983; Bachenko—Fitzpatrick 1990). No such rules have yet been implemented. Also, coarticulation and sandhi phenomena must be investigated in more detail, as there may be problems that our rule does not solve.

5. Extensions and limitations

The syntax-to-prosody interface described in the two previous sections is highly general, and, to a large degree, grammar-independent. All our system needs to know about syntactic structure is (a) how elements combine to form larger phrases, i.e. which element is the functor and which the argument; (b) whether or not a phrase is an XP. The pragmatic aspects of accent (i.e. focus) are currently modeled by simple, and rather crude, heuristics. However, only minor changes are needed to make the system work with a discourse model (Hirschberg 1990). This is one area for future research.

Another area for further research concerns the actual degree of grammar-independence. This is especially important if one wants to integrate text-to-speech systems with other types of NLP systems. In that case, synthetic speech is merely an alternative way of outputting information to the user, and the syntax-to-prosody interface should be able to hook into resources provided by the host system.

Also, there are issues of reversibility and declarativeness. In its present formulation, the syntax-to-prosody interface works only for generating prosody from syntax, and operates deterministically. It would be interesting to find out whether the system can be adapted to work in reverse, i.e. whether it might be used to constrain syntax.

So, our program holds considerable promise for further development, in that it can be expanded in several directions. However, there are also serious problems that might limit its practical application.

First, as most of the work is done by the syntactic parser, it makes a great deal of difference how exactly syntactic structure is conceived. This is not to deny the claim of grammar-independence. It simply means that different conceptions of syntactic structure may make different predictions about sentence prosody. This might become a problem if the syntax-prosody interface is to work with a grammar that was not specifically designed for this purpose.

Second, incorporation of a syntactic parser in a text-to-speech system introduces a number of related problems, among which are processing speed and memory use, coverage and sophistication of the grammar, syntactic ambiguity and robustness. We will briefly discuss these problems.

PROS2 uses chart parsing techniques (e.g. Gazdar—Mellish 1989) to improve efficiency. However, as the grammar grew larger and more sophisticated, processing time and memory use could not be kept within reasonable limits. Although further optimization is certainly possible, it seems necessary to scale down the grammar somewhat to improve on speed and memory use (at least, for practical applications). On the other hand, the coverage of the grammar is still rather limited. In a sense, this cannot be avoided: there is no complete solution to the grammar of any natural language. Still, we do want some improvement in this area.

Sophistication of the grammar is strongly related to the problem of ambiguity. In this chapter, we have illustrated syntax with very simple phrase structure rules using only atomic categories. Although such simple rules may be used to assign hierarchical structure, they do not disambiguate very well. Ambiguities arise almost everywhere in natural language processing: at the lexical level (many words have more than one syntactic category), locally (a substring of a sentence may have more than one analysis) and globally (a sentence may have several interpretations, with varying degrees of plausibility).[6] A (partial) solution to this problem is to replace atomic categories with complex categories, using features to encode context-sensitive properties of elements, and to augment phrase-structure rules with constraints on feature co-occurrences. In this manner, spurious ambiguities can be avoided, and a more fine-grained parsing results. However, the use of complex categories adds significantly to the complexity of the parsing problem. In addition, these more sophisticated grammars are much harder to design and test. The current PROS2 grammar uses complex categories to encode context dependencies, which is one of reasons why the program is rather slow. Thus, one of our short-term goals is to find a reasonable compromise between sophistication and efficiency.

Finally, robustness is an issue if a parser is to process unrestricted text. Many sentences necessarily fall outside the scope of the grammar, either because of limitations of the grammar itself, or because a sentence is ill-formed. Dealing with punctuation in a principled manner is also very difficult. Still, even if a sentence cannot be fully analyzed, we expect the parser to provide some kind of analysis. One of our reasons for using a chart parser is this requirement of robustness. A chart parser stores its intermediate results in a chart in order to avoid ever having to compute them again. If no analysis spanning the entire utterance can be found, the chart will at least contain information about those parts of the utterance that could be analyzed. Of course, the prosody assigned to these partial analyses is "phrase" prosody rather than sentence prosody. But this is preferable to having no prosody at all.

In conclusion then, if it seems that our "next generation" of prosodic analysis programs does not really come off, this is due to problems associated with syntactic parsing. Nevertheless, we are confident that these problems can be solved by finding a reasonable compromise between the "ideal" system and one that actually works. In fact, some of the problems mentioned here have found a solution in PROS3 (see note 1), which runs with fairly adequate speed on a modest PC. So, we think our confidence is warranted. Also, we firmly believe that our approach to sentence prosody is necessary if speech technology is to be integrated with endeavors of computational linguistics. One cannot ignore syntax forever.

Acknowledgements

While researching and developing PROS2, we were greatly assisted by Garmt Boekholt, Sidonne Bos, Gerrit Bouhuis, Eldrid Bringmann, Marieke van Cappellen and Hugo Voerman. We thank Bert Schouten for coaching, and our colleagues in the ASSP research program for their help and advice.

Notes

1. PROS2 has been developed for the Dutch text-to-speech system Speech Maker as part of the ASSP program. Dirksen is currently developing PROS3, a prototype and development system for prosodic analysis in a multi-lingual text-to-speech system. Thus, we will soon find out about the degree of language-independence.
2. It should be noted that the differences are not merely notational, but have empirical content. Baart (1987) argues for *integrative accent*, i.e. the possibility of one accent marking a long stretch of speech as +Focus. Our version of the theory seems more in

line with what speakers actually do (i.e. accent each major syntactic phrase which is not deaccented), and is in many respects closer to Gussenhoven (1984). See also Gussenhoven's (1988) review of Baart. However, a detailed evaluation of these differences is beyond the scope of this chapter.

3. Capitals indicate accent. Note that in the English translations of (2a) and (2b) the distribution of accents may be different. This is due to a difference in syntax: (2a) and (2b) are cases of Verb Raising, which does not occur in English.
4. The notation has been borrowed from categorial grammar. However, the interpretation used here is rather different. In categorial grammar, (X/Y) or (Y\X) represents a functor category which combines with a category Y to form a category X, and the slash represents the direction of combination (right or left). In our system, the slash merely indicates which element is the argument. It should be noted that we are appealing to an intuitive notion of "argument". From a strictly formal point of view, it does not make any difference which of two elements is the functor. For example, given a rule S ⇒ NP VP, we might say that NP is an argument of VP, but also that VP is an argument of NP. While the latter is counter-intuitive, it may sometimes be necessary to treat the subject NP as a functor in order to derive the correct quantifier scopings.
5. That issues of markedness are involved can be demonstrated in the following manner. If we replace *die man* 'that man' in (5a) and (5b) with a definite pronoun, e.g. *hem* 'him', then (5a) becomes ill-formed, whereas (5b) does not. On the other hand, if *die man* is replaced with an indefinite NP, e.g. *een man* 'a man', then (5b) becomes slightly odd (i.e. the NP cannot be understood non-specifically).
6. In PROS2, as it runs within the Speech Maker environment, the situation is even worse in that lexical category information is obtained from morphological parsing — see the chapter by Heemskerk—van Heuven (this volume). These morphological assignments are often highly ambiguous.

Part III

Building blocks for speech synthesis

Speech synthesis with accented and unaccented diphones

Rob Drullman—René C. Collier

Abstract

A complete inventory of accented and unaccented diphones, produced by a professional male speaker, was made. In order to evaluate the quality of synthetic speech using both types of diphones, we asked subjects to judge the naturalness and fluency of different versions of an utterance. Two experiments with isolated polysyllabic words indicate that the use of accented or unaccented diphones has a perceptual effect on long vowels only. In a third experiment, we evaluated the use of the different diphone types in short sentences with a fixed temporal structure. It appears that the use of unaccented instead of accented diphones for unaccented syllables does not result systematically in more natural-sounding speech.

1. Introduction

For the moment there are two methods for speech synthesis that lay at the basis of a Dutch text-to-speech system. Speaker-independent allophone rules have been developed at Nijmegen University (Loman—Boves, this volume), while at IPO in Eindhoven natural speech is used for the creation of so-called diphones. In order to give some insight into the generation of synthetic speech, a brief outline of the two synthesis methods will be given below. A general introduction to the basic principles and mechanisms of speech synthesis can be found in Holmes (1988).

In speech synthesis by rule (allophone synthesis) every phoneme, with its allophonic variations, is described in some parametric form, generally formant parameters. From a scientific point of view, allophone synthesis is more challenging, since it is the ultimate test of our knowledge of speech production. With very good rules one should be able to generate speech of a high quality. However, making artificial speech completely on the basis of rules requires detailed information about the many parameters that are involved. At the segmental level, one must have target values (e.g., default spectral identity, intensity, duration) for all speech sounds (allophones) to start with. Simply concatenating these targets leads to unintelligible speech. For example, if we were to synthesize the word *stoel* 'chair' by concatenating /s/, /t/, /u·/, and /l/ , respectively, the resulting speech signal would hardly be recognized as /stu·l/.[1] We must first apply rules that provide the transitions from one speech sound to the next and adjust adjacent speech sounds to each other (coarticulation). However, rules for the simulation of coarticulation are quite complex. Because of this problem, the idea of using fragments of natural speech as synthesis units has been put forward. One could think of storing entire words or syllables in a database. This might be a good compromise, but it would only work for a fairly limited set of utterances. If one wanted to be able to synthesize any utterance, one would have to store a few thousand syllables and even more words. Apart from this, there would still be problems at word/syllable boundaries where the resulting speech will not sound fluent. A better alternative is the use of units that include the transition regions between adjacent sounds. Such units are commonly called dyads, or diphones (cf. Witten 1982).

A diphone can be defined as a speech fragment which runs roughly from half-way one phoneme to half-way the next phoneme. In this way the transitions between two successive speech sounds are encapsulated in the diphone and need not be calculated. Each diphone can thus be considered as a building block of spoken language. In order to generate a word or a sentence one simply concatenates the appropriate diphones. After adding an intonation contour and adjusting the segmental durations, one can generate intelligible speech. A disadvantage of the diphone approach is the fact that one can generate speech of one specific speaker only; for every new speaker a completely new diphone inventory has to be made. The main advantage is that acceptable speech quality can be obtained with little processing effort (transitions and coarticulatory effects are already incorporated in a diphone).

2. Preparation of the diphone inventory

The first attempts at developing a diphone-based speech synthesis system for Dutch (Elsendoorn—'t Hart 1982; Elsendoorn 1984) proved to be quite promising. The preparation of the inventory was rather laborious and time-consuming, since the whole process of extracting a diphone from a (nonsense) word was done manually. Van Hemert (1985) developed a computer program that automatically generates the diphones by segmenting the words from which they have to be excised. The automatic procedure resulted in a considerable reduction in preparation time, while the quality remained at the same level (compared to manual editing).

Van Bezooijen (this volume) tested the intelligibility of a second Dutch diphone set (the so-called HZ diphones) based on the speech of a (non-professional) Western Dutch speaker. Van Bezooijen tested the intelligibility of monosyllabic nonsense words of the types CVC, VCV and VCCV.

Identification scores for the consonants ranged from 63.4 to 81.2 percent correct, depending on their position in the word. Identification scores for the vowels ranged from 84.3 to 97.5 percent correct, also depending on the position in the word.

Despite the good intelligibility of diphone speech, utterances sometimes suffer a lack from of naturalness and fluency. Part of this can be explained by the fact that the diphones are excised from accented syllables. Therefore, all the speech sounds that result from the concatenation of diphones have phonetic properties that are typical of this accented context only. In particular, their temporal and spectral characteristics are close to the target values that one finds in the production of carefully spoken, isolated, accented syllables (Koopmans-van Beinum 1980). Speech generated by means of such accented diphones often sounds over-articulated. To overcome this problem, one can extend the inventory with diphones extracted from unaccented syllables, which are likely to be spectrally reduced and shorter than accented diphones. It is expected that the combined use of accented and unaccented diphones will lead to more natural sounding speech.

In order to test the above expectation, we prepared a complete inventory of accented and unaccented diphones, produced by a professional native Dutch male speaker (referred to as the designated talker PB throughout this book). The diphones were extracted from isolated (nonsense) words. For the accented CV and VC diphones we used words of the type CəCVCə. For instance, the word /məmi·mə/ served as a carrier for the accented /mi·/ and /i·m/ diphones. For the unaccented CV and VC diphones we used words of the type CVCVCVCVCə, with accents on the first and fourth syllables and no accent on the second and third syllables. From these words we excised the third (unaccented) syllable.

All diphones were LPC-coded with 30 reflection coefficients per frame of 10 ms (analysis window of 25 ms) at a 20 kHz sampling rate (Vogten 1983). The diphones were generated automatically. Corrections of the amplitudes and voiced-unvoiced parameters were made by hand, where necessary. The diphones were excised from the syllables in such a way as to have fixed durations. This means that all phoneme parts belonging to the same phonetic class (short vowels, long vowels, plosives, fricatives, etc.) were made of equal length. In this quantization, accentuation differences were taken into account, too: unaccented vowels are shorter than accented ones. On the whole, the inventory consists of approx. 2,900 diphones (CV, VC, CC, VV), of which 1,300 are unaccented.

3. Perceptual evaluation

3.1. Experimental questions

Acoustic-phonetic factors play a major role in the temporal and spectral variability of a vowel. Among the local factors, the presence or absence of word stress to a large extent determines the quality of a vowel: unstressed vowels are more reduced (spectrally and temporally) than stressed ones (cf. Koopmans-van Beinum 1980). Phonologically, we can distinguish the following three degrees of lexical stress (Booij 1981): [1stress], for syllables bearing primary stress; [2stress], for syllables bearing secondary stress; [-stress], for unstressed syllables. We want to know how stress influences the choice of diphone type we will have to make. Assuming we use accented and unaccented diphones for [1stress] and [-stress] syllables, respectively, we still have to make a decision as to which type of diphone we use for [2stress] syllables.

Nooteboom (1972) found that the duration of a vowel depends, among other things, on its position in a word and on the number of syllables preceding and following it. Furthermore, he found that long vowels can be shortened relatively more than short ones (cf. Koopmans-van Beinum 1980). It is thus to be expected that long vowels in particular are influenced by the temporal aspect of accentedness. Taking syllable position and intrinsic vowel duration into consideration, we also want to know whether the choice of accented or unaccented diphones depends on the position of a syllable in a word and/or on the intrinsic duration of the vowel in the syllable.

3.2. Isolated words

In order to answer the above questions, we ran two experiments in which we used isolated non-compound polysyllabic words as stimuli (Drullman—Collier 1991). Each time we asked subjects to judge different versions of an utterance with regard to naturalness and fluency, using a paired comparison paradigm.

In the first experiment, we used three-syllable words with primary stress varying on one of the syllables (e.g. *olifant* /ˈoːliˑfɑnt/ 'elephant', *dictator* /dɪkˈtaːtɔr/ 'id', *sigaret* /siˑɣaːˈrɛt/ 'cigaret'. At the same time the intrinsic vowel durations of both non-primary stressed syllables were varied: short-short, short-long, long-short, and long-long. Each stimulus was produced by using accented diphones for the [1stress] syllable and either accented or unaccented diphones for the remaining two syllables. In this way, four versions of every word could be synthesized, with accented and unaccented diphones divided between the two non-primary stressed syllables. The primary stressed syllable always carried a rise-fall in pitch. No duration rules were applied. The four versions were presented in six different pairs. For each pair, subjects could state their preference for one of the versions (strong preference, slight preference, or no preference for either one).

The data were submitted to an analysis of variance for paired comparisons (Scheffé 1952). The results indicate that the phonological distinction between [2stress] and [-stress] does not lead to a preference for accented or unaccented diphones, respectively. On the other hand, an effect of syllable position was revealed, at least with intrinsically long vowels: they favor accented diphones in word-final position and unaccented diphones elsewhere. With short vowels no such preference was observed. The effect with long vowels is probably explained by durational requirements: accented diphones are longer than unaccented ones and therefore accommodate the listener's expectation of utterance-final lengthening better.

In a second experiment, we used non-compound five- and six-syllable words with [1stress] on the fifth syllable (e.g., *universiteit* /yˑniˑvɛrziˑˈtɛɪt/ 'university', *encyclopedie* /ɛnsiˑklo:pe:ˈdiˑ/ 'encyclopedia'). All words had [2stress] on the first and third syllable, and [–stress] on the second and fourth (and sixth) syllable. So, phonologically, all words revealed a rhythmical structure of alternating stressed and unstressed syllables. The intrinsic vowel durations of the two [2stress] syllables were varied as in the previous experiment. Each stimulus was produced by using accented diphones and a rise-fall pitch accent in the [1stress] syllable, unaccented diphones for the [-stress] syllables, and either accented or unaccented diphones in both [2stress] syllables. So, we could again make four versions of every word. The same paired-comparison design and procedure were used as in the previous experiment. The results are generally in agreement with what we found for the three-syllable words. As to the [2stress] syllables, we reach to the following conclusions: no preference for accented or unaccented diphones with short vowels, and a (slight) preference for unaccented diphones with long vowels. Note that, this time, the syllables under consideration were never in word-final position.

Taking the results of the two experiments together, one has to conclude that, with the current diphone inventory, there is no reason for choosing accented diphones in syllables that bear secondary stress at the phonological level. It remains to be examined why, at least with long syllables, the use of unaccented diphones improves speech quality. It may be that, in particular, the temporal features of the unaccented diphones contribute to the improvement. If that is of major perceptual importance (within the restrictions of LPC diphone speech), one could equally well use accented diphones only and make the syllables shorter when necessary, thus making the unaccented set superfluous. Conversely, by using fixed segmental durations of syllables or phonemes, one can find out whether the spectral aspects of the unaccented set are relevant to the production of more natural speech. In order to answer this question, a third experiment was carried out in which the temporal differences between the two sets were eliminated.

3.3. Sentences

We selected 26 short sentences, typically of 8 to 9 syllables from two phonetically balanced lists of 13 sentences (Plomp—Mimpen 1979). The sentences were read aloud by a trained male speaker (not the same one who had produced the diphones). They were digitized and submitted to an LPC analysis (Vogten 1983). The original intonation contours were automatically stylized (Hermes—'t Hart 1987; Hermes 1988). All phoneme boundaries were marked by hand, such that the duration of each phoneme was known with an accuracy of 10 ms. We will refer to these LPC-coded and stylized utterances as the original sentences.

For the generation of the diphone versions of the sentences, we decided to control the segmental durations in two different ways: alignment of the segmental durations with the originals and assignment of the duration of each segment by rule (cf. van Coile 1987). The adjustment of the durations was done by increasing or decreasing the duration of every frame that belonged to a phoneme. In this way the spectral content was preserved; no frames were inserted or deleted.

By listening to the original sentences and looking at their stylized pitch contours, we determined which syllables were accented. The diphone versions were synthesized either by using accented diphones only, or by using accented diphones in accented syllables and unaccented ones elsewhere. After concatenation, the segmental durations were adjusted according to the two methods described above. Subsequently, a pitch contour was generated, matching the contour of the original sentences as closely as possible (Terken—Collier 1989). To summarize, we had four diphone versions of every sentence:

1. Segmental durations according to rules; accented diphones in accented syllables, unaccented diphones elsewhere;
2. Segmental durations aligned to those of the original sentences; accented diphones in accented syllables, unaccented diphones elsewhere;
3. Segmental durations according to rules; accented diphones only;
4. Segmental durations aligned to those of the original sentences; accented diphones only.

Versions 1 and 3 on the one hand and versions 2 and 4 on the other had the same durational structure; they only differed spectrally in their unaccented syllables. The same paired-comparison procedure and data analysis was used as in the previous experiments.

The results indicate that appreciation of the four versions makes them fall into two sets of two. The preferences for versions 2 and 4 are significantly higher than those for versions 1 and 3. However, there is no significant difference within the two versions in a set. This means that the versions in which the segmental durations were aligned to the original sentences are preferred to the versions in which the segmental durations were determined by rule. This is of course not surprising.

The most interesting conclusion, though, is the fact that no significant difference was found between any two versions that had the same temporal structure. In other words, speech quality was not improved by using unaccented instead of accented diphones in unaccented syllables. This indicates that spectral reductions, if any, do not contribute to greater fluency and naturalness, even if the duration rules are still not perfect.

4. Spectral evaluation

The results of the last experiment indicate that the spectral differences between the accented and unaccented diphones are perhaps quite small. How spectrally different are the unaccented diphones and the accented ones? Spectral measurements were carried out in order to answer this question.

We had made an LPC version of the diphones with 5 formant-bandwidth pairs (robust formant analysis; Willems 1987). This version was used for the spectral analysis of the accented and unaccented vowel parts in the diphones. This was done as follows. The values of the first and second formants of the vowels /a:, ɑ, o:, u·, y·, i·, ɛ/ were taken from the initial frame of the VC diphones. These diphones contain a longer vowel part, including the steady-state segment, in comparison with the CV diphones. For the C part of the diphones we took the most commonly used consonants, i.e. /p, t, k, b, d, f, s, χ, v, z, m, n, ŋ, r, l, j, w/. For each vowel the mean F_1 and F_2 over the 17 consonant contexts were calculated. This was done separately for the accented and the unaccented diphones. In Figure 1 we have plotted the mean formant values (in Hz) of the accented and unaccented vowels in the F_1-F_2 plane. Lines have been drawn between the data points of two neighboring vowels in the figure (solid lines for the accented vowels, dashed lines for the unaccented vowels). In this way we can compare the contours of the vowel triangles more easily.

As can be seen in the figure, the unaccented vowels do differ spectrally from the accented ones. If we define the mean formants of the accented vowels as the targets, we see that the unaccented vowels tend to move away from their targets, but not clearly towards a more central position. We can instead observe a lowering of the F_1 (the unaccented area has mainly shifted to the left, except for /a:/).

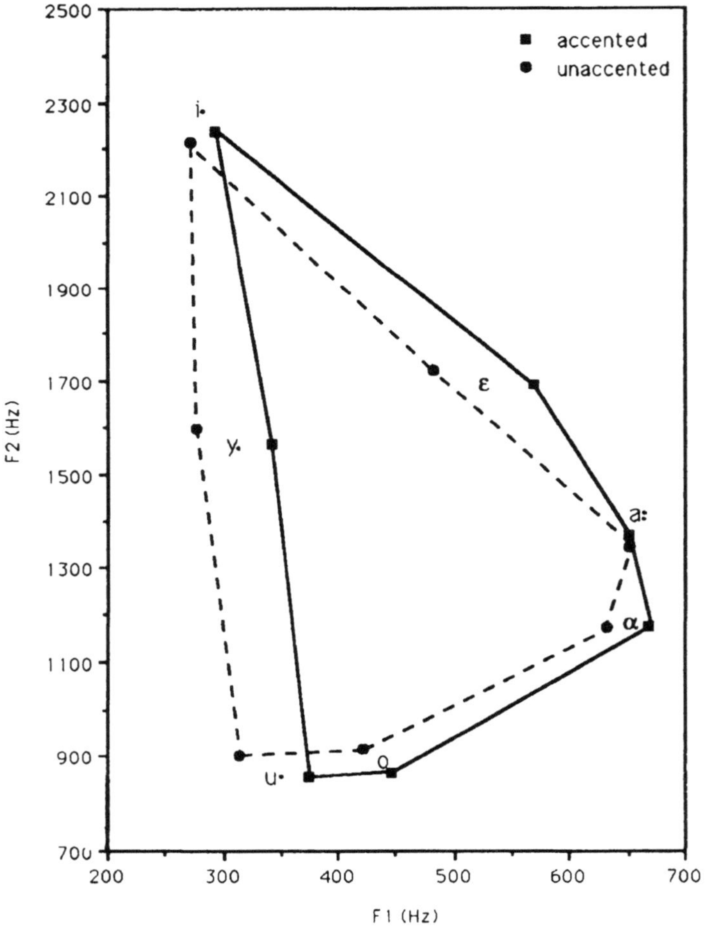

Figure 1. Mean F_1-F_2 values of the accented and unaccented vowels in the diphones (The data points are connected with solid lines and dashed lines, respectively.)

If we compare our data with those of other investigations which use the same speaker and analysis method for a read-out text, we observe a similar pattern (van Son—Pols 1990; Drullman—Collier 1991). Admittedly, different speech styles and acoustic measurements in different consonantal contexts may lead to different formant values. But the lack of centralization with the unaccented vowels, as well as the shift to a lower F1, seem to be typical of this particular speaker. Indeed, the unaccented diphones appear to be representative of vowels in unaccented syllables in a read aloud text. This holds at least for their average formant frequencies. On the other hand, one can argue that the formant positions of the entire set (accented and unaccented) are a bit too extreme. Koopmans-van Beinum (1992) recently carried out some acoustic measurements on a text read by this speaker. She showed that vowels in focus words (comparable to our accented diphones) are generally more centralized. This would imply the need of an overall spectral reduction, both for the accented and unaccented diphones.

One might expect unaccentedness to lead to more coarticulation with nearby phonemes (Lindblom 1963; Koopmans-van Beinum 1980). In this case, the spread in formant frequencies of the vowels would be larger with unaccented diphones than with accented ones. To estimate the magnitude of this effect, we computed the relative spread in F_1 and F_2 values of all accented and unaccented vowel parts in the diphones (in the 17 consonant environments mentioned above). They are listed in Table 1 as the ratio (in percentage) of the standard deviation and the mean formant frequency per vowel.

Table 1. Relative spread (defined as standard deviation/mean frequency) in F_1 and F_2 in percentages of the vowels in the accented and unaccented diphones

vowel	F_1		F_2	
	+ACC	−ACC	+ACC	−ACC
/ɑ/	6.2	6.5	6.3	7.9
/a:/	5.6	5.3	2.1	4.0
/ɛ/	4.5	10.8	3.8	5.7
/i·/	8.5	4.2	2.3	3.8
/o:/	6.7	4.0	5.9	10.4
/u·/	5.4	4.8	12.6	15.7
/y·/	5.2	5.3	4.2	7.3

One can see that there is a slightly larger spread in F2 for all vowels in the unaccented diphones relative to the accented diphones. This is not the case with the spread in F1; apart from /ε/, the spread in F1 is practically equal or even larger in the accented diphones. From these data we cannot conclude that the unaccented diphones are clearly more affected by coarticulation than the accented diphones.

5. Conclusions

In the experiments described above, we tried to assess the improvement in naturalness and fluency of synthetic speech that can be achieved by using accented and unaccented diphones. Accented diphones were extracted from accented syllables, unaccented diphones were extracted from unaccented syllables as pronounced in isolated nonsense words.

In the first two experiments we used isolated polysyllabic words that were synthesized in four different ways. The results obtained in those experiments demonstrated no correspondence between the metrical structure of a word and the preferred use of either type of diphone. Only for long vowels a preference could be found, depending on the position of the syllable in a word.

In a third experiment, we used short sentences with fixed segmental durations. The results indicate that if the temporal structure of the sentences is made independent of the durations of the individual diphones and only spectral differences remain, the use of unaccented diphones in unaccented syllables no longer yields more natural-sounding speech.

Acoustically, the difference between accented and unaccented realizations of the diphone vowels reflects the difference between accented and unaccented vowel realizations in a continuous text read out by the same speaker. That there is little or no centralization, in the sense that unaccented vowels do not move towards the center of the vowel triangle (to a neutral position), may be typical of this particular speaker. On the other hand, from our third perception experiment we know that the slightly different spectral properties of the unaccented diphones do not contribute to greater naturalness and fluency. This may be due to the fact that the vowels in the unaccented diphones display little coarticulation with nearby phonemes.

Notes

1. But see van Bezooijen—Pols (this volume) under neutrone synthesis.

Development of rule based analysis for text-to-speech

Henk Loman—Louis Boves

Abstract

This chapter reports on a project that aimed to improve the segmental quality of allophone synthesis for Dutch. We emphasize the importance of our rule development strategy, which comprises a six stage cycle: (i) collect natural speech utterances, (ii) analyze speech data, (iii) convert results to synthesis rules, (iv) synthesize copies, (v) compare synthetic and original utterances, and (vi) adjust rules where necessary. Each of these stages will be discussed at some length. The results of this project show that the strategy has led to a steady improvement of our synthesis.

1. Introduction

This paper is a summary of the results of the SPIN/ASSP project ALSYS (**al**lophone **sy**nthe**s**is). When the project started, it had two major aims, viz.

I. obtaining linguistic/phonetic knowledge through examination of speech samples produced by a human speaker;
II. improving the segmental quality of an existing rule based synthesis system using the newly obtained knowledge.

Thus, this project had both scientific and practical aspects. It is worth noting that the work in the ALSYS project has, in a way, been quite limited: we restricted our attention to the level of segments in simple phonetic contexts. We only studied CVC and VC(C)V utterances produced in isolation or in fixed carrier sentences. We have not been able to investigate segmental effects that are due to wider phonetic and phonological (especially prosodic) contexts systematically. However, when using our text-to-speech system in (simulated) applications, it appeared that it is quite difficult to predict sentence intelligibility from segmental intelligibility scores obtained with logatomes.

Although Dutch is among the better investigated languages, it still appeared that little acoustic phonetic knowledge was available in the literature that was useful for the development of a rule based synthesis system. Most of the literature data describe acoustic phonetic properties of stationary sounds, whereas for the purpose of speech synthesis information on dynamic aspects is much more important. Thus, most of the data needed to formulate rules had to be acquired from the analysis of natural speech that was recorded in the course of the project.

The constant pressure to improve the quality of the synthesizer has had a decisive influence on the direction of the work in the ALSYS project. Our decisions with respect to the phenomena to select for further investigation have strongly been influenced by the observed inadequacies in the segmental rules of our synthesizer, rather than by scientific curiosity and interest. In this sense the results of the evaluation studies carried out by van Bezooijen—Pols (this volume) have played a decisive role in the planning of the work in this project.

From the very beginning of the work it has been clear that the development of segmental synthesis rules is extremely dependent on the availability of good tools. Thus, it is not surprising that much effort has been spent in developing new tools and improving existing ones. Since only a small part of the tool development was done in the framework of the ASSP program, the results of this part of the work will only be mentioned in passing. A more detailed account can be found in Loman—Kerkhoff—Boves (1989). On the other hand, a large part of this paper will be devoted to a description and explanation of the overall strategy for rule development that was adopted in this project. This emphasizes our belief that the rule development strategy is at least as important as the development tools.

The work on rule development has, in a way, been frustrating. Even when one adheres to an efficient strategy, progress appears to be slow from time to time. Yet, we have obtained a considerable improvement of the intelligibility of our synthesizer, as will be briefly shown in the conclusions section of this chapter. The numerical data on segmental intelligibility are discussed in greater depth elsewhere (van Bezooijen—Pols, this volume, and references cited therein). We will not go into the details of the results of these tests, but we want to emphasize that these tests have been a central factor in our rule development strategy.

2. Method

In principle, the strategy that we followed in rule development is simple: make recordings of a comprehensive set of strategically chosen utterances produced by one or more human speakers, analyze the data, translate the analysis results into synthesis rules, make synthetic copies of the utterances, compare these to the natural ones, and update rules where the comparison fails. In the remainder of this paper we hope to show that much of the simplicity of this strategy is rather deceptive.

2.1. A strategically chosen set of utterances

For the natural speech utterances we restricted ourselves to recordings of one male speaker. Recordings consisted mainly of CVC, VCV, and VCCV words (V = vowel, C = consonant). Only a few sentences were recorded. Most of the CVC, VCV, and VCCV (nonsense) words were spoken in isolation. We did not bother to have the words spoken in carrier phrases, as we were primarily concerned with the description of dynamic spectral events at CV and VC phoneme boundaries, not with prosody. Moreover, our speaker was able to maintain a fairly equal pitch and articulation rate during a recording session and over different recording sessions, irrespective of the period of time between two sessions.

All the recordings used in this project were made in a professional sound recording studio, using analog taperecorders. The analog recordings were subsequently digitized using a sampling frequency of 10 kHz and a resolution of 12 bits. A considerable part of the digitized database was hand labelled in order to allow automatic signal processing procedures to select exactly those portions of the signals that were of interest.

In creating the speech database we tried to cover all phonotactically possible VC and CV combinations of Dutch. Unfortunately, consonant clusters could not be given the attention they deserve within the framework of this project. Since recordings of utterances containing a specific class of consonants were usually only made when we started developing rules for this class, and since the work on consonants could not be completed, the database contains only an incomplete set of clusters. As a matter of routine, all the words in a list used during a recording session were read twice. This strategy of distributed build-up of the database has the advantage that the quite tedious work is chopped into pieces that are so small that they do not demotivate. It has the obvious drawback that the speaker(s) must be persons who are easily accessible at many points in time.

It appeared that it is much better to model the speech of a single speaker, whose pronunciation is acceptably close to what is called "Algemeen Beschaafd Nederlands" (i.e. Standard Dutch) than to try and find average values over a large group of speakers for the acoustic parameters used to control the synthesizer. It is relatively easy to obtain group averages for parameters such as formant frequencies and bandwidths in steady state sounds, F_0, and sound durations. But what matters in rule based synthesis are not those gross averages, but the details of the transitions between target values of neighboring sounds. And those transitions seem to be speaker dependent in many ways that are not yet understood. The average values of e.g. formant frequencies, on the other hand, appear to be much less critical.

2.2. Analysis of the natural speech data

The purpose of analyzing natural speech data is, of course, to obtain estimates of the optimal values of the control parameters in our synthesizer. Thus, it is clear that the signal analysis techniques must be adapted to the kind of data needed to control the synthesizer.

2.2.1. The architecture of the synthesizer

The synthesizer architecture we use in our rule based text-to-speech system has been described in detail in Boves—Kerkhoff—Loman (1987). In its original form, it used the source model described in Klatt (1980). However, our vocal tract model was implemented as a cascade of six resonators and five anti-resonators. Compared with the serial-parallel configuration advocated by Klatt, our model has the advantage that it is not necessary to switch between two different "heads" at the boundaries between voiced and unvoiced sounds. Also, the presence of anti-resonators in the serial branch, used for synthesizing sounds like the lateral /l/, provides a filter structure that resembles the acoustic properties of the human vocal tract better than a structure that contains only resonators (Boves 1991).

Our intention to exploit knowledge of speech articulation as much as possible, which led us to the choice of the serial pole-zero structure, also motivated a change in the voice source model. Although the original model allows one to change the spectral properties of the glottal flow pulses, it appeared to be extremely difficult to derive a simple and insightful mapping between the parameters of that source model and knowledge of the physiology of voice production. It cannot be maintained that such a direct mapping is possible in the case of the Liljencrants-Fant (henceforth: LF) model (Fant—Liljencrants—Lin 1985) or the model proposed in Klatt—Klatt (1990). Yet, the parametric structure of these models is much closer to the parameters in a physiologically realistic voice source model. Since the model proposed in Klatt—Klatt is computationally much less expensive than the LF model (while having approximately the same modelling power) we decided to integrate it into our synthesizer. Unfortunately, this could only be done towards the end of the project. In a follow-up project it has been shown that the naturalness of the synthetic speech can be improved considerably by taking full advantage of this new source.

A nonnegligible disadvantage of our synthesizer architecture — a disadvantage that is shared by the serial-parallel architecture of Klatt — is that there is, as yet, no completely automatic procedure for extracting synthesizer control parameters from natural speech. The work described by de Veth—de Golstein Brouwers—Boves (this volume) has shown that a completely automatic parameter estimation procedure for a pole-zero system will be extremely difficult to obtain. Therefore, we were obliged to derive the control parameters in a semi-automatic way. Although such a procedure may seem to be time consuming and tedious, we believe that it has not slowed down the work. A rule-based synthesizer is essentially a knowledge based system, and as yet no reliable procedures exist for deriving "knowledge" from large sets of raw data.

Because it is not possible to obtain reliable estimates of the synthesizer control parameters directly from the analysis of natural speech, it appeared to be essential that one look at the natural (and synthetic) signals from a number of different perspectives, using different analysis and display techniques. Although it is time consuming and — perhaps more importantly — requires more than basic knowledge of speech acoustics and articulation, we are convinced that this way of approaching speech signals will remain fruitful (and necessary) for quite some time to come, if we want to really understand the acoustics of speech production.

The major analysis techniques used in our work on segmental rule development were (apart from the more exotic ones related to glottal inverse filtering and ARMA analysis) Linear Predictive Coding (LPC) formant tracking, short term spectral analysis using Fast Fourier Transforms (FFT) and Sonagram displays derived from FFT analyses. In what follows, we will give a short overview of our experiences with these analysis and display techniques in the framework of the development of rule-based segmental synthesis.

2.2.2. LPC formant tracking

Although our synthesizer architecture is not a straightforward formant synthesizer, formant frequencies and bandwidths remain among the most important control parameters. For rule development we need two kinds of data: (1) data on the influence of surrounding sounds on the formants in steady state portions of voiced sounds, and (2) data on the transitions from the steady state values for one sound to the next. A large number of (semi)automatic formant trackers have been described in the literature. None of these techniques appear to be error-free when applied to natural speech. Since we were not looking for a completely automatic procedure, we settled for a technique that is readily available in widely used signal processing packages (Markel—Gray 1976). This technique is based on LPC analysis, followed by a smoothing and selection procedure guided by the assumption that formant tracks should be smooth and continuous. The results of this procedure are then displayed in a so called resogram, which basically plots frequency (vertically) as a function of time (horizontally). An indication of formant bandwidth is also provided by using the vertical dimension as a double axis. Equally importantly, the results can also be printed in terms of numerical values of formant frequencies and bandwidths.

Conventionally, LPC analysis is carried out with windows of approximately 25 ms. Although this choice may be adequate in many situations, it is not for our purposes. Synthesizer control parameters are updated every 5 or 10 ms; therefore, we need information on the signal characteristics during intervals of approximately that size. Using 25 ms windows might cause considerable smearing of signal characteristics at points where the signal changes rapidly. For a high quality synthesizer it is probably essential to model these rapid changes accurately. For this reason, we used windows of 10 ms and a window shift of 2.5 ms in most of our analyses. The increase in frame-to-frame variation due to the short analysis window is compensated by the smoothing and selection procedure following the LPC analysis.

Usually, the LPC formant tracking was done in a batch process that could run overnight and that would produce annotated hardcopy plots of the results. In our rule development work the availability of sets of hardcopy pictures that can serve as a quick reference proved to be invaluable.

Probably the most important drawback of the representation of a speech signal in terms of frequencies and bandwidths of a set of poles is that information on overall spectral slope tends to get lost. This is not so much due to the all-pole character of LPC analysis; a similar problem was encountered with pole-zero analyses. The real cause of the problem lies in the fact that a representation in terms of just formant frequencies and bandwidths is usually incomplete, because it involves a selection of poles that are considered as formants out of a larger set of poles (and perhaps zeros) that describe the spectral envelope. Even if such an information reduction does not take place, it remains extremely difficult for a rule developer to estimate the spectral slope from a set of formant data only. Moreover, it is well known that LPC formants are probably not the best way to analyze voiceless consonants. For these reasons, it is worthwhile to complement LPC formant tracking with short-time spectra obtained through FFT analysis.

2.2.3. Short-time FFT spectra

FFT spectra form a non-parametric representation of the spectral structure of a speech signal. Although the non-parametric character may seem to be a drawback in the framework of a parametric synthesizer, FFT spectra proved to be indispensable. First of all, it must be remembered that our synthesizer architecture does not map directly on any parametric analysis technique that can be run automatically. Thus, for the human observer FFT spectra can be expected to give information that is not available in, for instance, LPC analysis. This applies among others to overall spectral slope, an important feature that is lost in LPC-based resograms, but that is fully retained in FFT spectra. Equally importantly, FFT spectra offer a quick and effective check on the appropriateness of parameter values used to control the synthesizer, especially for fricatives and bursts of plosives where LPC-derived poles may not be a good description. We used a VMS batch procedure to produce hardcopy plots of FFT spectra of the steady state portions of all sounds in our natural speech database. These plots were then used as reference material when checking the spectral structure of synthetic replicas of these sounds.

FFT spectra also played an important role in developing rules for transitions of the higher formants into and out of voiced consonants surrounding vowels. The spectral slope in consonants is usually much steeper than in vowels. One consequence of the steep spectral slope is that the estimates of the frequencies and bandwidths of the higher spectral maxima (not to use the term *formants*) derived from LPC analyses are quite unreliable, at least if they must be interpreted as formants. This may not be harmful if LPC parameters are used to resynthesize the signal without changing the parameters (or with some degree of parameter quantization) because an explicit interpretation of the LPC parameters is not required. If, however, a single set of optimal parameter values is selected for use in rule-based synthesis, the situation may become quite different. In a formant synthesizer like ours, these parameters are treated as formant values. Consequently, formant transitions can become erroneous. This may not be a problem in sustained consonantal sounds, where the high energy low frequency components will probably mask the weak high frequency components anyhow. But erroneous formant transitions into and out of vowels may be quite disturbing and may give rise to erroneous perception of place of articulation of the consonant. In practice, FFT spectra prove to be of great help in avoiding erroneous interpretations of the "formants" obtained from LPC analysis of consonants.

2.2.4. Sonagram displays

The traditional Sonagram display, computer generated in our case, is still a very convenient compromise between, on the one hand, the LPC based resogram display, that shows the dynamic aspects of the formant transitions but no spectral slope, and, on the other hand, the FFT based short-time spectrum, that shows the slope as well as the formant locations, but no dynamic changes over time. As with the other two spectral representations, a catalogue of hardcopy Sonagrams was produced for the natural utterances, that were then used as reference material when working on the rules.

2.3. Compare natural and synthetic copies of the utterances

Despite the availability of several complementary spectral and temporal displays of the natural and synthetic versions of the logatomes, auditory comparison of the versions is still essential. We did not succeed in finding a solution for the "his master's voice" problem: phoneticians who are working on rule development tend to hear the sounds they are trying to synthesize, even if naive listeners hear quite different things. Obviously, the rule developer very quickly learns to categorize and to identify sounds as speech sounds, irrespective of the objective resemblance of these sounds to natural speech sounds. This is the point where the colleagues, students and chance visitors come in as essential components of the rule development procedure.

We have made an attempt to replace frequent informal listening tests by objective measures of the distance between natural and synthetic copies of the utterances. To this end, the copies were first time aligned using Dynamic Time Warping techniques, after which local spectral distances could be computed. We hoped to be able to use the non-linearities in the time warp function, together with the local spectral distance to decide whether the synthetic version of the utterance was close enough to the natural one, and if not, what changes should be made (i.e., should the temporal structure be changed, the spectral structure, or both). This attempt failed, probably because it was not possible for the technique to distinguish perceptually significant differences between several versions of an utterance from equally large differences that are not perceptually relevant. Interestingly, it did not help if we used auditory based spectral distance measures in the computations. Apparently, distance measures are needed that take into account not only frequency masking but also temporal masking effects. Unfortunately, the implementation of such dynamically changing distance measures would have constituted a research program of its own. Thus, human judgments remained indispensable.

As indicated above, human judgments of the intelligibility of the synthetic logatomes were not limited to informal listening tests with colleagues. Instead, a number of formal intelligibility tests formed part of the development strategy. These tests played a decisive role in the first stages of the development. When the intelligibility approached that obtained with diphone concatenation, however, the contribution of logatome based intelligibility tests with untrained listeners became gradually less informative. It appeared that even naive listeners manage to discriminate and to identify sounds as (the intended) speech sounds in a quite reliable and consistent manner, even though phonetic experts will find that these sounds are different from natural speech sounds. It appeared to be very productive to use trained listeners in the tests, and to ask them to score naturalness of the synthetic utterances in addition to intelligibility, and to give detailed explanations of the causes of the lack of naturalness. In the later stages of rule development it also appeared to be useful to test segmental intelligibility with "unpredictable" sentences, i.e., sentences that are semantically meaningful and syntactically correct, but still very low in redundancy, for instance because of the use of infrequent words or because they express unusual events or situations. When trying to understand these sentences listeners can no longer rely on their ability to guess at the identity of sounds in short logatomes.

2.4. Update rules

In previous papers we have described the working environment that allows the rule developer to change formal rules, without having to go through the complete process of translating the new set of rules into a computer program, compiling that program, and linking it, before the updated rule set can be used to synthesize hopefully improved versions of the speech sounds under development (Kerkhoff—Loman—Boves 1989). Such a working environment is of crucial importance. Even using a state of the art work station or a very powerful PC, the compilation and load processes are so time consuming that effective rule development is not possible. The same would be true, of course, if the step of translating the formal rules into a computer program could be skipped, because a conventional programming language is used for expressing the rules. Due to the size of the resulting program it would become extremely difficult to keep track of all points in the program that might affect a specific speech sound in a specific context. Moreover, it is our experience that the time needed to compile the C-program generated by our parser generator is much larger than the time it takes the parser generator to translate a set of rules into a C-program.

3. Results

Probably, the best description of the results of our rule development activities can be found in the chapter by van Bezooijen—Pols (this volume).

In the present chapter, we confine ourselves to a short exemplary description of the rules for the /l/ sound. The lateral is known to have many different realizations in different phonetic contexts. For sounds that are strongly affected by the phonetic context one has, in principle, the choice between two alternatives: one can increase the set of sounds for which default specifications are available by including a (possibly large) number of allophones, each with its own set of default specifications; or one can write a large number of rules that adapt a single allophone on the basis of the surrounding sounds. We opted for the second strategy, mainly because we believe that eventually the number of rules operating on a large number of allophones will not be significantly smaller than with basically one allophone per phoneme.

The phonetic rules will be presented in the notational format described in Loman—Kerkhoff—Boves (1989). Phonetic rules have two inputs, viz. the enriched phonemic representation of the utterance computed by the linguistic part of the text-to-speech system on the one hand, and a table with default specifications of all sounds on the other. The default specifications come in two separate classes: the largest group comprises parameters that are used to control the synthesizer, like formant frequencies and bandwidths; the other group consists of parameters that determine the interpolation between target values of adjacent sounds. These target values are subject to modification by context rules, which are driven by the input phonemic representation. In our system phonetic rules follow the same crucial ordering conventions that are known from conventional Generative Phonology (Chomsky—Halle 1968). This means that the first rule that applies to a sound, acts on the default values read from the table; all subsequent rules that apply to this sound act on the output of the previous rules.

A subset of the default specifications of the /l/, i.e. of the formants, total duration and duration of the formant transitions, is given in Table 1. These specifications were derived from the results of LPC formant tracking.

Table 1. Subset of the default specifications for the sound /l/

dur	$trans_1$	f_1trans_1	$trans_2$	f_1trans_2	f_1	b_1	f_2	b_2	f_3	b_3	f_4	b_4
65	10	10	10	10	300	120	1700	120	2500	200	3300	400

Note: dur = Duration; $trans_1$ = Duration of initial transition for most parameters; f_1trans_1 = Duration of initial transition of F_1; $trans_2$ = Duration of final transition for most parameters; f_1trans_2 = Duration of final transition of F_1; f_n = Frequency of Formant n; b_n = Bandwidth of Formant n.

From analyses of /l/ in different vowel contexts it appeared that a number of vowel classes could be distinguished, each having specific effects on the formant target values of the lateral. One of these classes consists of the vowels with the features [front,unrounded]. The formant values in Table 1 apply to /l/ followed by one of the vowels from that class. The following set of rules takes care of the adaptation of word initial /l/ to other vowel contexts.

(1)	1 ⇒ 1	FORM2	−:= 200	/ --- [+voc,+back]
	1 ⇒ 3	SET F3	= F2	
		FORM3	+:= 200	
		BANDW3	:= 200	
(2)		FORM4	:= 2500	/ --- [+voc,+round]
(3)	1 ⇒ 1	FORM1	−:= 70	/ --- {u·/i·/y·/ə}

Rule (1) stipulates that the frequency of F_2 is lowered by 200 Hz if /l/ is followed by a vowel with the feature [+back]. Rule (2) first sets F_3 equal to F_2, after which F_3 is increased by 200 Hz; F_4 is set to 2,500 Hz. The value of F_2 used in the first operation in this rule is the one prevailing after rule (1) has done its work. The net effect of (2) is a lowering of F_4. In (3) the target frequency of the first formant is somewhat lowered when /l/ is followed by any of the vowels /u·/, /i·/, /y·/, or /ə/. The vowels which cause this effect are difficult to describe in terms of a particular phonetic class. Vowel height seems to be the most important characteristic these vowels share. Yet, /ə/ is less high than the other three vowels, and there are other vowels in Dutch which agree in terms of the feature [high] with /ə/, that do not have a similar effect on F_1 in a preceding /l/.

(4)	1 ⇒ 6	FORM1	:= 400	
		FORM2	:= 810	
		FORM3	:= 2750	
		BANDW3	:= 150	
		FORM4	:= 3375	
		BANDW4	:= 100	/ [+voc] ---

In (4) the single rule is given that determines the target frequencies and bandwidths of the four formants of final /l/. Listening tests showed that it is not necessary to distinguish between classes of vowels that affect the formant targets of syllable final /l/ in different ways.

Comparisons between speech spectrograms obtained from natural speech of /l/-Vowel and Vowel-/l/ sequences, and their synthetic counterparts showed that rules (1)–(4) adequately describe the synthetic speech signal as to the location of the target frequencies of /l/ and its spectral slope. Other important rules concern the determination of the dynamic character of formant tracks in /l/-Vowel sequences.

(5)	l ⇒ 2	TRANS2	:=70	
		F1TRANS2	:=10	/ --- {a:/ɑ/ɔ/o:}
(6)	l ⇒ 2	TRANS2	:= 5	
		F1TRANS2	:= 5	/ --- {ɪ/i·/ɛ/e:}
(7)	l ⇒ 2	TRANS1	:=30	
		F1TRANS1	:= 5	/ [+voc] ---

In (5) and (6) the time interval is determined during which the formant target values of /l/ move to the values in the following vowel. Rule (5) stipulates that transition duration for F_1 (F1TRANS) is different from the transition duration of the remaining formants. Very short formant transitions were found when /l/ preceded any of the front vowels, as specified by (6). Rule (7) reflects our findings that the duration of the formant transitions for postvocalic /l/ are not influenced by the type of vowel.

4. Conclusion

Consistent application of the rule development strategy outlined in this chapter has led to a slow but steady progress in the segmental quality of the allophone synthesis for Dutch. At the onset of the project segmental intelligibility was rather poor: 44, 76, and 55 percent correct phoneme identification for C_1, V, and C_2 in CVC nonsense words (cf. van Bezooijen 1986, van Bezooijen—Pols, this volume). At the conclusion of the project intelligibility had risen to 78, 90, and 81 percent phoneme identification, for comparable test materials. By this time the allophone synthesis was, in fact, more intelligible than even the best quality diphone synthesis available within the ASSP program (69, 85, and 82 percent correct for C_1, V, and C_2, respectively). Our performance level has reached its practical upper limit for vowels, since phoneme identification of vowels in LPC-resynthesis of natural token of the same test materials is 88 percent correct (van Bezooijen 1986). However, there is still considerable room for improvement for both initial and final consonants, as is suggested by the percentages reported by van Bezooijen (1986) for these segments in LPC-resynthesis (92 and 97 percent correct, respectively).

Part IV

Acoustic-phonetic data and synthesis rules

How does speaking rate influence vowel formant track parameters?

Rob J. J. H. van Son—Louis C. W. Pols

Abstract

Speaking rate and vowel duration are thought to affect the spectral features of vowels. Target-understood models of vowel production predict more spectral reduction and more level formant tracks in fast-rate speech and shorter vowels. To test this prediction, a meaningful Dutch text of 844 words was read twice by an experienced newscaster, once at a normal speaking rate and once as fast as possible. All realizations of seven vowels and some realizations of the schwa vowel were used to study the effects of speaking rate and vowel duration on formant frequency and track shape. Neither the formant frequency values nor the formant track shapes showed an increased target-undershoot in fast-rate speech. Only a uniform increase in F_1 frequency, irrespective of vowel identity, was found in fast-rate speech. A small correlation between shorter durations and more reduced and more level F_1 tracks was found only when realizations of the open vowels /ɛ, a:, ɑ/ uttered at a single speaking rate where compared. This indicates that if target-undershoot phenomena operate in read speech, they do so only when speaking rate is constant.

1. Introduction

1.1. General introduction

The question stated in the title is part of a tradition in phonetics that dates back at least to the paper of Lindblom (1963). In this paper, Lindblom tried to construct a (ballistic) model of articulatory dynamics that was based on the inertia of the speech organs. He found that there was a direct relation between the duration of a vowel and the difference between the actual articulation and the canonical articulation of that vowel.

Because the movements of the articulators are very difficult to observe directly, the frequencies of the first two formants are generally used instead to assess the articulatory movements or positions in a quantitative way. Lindblom (1963) concluded that the shorter a vowel realization is, the more the frequencies of the first two formants differ from the frequencies found in the ideal form (as measured in very long realizations). This ideal form is called the canonical target of the vowel. The model was called the target-undershoot model because in it the articulators, in normal speech, are thought to be stopped short of reaching their canonical target positions due to lack of time.

The target-undershoot model tries to account for two important and well attested phenomena of vowel articulation: Coarticulation and spectral vowel reduction (see e.g. the textbooks of O'Shaughnessy 1987; Clark—Yallop 1990). The target-undershoot model predicts that when phoneme realizations get shorter, there will come a point where the articulators will not have enough time to complete the movements from one phoneme target to the next. The articulatory positions that are actually reached in a sequence of speech sounds will be drawn closer together in time, thereby increasing coarticulation. Also, the articulatory movements will be shorter, resulting in leveled-off formant frequency tracks, which means that formant frequency differences (e.g. between on/off-set and target) within a single vowel realization will diminish. Furthermore, when uttering a vowel, the articulators will travel less far from the relaxed, neutral position (i.e. the schwa /ə/), which is spectral reduction.

After Lindblom (1963), the target-undershoot model has been modified by Gay (1981) and Lindblom (1983) to include speaking effort as a factor that will modify the effect of duration on the amount of coarticulation and spectral vowel reduction. The matter is of more than only academic interest. To synthesize high quality speech, correct variation in the duration of phonemes is necessary. If the spectral characteristics of natural speech change with phoneme duration, neglecting these changes in synthetic speech may impair naturalness and even intelligibility.

Since the study of Lindblom (1963), a multitude of studies were performed to investigate the influence of vowel duration on the spectral characteristics of vowels. The results were ambiguous. On the one hand, several papers support the notion of more target undershoot with shorter vowel durations (Lindblom 1963; Broad—Fertig 1970; Gay—Ushijima—Hirose—Cooper 1974; Broad—Clermont 1987; Lindblom—Moon 1988). Other studies, however, were unable to detect such undershoot (Gay 1978; Nord 1987; Gopal—Syrdal 1988; den Os 1988; Engstrand 1988) or found the effect of speaking rate on vowel undershoot to be speaker dependent (Kuehn—Moll 1976). Support for the target undershoot model is most frequently found when vowel realizations from only one speaking rate and style are studied, whereas it seems to be difficult to find support for it when differences between speaking rates or styles are studied.

There are practical difficulties in eliciting vowel realizations that differ only in duration. The natural variation in vowel duration is strongly coupled to other features of speech that are known to influence vowel spectra, e.g. stress (sentence and word stress), position in word, information content, phoneme context, speaking style, and familiarity with words (see e.g. the textbooks of O'Shaughnessy 1987; Clark—Yallop 1990). It is difficult to control all these factors and still elicit variation in vowel duration (but not impossible, see Lindblom—Moon 1988), even more so when the speech uttered should be close to natural speech, or at least should be close to read speech. It is much easier to obtain vowel realizations that differ only in duration when different speaking rates are used. It suffices then to instruct the speaker to speak the same materials at different rates. This keeps context, stress and all other factors identical for every realization of the utterance. Also, a long, normal text can be used to be read, preventing short term adaptations of articulation strategies to difficult speaking conditions. Such short term adaptations were suggested by Gay (1981) to explain the lack of reduction often found in fast rate speech.

Using a read text in an experiment is not without problems. Reading a text aloud is not the natural way of speaking. Results of experiments using this kind of speech cannot readily be extrapolated to free conversation. In this scheme, reading errors (e.g. deletions and stress assignment errors) will thwart a comparison between vowel realizations from different readings of the same text. Error free reading is a difficult task and good speakers (or better: readers) are hard to find. Despite these potential problems, we opted for a relatively long text, read at a normal rate and at a fast rate. We were able to engage a professional speaker with a long experience as a news caster and narrator. We are aware that by using only a single, very experienced, speaker, the results of our study will not be representative for the average speaker. But in this paper we are dealing with basic models that describe what is possible in speech. With such general models, a case study of a single speaker producing highly intelligible continuous speech can be enough to show at what point the prevalent models are deficient or even invalid as general models, and which parts of the models (if any) are supported by this (one) speaker. Furthermore, if a speech synthesizer can produce speech that is of the same quality as that of a professional speaker, it will not matter when this is different from the average speaker in the street.

Two, potentially independent, questions were investigated in our study. First, does the vowel target show more spectral reduction, i.e. more schwa-like formant frequencies, or more coarticulation, i.e. formant frequency shifts toward neighboring phonemes, in fast-rate speech than in normal-rate speech? Second, are formant frequency tracks of fast-rate vowels more level (i.e. have smaller differences between vowel on/off-set and target) than those of normal-rate vowels, indicating that articulation movements are shorter in fast-rate speech? Our speaker was, of course, not informed about the aims of our research.

1.2. Speech material

Our text was 844 words long. The text had been used originally in a radio broadcast and was informative (concerning economics). The text was read twice, once as for an audience, once as fast as possible. Reading this text took 330 seconds when reading at a normal rate, and 220 seconds when reading at a fast rate. When pauses over 200 milliseconds were excluded, the overall reduction in duration of the fast-rate realization as compared to the normal-rate realization was one fourth (i.e. 25 percent). The speech was recorded on a commercial PCM-recorder, low-pass filtered with a 4.5 kHz cut-off frequency, and then digitized at 10 kHz and 12 bits resolution.

For practical reasons, we did not use all Dutch vowels. Out of the 12 Dutch monophthongs, 7 were used: the vowels /iˑ, yˑ, uˑ, oː, ɑ, aː, ɛ/. Two vowels are long vowels (/aː, oː/), the other five are short or half-long vowels (/iˑ, yˑ, uˑ, ɑ, ɛ/). We sequenced realizations of these vowels from the text readings (based on their orthographic form) and labeled them according to their actual spoken form. Both readings of the text were labeled for sentence stress by an experienced phonetician. We also used some realizations of the schwa (/ə/), from the words *het* /ət/ 'the' and *er* /ər/ 'there'.

The vowel realizations were isolated with a leading and trailing margin of 50 milliseconds. The LVS software package for speech analysis (Vogten 1985) was used for LPC analysis. The vowel segments were analyzed with a 10-pole LPC-analysis, using a 25 ms Hamming window. The window was shifted in one ms steps. This was the basis for formant extraction. The LPC-analysis was based on the Split-Levinson algorithm, which gives continuous formant tracks (Willems 1986).

A grand total of 1,178 vowel realizations was isolated from the two readings of the text, existing of 587 pairs of realizations of the same text item at different speaking rates and 4 unpaired realizations resulting from insertions and deletions. For various reasons (e.g. segmentation problems, speaking errors), 38 vowel pairs could not be used in this study. Therefore, there remained 549 pairs of realizations of the same text item and vowel at a normal- and at a fast-speaking rate, these are summarized in Table 1.

2. Formant targets

2.1. Introduction

First of all, we examined the effects of speaking rate on the vowel formant target frequencies. The target undershoot model predicts that as vowel realizations become shorter, they become more schwa-like (i.e. reduction) and more like their neighbors (i.e. coarticulation). Generally, no preference for either of these two (often conflicting) tendencies is given.

Often, reduction is measured as a change in the distance between an vowel and the schwa in the formant space. Also, combinations between different formants and between F_1 and F_0 are used to characterize vowels.

Table 1. Number of vowel pairs matched for normal versus fast rate. Both realizations in each pair are from the same text item (see text)

	Stressed	Unstressed	Unequal	Total
ɛ	23	85	12	120
ɑ	23	79	8	110
a:	21	70	11	98
i·	23	57	4	84
o:	17	56	11	84
ə	0	21	0	21
u·	4	7	5	16
y·	5	6	1	12
Total	116	381	52	549

However, different formants are generally influenced by different articulators and therefore can be expected to react differently to changes in speaking rate. This means that combined measures might hide changes in articulation. Afterwards, it is also difficult to disentangle any differences found and to decide what happened (or did not happen). A further drawback of combining formants is that this is only possible when a metric is defined in the formant space (e.g., linear, logarithmic, Bark). Chosing the wrong metric will invalidate all results. As there is no consensus about what is the best metric for formant space we decided to use rank-order statistic methods only. However, rank-order statistics preclude the use of differences between formant values (or durations), distances between vowels or any combination of formants values. A practical problem when studying vowel target frequencies is the lack of a good, operational, definition of the point in time where in a vowel realization the target is reached or at least approximated most closely. A survey of the available literature shows that there are hardly two papers using the same "point" in the realization (compare e.g. Lindblom 1963; Delattre 1969; Gay 1978; Koopmans-van Beinum 1980; Lisker 1984; Vaissière 1987; Engstrand 1988; den Os 1988; Gopal—Syrdal 1988). Because the method with which the formant target frequencies are measured could influence the outcome of the comparisons between speaking rates, we adopted a selection of methods for determining vowel formant target frequencies. We used (a) the maximal or minimal formant frequency, (b) the point of maximal energy, (c) the most stable part of the vowel, (d) the values at the center of the vowel (i.e. the midpoint), and (e) the mean formant frequency within the realization. For the problem we were concerned with, the choice of measuring method turned out to be immaterial. All methods used essentially gave the same results, although with a difference in sensitivity. In this paper we will limit ourselves to the most sensitive method, using the average formant frequency (averaged over the complete vowel realization). For a more exhaustive discussion of the differences between measuring methods we refer to van Son—Pols (1990).

2.2. Differences in duration between speaking rates

Vowel realizations from the fast-rate reading of the text are, on average, only 15 percent shorter than vowel realizations from the normal-rate reading. The mean duration of the normal-rate vowel realizations was 99ms (s.d. 41ms) and the mean duration of the fast-rate realizations was 84ms (s.d. 31ms). If we compare median durations (instead of mean durations), the differences in duration between normal-rate and fast-rate realizations are statistically significant (at the 0.1 percent level) for all realizations pooled (89 ms versus 78 ms). Closer inspection reveals that the effect of rate is significant for the volwels /a:, o:/ only (Mann-Whitney U test, $p \leq .001$). We will use pair-wise comparisons between the two realizations of each text item (one realized at a normal speaking rate and one at a fast speaking rate). On average, in 75 percent of all vowel pairs, the fast-rate realization is shorter than the corresponding normal-rate realization. A sign test on the number of pairs for which the fast-rate realization is the shortest of the two, gives a statistically significant difference (at the 0.1 percent level) for /ɛ, ɑ, a:, i·, o:/ and all vowels pooled. From this we can conclude that, in general, fast-rate realizations of vowels are indeed shorter than their normal-rate counterparts.

This discussion may seem superfluous, but the small difference found between the average duration of normal-rate vowels and fast-rate vowels leaves the possibility that not all fast-rate realizations of vowels were shorter than their normal-rate counterparts. Using a pair-wise test, we are able to show that the fast rate vowel realizations are indeed shorter than their normal-rate counterparts.

2.3. Formant target values

2.3.1. Median target frequencies

The effect of speaking rate on vowel formant targets can be illustrated by a plot of second versus first formant frequency of the median formant target frequencies. This is done in Figure 1. It can clearly be seen that the fast-rate realizations have a higher F_1 target frequency than the normal-rate realizations for all vowels used. There may be a tendency of a more centralized F_2 frequency, but this is difficult to see.

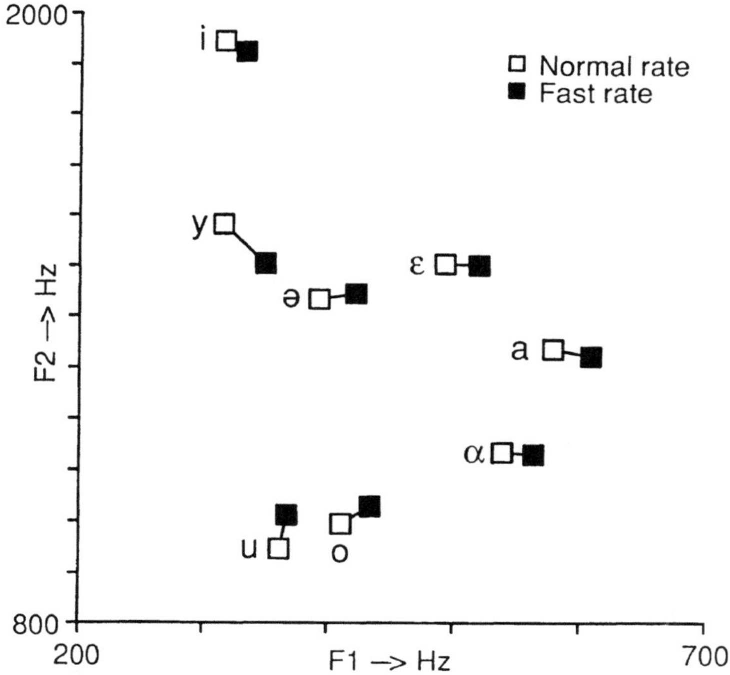

Figure 1. Median values of the first and second formant frequencies for the 7 vowels studied
Open squares: Normal speaking rate values
Closed squares: Fast speaking rate values

The actual median values are presented in Table 2. Statistically significant differences are only found for the F_1 frequencies of the vowels /ɛ, ɑ, a:, o:/. None of the vowels shows a significant difference between the F_2 target frequencies.

Table 2. Median values for formant frequencies (Hz)

	ɛ	ɑ	aː	i·	oː	ə	u·	y·	tot
F_1 N	$\underline{493}$	$\underline{539}$	$\underline{579}$	316	$\underline{411}$	393	362	316	476
F	$\underline{520}$	$\underline{564}$	$\underline{609}$	333	$\underline{434}$	422	368	350	501
F_2 N	1503	1133	1335	1946	995	1433	947	1582	1345
F	1501	1129	1321	1925	1029	1444	1012	1504	1360

Note: Statistical significance of differences between speaking-rate is determined by a Mann-Whitney U test. Pairs of median frequencies that are significantly different between speaking rates at the level of 0.1 percent are underlined.

2.3.2. *Pair-wise comparisons*

When pair-wise comparisons of formant frequencies are used (see Table 3), the effect of speaking rate is much more pronounced. In about three quarters of all vowel pairs, the fast-rate vowel realization has a higher F_1 frequency than the corresponding normal-rate vowel realization (Table 3), irrespective of vowel identity. A, statistically not significant, exception is the vowel /u·/, probably due to the low number of realizations used. All results for the F_1 frequency values are significant at the 0.1 percent level, except for the vowels /ə, u·, y·/, of which only a few realizations were available.

The results for the F_2 frequency values are in line with the spectral reduction hypotheses, i.e. higher F_2 fequency for low F_2-target vowels, lower for high F_2-target vowels, but only for the vowel /oː/ the difference is statistically significant.

Table 3. Percentage of pairs for which the fast-rate realization has a higher formant target value than its normal-rate counterpart

	ɛ	ɑ	aː	i·	oː	ə	u·	y·	tot
F_1	$\underline{80}$	$\underline{76}$	$\underline{77}$	$\underline{71}$	$\underline{88}$	76	55	91	$\underline{78}$
F_2	44	63	46	42	$\underline{71}$	67	73	9	53

Note: Significance is given for a sign test, ties (fast-rate value = normal-rate value) are omitted. Statistically significant entries (at the 0.1 percent level) are underlined.

2.4. Correlations

The strength of the correlation of formant values between members of a pair indicates the degree with which variations in formant target values within the reading of a text is reproduced when the text is re-read. A strong correlation (i.e. a high correlation coefficient) indicates that the variation in formant target frequencies is systematic and not random. A weak correlation could be the result of random variation in the formant values, but this is not necessary. Variation in vowel duration can be assessed in the same way.

The correlations between formant values within pairs (i.e. between corresponding vowel realizations) and durations within pairs are high for almost all vowels (Spearman rank correlation coefficients ≥ 0.6, not shown). The correlation coefficients are highest for F_2. The pair-wise correlations between durations at fast and normal speaking rates are statistically significant (level 0.1 percent) for all vowels except /ə, u·, y·/. The pair-wise correlations are statistically significant (level 0.1 percent) for F_1 and F_2 for all vowels except for the F_1 of the vowels /ə, u·, y·/ and the F_2 of the vowels /i·, u·, y·/.

The fact that the correlation between formant frequencies (especially for F_2) is generally higher than between durations suggests that the variation in duration is not the explanation of the systematic variation in formant target frequencies.

The relation between formant frequencies and vowel duration can be tested directly by testing the correlation between these values. The correlation coefficients between formant frequencies and vowel durations are very small (Spearman rank correlation test, data not shown). For both speaking rates pooled the correlation coefficients are all smaller than 0.4 (significant at 0.1 percent level only for /ɑ/, both F_1 and F_2). For the fast-rate realizations only, the largest correlation coefficient is 0.45 (significant at 0.1 percent level only for F_1 of /a:/).

2.5. Stress and phoneme context

It is possible that stress influences the effects of speaking rate on vowel formant target frequencies. To test this, we divided the vowel realizations into two sets based on stress. There were not enough stressed vowels to analyze all the vowels individually so we pooled all vowel realizations. We did not find any speaking-rate related differences between the stressed and the unstressed vowel realizations.

Different vowel contextual phonemes may alter the direction of change under a higher speaking rate depending on the vowel identity, i.e. speaking rate may affect coarticulation and not reduction. By pooling all vowel realizations irrespective of their context we may have averaged out any effect of speaking rate.

To check the effects of speaking rate on coarticulation we selected all the vowel realizations that were followed by an alveolar consonant (i.e. *VC in which C is one of /n, t, d, s, z, l, r/). This context was chosen because it is most frequent and the trailing consonant is known to have the greatest importance in vowel coarticulation (Pols 1977). The vowels were divided into four, overlapping, sets: [+closed] (/i˙, y˙, u˙/), [+open] (/ɛ, ɑ, a:/), [+front] (/i˙, ɛ/), and [+back] (/u˙, o:/). A sign test on the pairs (see Table 4) revealed that there was no difference between the four sets in their response to a higher speaking rate. Neither was their a difference between the vowel realizations in this context and those used in Table 3.

So neither stress nor context influence the differences between normal-rate vowel realizations and fast-rate vowel realizations found in this study.

Table 4. As Table 3, but only vowels uttered in *VC context are used, where the C is an alveolar consonant (one of /n, t, d, s, z, l, r/) and the * can be any context

	Closed	Open	Front	Back
F_1	67	<u>79</u>	<u>75</u>	<u>87</u>
F_2	43	52	45	70
Duration	<u>73</u>	<u>79</u>	<u>75</u>	<u>85</u>

Note: The vowel pairs are pooled on the features [+closed] (/i˙, y˙, u˙/, n = 60), [+open] (/ɛ, ɑ, a:/, n = 255), [+front] (/i˙, ɛ/, n = 141), and [+back] (/u˙, o:/, n=46).

2.6. Discussion and conclusions

In this chapter we investigated the effects of speaking rate differences on vowel formant targets. We found that vowels spoken at a fast rate did differ in their measured formant target frequencies, but that these differences were small. Furthermore, the differences (a higher F_1 frequency with a higher speaking rate) are independent of vowel identity, stress, or flanking consonants.

All the articulatory models described in the introduction predict a change in formant target values with speaking rate that depends on vowel identity. Furthermore, none of the models can incorporate a rising F_1 frequency with rising speaking rate of the vowel /a:/. Therefore we must conclude that all models mentioned before have severe deficiencies with respect to the effects of speaking rate on vowel formant target frequencies.

A possible explanation for the rise in F_1 in fast-rate speech is that our speaker speaks louder when speaking fast. Schulman (1989) and Traunmüller (1988) found that louder speech indeed can have a more open articulation than normal speech. A more open articulation results in a higher F_1 target frequency. Our recordings were not made to compare speech loudness and are not calibrated for sound levels (the readings were even recorded at different sessions). Therefore we are not able to check the suggestion that the speech in the fast rate reading was louder.

3. Formant tracks

3.1. Introduction

Whereas a lot of work has been done on the relation between vowel-formant *target* frequencies and vowel duration (see introduction), relatively few studies have been performed on the relation between vowel formant *dynamics* and vowel duration (e.g. Broad—Fertig 1970; Broad—Clermont 1987; Di Benedetto 1989). From these studies it is still not clear whether fast rate speech is just "speeded up" normal rate speech or that the articulatory dynamics change. Current theories on formant dynamics are not conclusive on the importance of formant track slope and how it reacts to vowel duration. An often heard hypothesis is that shorter vowels should have more level (i.e. flatter after time normalization) formant tracks with a smaller difference between vowel formant on/offset frequency and formant target frequency. This leveling would be the result of a smaller amplitude of the articulatory movements due to lack of time (cf. the target-undershoot model, Lindblom 1963). The results of Di Benedetto (1989) suggest that this might not be true and that the slopes of the formant track are steeper with shorter duration, so as to preserve the articulatory amplitude.

3.2. Methods

A problem with the study of formant dynamics is that it is not clear what should be measured. In most studies, the durations and slopes of vowel on- and off-glide, and the stationary part of the vowel realizations are measured using two to four points along each formant track (Di Benedetto 1989; Strange 1989a,b; Duez 1989; Krull 1989). This approach is hampered by the fact that formant tracks are almost always strongly curved. It is very difficult to determine the boundaries of the stationary part (Benguerel 1989) and to measure formant track slopes in the on- and offglide parts of the vowels. As a result the slopes measured are unreliable. A different approach that is free of the problem of formant track curvature, is to fit a model function onto a sampled version of the formant tracks (Broad—Fertig 1970; Broad—Clermont 1987). The choice of a single model function to fit the formant tracks is tightly linked to the articulatory model under investigation, a generalization of the results is therefore difficult.

In view of the problems mentioned above, we chose a different approach in which the strong sides of the traditional methods, the transparant meaning of the formant mean value and slope and the reliability of high order poly nomial fits, are combined. After a polynomial of suitable order is fitted on the formant track, it is decomposed into a set of simple, independent or orthogonal, functions that each represent a single "feature" of the formant track. This procedure is much like a Principal Components Analysis. Based on their simplicity and computational efficiency we chose the Legendre polynomial functions (Abramowitz—Stegun 1965: 773–802). Any polynomial can always be written as the sum of a finite number of Legendre polynomials. Individual polynomial coefficients can be interpreted in familiar terms. They represent the mean value, the mean slope, the parabolic deviation (excursion size) and higher order components of track shape (e.g., length of the vowel nucleus). Other measures can be calculated from the original polynomial, e.g., the maximum (minimum) value and its position and slopes at every point along the track. Legendre polynomial functions are therefore able to give both a meaningful and a complete description of formant tracks. They can also be determined very accurately and can easily be translated to formant tracks for speech synthesis. In Figure 2 an example is given of the use of the Legendre polynomials in modeling track shapes.

In the target-undershoot model, vowel articulation cannot completely compensate for changes in vowel duration. The result should be a change in articulation speed, and therefore formant track shape, that does not match the change in duration. This lack of accomodation of articulation speed to duration can be found by normalizing the formant tracks for duration. Any differences that remain between the formant tracks, points to a difference in articulation. In this study we normalized the vowel tracks by sampling each vowel realization at 16, evenly distributed point (equidistant within each individual realization). With 16 data points, the contributions of the first five orders of the Legendre polynomials (0–4) could be calculated reliably. The calculations were done using the Newton-Cote formulas for numeric integration (see Abramowitz—Stegun 1965: 886). The contribution of coefficient (P) of each order (i) Legendre polynomial is related to the variance (V) of the polynomial by the formula: V =

P∗P/{1+2∗i} (Abramowitz—Stegun 1965: 773–802). This is also the amount of variance in the original track that is "explained" by this polynomial.

We also used the sample points themselves for a point to point analysis. This analysis gave no results that were not also obtained with the polynomial analysis and we will limit the present paper to the polynomial analysis (for details see: van Son—Pols 1989; van Son—Pols, in press). Using the Legendre polynomials, we also calculated the formant track slopes at points in the on- and offglide of the vowel realizations (points at 1/4 and 3/4 of the formant track). The resulting slopes were difficult to interpret and an analysis gave no new information on the effects of speaking rate on vowel formant tracks (not shown, but see van Son—Pols 1991).

3.3. Results

3.3.1. Goodness of fit

When using modeling functions, it is important to know how well the model constructed from these functions fits the original formant tracks. To assess the fit of the first five orders of Legendre polynomials, we calculated the percentage of the variance around the mean that is explained by the contribution of each order Legendre polynomial to the model function and the percentage of the variance that remains unexplained after the polynomials are fitted on the tracks (i.e. the error in the fit), see Table 5. For clarity, this was done without using the contribution of the zero order component (i.e. the mean value, we already know that this is non-zero).

The bulk of the variance around the mean is explained by the first and second order polynomials (first order: 25–82 percent, second order: 10–66 percent). Together they explain 80 percent and more of the variance of F_2 tracks, and 65 percent and more of the variance of F_1 tracks (> 90 percent in /ɛ, ɑ, a:/). The worst fit after using all five polynomials is found with the F_1 tracks of the vowel /u·/ (12 percent of the variance remains unexplained). This bad fit can possibly be explained by the fact that the F_1 of the vowel /u·/ is almost constant, except at the vowel boundaries. This leaves very little variance to explain.

Because the contribution to the total track shape of third and fourth order polynomials is only small, we will limit our discussion here to the zero, first, and second order polynomial contributions.

3.3.2. Interpretation of polynomial coefficients

The mean values of the Legendre polynomial coefficients (i.e. the mean size of the contributions of each order) are given in Table 6. The mean coefficients

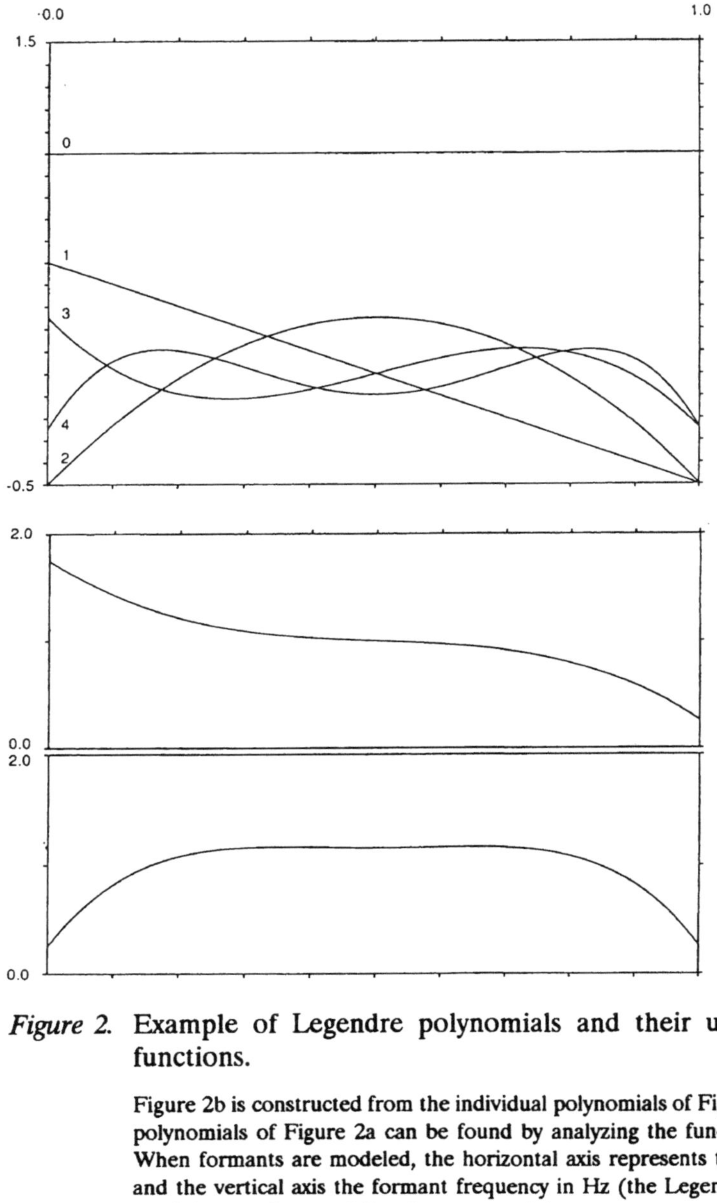

Figure 2. Example of Legendre polynomials and their use in modeling functions.

Figure 2b is constructed from the individual polynomials of Figure 2a, but also the polynomials of Figure 2a can be found by analyzing the functions of Figure 2b. When formants are modeled, the horizontal axis represents the normalized time and the vertical axis the formant frequency in Hz (the Legendre coefficients are much larger when modeling formant tracks).

a. The first 5 Legendre polynomials, L0-L4. The polynomials are drawn with different legendre coefficients P_i (i.e. size):
1∗L0, −0.5∗L1, −0.5∗L2, −0.25∗L3, and −0.25∗L4

b. Tracks constructed by adding the polynomials 1∗L0 −0.5∗L1 −0.25∗L3 (top) and 1∗L0 −0.5∗L2 −0.25∗L4 (bottom), i.e. the Legendre coefficients in Figure 2b are the same as in Figure 2a.

Table 5. Mean percentage (%) of formant track variance around the mean formant frequency (i.e. excluding the zero order Legendre coefficient)

order		ɛ	ɑ	a:	i·	o:	ə	u·	y·
1	F_1	39	31	25	51	40	58	47	37
	F_2	51	67	62	38	47	56	60	82
2	F_1	54	61	66	21	29	32	18	37
	F_2	32	17	23	42	32	26	31	10
3	F_1	3	5	4	15	17	6	14	14
	F_2	9	8	7	7	10	9	4	3
4	F_1	2	2	2	6	5	3	9	6
	F_2	4	3	4	5	7	5	3	2
R	F_1	2	2	3	7	9	1	12	6
	F_2	4	5	5	7	5	4	2	3

Note: Order 1–4, rows: explained by the higher order Legendre polynomials, columns: for each vowel. In the last row (marked "R") the mean percentage of the remaining (i.e. not explained) variance is given. Vowel realizations from both speaking rates are pooled.

of zero order are much larger than the mean coefficients of the other orders. The mean second order coefficients are often much larger than the mean first order coefficients. Mostly, the mean first order coefficients are around zero, and in only a few cases are they statistically significant different from zero (7 out of 32 values at level 0.1 percent).

From Tables 5 and 6 we can see that the mean size of the coefficients of the first order Legendre polynomial is rather small (Table 6) and its importance for explaining the shape of the track is rather large (Table 5). This can be explained by assuming that the actual size of the contribution of the first order polynomial in each individual vowel realization is generally large, but that the Legendre coefficient can be both positive and negative in every vowel, averaging out the mean coefficient value to almost zero.

Table 6. Mean values of Legendre polynomial coefficients for the first three orders (0–2, rows)

FIRST FORMANT (F_1)

order		ε	ɑ	aː	i·	oː	ə	u·	y·
0	N	**499**	**544**	**573**	**319**	**410**	**400**	**366**	**327**
	F	**520**	**567**	**595**	**334**	**430**	**423**	**373**	**343**
1	N	**-33**	-21	**-24**	**-12.2**	**-14**	-32	-11	13
	F	-9.3	-15	-10	-10.5	-10.4	-33	-26	5.3
2	N	**-77**	**-92**	**-116**	-1.9	-5.8	-28	-3.1	4.6
	F	**-74**	**-86**	**-98**	-4.9	**-15**	**-31**	-9	-5.9

SECOND FORMANT (F_2)

order		ε	ɑ	aː	i·	oː	ə	u·	y·
0	N	**150**	**1146**	**1349**	**1929**	**1009**	**1396**	**960**	**1568**
	F	**150**	**1159**	**1329**	**1892**	**1031**	**1414**	**962**	**1487**
1	N	**-55**	**-51**	-38	-67	-30	-7.4	-35	-157
	F	-35	**-40**	-26	-40	-35	1	1.8	-157
2	N	**-53**	31	-16	**-196**	**132**	-15	**187**	-49
	F	**-49**	11.2	-23	**-162**	**111**	-4	**203**	-0.9

Note: Mean values that are statistically different from zero are printed in bold-face (Student t-test, $p \leq 0.1\%$). Whenever the fast-rate value differs significantly from the normal-rate value, both values are underlined (Student t-test on difference, $p \leq 0.1\%$). For each order, normal-rate values are printed on the top row (N), fast-rate values on the bottom row (F).

For the second order Legendre polynomials it can be seen that the importance of this order for explaining the shape of the track (Table 5) is related to the mean value of the coefficient (Table 6). This means that the value of the coefficient of the second order Legendre polynomial changes systematically with the vowel identity. This can be seen most clearly when the mean values of the second order Legendre polynomial coefficient from Table 6 are plotted, i.e. the second order Legendre coefficient value for the F_2 against the value for the F_1 (Figure 3).

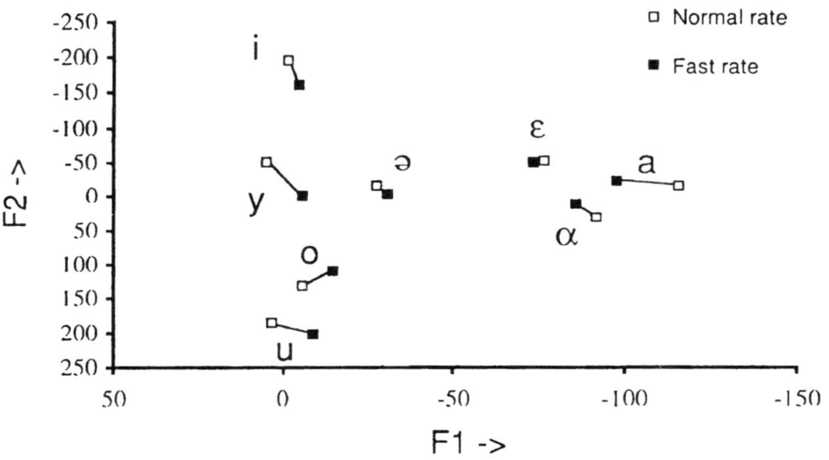

Figure 3. Vowel space constructed by plotting mean second order Legendre polynomial coefficient values for the F_2 against the mean values for the F_1 (Note the reversed axes)
Open squares: Normal speaking rate values
Closed squares: Fast speaking rate values

The vowels occupy an area that is almost identical to the vowel triangle as is shown in Figure 1, which is based on the mean formant values (i.e., comparable to zero order Legendre coefficient values). The ordering of the vowels in the F_1/F_2 plane in Figure 3 is identical to that of a normal vowel triangle (e.g. Figure 1), apart from an obvious sign inversion. The only difference is the variance of the values within each vowel, the variance is much larger with second order coefficients than with mean values (not shown) and the shape of the area occupied by the vowels which does resemble a T more than a triangle. The bars of the T lie at zero value coefficients for both formants. This T-shaped vowel space indicates that, generally, only one of both formant tracks has a strong second order component, the other track shows at most a shallow deviation from a straight line.

Figure 3 suggests that the second order coefficient could be interpreted as a measure of openness in the F_1 direction (closed has value zero, e.g. the vowels /uˑ, yˑ, iˑ/) and as a measure of front- versus back-articulation in the F_2 direction (schwa has value zero, /uˑ/ is positive and /iˑ/ is negative). Figure 3 and Table 5 suggest that the second order coefficient could be an important clue on the relation between vowel identity and formant track shape dynamics.

3.3.3. *Effects of speaking rate and duration*

The differences between Legendre coefficient values of vowel realizations spoken at fast rate and at normal rate are only sizable (and statistically significant, level 0.1 percent) for the zero order coefficient (Table 6). The change in the zero order coefficient values due to the change in speaking rate is the same as found before (section 2). This is to be expected because the zero order coefficient value is identical to the mean formant value. A change in speaking rate only results in a statistically significant difference (level 0.1 percent) in first order coefficients for the F_1 of the vowel /ε/. For the second order coefficient, statistically significant differences are found only for the F_1 of the vowel /a:/ and the F_2 of the vowel /ɑ/.

The relation between coefficient value and duration can also be studied by measuring the correlation between duration and coefficient value. The correlation between Legendre coefficient values and vowel duration must be compared with the amount of systematic variation in Legendre coefficient value (i.e. some kind of maximum correlation). The systematic variation can be estimated by calculating the correlation between coefficient values from corresponding vowel realizations uttered at different speaking rates (Table 7). These correlation coefficients indicate what part of the variance in the coefficient values can be explained by the context of the realization, because the context is the same in both readings of the text. From Table 7 we see that the correlation coefficients between speaking rates are 0.5 or more for most vowels, which means that 25 percent or more of the variance in most vowels is systematic.

Vowel duration also correlates strongly between speaking rates (see section 2). It can therefore be predicted that the correlation between Legendre polynomial coefficients and vowel durations at least should rival the correlation coefficients shown in Table 7 if vowel duration is a strong determinant of formant track shape. In Table 8 we can see that quite the opposite is true. The correlations between Legendre coefficient values and vowel durations are much weaker than the correlations between speaking rates. The correlation coefficients between speaking rates for the F_2 Legendre coefficients are often over 0.7 (i.e. explaining 50 percent or more of the variance).

Table 7. Linear correlation coefficients between the Legendre coefficient values of corresponding vowel realizations uttered at fast and at normal speaking rate (i.e. pair-wise correlation)

order		ɛ	ɑ	a:	i·	o·	ə	u·	y·
0	F_1	$\underline{0.62}$	$\underline{0.86}$	$\underline{0.71}$	$\underline{0.57}$	$\underline{0.85}$	0.55	0.04	0.73
	F_2	$\underline{0.87}$	$\underline{0.91}$	$\underline{0.85}$	0.32	$\underline{0.87}$	$\underline{0.95}$	0.73	$\underline{0.84}$
1	F_1	$\underline{0.47}$	$\underline{0.67}$	$\underline{0.59}$	$\underline{0.69}$	$\underline{0.69}$	0.36	$\underline{0.75}$	0.62
	F_2	$\underline{0.76}$	$\underline{0.86}$	$\underline{0.85}$	$\underline{0.50}$	$\underline{0.78}$	$\underline{0.83}$	$\underline{0.86}$	$\underline{0.88}$
2	F_1	$\underline{0.47}$	$\underline{0.46}$	$\underline{0.55}$	$\underline{0.46}$	$\underline{0.70}$	0.40	0.26	0.54
	F_2	$\underline{0.54}$	$\underline{0.68}$	$\underline{0.67}$	0.25	$\underline{0.76}$	0.19	0.73	0.72

Note: Coefficients for which the correlations are statistically significant are underlined (at level 0.1%).

Table 8. Linear correlation coefficients between the Legendre coefficient values and the duration of vowel realizations

order		ɛ	ɑ	a:	i·	o:	ə	u·	y·
0	F_1	0.19	0.23	$\underline{0.37}$	-0.11	0.18	-0.15	-0.08	0.62
	F_2	-0.23	-0.27	0.09	0.04	-0.14	0.25	-0.12	0.62
1	F_1	0.18	$\underline{-0.32}$	-0.11	-0.24	-0.21	-0.29	0.19	0.40
	F_2	-0.16	-0.21	0.01	0.12	0.14	-0.24	-0.14	-0.42
2	F_1	$\underline{-0.48}$	$\underline{-0.43}$	$\underline{-0.52}$	0.02	-0.14	-0.53	0.17	0.11
	F_2	-0.04	0.26	-0.06	-0.24	-0.02	0.19	0.61	-0.58

Note: Only fast rate realizations are used, the correlations are somewhat weaker for normal rate realizations. Coefficients for which the correlations are statistically significant (at level 0.1%) are underlined.

In contrast, the correlation coefficients between Legendre coefficient values and duration for the F_2 are all smaller than 0.7 for all vowels and none of them is statistically significant (level 0.1 percent).

There is an exception to this low correlation between Legendre coefficient value and vowel duration. The second order Legendre coefficient values of the F_1 of the high F_1-target vowels /ɛ, ɑ, a:/ are correlated with vowel duration (Table 8) with a strength that is comparable to the correlation between speaking rates (Table 7). For this second order polynomial, duration could be a determinant of vowel shape. The correlation is directed in such a way as to make formant tracks of shorter vowel realizations more level (after time normalization). So for the F_1 there could be an influence of vowel duration on vowel track shape that makes shorter vowel realizations more level than longer vowel realizations. However, the size of the effect is minimal, it explains only a quarter of the variance or less.

3.4. Conclusions

A quantitative comparison of the shapes of vowel formant tracks of vowel realizations from fast-rate and normal-rate speech, does not show differences that are in accordance with target-undershoot models of articulation. The only change found is the same as was found in section 2, a uniformly higher F_1 frequency in fast-rate speech, independent of vowel identity.

Within each individual speaking rate we could find a small effect of vowel duration on the second order Legendre coefficient (i.e. the parabolic component) of the first formant. This effect indicates that shorter vowel realizations have somewhat more level formant tracks when speaking rate is constant.

4. General conclusions

With the limitations that only one speaker was used who read aloud a single text, the conclusion must be drawn that the only confirmed effect of a high speaking rate on the spectral structure of vowels is a uniformly higher frequency of the first formant. Our study does not find any difference between vowels uttered at different speaking rates (once the data are time normalized) that in any way confirms theories of vowel articulation that are based principally on vowel duration. From these results we can now answer the question stated in the title: how does speaking rate influence vowel formant shape? When speaking faster, our speaker completely compensates for the shortening of the available time for pronunciation by articulating faster. This means that the time normalized formant track shape is independent of speaking rate.

Acknowledgments

The authors wish to thank A.C.M. Rietveld of the Catholic University of Nijmegen for performing the sentence accent labeling of the speech material and D.R. van Bergem of the University of Amsterdam for providing the method for measuring vowel formant values at near stationary positions of the realizations. We also thank J. Stam for her work in the pilot phase of this project. The text used was selected by W. Eefting of Utrecht University, and the speech was recorded by her and J. Terken of the Institute for Perception Research, Eindhoven.

From data to rules: A background survey

Louis F. M. ten Bosch

Abstract

This chapter presents a description of the approach followed and results obtained in a research project that aimed at the automatic extraction of allophone rules from diphone sets.

1. Introduction

From speech perception experiments, it is well-known that the proper modeling of speech *transients* is crucial for the perceptual quality of synthetic speech. Transients, which correspond to the dynamic spectral events in the speech signal, result mainly from coarticulatory processes. Their exact realizations are determined by a number of factors, such as phonetic context, speaker identity, speaking rate, and speaking style. If we aim at speech synthesis representing one speaker and one speaking style, the transients are determined by context and speaking rate and they can be modeled by a proper, possibly very extensive collection of context-dependent rules. In principle, these rules can be found by analyses of natural speech. Unfortunately, this is not a trivial task. As is well known, Dennis Klatt spent more than 15 years in producing his version of Klatt-talk (which is now commercially available as DEC-talk). In order to cope with the problem of modeling transients, different approaches have been devised, of which *diphone synthesis* and *allophone synthesis* represent two important lines of research.

Diphone synthesis. Diphone speech synthesis employs a database containing many specific speech transients ("diphones"). Broadly speaking, a diphone is a small segment of the speech signal starting at the phonetic "midpoint" of a phoneme and extending to the "midpoint" of the next phoneme. Speech synthesis by means of diphones is a matter of concatenation of appropriate diphones, in combination with an appropriate prosodic structure. Diphones are usually excerpted from carefully realized utterances. The intelligibility of diphone synthesis can approximate the intelligibility of natural speech. For Dutch, diphone speech synthesis is employed at the Institute for Perception Research (IPO) in Eindhoven (cf. Elsendoorn—'t

Hart 1982). Instead of diphones, longer speech segments, such as syllables or demi-syllables, and shorter segments, such as sub-phonemic speech units, can be used as well (cf. Olive 1990). Obviously, these implementations differ with respect to memory requirements and synthesis flexibility.

Allophone synthesis. Allophone synthesis is based upon *rules*, rather than a database. In principle, rule-based synthesis can sound very intelligible and natural: DEC-talk provides a good example. A significant advantage of rule-based synthesis over diphone synthesis is the parametric freedom of the resulting speech output. A disadvantage is that the search for rules is a tedious task: rules often result from a trial-and-error process. Examples of allophone synthesis are provided by e.g. the Dutch SPIN/ASSP-project ALSYS, carried out at the Catholic University of Nijmegen (cf. Loman—Kerkhoff—Boves 1989; Loman—Boves, this volume), by MITalk (for American English, Allen—Hunnicutt—Klatt 1987) and in the Hungarian MULTIVOX-system (Olaszy—Gordos—Nemeth 1990).

ALLODIF was set up as a bridging project between these two approaches to speech synthesis. The question was posed how rule improvement (carried out in the allophone synthesis project) might be helped by careful analyses of the diphone set (developed at IPO, Eindhoven). The concrete problem became, how to extract allophone rules from diphone data in a (semi)automatic way. "Semiautomatic" means that an algorithm yields a solution for an optimization problem in which the search strategy is supervised interactively by an expert.

The main result of the project ALLODIF can be formulated as follows. The rule extraction problem is solvable; however, the search for a solution might be cpu-time-consuming and there are some methodological restrictions:

I. We have to define the *rule format* in advance.
II. We must consider the problem of the *perceptual relevance* of rules.

Additionally, we face the problem of the *different characteristics* of the Nijmegen and Eindhoven synthesizers. One of the differences is that the allophone synthesizer is able to handle specifications of spectral zeros. Zeros are absent in the diphone parameter descriptions.

In order to be able to relate the data on the one hand and rules on the other, we first consider the available diphone data set and the Nijmegen rule set (next section). After that, we discuss the rule-extraction problem.

2. The diphone data set and the allophone rule set

2.1. The data set

The Eindhoven diphone set used for rule extraction purposes contains about 1500 diphones. These diphones were segmented from stressed syllables in utterances spoken by the Dutch speaker HZ (see van Bezooijen—Pols, this volume). A diphone is characterized by the behavior over time of a specific set of speech parameters, which are stored in *frames* and updated every 10 ms. The twelve most important parameters are the first five formant frequencies, the corresponding bandwidths, the overall energy, and a parameter indicating voicing. In the sequel, we will concentrate on these parameters. Other parameters, of secondary importance for us, determine e.g. the pre-emphasis and the frame duration (cf. Elsendoorn—'t Hart 1982).

Allophone rules that are constructed to "simulate" diphone data must prescribe the behavior of all these parameters over time. It is not necessary to code all spurious details in parameter tracks: perceptually irrelevant details can be omitted in this simulation.

2.2. The rule set

Since we aim to construct a tool for the allophone rule development, we now consider the Nijmegen rule set in some detail. For us, the essential feature of an allophone rule is its capability of transforming ("mapping") a linear input symbol string into a context-dependent list of target values for synthesis parameters. The rules are sequentially ordered in one file. This rule file contains about 2,000 lines.

A *rule* consists of a focus specification, a context specification and an "action" (often a numerical assignment). Rules make use of a format that was introduced in linguistic research in *The Sound Pattern of English* (Chomsky—Halle 1968). Here we show a rule concerning the labial /m/:

```
m  ⇒  1 FORM1        := 130 / {y·/œ/u·/ə} [nonseg]0 ---
m  ⇒  2 EQFORM2      := -1
        FORM2       -:= 200 / {ɸ/ɑ/ɔ/a:/o:} [nonseg]0 ---
m  ⇒  3 EQFORM2      := -1
        FORM2       -:= 50
        FORM3        := 2100 / u· [nonseg]0 ---
m  ⇒  1 FORM3        := 2100 / ə [nonseg]0 ---
```

/m/ before the assignment symbol '⇒' is in the focus position. After '⇒', an integer denotes the number of numerical assignments to come. Between the focus and '/' the action (numerical assignment) is specified. After '/', the context is given in some format. (The precise format is not relevant for our present exposition.) Since the Nijmegen rule set has as its input a *linear* symbol string, the context specification is enriched by non-segmental, higher level information. In the example, the symbol [nonseg] denotes the set of all non-segmental symbols.

The Nijmegen rule set contains four types of numerical assignments.

Type 1. An assignment may have the simple form F_1:= 130. This means that, if the rule fits, the target value of the first frequency is set to 130 Hz. This action is of the general form $p(\phi) := c$ where ϕ denotes the segment (here /m/), p is a parameter (here F_1) and c is a constant (here 130).

Type 2. In the third line of the example, we observe another type: FORM2 -:= 200, which is equivalent to the assignment $F_2 := F_2$ -200. This rule is of the general form $p(\phi) := p(\phi) + c$, here with $c = -200$.

Type 3. The third type is present in the second line of the example: EQFORM2 := -1 / ... This action sets the F_2 of the current focus (here /m/) to the *table value* of F_2 of the preceding segment. (The value -1 points to the preceding segment. Other values (-2, 1, 2) are possible as well.) All actions of type 3 are of the form $p(\phi_1) := p(\phi_2)$, in which ϕ_1 and ϕ_2 are adjacent or pen-adjacent segments. Here, ϕ_1 = /m/; ϕ_2 depends on the context.

Type 4. The fourth and last type occurs in the following example, regulating the vowels before /h/:

```
[+voc] ⇒  4 SET Z1       = F1
            SET Z3       = F4
            BANDBRZ1 := 2000
            BANDBRZ3 := 2000/ --- [nonseg]0 h
```

The SET command makes the frequencies of the first and third *zeros* Z_1 and Z_3 equal to the *current values* of the first and fourth *formant* frequencies F_1 and F_4. These actions are of the type $p(\phi) := p'(\phi)$, where e.g. $p = Z_1$ and $p' = F_1$, and ϕ vocalic before '[nonseg]0 h'.

We may summarize these types of action as follows:

type of assignment		description	right-hand side
1	$p(\phi)$:= c	simple	
2	$p(\phi)$:= $p(\phi) + c$	simple	current
3	$p(\phi_1)$:= $p(\phi_2)$	between segments	table
4	$p(\phi)$:= $p'(\phi)$	within segments	current

Type 1 actions are simple redefinitions. Of all the 1139 assignments found in the rule set, 611 (about 54 percent) are of type 1, while 349 assignments (31 percent) are of type 2. It is a crucial observation that the assignments of types 1 and 2 turn out to be the easiest to find. This will not be shown here; the reader is referred to ten Bosch (1991) instead. Assignments of the third (111 cases) and fourth types (68 cases) are much more difficult to find.

As the above four action types structurally cover all numerical assignments in the Nijmegen rule set, it is of importance to look for methods to extract them from speech data. In order to be able to do so, we first appropriately preprocess the diphones such that the rules can be derived more easily. This preprocessing method will be discussed in the next section. Next, we will discuss the background of the actual rule extraction method.

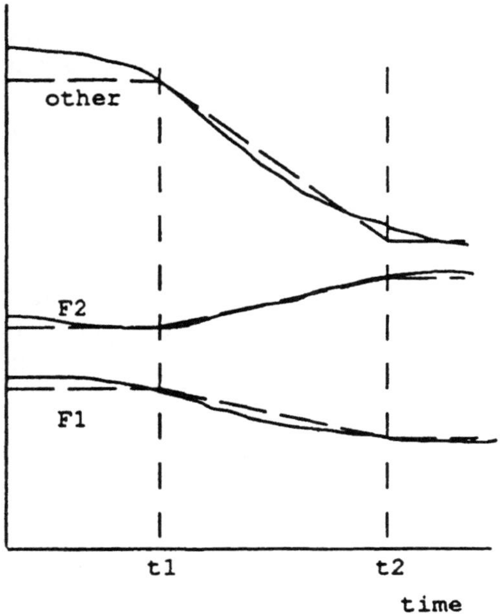

Figure 1. The stylization of a diphone

The full lines represent the original tracks; the dotted lines indicate the stylized version

3. Diphone preprocessing

In order to extract rules from a diphone database, a diphone *stylization* is required to get rid of the data-intrinsic "noise".

Figure 1 shows the principle of diphone stylization. The dotted lines indicate original parameter tracks, solid lines represent the stylized version. Time is plotted along the horizontal axis. The stylization results in parameter tracks such that all spectral parameters F_i and B_i, (i = 1, ..., 5) fulfill the following properties:

— All parameters are either constant or change linearly over time.
— Time intervals during which all parameters are constant may occur diphone-initially and diphone-finally.
— In between, they all move linearly over time.

The stylization allowed us to code each diphone with a set of well-defined parameters, so-called anchor points: parameter target values and three specific time constants. This coding yields an overall reduction of about a factor five compared to the "original" diphones. The anchor points (there are 23 of them) represent a "stylized diphone". They can be used as input for an optimization algorithm. This algorithm looks for relations between those anchor points (that are phonetically specified) and the context, i.e. the diphone "label". We go into detail in the next section. In practice, the algorithm is capable of dealing with *discontinuous* parameter tracks, such as in the case of plosives.

In order to find optimal stylization settings, utterances resulting from concatenation of stylized diphones were informally judged by a panel. From these tests, the conclusion was drawn that better stylization techniques could probably be obtained only if the stylization method is *diphone-specific*. In other words, it is argued that the present stylization is among the best that are valid for all diphones simultaneously. Van Bezooijen (1990) reports that stylized diphone sets perform about 10 percent worse than the original sets in a well-controlled open response segment identification task (see also van Bezooijen—Pols, this volume).

4. Automatic rule extraction

Once we have a stylized diphone set, we are ready to look for relations between the anchor points in the stylized diphones on the one hand, and the diphone label on the other. In this section we will discuss a method to explicitly find these relations. The method that we will propose will be referred to as the Eindhoven-Nijmegen method (or EN-method for short). Other methods will be mentioned in section 4.2 (see also ten Bosch 1991).

All rules we encountered so far have the form

$$\text{if } C \text{ then } A$$

where C and A denote the context specification (including focus specification) and the action, respectively. The context specification yields a unique condition for the application of the rule.

Our method is based on the idea that rules of the form 'if C then A' can be translated to a *condition-free* rule consisting of an action 'A_2' only. In the latter case, the action A_2 is more elaborate, more "compound" than is the action A. The action A_2 in the new rule combines the condition C *and* the action A that were present in the old rule. Conversely, a condition-free rule with complicated action A_2 can be translated into a rule of the form 'if C then A'. Since this latter rule has a format close to the format of the Nijmegen rules, it is called "phonological". The compound version A_2 will be called "numerical".

The EN-method consists of two steps:

I. a translation from phonological rules to numerical rules and vice versa;

II. the algorithmic search for numerical rules in a database.

The line of thought is as follows. Assume we want to govern by rule some phonetic parameter, say F_1. By means of the algorithm in the second step, we look for numerical F_1-rules that are valid for the whole database or an appropriate subbase that is as large as possible. Once such a rule is found, we use the first step to translate the numerical F_1-rule into a phonological F_1-rule, and we insert the discovered rule into a rule set. And conversely, once we have found a phonological rule, we can use the first step to transform it into a numerical rule.

In section 4.1, we will deal with the first step. We only consider a simple example; for more details we refer to ten Bosch (1990). The second step will be discussed in section 4.2.

4.1. Conversion from phonological rules to numerical rules and vice versa

In this section, we give an example of the relation between phonological and numerical rules. Suppose we have a rule:

if focus = [a] and the syllable is unstressed then $F_1 := 650$
if focus = [a] and the syllable is stressed then $F_1 := 700$

This rule has a "numerical" variant:

if F_a(focus) then $F_1 := 650 + 50$ [stress](syll)

or, explicitly,

(1)
$$\begin{aligned} F_1 &:= (650 + 50\,[\text{stress}](\text{syll})) * F_a(\text{focus}) \\ &= 650 * F_a(\text{focus}) + \\ &\quad 50 * [\text{stress}](\text{syll}) * F_a(\text{focus}) \end{aligned}$$

Here we formulated '[stress]' as a predicate with 'syll' as its argument. In this example, [stress] is a binary-valued function. The binary-valued predicate 'F_a' has 'focus' as its argument (cf. ten Bosch 1991).

By this type of conversion, most phonological rules can be translated into their numerical variants, and vice versa. There exists a trade-off between context specification and action specification in the rules. In the rule we started with, the context specification is rather elaborate ('focus must be [a]', 'syllable must be stressed or unstressed') while the action is very simple: F_1:= 650 or F_1:= 700. In the latter rule, we do not have *any* context specification, but the action is rather elaborate. Schematically, there is a balance between actions and contexts:

phonological rule		numerical variant
context } action }	⇔	action

On the strength of this relation, we can reduce the problem to the search for numerical rules. In the next section, we discuss how to find such "numerical" rules in a semi-automatic way.

4.2. Algorithmic search for numerical rules on a database

The method that we developed to solve the rule-extraction problem is based upon interpretation of the solution of a minimization problem, and it makes use of a matrix formalism (ten Bosch 1989, 1990). Our method is not the only possible one to extract numerical information from databases. Other methods include: cluster analysis (CA), the CART-method, discriminant analysis (DA), the covariance method (COV), and neural network approaches (NN). Our method is a kind of combination of the CART-method and discriminant-analysis. In ten Bosch (1991) we discuss the specific differences between these methods.

The second step, viz. the search for numerical rules, requires three substeps:

— (re)arrangement of the data
— algorithmic search for an adequate minimizing expression
— interpretation of the expression obtained.

First substep: rearrangement
The first step involves a representation of the speech database in a tractable way. One possible representation is shown in Table 1.

Table 1. A matrix representation of a speech database

Functions					Parameters	
F_a	...	[stress]	...	...	F_1	...
0	...	0	...	...	510	...
0	...	1	...	...	350	...
1	...	1	...	...	700	...
1	...	1	...	...	700	...
1	...	0	...	...	650	...
⋮						
0	...	0	...	...	405	...

Such a matrix representation is very basic and often used in other methods as well (e.g. in the covariance method by van Santen—Olive 1990). In the matrix presented, we read the values of the F_1 in the F_1-column at the right side. These and similar entries referring to values of phonetic parameters will be denoted by the overall term "parameters". The left-hand side consists of the values of phonological features and other relevant context features; all these linguistic features will be denoted by the general term "functions". We here assume that the data concerning [a] are accurately described by the [a]-rule.

Second substep: algorithmic search

The second step essentially deals with the search for a relation between function values and parameter values. This search is performed by minimization of some numerical expression. In order to extract the above F_1-rule from Table 1, all lines in the table must be considered that contain a '1' in the function column F_a. Two aspects are of importance here: (a) The construction of a specific matrix A by appropriate selection of columns from the left-hand side of Table 1; consequently, the matrix A is not of arbitrary form but is subject to severe restrictions; (b) next, the minimization of a vector norm $\| Ax - b \|$, in which b is a known parameter vector containing the parameters in the F_1-column in the right-hand side, and x is an unknown vector consisting of the coefficients weighing the function values (Golub—van Loan 1983).

The *crucial question* is how to appropriately construct matrix A so as to minimize $\min_x \| Ax - b \|$ for a given data table.

With respect to our example, we come to an essential observation: *If* A contains at least the three columns F_a, [stress] and their column product, *then* the expression $\| Ax - b \|$ can be minimized towards zero. In other words, in that case we have found a matrix A such that $\min_x \| Ax - b \|$ is minimized; no other matrix A will outperform this result.

If a minimizing A is found, the expansion of Ax yields an approximation of phonetic parameters in terms of phonological functions of the following polynomial form:

$$(2) \quad p := \overbrace{a_0}^{\text{constant}} + \overbrace{a_i[\text{fun}]_i + \ldots}^{\text{linear terms}} + \overbrace{a_{ij}[\text{fun}]_i\,[\text{fun}]_j + \ldots}^{\text{quadratic terms}} + \ldots$$

where p and [fun] denote a parameter from the vector b, and a function value, respectively.

Third substep: interpretation

The algorithm searches for the matrix A such that there exists a vector x such that Ax optimally approximates b. By relaxing constraints on A, the expansion of Ax will in general yield a better approximation to b. However, relaxation does not necessarily improve interpretability.

The constant in equation 2 represents the table default value of the parameter p. The linear terms correspond to the correction of the table value by one if-statement, the second order terms correspond to the correction by two compound if-statements, and so on.

In the present algorithm we impose two restrictions on the structure of the matrix A, one dealing with the number of columns and the other dealing with the degree of the columns. For this purpose, two integers M and E

were defined. The number M denotes the maximal number of columns of A; this corresponds to the maximal *length* of the corresponding phonological rule. The second number E denotes the *maximal degree* of columns of A, more precisely, of the entries in those columns. By restricting M and E a priori, we can reduce the search space to a manageable size. The number of columns in the input data matrix (left-hand side of Table 1) is not restricted.

In ten Bosch (1991), a concrete example of the rule extraction is discussed. This example deals with the so-called "l-rule". It was observed that the Nijmegen l-rule, which states that F_3 approximates F_2 up to 200 Hz before round vowels, cannot be traced back in the particular diphone set used. From an optimization point of view, the feature [round], which is chosen in the modification rule in the Nijmegen set as a prime context specifier, cannot be found either. The data in the diphone set, however, *can* of course be described by other rules.

We make two observations. Firstly, this suggests that, in general, the Nijmegen-rule set *cannot be improved* by the present rule-extraction approach on the basis of this particular diphone set. Most probably, it cannot be improved directly by any other automatic approach either. Secondly, the rules that result from the present rule-extraction method may yield acceptable output *without* being satisfactorily interpretable in a phonetic way. We return to this point in section 6.

5. Application in rule sets

In the preceding sections, we examined a method to extract rules from a speech database. These rules have to be of a special form, as we have seen above. This form results from the rule derivation by means of matrices. Each approximation Ax to b yields a rule for the phonetic parameter corresponding to b.

In this section, we will consider *rule sets* rather than separate rules. Since the term "rule set" suggests that rules are to be applied without any specified ordering, the term "rule sequence" is to be preferred. However, since the term "set" is widely used, we will here adopt this convention. In the following, "set" is to be interpreted as "sequence".

A rule will be denoted by R_i. We have seen that the rule R_i is decomposable into one parameter setting and a sequence of compound if-statements. A rule set, such as the Nijmegen set, can be represented by an ordered sequence of rules

$$(R_1, R_2, ..., R_k)$$

where R_{i+1} appears "later" than R_i.

The proper construction of such a sequence is not trivial. This statement can be refined in the following manner. The rule set can be provided with a tree-structure, as follows. Rule R_1 is said to be "mother" of rule R_2 if any context fitting R_2 fits R_1; in that case, R_2 is "daughter" of R_1. *Comparable* contexts define mother and daughter. Every rule has a mother, since the *default table* can be interpreted as a collection of the broadest rules which are all sisters. From the view point of rule optimization, a rule sequence is optimal if all sisters have disjoint contexts. In ten Bosch (1992) it is shown how an arbitrary rule set can be transformed to satisfy this condition. A practical drawback is the increasing number of rules in the rule set.

In the present research, we have investigated the optimal theoretic structure of a rule sequence aiming at the transformation from linear symbol strings to actions on phonetic parameters. The Nijmegen rule set does not fully satisfy this optimality condition (ten Bosch 1991).

6. Discussion

In our research we have pointed out what aspects are relevant in order to design algorithms for rule extraction from diphone databases. The following points might be of importance:

— Rule extraction from data is possible, provided that (a) the speech database is sufficiently rich (i.e. contains several versions of allophones in comparable contexts), and (b) the rules have a very strict format.
— (Semi-)automatic extraction of a rule *sequence* is possible if the sequence is structured along trees with conditions on the motherdaughter and sister-sister context specifications.
— The algorithm to find rules is cpu-time consuming but is capable of extracting "phonological rules".[1]
— A fast rule *interpreter* is required to optimize the rules perceptually and interactively.[2]

Some questions, however, remain to be answered:

— What can we say about the *convergence* of a derived rule set towards the Nijmegen rule set? In other words, under what circumstances are the rules in the Nijmegen set the concrete outcome of any numerical algorithm? The development of such an algorithm will be a difficult task. Firstly, as we observed, the structure of the Nijmegen set does not precisely fulfill the specifications under which a (semi)automatic rule optimization is possible. Secondly, it is not clear in what sense the Nijmegen rule set is unique given its rule format. In other words: given the format of the Nijmegen synthesizer, a *lot of* rule sets may produce perceptually identical acoustic output, and there is no simple criterion to decide which of the rule sets is to be preferred over alternative sets.

Notes

1. This may be of importance when rule extraction methods are compared to the neural network approach.
2. Recently, a dedicated rule interpreter has been implemented at IPO.

Collecting data for a speech database

Ellen van Zanten—Laurens Damen—Els van Houten

Abstract

This chapter reports on the collecting and storing of speech data in a database. To this end, running speech was described on a linguistic and on a phonetic level as well as orthographically and acoustically. Some of the problems which were encountered during the phonetic labeling process are mentioned, and discrepancies between the original phonetic transcription by ear and the corresponding labeled segments are discussed.

1. Introduction

The aim of the ASSP Speech Database Project was to create a database containing linguistic, phonetic and acoustic descriptions of texts read aloud by one speaker. The emphasis was on segmenting the acoustic signal into discrete segments, in order to acquire data which could be used in research on duration.

Speech researchers in many different countries feel the need for collecting phonetically labeled speech material and storing this in acoustic-phonetic databases. Apart from acoustic-phonetic information, such databases may also contain information concerning phrase structure, stress position and other linguistic information. The type of information that is included in a database depends on the specific purpose the database is going to be used for (Hendriks—Boves 1988).

Within ASSP, the need was felt for a database with speech material that could be used in research on the relation between linguistic, especially prosodic, structures and phonetic realizations. Such a database will have to contain information on prosody in running speech. In particular, it will be aimed at research on duration rules in running speech and on sentence phonology, assimilation, reduction, and so on. To serve these purposes, the database will contain sentences spoken as part of a larger text. To be able to compare the labeled speech material with the data of several ASSP research projects, the speech material was restricted to texts read by ASSP's designated speaker, PB.

Section 2 of this paper gives some information on the structure of the database environment that was used. Section 3 reports on the data collecting and storing. Section 4 contains some concluding remarks.

2. The framework

Most linguistic-phonetic studies in the past were based on disparate sets of speech utterances, thus impairing the possibility to compare the results and consequently slowing down the progress of knowledge on speech processes. It is hoped that such problems can be overcome in the future by the use of more comprehensive speech databases which contain linguistic, phonetic and acoustic descriptions of speech utterances. These databases will serve to facilitate the comparison and integration of the results of studies hitherto incompatible (Hendriks—Boves 1988).

Our speech data were stored in the acoustic-phonetic database environment called DEMSI (Database Environment for the Manipulation of Speech related Information); for the structure of DEMSI we refer to Hendriks—Boves (1988) and Hendriks—Houben (1988). DEMSI is considered adequate for the management of data which are relevant for the ASSP research projects concerned. In the future, all data which are now stored in DEMSI may be transferred to the more powerful database system which is being developed at the Speech Processing Expertise Centre SPEX (Hendriks—Boves—Swagten—Lagendijk—van der Griendt 1990).

The information within DEMSI can be divided into text-related linguistic information on the one hand and utterance-related acoustic-phonetic information on the other. Text-related information may be derived from the written version of the text and is independent of the speaker actually pronouncing the text. Utterance-related information depends on the actual realization of the text and may itself be subdivided into essentially continuous acoustic data and discrete phonetic data (Hendriks—Houben 1988). The division of the data into the linguistic, phonetic and acoustic areas, is illustrated in Figure 1.

3. Data collecting

The aim of the project was to collect and store data which can shed light on the relation between language structures and phonetic realizations. To achieve this aim, the speech material had to be described on a linguistic and on a phonetic level. Furthermore, it had to be stored acoustically and orthographically.

The speech material was selected from written texts read at normal speed by PB, a highly experienced professional reader (see further van Son—Pols, this volume). The texts (approximating one hour of speech; 11,000 words) were recorded at the Institute for Perception Research, Eindhoven, under the supervision of J. Terken in 1987. They consisted of newspaper articles

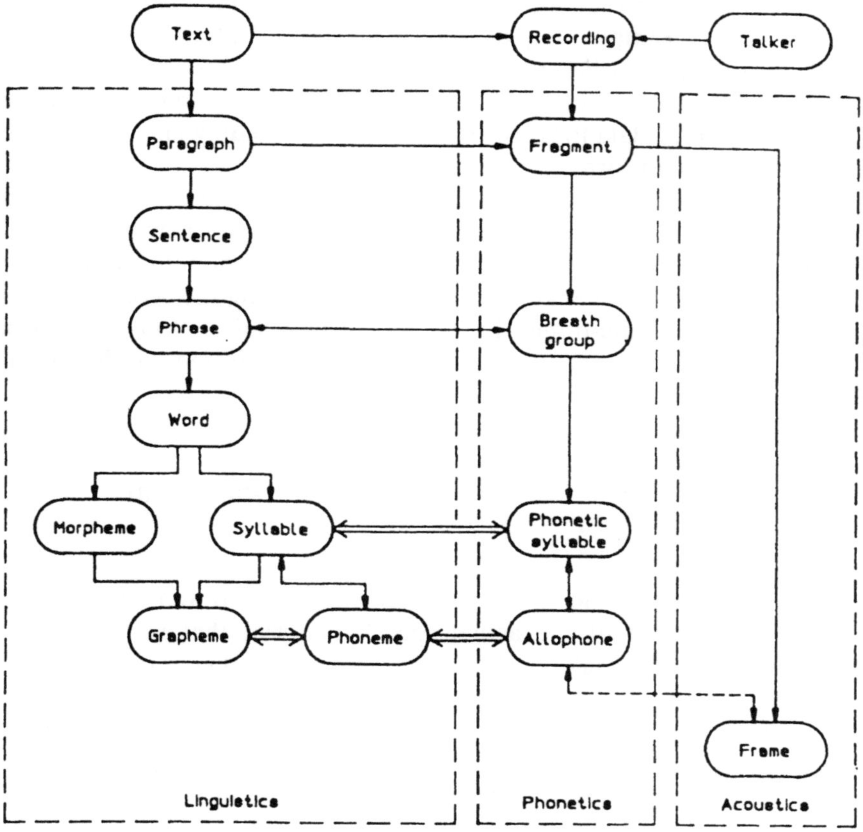

Figure 1. The structure of the database (Hendriks—Houben 1988)

articles and bulletins (Eefting—Nooteboom, this volume; van Son—Pols, this volume; Terken, this volume), and were to be used in several ASSP research projects on prosody. An orthographic representation of all the texts is provided by Bringmann (1990b).

To be able to implement the required information into the database, DEMSI needs to be provided with data pertaining to all tables in the linguistic, phonetic and acoustic areas of Figure 1. Sections 3.1, 3.2 and 3.3 provide some information on the derivation of these data.

3.1. Acoustic information (cf. Figure 1, right-hand part: Acoustics)

The speech material was digitized and stored using a 12 bit analog-to-digital converter with a sample frequency of 10 kHz (LP-filter 4.8 kHz). To facilitate further processing, the material was subsequently converted into sampled data files, each containing one sentence. In the final stage of the project, the sampled data files, as well as the corresponding label files, were concatenated back to form one large file.

The acoustic waveform is not included in the database itself, but a reference to a standard datafile exists, so that the samples may be accessed by the user. In DEMSI, the smallest unit in acoustic-phonetics is called a frame. This is a full set of analysis parameters describing the acoustic signal during a particular time-frame. Frame length is usually 10 ms. Within a sentence, the frames form a quasi-continuous description of the signal (Hendriks—Houben 1988).

3.2. Linguistic information (cf. Figure 1, left-hand part: Linguistics)

The orthography of all the speech material was checked and corrected to make an exact match of the actual speech material that was analyzed, including speaker's mistakes. The orthography was then enriched with linguistic information as required by DEMSI.

Paragraph boundaries were copied from the written texts which had been used in the recording sessions. Sentence, phrase and word boundaries were allocated manually (Bringmann 1990a), as is indicated in Figure 2, 1st and 2nd column.

Word class information was provided by the MORPA lexical classification (Heemskerk—van Heuven, this volume), and the MORPA analysis formed the basis for further linguistic description of the material. The MORPA lexicon supplied us with an automatic morphological decomposition of some 3,000 word types of the material. MORPA's automatic lexical classification was matched with Bringmann's analysis, as this last analysis was based on context. In case of discrepancy between these two analyses, lexical classification and morphological decomposition were checked by hand. This is illustrated in Figure 2, 1st and 4th column (ng: unbound morpheme; lg: left bound morpheme).

Furthermore, MORPA provided an underlying phonemic representation for the set of word types which was mentioned above. From this abstract representation a surface phonemic representation was derived by the

MORPHON program modules for phonemic syllabification, assimilation and main stress allocation (cf. Nunn—van Heuven, this volume). This surface representation was subsequently encoded in (COST) C.P.A., the Computer Phonetic Alphabet which is used in DEMSI (van Erp 1988). This is shown in Figure 2, 3rd column.

Finally, graphemes were mapped onto phonemes, i.e., two or more graphemes which map onto one phoneme were linked with the symbol "+" (Figure 2, 2nd column). All linguistic information was checked by hand before being stored in an orthographic file. Figure 2 contains the enriched orthography of one sentence which can be found in the database.

[zin,phi,pro]	"Ik	"Ik	ng
[vfin]	w"o+u	w"A>u	ng
[pro]	"u	"y	ng
[det]	e+en	@n	ng
[adv]	mis+-sc+h"i+en	mI$sX"in	ng
[adv]	w"at	w"At	ng
[adj]	r"a-r#e	r"a$r@	ng,lg
[noun]	vr"a+ag	vr"aX	ng
[vinf]	v"o+or-#leg+-g#en	v"orlEG@n	ng,ng,lg

Figure 2. The orthography of the sentence *Ik wou u een misschien wat rare vraag voorleggen* 'I would like to put to you a perhaps somewhat queer question', enriched with linguistic information

3.3. Phonetic information (cf. Figure 1, middle part: Phonetics)

No information was collected for the Fragment and Breath group tables. A (phonetic) fragment always corresponds to a single (linguistic) paragraph. It contains, however, references to phonetic entities, while non-speech noises, such as coughs, are disregarded. Similarly, a breath group corresponds to one or more linguistic phrases, and beginning and end of a breath group are determined on the basis of phonetic data.

Of all the speech material which was to be phonetically labeled, a fairly broad phonetic transcription was made by ear by the third author, an experienced transcriber. The narrowness of the transcriptions was defined by the needs of research projects on prosody which may use the database in the future. Vowel length and "weak realization" were indicated, for instance, and so were "inserted" glides and (de)voicing of consonants. The symbols were restricted to the symbols and diacritics of the DEMSI-compatible (COST) C.P.A. (Van Erp 1988).

The acoustic signal of the speech material was segmented into discrete elements which were then labeled with the allophone symbols obtained from the phonetic transcriptions.

Labeling took place with the aid of the computer program SESAM (cf. Broeder 1991), a high resolution waveform editor which provides for manipulation of audio signals and segments. Notwithstanding SESAM's user-friendliness, which provides for easy control and modification of labels, labeling proved to be an arduous task. As a consequence, only approximately 30 minutes of speech material were labeled.

The waveforms of speech are essentially continuous in nature, and co-articulation between adjacent segments makes it often impossible to determine exact boundaries between segments. To guarantee adequate within and between labeler consistency, all three labelers, in the initial stage of the project, independently segmented and labeled one text (11 files). Results were compared, and on the basis of this comparison a number of explicit rules for segmentation and labeling were decided upon. The most important segmentation criteria are summarized below.

— Segment boundaries are determined visually, not by ear.
— The primary criterion for boundary marking is change in amplitude. In those cases where the amplitude changes gradually (or not noticeably), a change in periodic structure determines the boundary.
— If a boundary between two phones is neither marked by a change in amplitude, nor by a change in periodic structure, it is marked halfway the transition between those two phones.
— If determination of a boundary between two segments is impossible, both segments are marked for uncertainty.
— To facilitate future signal processing, segment boundaries are always set at positive zero crossings of the audio signals, the only exception being (final) boundaries of plosive bursts.

Any deviations from the transcriptions during the labeling proces were indicated in the database. In those cases where an element from the transcription was not traceable in the acoustic signal, it was attributed zero duration.

Phonetic syllables are independent of lexical boundaries. Phonetic syllable boundaries were automatically inserted into the label files, in accordance with the maximal legal onset principles for Dutch, with the aid of a phonetic syllabification algorithm. For the purpose of phonetic syllabification, glottal stops were considered as consonants which can only occur immediately before a vowel in first position in a syllable. Syllable boundaries were also placed between any two consecutive vowels. All syllable boundary decisions were checked by hand.

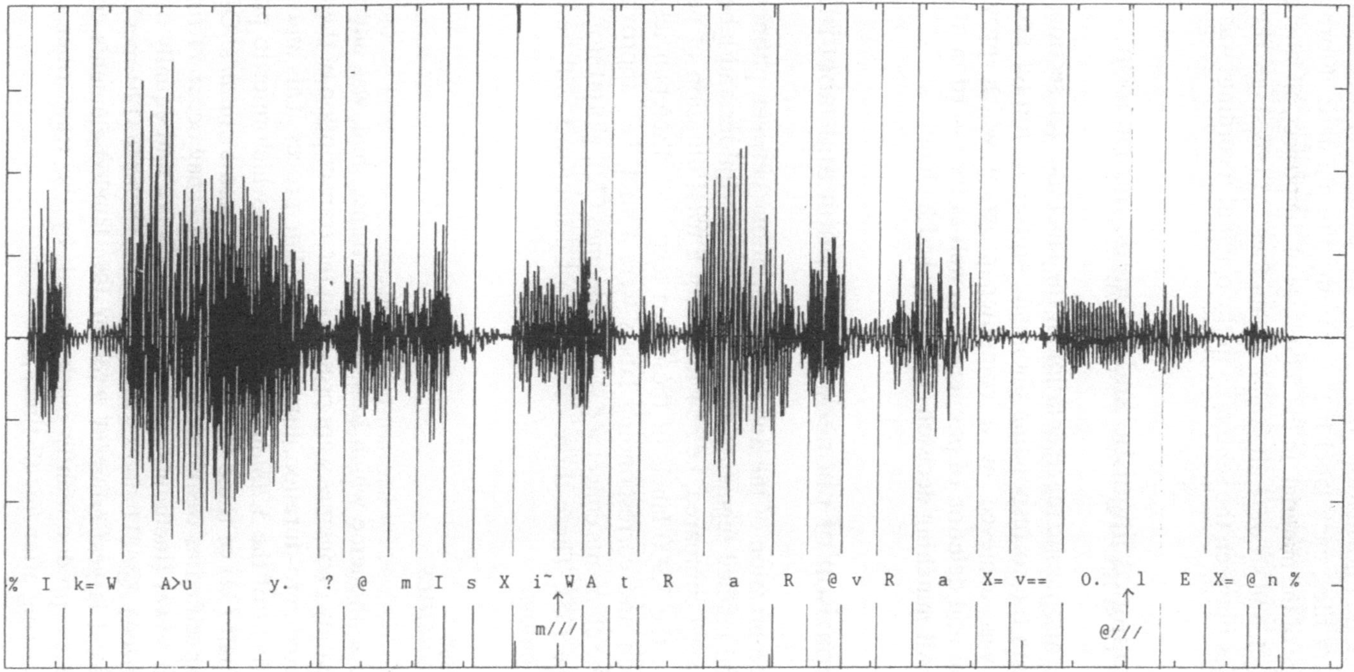

Figure 3. The acoustic signal and the labeled segments of the sentence *Ik wou u een misschien wat rare vraag voorleggen* 'I would like to put to you a perhaps somewhat queer question.'

The phonetic information was initially stored in label files matching the sampled data files, each label file containing the phonetic information on one sentence of the material. In the final stage of the project, all label files were concatenated, and so were all sampled data files. At this stage, the duration of the pauses between the sentences in the original recordings was included.

3.4. Matching of linguistic and phonetic information

Finally, the allophonic representation of the label files (cf. section 3.3), was matched with the corresponding phonemic representation (cf. section 3.2). Matching was achieved by a computer program which provided for assimilation and deletion of phonemes, as well as for insertion of phonetic segments. All matching decisions were checked by hand.

3.5. Comparison of phonetic transcription and label file data

To get an impression of the number of deviations between phonetic transcription and labeled segments, the original transcriptions and label files of two texts were compared, i.e., 54 files with a total duration of nearly five minutes. In the 3,900 labels of these two texts 152 discrepancies between transcription and corresponding labels were found, i.e., approximately 4 percent. The elements concerned were phonemes (72), glottal stops (45) and silent pause (35). These three categories of discrepancy will be discussed separately below.

3.5.1. Phonemes

Only twice a phoneme which had not been transcribed, was added by the labeler. Seventy phonemes were present in the transcription of the two texts but attributed zero-duration during the labeling proces. This amounts to a scant 2 percent of the 3,700 labels in the sample which refer to phonemes.

Nearly half (34) of these "zero-duration" elements are /n/'s. Of these, 8 had been specified as weak in the transcription. They occur 11 times after a nasalized vowel (including nasalized schwa /@/), and equally often after (non-nasalized) /@/ (11 times), and after other vowels (12 times).[1]

The second largest group of zero-duration labeled elements consists of /r/'s: 11 cases, predominantly marked weak by the transcriber (7 times) and/or occurring after /@/ (7 times).

The only vowel phoneme which was present in the transcription but which was attributed zero-duration in the label files is /@/, in words like *werkt* 'works' [wER@/kt] (in IPA: [wɛrəkt) (epenthetic schwa; 8 times, of which 5 specified as weak: /@/).

3.5.2. *Glottal stops*

Glottal stops do not belong to the Dutch phoneme inventory, and our transcriber had already expressed some uncertainty about her ability to detect these elements. Glottal stops may occur at the so-called hiatus position, i.e., the onset of any word or morpheme initial vowel (Jongenburger—van Heuven 1991). Our sample contains 252 hiatus positions. We counted 34 glottal stops in the two texts which were transcribed as well as labeled, and as many as 45 discrepancies between transcription and labeling (nearly 18 percent): twelve times, a glottal stop was present in the transcription but could not be traced in the signal, and 33 elements which were labeled as glottal stop were not present in the original transcription, including one which had been transcribed as a pause; cf. Table 1. The cell "not transcribed, not labeled" in Table 1 therefore includes hiatus deletion by means of coarticulation or otherwise.

Table 1. Frequencies of glottal stop transcription and labeling (54 files)

	transcribed	not transcribed	total
labeled	34	33	67
not labeled	12	173	185
total	46	206	252

The total number of discrepancies (45) is higher than the number of transcribed as well as labeled glottal stops (34) found in the two texts. Therefore, we decided to compare our data with the transcription data of two researchers who had independently analyzed the distribution of the glottal stop in 24 of the 54 files of our sample (Jongenburger—van Heuven 1991). Table 2 presents the glottal stop transcription and label file data for these 24 files.

Table 2. Frequencies of glottal stop transcription and labeling (24 files)

	our transcription			Jongenburger—van Heuven		
	transcr.	not tr.	total	transcr.	not tr.	total
labeled	26	10	36	31	5	36
not labeled	2	84	86	27	59	86
total	28	94	122	58	64	122

The Jongenburger—van Heuven transcription data in this sample are closer to our label file data: 31 as compared to 26 glottal stops transcribed and labeled; only 5 as opposed to 10 glottal stops are absent in the transcription but present in the label files.

The number of glottal stops which were reported by Jongenburger—van Heuven but which were not present in our label files is, however, relatively high (27). An explanation of this discrepancy may be found in the definition of the glottal stop. In our segmentation criteria, glottal stops were defined as "some glottal periods at irregular distances". Only these irregular periods were segmented and labeled; for some examples cf. Figures 4a and 4b.

The aim of Jongenburger—van Heuven, on the other hand, was to define vowel onset rules for text-to-speech systems. To this end, they employed a fairly broad glottal stop definition, including any fast attack following a silent pause, with or without irregular glottal periods. (cf. Figure 5a; for the sake of comparison, Figure 5b presents an example of a smooth vowel onset.) Twenty-two of the 27 transcribed but not labeled pauses occurred after a (long) pause and thus may fall within this category. We may conclude that our glottal stop data should be regarded with some caution.

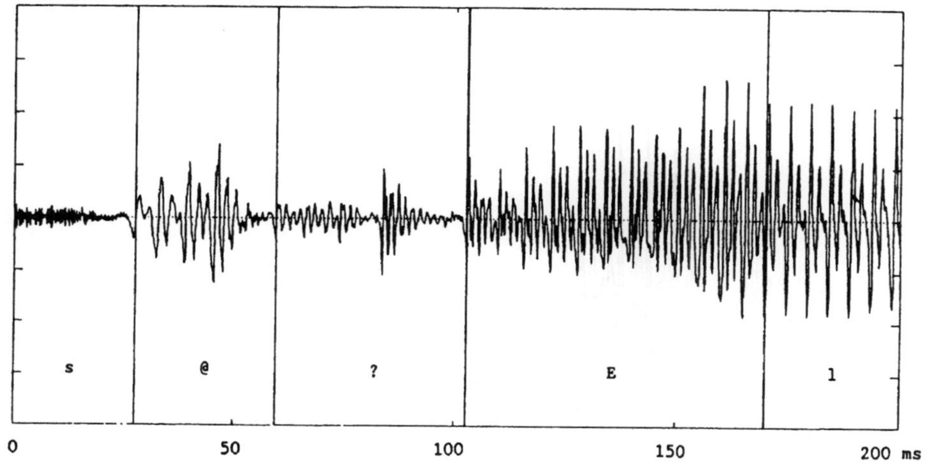

Figure 4a. Glottal stop present in our transcription as well as in the Jongenburger—van Heuven (1991) transcription

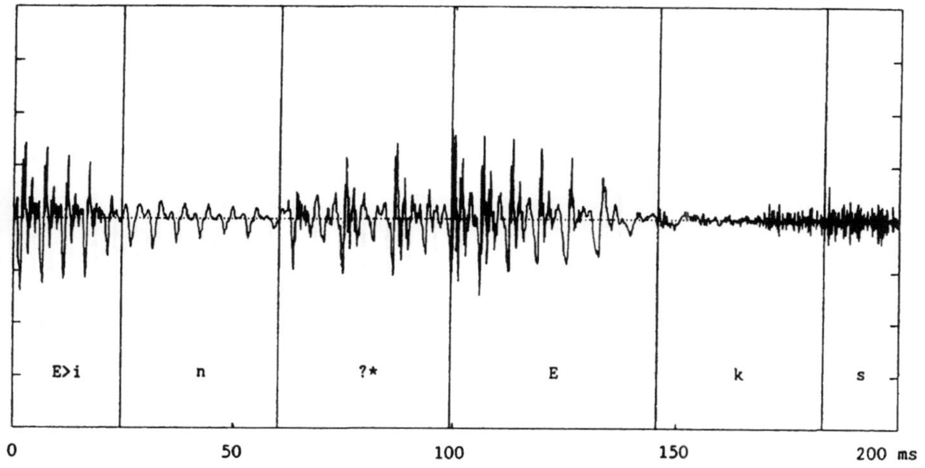

Figure 4b. Glottal stop not present in our transcription, but added by the labeler; present in the Jongenburger—van Heuven (1991) transcription

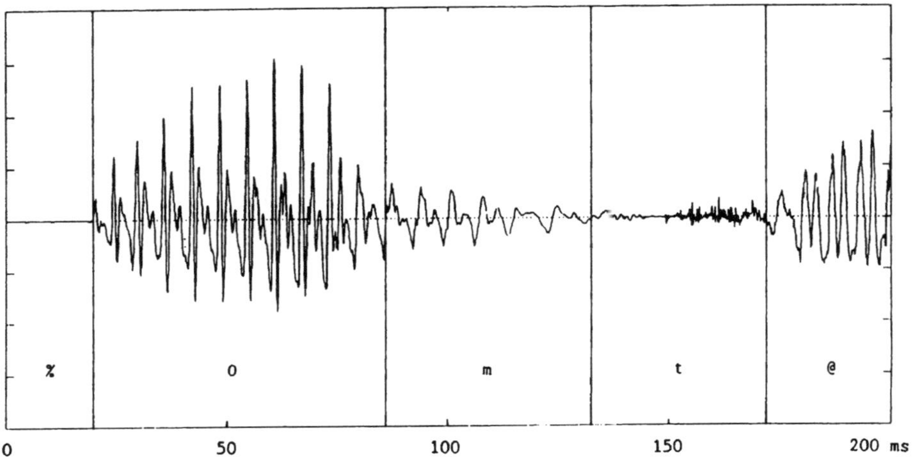

Figure 5a. An example of "fast attack" following silent pause (%); transcribed as glottal stop by Jongenburger—van Heuven (1991); not present in our transcription and labeling

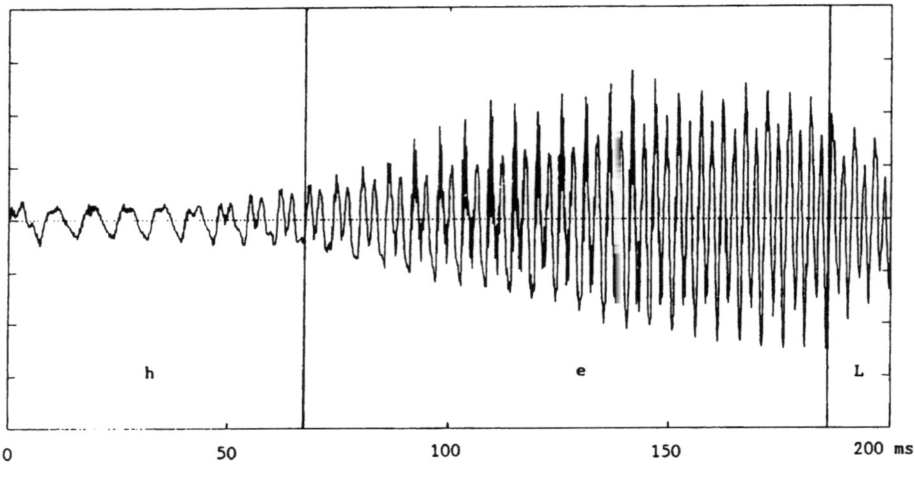

Figure 5b. An example of "smooth" vowel onset

3.5.3. Silent pauses

In our comparison of transcription and labeling, we took into account silent intervals within files only, disregarding between sentence pauses. The sample contained 847 word boundaries, and we were interested to know how many of these potential pause positions were actually filled with silent pauses. We found a total of 101 pauses which were transcribed as well as labeled, and 35 discrepancies, i.e., just over 4 percent. Table 3 presents the frequencies of (potential) silent pause in transcription and label files.

Table 3. Frequencies of silent pause transcription and labeling (54 files; between sentence pauses not included)

	transcribed	not transcribed	total
labeled	101	31	132
not labeled	4	711	715
total	105	742	847

Four transcribed pauses were not traceable in the signal and were accordingly attributed zero duration. These "misperceptions" may have been caused by preceding syllable lengthening (Martin 1970). Not present in the transcription but found in the label files were 31 silent intervals. Five of these had originally been transcribed as glottal stop. A preliminary investigation showed that some of the labeled pauses were very short, and might not be identified with word boundaries. We wished to find out how many of the labeled pauses could be identified with word boundaries.

We also wanted to investigate to what extent there was a relation between pause duration and presence or absence of the pause in the transcription. Bringmann (1991), in her research on the distribution of Dutch reading pauses, defines pause as "an audible interruption of the flow of speech, consisting of a silence of minimally 100 ms." We were interested to see whether the criterion "audible interruption" actually coincided with the "correct" silent pauses of minimally 100 ms in our sample.

Silent intervals of less than 50 ms are usually ignored in the literature on silent pause perception; cf. Martin (1970). But, as pauses of less than 50 ms had occasionally been indicated in the transcription, we decided to look into these extremely short silent intervals. Some researchers assume that pauses of between 50 and 100 ms are used by listeners to parse syntactically ambiguous sentences (Bringmann 1991:7). Thus, we quantisized pause occurrences into the following three durational categories: under 50 ms, 50 to 100 ms, and over 100 ms; cf. Table 4.

Table 4. Frequencies of silent pause transcription and labeling divided into three durational categories (54 files; between sentence pauses not included)

	<50ms	50-100ms	>100ms	total
transcribed and labeled	5	9	87	101
labeled but not transcribed	10	12	9	31

Not surprisingly, Table 4 shows that the shorter the silent pause, the higher the number of discrepancies in the sample. However, no less than 8 of the 96 silent intervals of over 100 ms had not been indicated by the transcriber, one having been originally transcribed as a glottal stop. All of these 96 silent intervals seem to be planned pauses, meant to help the listener to understand the meaning of the sentence.

Three of the five silent pauses shorter than 50 ms which were transcribed and labeled may possibly be interpreted as planned pauses, as for instance in the sentence *Vijf "ja, maars"* 'Five "yes, buts"', with a silent interval of 40 ms between *vijf* and *ja*. The two other pauses in this category, as well as the 10 silent intervals which were not indicated in the transcription, do not seem to have such a significance. Moreover, they all occur immediately before either a glottal stop or a (word or morpheme initial) vowel. Vowel onset following a pause is the most favored position of the glottal stop (Jongenburger—van Heuven 1991). Extending our definition of the glottal stop to include an (optional, short) silent interval as closure time would enable us to relabel at least 12 out of the 15 silent intervals shorter than 50 ms as glottal stop closures. This would, at the same time, reduce the number of silent pause discrepancies.

We found a total of 21 silent intervals of between 50 and 100 ms. As many as 9 of these, all seemingly planned pauses, had been perceived by the transcriber, suggesting that the 100 ms minimum duration for pause definition may be too short.

Twelve silent pauses in the 50-100 ms category had not been transcribed and were added by the labeler. Nine of these may, if we re-define the glottal stop, be identified as glottal stop closures on account of their position. We subtracted these nine pauses from the total of 31 "labeled but not transcribed" pauses of Table 3. We also subtracted the twelve pauses of less than 50 ms which may be seen as glottal stop closures. The remaining 12 labeled but not transcribed pauses are true inter-word pauses. Table 5 presents these 12 pauses set against the total number of word boundaries in the sample. The total number of discrepancies, including the four transcribed pauses which were not traceable in the signal, is now 16, i.e., less than 2 percent of the 847 potential pause positions.

Table 5. Frequency of inter-word silent pause transcription and labeling (54 files; between sentence pauses and intra-word pauses not included)

	transcribed	not transcribed	total
labeled	99	12	111
not labeled	4	732	736
total	103	744	847

3.5.4. Summary of comparison of transcription and label file data

Overall agreement of transcription and label file data in the sample is 96 percent. Agreement as regards phonemes is even higher, viz. 98 percent. Only the detection of the glottal stop and the confusion of glottal stop and (short) silent pause caused some problems in our sample. Future users of the database should be aware of this.

On the basis of our data we conclude that our glottal stop definition should be changed to allow for closure time. Pauses shorter than 100 ms immediately before a glottal stop, as well as pauses shorter than 50 ms immediately before a vowel, may be regarded as glottal stop closures.

Finally, the Jongenburger—van Heuven (1991) glottal stop definition includes any "fast attack" of a vowel following a silent pause of any duration. If this view is correct, "fast attack" should be specified in physical terms, possibly as a rise time of maximally 30 ms (cf. van den Broecke—van Heuven 1983).

4. Concluding remarks

The aim of the Speech Database Project was to create a database with speech material that could be used in research on the relation between linguistic structures and phonetic realizations. It was hoped that the complete set of texts which are used in the ASSP research projects on prosody would be labeled and stored. This would include approximately one hour of speech by ASSP's designated speaker, PB.

All the available texts were linguistically analyzed. The labeling task, however, proved more complicated and, consequently, more time consuming than had been estimated. Consistency in the phonetic description was considered essential for future use of the material. In Section 3.3, some of the difficulties are mentioned which, especially in the initial stages of the project, slowed down the labeling process. As a consequence, only some 30 minutes of speech material were labeled and stored in the database. Overall agreement between phonetic transcription and label file data appears to be good: 96 percent in the analyzed sample. Agreement as regards phonemes is even higher, but for glottal stop and silent pause it is slightly lower.

If extension of the data is considered necessary, it should be investigated to what extent the labeling proces can be automated, using the existing database as a reliable training set for an automatic segmentation algorithm. Automatic segmentation, if sufficiently accurate, would provide a method, using the existing database as a reliable training set for an automatic segmentation algorithm which is both fast and consistent.

Acknowledgements

Many people cooperated in the ASSP Speech Database Project. We specifically acknowledge the support of Daan Broeder, Josée Heemskerk, Vincent van Heuven, Maarten Hijzelendoorn and Jos Pacilly.

Notes

1. In eight instances, a non-nasalized vowel followed by /n/ in the transcription was labeled as a nasalized vowel followed by "/n/-zero". These cases were each counted as one discrepancy.

Part V

Prosody

Accentuation, information value and word duration: Effects on speech production, naturalness and sentence processing

Wieke Eefting—Sieb G. Nooteboom

Abstract

This chapter describes several production and perception experiments that focus on tempo variation in speech. Our basic assumption is that speakers adapt their speech production to the needs of their audience. This is what we call "the adaptation principle". We investigated whether speakers base their tempo variation on the closely related factors INFORMATION VALUE and ACCENTUATION. The results of a production study reveal that speed of articulation is not immediately controlled by information value. However, the measurements of segments and syllables show that the duration changes are not caused by the extra time needed for the realization of the pitch movement invoking accentuation. The results of perception experiments show that tempo variation contributes to the perceived naturalness of speech. Further, correct tempo variation results in faster speech processing than incorrect tempo variation. The results of this study demonstrate that, to a certain extent, speakers indeed adapt their pronunciation to the needs of their audience.

1. Background and aims of the study

In the project "Tempo variation in natural and synthetic speech", we concentrated on the durational variation of speech fragments larger than segments. More specifically, we focused on tempo variation that is assumed to be brought about intentionally by the speaker in order to improve speech communication. This project was geared towards fundamental research. We realized that at the end of the project, we would not yet be able to formulate a set of simple rules that would result in an improvement of the quality of the synthetic speech. The speech in the text-to-speech system that was developed within the framework of the program "Analysis and Synthesis of Speech", would not profit directly from the outcome of this study before the ending of that program. The choice of this outline was based on the state of the art of our knowledge about the (ir-)regularities in tempo changes at levels above the segment, the quality of the synthetic speech, and the manipulation techniques available at the time. Not much was known about the factors on which speakers base the variation in articulation rate, and what is the domain over which tempo remains constant. Further, little was known about the consequences of tempo variation for speech perception. Moreover, variation in tempo with a communicative function will only then pay a valuable contribution to the quality of synthetic speech, when other characteristics like intonation, accent placement, and pause locations are optimal. When the project started, no adequate manipulation techniques were available, which made systematic investigation of the perceptual consequences of changes in duration very difficult. Fortunately, during this project, the quality of synthetic speech improved and new developments in manipulation techniques allowed us to perform several perception experiments about naturalness and processing of correct as opposed to incorrect temporal structure in natural speech. In this paper, we will describe the assumptions and statements that formed the basis of our study. We suggest the existence of a strategy on the part of the speaker to adapt his speech to the needs of the listener. From that point of view, we performed several experiments. Here we will describe to what extent the results of these experiments provide evidence for the existence of such a strategy. Finally, we will draw some conclusions and indicate what is the relevance of this study for more fundamental research, and how the quality of synthetic speech can profit from the insights obtained in this study.

2. The adaptation principle

This study is based on the assumption that speakers speak in order to be understood. For this purpose, a speaker continuously adapts his pronunciation to the estimated needs of his audience. When speaking to a big audience, he has to speak louder and more clearly than when speaking to a single person sitting next to him in a quiet room, in order to be understood. Similarly, when speaking through a bad and noisy telephone line, he has to speak more slowly and articulate more carefully than when the transmission line is quiet.

The precise ways in which such listener oriented behavior of speakers affects the global characteristics of speech, such as overall loudness, speech rate, pitch level and articulatory precision, would constitute an interesting domain of acoustic-phonetic research. However, in the present study we are not so much interested in the global characteristics of speech.

It is quite conceivable that speakers do not only adapt the global characteristics of their speech to the estimated needs of their audience, but also adapt more local properties of speech. For example, if a particular word in a sentence is very important for the communication, and is not easily predictable from the preceding context, the speaker may well pronounce this word more slowly and more carefully than other words in the same sentence that are less relevant and/or more predictable.

This situation differs markedly from the earlier examples, because here the speaker can estimate the needs of his audience at least partly from the properties of the message itself. The extent to which a particular sound, syllable, word, or group of words is predictable from the context, can be estimated by the speaker in an on-line fashion from what he himself is saying. For this purpose, he may ignore all aspects of the communicative situation other than the general assumption that he shares with his audience knowledge of the language and of the universe of discourse.

In a text-to-speech system, in which synthetic speech is used for the acoustic realization of written text, global characteristics such as playback volume and overall speech rate can be adapted relatively easily. However, modification of local characteristics is not so straightforward. It is unclear what characteristics should be adjusted and by what factors these adjustments are caused. In the present study, we made a start with the investigation of this matter. We examined variation in temporal structure as a result of the information value of the fragments, based on the statement with which we opened this paper.

Against this background we can now rephrase the principle of listener adapted pronunciation as follows: Local speech rate and carefulness of articulation are controlled by the extent to which the units to be pronounced are predictable from context. In what follows we will explore some consequences of this hypothesis. Several experiments that we performed in order to gain evidence in favor of this assumption will be described.

3. Time compression at the word level

A monosyllabic word like English *pat* contains little lexical redundancy. Each of its constituting phonemes is not fully predictable from the other ones. This is different for a polysyllabic word like *hippopotamus*, which is highly redundant, in the sense that the word remains recognizable even when a few of its constituting phonemes are completely missing.

From a listener's point of view this means that the word *hippopotamus* remains recognizable when it is rapidly and sloppily pronounced, whereas the word *pat* can only be recognized correctly when it is pronounced carefully, and therefore, we assume, more slowly, such that all three phonemes are identifiable.

In general, lexical redundancy increases with word length. Therefore the need for slow and careful articulation decreases with increasing word length. From this we may predict that speed of articulation increases with increasing word length. Figure 1 shows some data corroborating this prediction. Average duration per phoneme is plotted as a function of word length in number of phonemes.

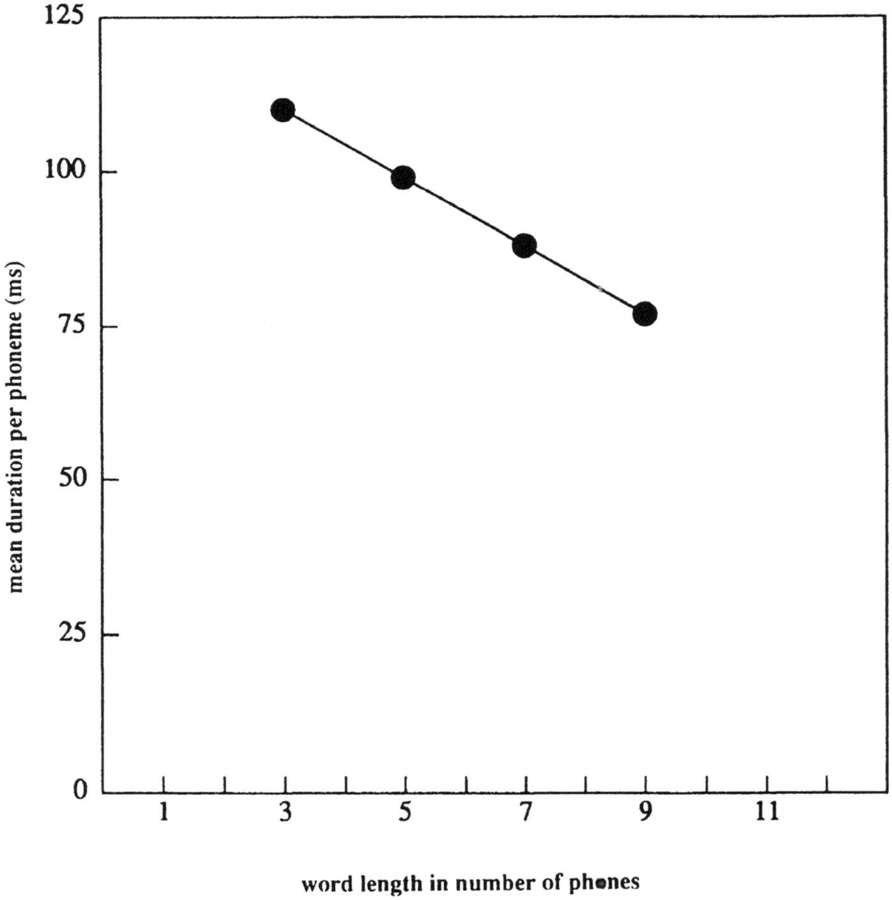

Figure 1. Average duration (in ms) per phoneme as a function of word length in number of phonemes (Measurements were performed on reiterant speech. Adapted from Nooteboom 1985.)

Of course compression of phoneme duration as a function of word length is a well known phenomenon. There are at least two other explanations that have been put forward to account for this regularity. One is in terms of "word level isochrony", i.e. a tendency to make all words equally long (cf. Lindblom 1963). The other is in terms of time compression on the level of short term storage of motor commands in the minds of speakers: consecutive planned motor commands are supposed to come closer together on the mental schedule for execution as there are more motor commands yet to be executed (Lindblom—Lyberg—Holmgren 1981).

Both earlier explanations suffer from the fact that they are, in some sense, begging the question. Why would speakers strive for isochrony, or why would motor commands follow each other more rapidly as there are more yet to come?

In this sense, the causal relation between lexical redundancy and speed of articulation proposed here seems to be more satisfactory. But an independent test of this relation is still lacking. We will not pursue this here, but rather turn to possible effects of contextual redundancy.

4. "New" versus "given" and speed of articulation

If it is correct that speed of articulation is controlled by redundancy or its inverse, information value, one would expect this principle not only to operate on lexical redundancy but also according to contextual redundancy. More particularly, one would expect that a word that is to some extent predictable from its preceding context, will be pronounced more rapidly and less carefully than a word that can not be predicted from context.

This expectation at first sight seems to be in agreement with Lieberman (1963), who found that predictable words are spoken with less care and more rapidly than unpredictable words. Lieberman's findings were more recently confirmed by Hunnicutt (1985) who repeated his measurements with more extreme differences in contextual redundancy. Further, Fowler—Housum (1987) showed that "old" or "given" words, i.e., words produced for the second time in a monologue, are shorter than "new" words, i.e., words produced for the first time in a monologue.

There is, however, a problem here. We know that in languages such as English or Dutch informative or new words are liable to receive a pitch accent, whereas predictable or given words are more often produced without such a prominence-lending pitch movement. In none of the above studies information value was separated from accentuation. It is therefore hard to tell whether the durational effects reported are due to accent structure or independent effects of information structure.

We have attempted to study the effects of accent structure and information structure independently.

A word can be made more predictable by turning it into old or given information, for example because it has been used in the same sense in the immediately preceding sentence. By varying the precursor sentence, we can manipulate the "newness" versus "givenness" and simultaneously, the accentedness of a particular word in a particular sentence, as in the following example:

I. [Target word *John* is new & accented]:
(Question: What did you say?)
Answer: JOHN is ill.

II. [Target word *John* is given & unaccented]:
(Question: What did you say about JOHN?)
Answer: John is ILL.

In these examples capitalized words are accented. In general, informationally new words carry an accent and informationally given words tend to be unaccented. In order to separate accentuation from givenness, we made use of the phenomenon of unit accentuation. If, in the above examples, we replace *John* with *John Miller*, the whole combination *John Miller* will be marked as containing new information by a single accent on *Miller*:

I. [Target word *John* is new & unaccented]:
(Question: What did you say?)
Answer: John MILLER is ill

II. [Target word *John* is given & unaccented]:
(Question: What did you say about John MILLER?)
Answer: John Miller is ILL

By comparing realizations of *John* in these two contexts, the effect of information value on speed of articulation can be studied where there is, at least on the word level, no difference in plus or minus accent.

By contrasting *John Miller* with *Pete Collins* in a single sentence we also can get a realization in which both *John* and *Miller* are correctly accented:

I. [Target word *John* is new & accented]:
(Question: What did you say?)
Answer: JOHN MILLER and PETE COLLINS are ill.

II. [Target word *John* is new & unaccented]:
(Question: What did you say?)
Answer: John MILLER is ill.

By comparing these two realizations of *John*, we can study the difference between plus and minus accent, where there is no difference in information value.

In this way we studied the effects of both accentuation and information value on word durations for eight one-syllable and eight three-syllable

Dutch words in three comparisons, one for plus versus minus accent, one for new versus given, and one for plus accent & new versus minus accent & given. Target words were always embedded in the second sentence. We used a single highly experienced professional speaker, who repeated everything five times in random order.

Main results are given in Figure 2, in terms of percentages durational difference. Durations were expressed as a percentual difference relative to the accented versions, so the figure can be read as showing the percentage shortening when going from plus to minus accent, going from new to given, or going from plus accent & new to minus accent & given.

These data tell us that there is a considerable effect of plus versus minus accent on word duration, but there appears to be hardly any independent effect of new versus given. Also it is the case that the combined effect of plus versus minus accent and new versus given is not greater than the effect of plus versus minus accent alone.

Obviously, we must conclude that our hypothesis that speed of articulation is immediately controlled by contextual redundancy is not generally valid. If, in a word combination like *John Miller*, or *French cheese* both words contain new information, the first, unaccented, word is not lengthened in comparison to a reading where it contains old or given information. Only the second, accented, word, is lengthened. Lengthening seems to be a concomitant side-effect of pitch accent realization and not an immediate consequence of information value.

These results point into the direction that information value has no effect at all on word durations, and that the effect we found for the new, accented and old, unaccented words are the result of the extra time needed for the realization of the prominence lending pitch movement. If this is true, only those segments or syllables on which a pitch accent occurs will undergo a change in duration.

Figure 3 gives a more detailed analysis of the data in Figure 2, for CVC-monosyllables only. We see the relative shortening in percent of the first consonant, vowel and second consonant, when going from plus to minus accent, going from new to given, and going from plus accent new to minus accent given.

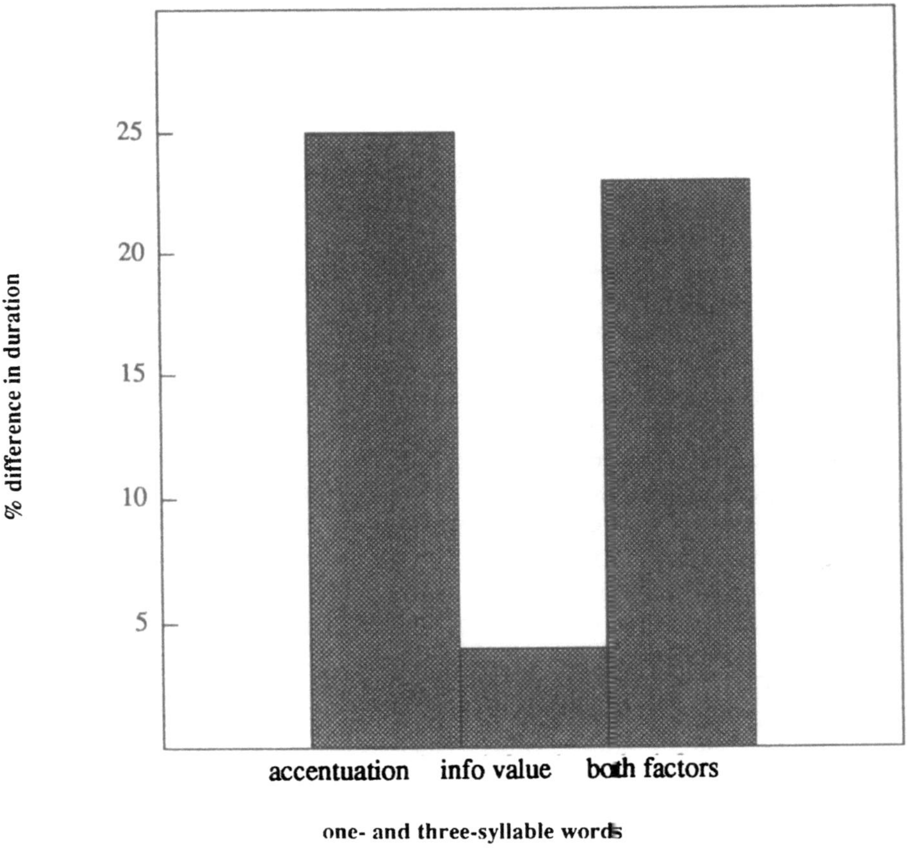

Figure 2. Percentage difference in word duration in the three comparisons
One hunderd percent provided by the duraticn of the [+accent] version ("Accentuation"), the [new] version ("Info value"), and the [+accent, new] version ("both factors")

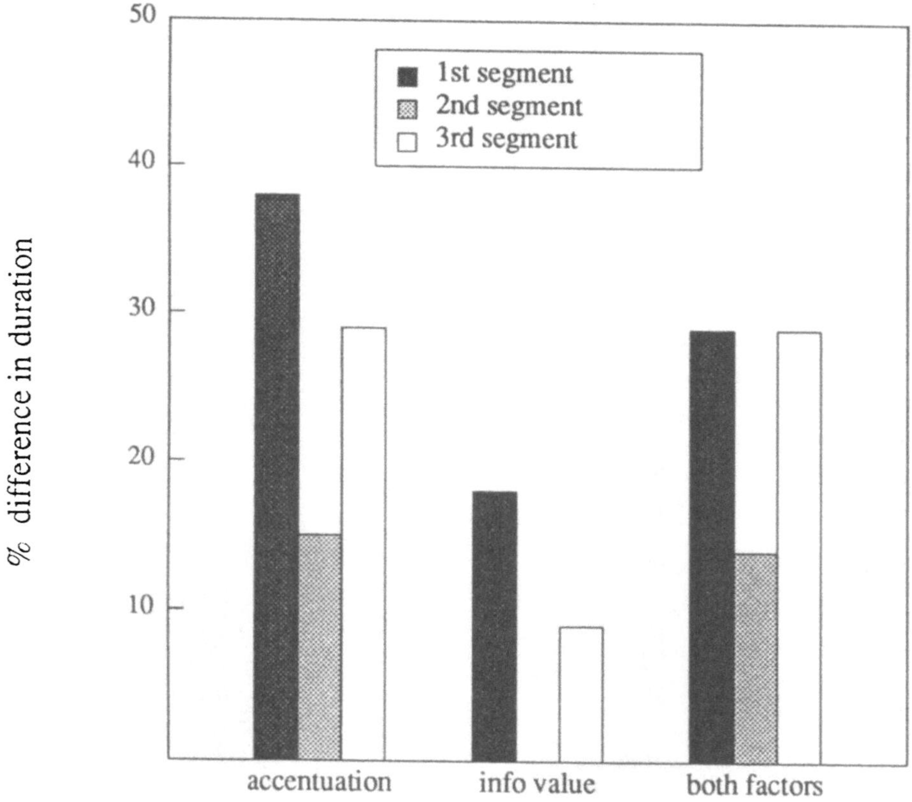

Figure 3. Percentual difference in duration of the individual segments of the one-syllable words

The percentages are computed with the following formula: [(D1-D2)/D1] * 100, in which D1 is the segment duration in the condition that is hypothesized to cause the longest duration, and D2 the segment duration in the condition that was expected to cause shortest duration

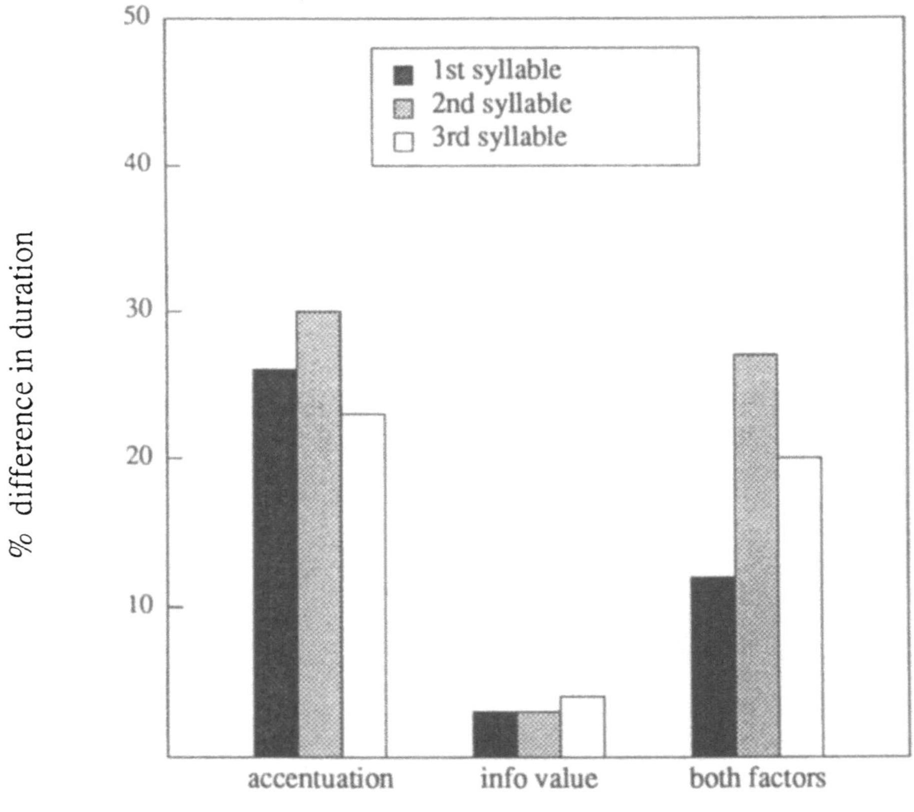

Figure 4. Percentage differences in duration of the separate syllables of the three-syllable words (Further see Figure 3.)

We see that in the first and third set the vowel segment, being most relevant for the realization of accent, is affected less by the presence or absence of accentuation than the word boundary consonants. Apparently, durational changes are not only caused by the extra time needed for the realization of the pitch movement.

The durational behavior of the syllables in the three-syllable words as displayed in Figure 4 confirms this conclusion. All syllables, whether carrying accent or not, are affected considerably as a result of variation in accentuation.

When examining the durational behavior of the segments in the one-syllable words, it catches the eye that the boundary consonants undergo the biggest change. This observation is also true for the words in which only information value was changed. The word boundary consonants are considerably shorter in the given than in the less predictable new realizations. One interpretation of these data is that the realization of word boundary consonants, at least in words with little lexical redundancy, is affected by word predictability. The more predictable a word is, the more easily it is run together with preceding and following context. Boundary consonants of words with a relatively low degree of contextual predictability are pronounced more carefully and, as a consequence, have a longer duration. With this interpretation, the data provide some evidence for the observation that informationally unimportant function words tend to be pronounced rapidly and sloppily, even to the extent that they loose their identity in the stream of speech.

Figure 5 gives similar data for the three-syllable words, showing the relative shortening for the individual segments. Although there seems to be some effect of information value alone, we do not find a similar clear pattern of results as in the monosyllable words. We assume, however, that the potential effect of contextual predictability is counteracted by the rather great lexical redundancy, which makes recognition easy anyway, and special actions on the part of the speaker to help the listener superfluous.

5. Accent patterns, word durations, and perceived naturalness

Of course, whatever we have said sofar, in these production data the effects of information value alone are minor as compared to the effects of accentuation. We have suggested earlier that information value does not get much chance to affect word duration because durational structure would be too severely constrained by accent patterns. If this is correct, one would expect that such constraints are perceptually relevant. More particularly, one would expect that speakers cannot stretch unaccented words or shrink accented words, without their speech becoming unacceptable.

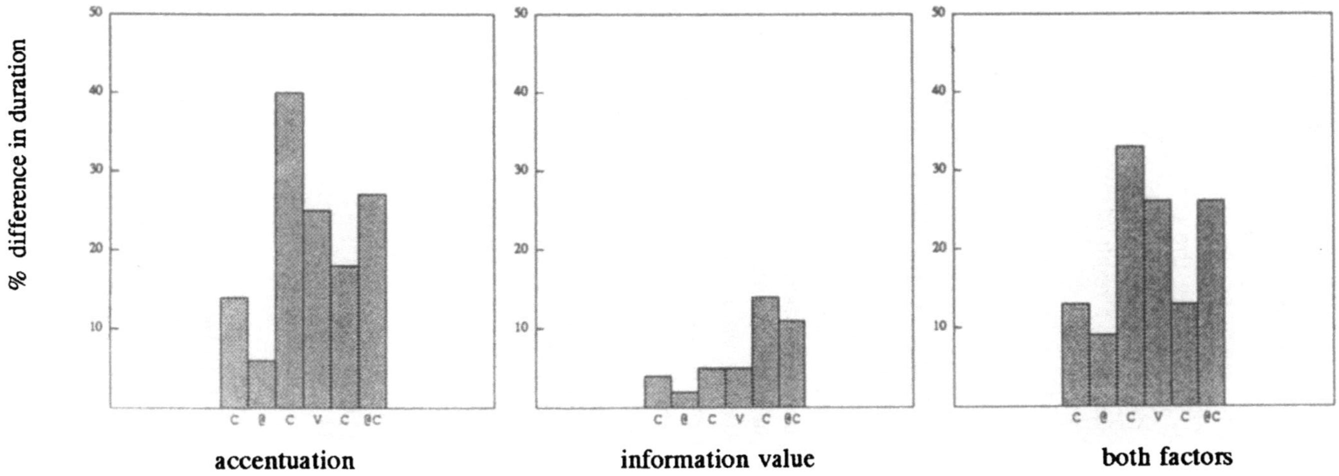

Figure 5. Percentage differences in duration of the separate segments of the three-syllable words (Further see Figure 3)

In a perception study we have investigated whether adjustment of word durations to plus or minus accent is relevant to the perceived naturalness of speech.

The results of this scaling experiment are presented in Table 1. With the Pitch Synchronous Overlap and Add technique (PSOLA; Charpentier—Moulines 1989) we manipulated durations of target words in sentences, while preserving high quality speech. In one of our experiments plus and minus accent were always correct, i.e., in accordance with context, and target words duration alone was varied.

Table 1. Average scale values and standard deviations

target word duration:	new [+accent]	old [-accent]
long	7.9 (2.2)	5.0 (3.1)
short	4.8 (2.6)	8.1 (2.1)

Note: Values are given on a scale from 1 (very unnatural) to 10 (very natural), for long and short durations of accented and unaccented words. Accent was always correct. N per cell = 256

Target words were the same 16 words used in the earlier production experiment, embedded in sentences, and either being new and accented or given and unaccented, depending on a precursor sentence. New and accented versus given and unaccented were orthogonally combined with long and short word durations. In the plus accent condition long durations preserved the original durations produced by our speaker and short durations were, by PSOLA manipulation, made equal to durations produced in the minus accent condition. In the minus accent condition this was the other way around.

Sixteen subjects listened to the sentence pairs and were asked to judge naturalness of the second sentence, with special attention for the target word, on a scale from 1 to 10 (with 1 least acceptable).

Results clearly show that naturalness suffers considerably when overall word duration is not in accordance with accentuation. This confirms our earlier suggestion that, at least for content words, accent patterns severely constrain durational patterns. Listeners object when we stretch unaccented words or shorten accented words.

6. Temporal structure and speed of perceptual processing

The above results do not give us insight in the effect of a correct temporal structure on the process of speech perception. It still remains unclear whether appropriate word durations are exploited by the listener for faster interpretation, such as is suggested by the adaptation-principle. In an attempt to obtain information about this matter, we performed a phoneme-monitoring experiment. In this experimental task, that was developed by Foss (1969), listeners are asked to listen to a specified sound in the sentence they are processing. At the same time, they are told to pay attention to the meaning of that sentence. It is assumed that when comprehension is difficult, a relatively large amount of processing time is needed for the comprehension task. Consequently, less capacity will be available for the detection task, which will result in relatively long reaction times. Extensive research concerning this matter has shown that the reaction times to detect a target-phoneme, are correlated positively with the difficulty of processing the sentence at the point where the target phoneme occurs. In other words, the detection latency reflects the ease of processing of the immediately preceding speech. In our experiment, this implied that the reaction time on a phoneme immediately following the target word will reflect the ease of processing of that target-word. We used the same material on which the naturalness judgments were elicited: Target-words, in this type of experiment called critical words, were either new and accented or given and unaccented, and they were orthogonally combined with long and short word durations, using the PSOLA-technique. This resulted in four versions of each sentence. The target-phoneme (either /b/ or /d/) occurred immediately after the critical word.

Care was taken that factors like predictability, ambiguity, and phonetic similarity of both the critical and the target-bearing words were kept similar (for a detailed overview, see Cutler—Norris 1979; Foss—Gernsbacher 1983). Consequently, the effect of these artifacts that have proven to affect reaction times were kept constant across all stimuli and conditions. The target-fragments were placed in a list with 64 filler fragments, in which the target phoneme occurred at other places in the sentence (32 times) or did not occur at all (32 times). This was done to prohibit the listeners from detecting regularities in the material and developing a strategy to come to their responses. Four stimulus sets were constructed, each set comprising one version of each target sentence, and all the filler items. Sixty subjects participated in the experiment, fifteen per stimulus set. The main results are presented in Table 2. Even though inappropriate duration has proven to cause a decrease in naturalness in the experiment described before, in this experiment the subjects indicated that they had not noticed the manipula-

Table 2. Mean reaction times

	duration		
critical word:	appropriate	inappropriate	total
one-syllable	519	523	521
three-syllable	490	510	499
total	505	517	510

Note: Values are given in ms after the critical words with appropriate and inappropriate duration. N per cell = 240

tions of duration. Apparently, this observation is caused by the different experimental task.

However, the results show that ease of processing is affected by appropriateness of duration, even though the listeners had not noticed the manipulations. The overall difference in response latency between appropriate and inappropriate duration was significant, $F(1,59)=5.7$ ($p=.020$). This difference is reflected clearly after three-syllable words. After the one-syllable words the effect is less obvious. Here, the context prior to the critical words might have had an effect on the reaction times, the critical words being so short. That context was not controlled for the artifacts as mentioned above, and it is unclear to what extent they played a role. But in general, these data point into the direction of an advantage of correct duration in the process of speech processing, which supports our hypothesis, that the listener really uses the variation in temporal structure in the process of speech perception. However, more evidence should be gathered with more target phonemes and more stimulus material in order to form a solid proof of this assumption.

7. Conclusions

The main point we want to make is this: We all know, and it has often been said, that speakers speak in order to be understood. But there is very little phonetic research that has taken this truism as a vantage point from which it may be systematically explored how the speaker's wish to make himself understood shapes the sound of his speech.

This should not be misunderstood. There are plenty of demonstrations in the experimental literature confirming that speakers indeed adapt their pronunciation, also locally, to the needs of their audience. Our own data provide such a demonstration. But what we are in need of is a set of rules generating such adaptations over a much wider range of aspects of pronunciation than is covered by such demonstration experiments.

We have suggested that lexical redundancy affects pronunciation. We have not shown this to be true. It would be of interest to find out whether there is a systematic quantifiable relation between lexical redundancy and articulation.

We have also suggested that contextual redundancy affects pronunciation, and that this interacts with lexical redundancy. Here again data are scarce, but there is plenty of room for further systematic exploration of such effects.

We have shown that immediate effects of contextual redundancy on pronunciation can be constrained by accent patterns. Accent patterns are generated by linguistic rules operating on semantic and syntactic structures. One of their functions is to signal information value.

The close association, both in speech production and speech perception, between accent patterns and temporal patterns, possibly shows us the adaptive principle in frozen, linguistically standardized form. If this is correct, it would be one example of how the principle of listener-oriented adaptation not only shapes the momentaneous pronunciation, but also the more permanent properties of the language (cf. Lindblom 1989, for other examples).

We know only little about the detailed effects the demands of communication have on the acoustic shape of our speech. Consequently, research about this matter is needed before the quality of the synthetic speech in a text-to-speech system can profit from the results. Research performed recently on the quality of synthetic speech has resulted in considerable improvement of that speech. But a system that adapts its speech automatically anticipating on the audience and the circumstances, and that also pronounces the more informative words carefully, watches the accent and temporal patterns, and pauses at appropriate positions in a way human beings do, is still far away.

Human and synthetic intonation: A case study

Jacques M. B. Terken

Abstract

An algorithm for the automatic generation of intonation, which had been developed within the framework of the SPIN/ASSP program, was applied to a sample text. This text was presented to four expert listeners. Their comments inspired several comparisons between the intonation in the synthetic version and the intonation in a version of the text read by a human speaker. The results showed that intonational choices in reading aloud appear to be guided by syntactic and phonological factors. In particular, the following results were obtained. With respect to declination, a distinction should be made between intonation phrases in sentence-initial, medial and final position. The size of sentence-internal declination resets appeared to be related to syntactic structure. F_0 maxima for the first accent of intonation phrases should not exceed an upper limit: high onset frequencies of the baseline should be associated with relatively small accent-lending pitch movements for the first accent.

With respect to the distribution of melodic configurations the following results were obtained. The $\overset{*}{R}\,\overset{*}{F}$ configuration in the human version occurred mainly in sentence-final position. The choice between different melodic boundary markers appeared to be related to syntactic characteristics of the boundary: the *LR%* sequence appeared to be associated with deeper syntactic boundaries than the *RH%* sequence. Also, there appeared to be a considerable perceptual tolerance: boundaries which were marked with *LR%* by the speaker and for which the algorithm had generated the *RH%* sequence, were approved of by the listeners; boundaries which were marked with *RH%* by the speaker and for which the algorithm had generated the *LR%* sequence were disapproved. It is concluded that the comparison of synthetic and human intonation, governed by expert comments on the shortcomings of synthetic intonation, provides a valuable tool to guide research concerning the tune-to-text association in human speakers and to improve rules for the automatic generation of intonation.

1. Introduction

A serious problem in the development of rules for the automatic generation of intonation for text-to-speech conversion is the lack of knowledge about factors governing the tune-to-text association in human speakers. The present contribution describes one possible approach to this problem. We describe how expert listeners' intuitions about the contextual inappropriateness of synthetic intonation in a sample text can be used as a guideline to examine some of the factors governing the tune-to-text association in a human reading of the same text.

Within the framework of the SPIN/ASSP program, an algorithm for synthetic intonation was developed and evaluated. The evaluation proceeded in the following way. Listeners were presented with several versions of a text, differing with respect to intonation only. They were asked to rate the naturalness of the intonation of the different versions on a 10-point scale, under two presentation modes: textwise presentation and sentence-by-sentence presentation. In the latter mode, all utterances making up the text were presented in scrambled order, and listeners rated each individual utterance. In the textwise presentation, the algorithm was given inferior ratings in comparison with a version in which the intonation was modelled on a human speaker. In the sentence-by-sentence presentation the algorithm obtained the same mean rating as the human version.

The results of earlier experiments (Collier—Terken 1987) suggest that the naturalness of synthetic intonation in longer utterances and coherent texts is judged primarily with respect to global characteristics such as overall F_0 variation, peak scaling and the scaling of contours in the relevant pitch range, provided that the distribution of accents and boundaries is adequate. Therefore, the finding that the synthetic intonation compares well with human intonation in the sentence-by-sentence presentation does not automatically imply that the intonation is appropriate in all details such as the choice of accent type, the size of declination reset and the relative prominence of accented words.

There is no good insight into the perceptual function of these detailed aspects of intonation. For instance, with respect to the type of accent there is evidence that the choice of a particular accent type does not contribute to comprehension or naturalness (Nooteboom—Kruyt 1987; Collier—de Zitter—Terken 1989). However, utterances differing only in the choice of accent type are perceptually very dissimilar (Collier et al. 1989) and it has been shown that the choice between different accent types may strongly affect the interpretation of an utterance (Pierrehumbert—Hirschberg 1990). Thus, it appears that the choice between different accent types has more to do with contextual appropriateness than with naturalness. For these reasons, it is desirable to gain insight into the factors governing the choice between different intonational options in human speakers, both from the point of view of accounting for human behavior and from the point of view of synthesizing appropriate prosody. If we can find out what factors make a certain choice more or less appropriate in a given context, we can attempt to develop ways to derive this information automatically in the process of text-to-speech conversion.

In order to investigate what factors make intonational choices more or less appropriate in a given context, a second evaluation was conducted with the same materials. Four intonation experts were presented with the version of the text in which the intonation was synthesized with the experimental algorithm, which we will refer to as the *test* version. They were explained that a text had been provided with synthetic intonation by means of an experimental algorithm, and they were asked to listen critically to the text and to mark in a written version of the text all the places where they judged the synthetic intonation to be inappropriate, and — if possible — to indicate why.

This evaluation should serve two aims. In the first place, it should indicate which aspects of the synthetic intonation need to be improved. In the second place, it should help to deepen our insights into factors governing intonational behavior in human speakers for the following reason. Since the synthesized pitch contours comply with the rules in the Grammar for Dutch Intonation ('t Hart—Collier—Cohen, 1990), we may suppose that they are phonologically well-formed. Therefore, if we ask expert listeners to give detailed comments on inadequacies of the intonation for a given text, we may suppose that their comments are based on intuitions about what would count as adequate intonation for a given text fragment. These comments can then be classified and used to examine the intonational characteristics of a human speaker for these text fragments. In this way, hypotheses can be formulated about the factors governing tune-to-text association in reading aloud by human speakers.

Our intonation algorithm takes as input the prosodic structure of a sentence. The prosodic structure represents the division of the sentence into prosodic domains and the location of pitch accents. This information can be included in the input text by the user, or can be generated by an algorithm (Dirksen—Quené, this volume; Quené—Kager, this volume). We assume that short sentences are treated as one prosodic domain, uninterrupted by pauses. We will refer to such a domain as an intonation phrase (for the purpose of automatic intonation synthesis, there is no splitting up of intonation phrases into smaller domains such as intermediate phrases). Longer sentences are divided into several phrases, corresponding to clauses; in longer clauses, one or more additional boundaries are inserted, coinciding with major constituent boundaries (NP, PP, AP, VP) and obligatory boundaries such as those between N and a non-restrictive relative clause.

The algorithm contains the following rules.

1. For each intonation phrase, a separate intonation contour is generated, consisting of a sequence of pitch movements which is superimposed on a declining baseline. The declination for this baseline is computed for each intonation phrase separately. A distinction is made between phrases in final and non-final position, on the basis of the offset frequency of the baseline: sentence-final phrases have a lower offset frequency than non-final phrases. The onset frequency of the baseline is always higher

than the offset frequency and is computed on the basis of offset frequency and phrase duration.

2. The size of the pitch movements in the intonation phrase decreases in a simple left-to-right manner, so that movements at the end of the phrase are smaller than movements at the beginning of the phrase.
3. Different ways to mark sentence-internal boundaries are selected on the basis of the distance between the last accented syllable before the boundary and the boundary itself: if the last accent before the boundary is followed by at least two unaccented syllables, the *LR%* sequence is selected (in traditional IPO notation Ø 2); in other cases the $\overset{*}{R}H\%$ sequence is selected (in traditional IPO notation 1 Ø). The notational conventions are explained in the appendix to this chapter.
4. For the last two accents of intonation phrases a simple form of alternation is applied, by selecting the $\overset{*}{R}\ \overset{*}{F}$ pattern (in traditional IPO notation 1 A) and the $\overset{*}{R}\ FF\ \overset{*}{R}\&F$ pattern (in traditional IPO notation 1 D 1A) in turn. For non-final phrases this rule does not apply when the previous rule has produced the $\overset{*}{R}H\%$ sequence.

The remainder of this chapter is structured as follows. First we will describe the materials which were used for the diagnostic test and for the comparison of human and synthetic intonation. Secondly, a brief overview of the results of the diagnostic test will be presented. Thirdly, the findings of the diagnostic test will be used as a heuristic tool for making comparisons between human and synthetic intonation.

2. Materials

A Dutch newspaper text was selected, consisting of 19 sentences. The mean number of words per sentence was 17, ranging from 9 to 30 (standard deviation = 7.0). The text was read at a normal rate by a professional speaker (designated talker PB), who was aware of the fact that the speech materials would be used for purposes of intonation research. A transcription was made of the intonation with prosodic markers for accent and boundary locations as produced by the human reader. No distinction was made between primary and secondary accents. The text, augmented with diacritic marks for locations of sentence accents and prosodic boundaries, was given as input to an experimental system for text-to-speech conversion. The system uses an inventory of diphones, which are stored as LPC parameter files, and performs durational and F_0 adaptations dependent on the locations of accents and boundaries (van Rijnsoever 1988a). The intonation contours for the synthetic speech were generated by means of the algorithm summarized above. At the temporal level, accented syllables and preboundary segments are subject to lengthening; prosodic boundaries are realized as pauses with a duration of 250 ms.

In order to simplify the comparison between the synthetic intonation contours and the human contours, a data reduction was applied to the F_0 contours in the text read by the human speaker, in the following way. Small F_0 variations in the human contours were smoothed out, i.e., replaced by straight lines in log-frequency by linear time plane, (cf. 't Hart—Collier—Cohen 1990). This procedure was repeated until further smoothing would induce perceptual differences between the original and smoothed versions. In this way, stylized versions of the original F_0 trajectories were obtained which were perceptually identical to the original ones but contained only the perceptually relevant F_0 changes. In this way a better impression was obtained of the sentence melody which the speaker intended to produce. Since the human version had a higher average F_0 than the synthesized version, F_0 in the human version was scaled down by a constant factor of .72 in order to allow for a better comparison of F_0 values in the two versions. The choice of a constant division factor ensures that the intervals remain constant on a logarithmic scale, which is traditionally used as the measurement scale for musical pitch perception. The value of .72 was chosen so as to make the average end frequency in the human version equal to the end frequency of the synthetic contours. These manipulations apparently left the naturalness of the intonation intact: in the formal perceptual evaluation mentioned before, which made use of synthetic speech, these F_0 trajectories were used to generate a version of the text with human-like intonation; it was awarded a naturalness rating of 7.5 on a 10-point scale. In the following, we will refer to this version as human.

3. Diagnostic evaluation: preliminary remarks

Four experts in the field of intonation research were asked to annotate the version of the text with synthetic intonation. The text was recorded on tape; each judge performed the test individually. The judges were asked to listen to the text carefully, both as a whole and sentence by sentence, and to replay the tape as often as needed. They were encouraged to criticize any aspect of the intonation which they judged inappropriate; they were explicitly instructed to give careful attention to the following aspects: (i) *sentence melody* (this concerns the question whether the specific accent types and boundary markers are appropriate); (ii) *prominence relations between accented words* (this concerns the question whether accented words receive enough emphasis in relation to each other); it was mentioned that the locations of accents were derived from the human speaker and were not under discussion; (iii) *declination* (this concerns the question whether the scaling of intonation phrases in the overall F_0 range domain is appropriate, and whether the size of declination resets between intonation phrases is appropriate).

In addition, they were asked to comment on global characteristics of the synthetic intonation, such as the global course of pitch in the utterances, the onset and offset pitch of successive utterances, the variation in the size of pitch movements and the overall variation in the sequence of pitch movements.

Performing the test posed few difficulties for the judges. In all, 177 comments were collected. Seventy comments were discarded: 49 remarks concerned the location of pauses, segmental durations and positive or neutral comments; 21 remarks concerned the distribution of accents. Since the listeners had been instructed to take the distribution of pauses and sentence accents as given, these comments were irrelevant to the present concerns. This left 107 comments, which were distributed as follows: 13 remarks on aspects of declination; 49 remarks on the prominence of accented words (4 remarks explicitly linked word prominence to the size of declination resets); 20 remarks on the choice of pitch movements; 14 remarks on melodic marking of boundaries; 11 remarks on the realization of movements.

In the following, we shall consider the individual categories in detail, and relate the observations to differences between the *human* and synthetic (*test*) intonation.

4. Declination

Thirteen diagnostic comments concerned the size of declination resets. All stated that specific sentence-internal declination resets were too large. The specifics of the declination resets are as in (1):

(1) For phrases in final position, the baseline has an end frequency of 75 Hz; for phrases in non-final position, the end frequency is 90 Hz. The onset frequency of the baseline is computed on the basis of the end frequency and the duration of the phrase, and is bound to upper and lower limits. Since the size of a declination reset is determined by the offset frequency of the baseline of a phrase and the onset frequency of the baseline of the next phrase, the size of declination resets also varies between upper and lower bounds.

The expert comments suggest that the distinction between non-final and final phrases may be too simple. Therefore, onset and offset frequencies of the baseline and the size of resets were measured, both in the *human* and *test* version, separately for phrases in utterance-initial, utterance-medial (i.e.

neither initial nor final) and utterance-final position. The size of a declination reset at the prosodic boundary between $phrase_i$ and $phrase_{i+1}$ is obtained in the following way. The offset frequency of the baseline of $phrase_i$ is subtracted from the onset frequency of the baseline of $phrase_{i+1}$. Next, the difference is converted to semitones. The data are shown in Table 1.

Table 1. Mean onset (bfr) and offset (efr) frequencies for baselines (in Hz), baseline resets (in semitones), and corresponding standard deviations

	Human								
	Initial (n=16)			Medial (n=13)			Final (n=16)		
	set	bfr	efr	reset	bfr	efr	reset	bfr	efr
mean	5.3	111.3	92.6	2.4	106.4	94.0	2.0	105.7	81.8
s.d.	2.0	11.0	7.4	1.3	6.8	7.4	1.6	10.7	4.0
	Test								
	Initial (n=16)			Medial (n=13)			Final (n=16)		
	set	bfr	efr	reset	bfr	efr	reset	bfr	efr
mean	7.1	115.3	92.1	3.8	115.0	92.2	3.3	111.8	76.4
s.d.	0.7	3.8	2.5	0.7	4.2	2.5	1.2	6.5	1.9

Note: "Set" is the difference (in st) between the sentence-initial onset frequency and the sentence-final offset frequency of the previous utterance.

Overall, declination (re-)sets are greater in the synthetic version than in the human version. This observation can be accounted for in two ways. One possibility is that the downscaling of the original human F_0 trajectories by a constant factor was wrong: it implies equal distances on a logarithmic scale. Recent evidence suggests that an Equivalent Rectangular Bandwidth (ERB) scale would be more appropriate (Hermes—van Gestel 1991). Another possibility is that the formulas by which the declination is computed must be adjusted. The latter interpretation is supported by outcome of the diagnostic evaluation: a number of sentence-internal declination resets in the *test* version were judged to be too large.

As can be seen in Table 1, the data of the human speaker and the algorithm compare reasonably well with respect to offset frequencies: here, a distinction between non-final and final phrases appears to be valid. The *human* and the *test* version compare less well with respect to onset frequencies: here, a distinction between initial and non-initial phrases would be more appropriate. This suggests that a ternary distinction is called for between initial, medial and final phrases: initial and medial phrases contrast with final phrases with respect to end frequency; medial and final phrases contrast with initial phrases with respect to onset frequency.

Further inspection of the data in Table 1 shows that the standard deviation for end frequencies is smaller than for onset frequencies. This is in line with the claim by Cohen—Collier—'t Hart (1982) that the end frequency is relatively stable and the onset frequency varies as a function of phrase duration. However, no good polynomial fits were found for the difference between onset and end frequency in the *human* version as a function of phrase duration. Closer inspection of the data suggested that there might be a relation between the size of the declination reset and the type of syntactic boundary with which it is associated. Therefore, the size of sentence-internal declination resets in the *human* version was examined as a function of the syntactic properties of the prosodic boundaries marked by declination resets.

Inspection of the speech materials indicated that there are preferred structural locations for prosodic boundaries. These prosodic boundaries often coincide with boundaries between units which can be classified as in the following examples. For convenience, we will use a much "flatter" structural description than the hierarchical representation that is normally used.

P1	P2	Middle				Pn
Martha	heeft	vorige week	een	lange	brief	gestuurd
Martha	has	last week	a	long	letter	sent

(P$_n$)	Extraposed				
...	naar	haar	broer	in	Parijs
...	to	her	brother	in	Paris

Dutch is basically an SOV language. In the main clause, the Finite Verb (P2) surfaces at the beginning of the VP. Here, its position is fixed: it can only be preceded by one other constituent (P1), which can be the subject or another argument of the verb, an adjunct, but also a subordinate clause. Other verb elements cluster at the end of the sentence (Pn) and can only be followed by right-dislocated expressions (Extraposed).

The vertical bars indicate preferred locations of prosodic boundaries. The decision to actually insert a boundary depends on a number of considerations which are beyond the scope of the present contribution.

Onset and offset frequencies and the size of declination resets at prosodic boundaries were analyzed as a function of the syntactic properties of these prosodic boundaries. The results are shown in Table 2.

Table 2. Means, standard deviations and number of observations for offset frequencies (in Hz) preceding prosodic boundaries (efr), onset frequencies (in Hz) following the boundaries (bfr), and resulting declination resets (in semitones) as a function of the type of syntactic boundary

Boundary		efr	reset	bfr	n
S-S	mean	83.3	3.6	102.7	3
	s.d.	3.1	1.0	5.5	
P1 - P2	mean	96.0	2.2	109.3	12
	s.d.	8.3	1.3	10.5	
Within Middle Group	mean	93.0	2.9	109.0	5
	s.d.	8.2	1.0	6.4	
Pn - Extraposed	mean	92.5	1.2	98.8	6
	s.d.	5.2	1.4	5.2	
Other	mean	95.7	1.6	105.3	3
	s.d.	2.5	1.9	9.3	

Note: S-S denotes boundaries between conjoined main clauses. Further explanation of the terminology for syntactic boundaries is given in the text.

As can be seen, the resets between conjoined main clauses (S-S) are relatively large. This is due to the low offset frequency of the intonation phrase before the boundary, which comes close to the end frequency for phrases in utterance-final position. It appears, therefore, that for main clauses no distinction needs to be made between final and non-final position. Furthermore, resets between the verbal end group (Pn) and the intonation phrase containing extraposed expressions are relatively small, due to the low onset frequency after the boundary. Finally, it appears that no further differentiation is required between the P1-P2 boundary and the boundaries within the middle group. It appears that these can be treated as a single category. In summary, the data suggest that rules for computing declination should be sensitive to properties of the text that can be captured by a rather flat syntactic description.

5. Size of accent-lending pitch movements

The rule for computing the size of accent-lending pitch movements is as follows:

(2) In intonation phrases containing one sentence accent, the distance between the peak in the accented syllable and its projection onto the baseline is 6 semitones. In phrases containing two or more accents, the initial peak is always 7.5 semitones above the baseline and the final peak is 3 or 4.5 semitones above the baseline, depending on whether the last accent is realized by $\overset{*}{F}$ or $R\overset{*}{\&}F$; the peaks of additional accented syllables are in between.

In all, 49 comments in the diagnostic analysis concerned the prominence of accented syllables. Most remarks stated that a word was too prominent. Thirty-nine of these 49 remarks (i.e. 80 percent) concerned the first accented word of a phrase. In all, the text contained 156 accented words distributed over 54 intonation phrases. This gives an average of 2.89 accented words per phrase. If the comments were distributed evenly over the different positions of accented words in the phrase, one would expect that 49/2.89 = 17 comments would concern the first word of the phrase. Since 39 comments concerned the first word of the phrase, it appears that something is wrong with the way in which the size of the accent-lending movement on the first word is computed. Three properties of the synthetic version may have contributed to this inadequacy.

Firstly, no distinction was made between primary and secondary accent. Consequently, words which obtained secondary accent in the *human* version obtained primary accent in the synthetic version. Some of these words occurred as the first accented word of a phrase containing several accents, so that the accent-lending movements had a size of 7.5 semitones and were associated with maximal prominence. The words involved are, for instance, modal auxiliaries such as *mag* 'may, be allowed'. These cases can be solved by making a distinction between primary and secondary prominence or by leaving such words unaccented.

Secondly, the first accent in a sequence of two or more accented words was always realized by means of an $\overset{*}{R}$ *FF* or an $\overset{*}{R}$ with following high level tone. This means that the pitch remains relatively high throughout the accented syllable, relative to the *R&F* realization. This may have enhanced the prominence associated with the accent-lending pitch movement, so that it was judged to be too prominent.

Thirdly, the size of the first accent-lending movement was fixed at 7.5 semitones and the peak was not bound to an upper limit. Consequently, the frequency of the peak was a direct function of the onset frequency of the phrase: higher onsets resulted in higher peak frequencies. Apparently, this rule needs adjustment, for two reasons. Analysis of the data of the *human* version suggests that the frequency of the first peak of the sentence is bound to an upper limit, which means that as the onset frequency of the baseline increases, the distance between the baseline and the peak becomes smaller. A linear regression equation was computed for the distance between the first peak (P1) and the onset frequency (bfr, in Hz), as a function of onset frequency. This gave the following equation:

$$\text{distance (P1} - \text{bfr)} = 176.5 - 1.03.\ \text{bfr}$$

with an associated correlation coefficient of .61. In words, this means that there is a tendency in the *human* version for higher onset frequencies to be associated with smaller sizes of accent-lending pitch movements. Furthermore, if we compare average frequencies of the first peak of phrases in initial, medial and final positions in the utterance in the *human* version, we obtain means of 174, 149 and 154 Hz for initial, medial and final phrases, respectively. This supports the conclusion which was drawn in relation to the results for declination, that for non-final phrases a further differentiation should be made between initial and medial phrases: not only is the onset frequency of medial phrases different from the onset of initial phrases; also the average frequency of the initial peak is different. In both respects medial phrases look more like final phrases. This suggests that medial and final phrases are different mainly with respect to the end frequency of the baseline and the slope of the baseline.

In summary, the results show that information about declination is relevant for computing the size of accent-lending pitch movements, due to general constraints on pitch range and register.

6. Melodic aspects

6.1. Alternation of melodies

Our algorithm contains the following rule for selecting different melodic realizations of the last two accents of each intonation phrase:

(3) for the last two accents of intonation phrases a simple form of alternation is applied, by selecting the $\overset{*}{R}\,\overset{*}{F}$ (1 A) and the $\overset{*}{R}\ FF\ R\overset{*}{\&}F$ pattern (1 D 1&A) in turn.

In the diagnostic evaluation, 18 out of 20 comments on the choice of pitch movements concerned this rule. The algorithm generates the two different realizations in turn. By contrast, the human speaker may be expected to choose different tunes on the basis of what he intends to express; that is, the human speaker will select both $\overset{*}{R}\,\overset{*}{F}$, $\overset{*}{R}\ FF\ R\overset{*}{\&}F$, and so on, in accordance with properties of the text. Consequently, there will be phrases in which the *human* and *test* versions match by accident, but other cases in which the two versions do not match. Table 3 shows the number of diagnostic comments in the matching and non-matching categories. Only those cases are included where the algorithm might select one of the two configurations; those cases in which application of rule 3 is blocked due to rule 4, are not included (n=9); also, two other cases, where the *test* version contained a pause but no phrase boundary, are not included.

As can be seen, the *human* speaker uses the $\overset{*}{R}\,\overset{*}{F}$ version in less than half of the cases: categories A + B yield 13 $\overset{*}{R}\,\overset{*}{F}$ versions, categories C and D yield 18 "other" versions. Most comments on the *test* version concern cases where the speaker uses the $\overset{*}{R}\,\overset{*}{F}$ version and the algorithm produces the $\overset{*}{R}\ FF\ R\overset{*}{\&}F$ version (category B). Here, we observe a much higher number of rejections than expected on the basis of the overall number of rejections and the distribution of observations for each category.

On the basis of these results one might be tempted to conclude that, in order to prevent failures of the type in category B, we should do away with the "by turns" alternation of the $\overset{*}{R}\,\overset{*}{F}$ and $\overset{*}{R}\ FF\ R\overset{*}{\&}F$ configurations and always generate the $\overset{*}{R}\,\overset{*}{F}$ configuration. But this decision would not do justice to the fact that the speaker uses the $\overset{*}{R}\,\overset{*}{F}$ configuration in less than half of the cases. In addition, it would have the undesirable consequence of generating the same variant over and over. In order to gain more insight into the factors affecting the speaker's behavior, we analyzed the speaker's behavior in relation to syntactic factors. In this analysis, all phrases containing two or more accents were taken into consideration (n=42).

Kruyt (1985) has argued that the syntactic relation between the two accented words influences the speaker's decision to select one of the configurations: if the accented words belong to the same syntactic constituent, the tendency to select the $\overset{*}{R}\,\overset{*}{F}$ configuration is fairly strong. Furthermore, in Kruyt's material there appears to be an influence of whether a given syntactic structure occurs at the end of the sentence or not: speakers produced considerably more $\overset{*}{R}\,\overset{*}{F}$ configurations at the end of sentences

Table 3. Rejection rate of synthetic intonation configuration over final two accents, broken down by human and test contours (further see text)

	(A)	(B)	(C)	(D)	Overall
human	$\overset{*}{R}\,\overset{*}{F}$	$\overset{*}{R}\,\overset{*}{F}$	other	other	
test	$\overset{*}{R}\,\overset{*}{F}$	$\overset{*}{R}$ *FF* *R*$\overset{*}{\&}$*F*	$\overset{*}{R}\,\overset{*}{F}$	$\overset{*}{R}$ *FF* *R*$\overset{*}{\&}$*F*	
number of phrases (K)	9	4	8	10	31
rejections (N)	1	9	4	4	18
expected (E)	5.2	2.3	4.7	5.8	18
percent rejections	3	56	12.5	10	15

Note: $\overset{*}{R}\,\overset{*}{F}$: ; $\overset{*}{R}$ *FF* *R*$\overset{*}{\&}$*F*:  "human other" refers to phrases in which the human speaker used another melody than $\overset{*}{R}\,\overset{*}{F}$; this can be $\overset{*}{R}$ *FF* *R*$\overset{*}{\&}$*F* or another choice. K: number of phrases. N: observed number of rejections of test version, summed over 4 judges (this means that the maximal number of rejections equals 4 x K). E: expected number of rejections: K x 18/31. %: percentage rejections in each category, i.e. 100 x N/(4 x K).

However, Kruyt's finding may be an artefact of restrictions on the distribution of $\overset{*}{R}\,\overset{*}{F}$ configurations. It can only occur at the end of an intonation phrase, but Kruyt did not take this restriction into consideration for non-sentence-final expressions. In the present analysis only those cases where considered where two accented words were the last accented words in the intonation phrase; only in these cases can the speaker in principle select a $\overset{*}{R}\,\overset{*}{F}$ configuration. The results are shown in Table 4.

Table 4. Distribution of $\overset{*}{R}\,\overset{*}{F}$ and other configurations in the *human* version for the last two accents of intonation phrases as a function of position of the phrase in the sentence and syntactic cohesion (further, see text)

		$\overset{*}{R}\,\overset{*}{F}$	other
End of Sentence	One constituent	6	4
	Two constituents	4	3
End of Full clause	One constituent	1	–
	Two constituents	–	3
Other	One constituent	2	12
	Two constituents	–	7
Sum		13	29

Two remarks can be made about these data.
Effect of position in the sentence. As can be seen, there is a strong association between the $\overset{*}{R}\ \overset{*}{F}$ configuration and sentence-final position: out of 17 sentence-final configurations 10 are $\overset{*}{R}\ \overset{*}{F}$ configurations; out of 25 sentence-non-final positions only 3 cases are $\overset{*}{R}\ \overset{*}{F}$ configurations. This produces a χ^2 of 10.39 with $df = 1$, $p < .01$.
Effect of syntactic cohesion. Nine out of 25 "non-constituent" cases were marked by $\overset{*}{R}\ \overset{*}{F}$, as opposed to 4 out of 17 "two-constituent" cases. This produces a χ^2 of .73 with $df = 1$, which is insignificant. It may be difficult, however, to assess the effect of syntactic cohesion, due to the strong association between the $\overset{*}{R}\ \overset{*}{F}$ configuration and sentence-final position. More recent data suggest that syntactic cohesion may affect the choice of a melodic configuration for the last two accented words of a phrase (Mallant 1992).

6.2. Intonational marking of sentence-internal boundaries

Our algorithm contains the following rule to select a melodic boundary marker:

(4) Different ways to mark sentence-internal boundaries are selected on the basis of the distance between the last accented syllable before the boundary and the boundary itself: if the last accented syllable before the boundary is followed by at least two unaccented syllables, the *LR%* sequence is selected (Ø 2); in other cases the *RH%* sequence is selected (1 Ø).

There were 14 comments on the choice of melodic boundary markers. Table 5 shows the number of phrases in which *human* and *test* have the same or different types of boundary marking, and the number and percentage of rejections of the *test* version.

A clear pattern can be observed in the distribution of rejections of the *test* version. If *test* produces the *LR%* realization, it is relatively often judged inappropriate except when the speaker has produced *LR%* as well. The main reason which is mentioned for rejecting the *test* version is that $\overset{*}{R}H\%$ is a strong boundary cue, which is judged too strong for the boundaries involved. This fits in with evidence provided by de Zitter (1989), who showed that listeners prefer *LR%* for deeper syntactic boundaries and $\overset{*}{R}H\%$ for less deep syntactic boundaries. If *test* produces the $\overset{*}{R}H\%$ realization, the choice of the *human* speaker is irrelevant: $\overset{*}{R}H\%$ seems to be alright for the experts in almost all cases.

Table 5. Number of phrases in which *human* and *test* have the same or different types of boundary markers, and the number and percentage of rejections of the *test* realization

		(A)	(B)	(C)	(D)	(E)	(F)
test		LR%	LR%	LR%	*RH%	*RH%	*RH%
human		LR%	*RH%	other	LR%	*RH%	other
number of phrases	(K)	6	2	7	1	3	9
rejections	(N)	1	5	7	–	–	1
expected	(E)	3.0	1.0	3.5	0.5	1.5	4.5
percent rejections		4	63	25	0	0	3

Note: LR%: ; *RH%: ; "*human* other" refers to phrases where the human speaker has a different realization than LR% or *RH%. K: number of phrases (sum = 28). N: observed number of rejections of *test* version, summed over 4 judges (this means that the possible number of rejections equals 4 x K). The sum of observed rejections is 14. E: expected number of rejections: K x 14/28. %: percentage rejections in each category, i.e. 100 x N/(4 x K).

One might be tempted to conclude from these findings that it would make sense to drop the LR% option altogether. However, since the same materials have not been tested with both LR% and *RH%, it cannot be assumed without additional evidence that *RH% would have been acceptable in cases where LR% is rejected; for instance, category (c) contains three cases of coordinated clauses where the human speaker does not use any intonational boundary marker to signal continuation; it is questionable whether *RH% would be more acceptable than LR% in these cases.

Alternatively, it may be that rejections of the synthetic LR% concern its realization rather than its phonetic occurrence as such: all LR% realizations in the *human* version were much smaller than the LR% realizations in the *test* version. However, we will not pursue this point further. Instead, we will look for possible relations between syntactic properties and the occurrence of different melodic boundary markers.

As was mentioned above, listeners appear to prefer a given type of melodic boundary marker in relation to the depth of the syntactic boundary. It was decided, therefore, to look whether there is a preference on the part of the speaker for a given type of melodic boundary marker as a function of the type of syntactic structure. The results are shown in Table 6. The same structural description is adopted as in the section on declination.

Table 6. Distribution of different types of melodic boundary markers as a function of syntactic structure in the *human* version

	melodic marker			
Boundary	none	*LR%*	*RH%*	other
S-S	3	–	–	–
P1 - P2	1	6	–	2
Within middle group	–	–	4	2
Pn - Extraposed	1	1	1	2
Other	3	–	–	2
Sum	8	7	5	8

Note: S-S: boundary between conjoined main clauses; P1-P2: boundary between first major constituent and the remainder of the utterance (usually beginning with the Finite Verb); Within middle group: boundaries within the part between the finite verb and the verbal end group (usually boundaries between major constituents); Pn - Extraposed: boundary between the verbal end group and right-dislocated, extraposed constituents.

The following observations can be made with respect to these data. The boundary between conjoined main clauses is not marked intonationally, although it is prosodically marked by the occurrence of a pause. This supports the conclusion drawn in the section on declination that the first of two conjoined main clauses may be treated intonationally as sentence-final. The P1-P2 boundary between the first constituent and the remainder of the utterance is marked mainly by *LR%*. Boundaries within the middle group are mainly marked by *RH%*; these cases involve boundaries such as those between Adverbial Phrases or between an Adverbial Phrase and the Direct or Indirect Object. Boundaries between the verbal end group and extraposed constituents are marked in several ways The number of cases is too small to look for meaningful subdivisions here.

Thus, it appears that there is some relation between syntactic factors and the choice of melodic boundary marker. At least three levels of depth appear to be involved:

1. boundaries between sentences and sentence-internal boundaries between main clauses: here, no melodic continuation marker is used (of course, this finding cannot be generalized to all sentence-internal boundaries between conjoined main clauses; it is easy to invent examples where some type of continuation marker is required);

2. boundaries between the first constituent and the remainder of the utterance;
3. boundaries between major constituents within the middle group.

Moreover, Table 6 shows that *LR%* and *RH%* together account for less than half of the boundaries: 12 out of 28 cases; apparently, there is considerable freedom either not to intonationally mark a sentence-internal prosodic boundary, or to use other types of boundary marker. Further investigations are needed to test and extend these preliminary results. In summary, the results in this section provide evidence that the selection of melodic configurations in human speech is governed by positional and syntactic factors.

7. Conclusion

The algorithm which had been developed in the framework of the SPIN/ASSP program was used to synthesize intonation for a sample text. The synthesized text was presented to four experts in the field of intonation, who were asked to listen to the text critically and to give comments on all details which were judged inappropriate. Their comments were classified and the outcomes of the diagnostic evaluation were used to make comparisons between the melodic properties of the synthetic version and a human reading of the same text.

In most cases where the judges had criticized properties of the synthetic version, the melodic properties of the rule-based version differed from those of the human version. Close inspection of the human version showed that melodic characteristics appeared to be associated with properties of the phonological, lexical and syntactic properties of the text. The following results were obtained.

In order to compute the baseline declination, a distinction should be made between three positions of the prosodic phrase in the utterance: initial, medial and final. In initial and medial positions, the baseline has the same end frequency; in medial and final positions, the baseline has, on average, the same onset frequency.

The size of pitch movements should be computed such that F_0 maxima are bound to an upper limit; moreover, a distinction between primary and secondary prominence would be useful: some types of words such as modal auxiliaries should receive only secondary accent.

The distribution of different melodic configurations depends on positional and structural constraints: the $\overset{*}{R}\overset{*}{F}$ configuration is most likely to occur in utterance-final position; in addition, there may be an influence of structural properties: $\overset{*}{R}\overset{*}{F}$ seems most appropriate when the two accented words belong to the same syntactic constituent. The distribution of melodic boundary markers appears to be related to some extent to syntactic factors. From the present findings it appears that the type of structural description which is required is less hierarchical than the descriptions which are generated by traditional phrase structure grammar (cf. Gee—Grosjean 1983). In particular, within the part of the utterance which is traditionally known as VP, less hierarchical structure seems to be required.

The preliminary conclusions drawn here must be considered as hypotheses which can only be confirmed by further investigations. As far as the application of these insights for text-to-speech conversion is concerned, the present findings indicate what type of syntactic information is required, and — consequently — how syntactic parsers should be designed so that they provide the required information. Keijsper (1989) rightly points out that text characteristics do not determine the distribution of accents. This applies also to intonational characteristics: they are not determined by the formal properties of the text. Instead, particular intonational characteristics may support particular interpretations while ruling out other ones. Yet, the present results suggest that some melodic properties tend to be associated with certain formal text properties. There are several reasons why this discrepancy between the two points of view is only apparent. In the first place, professional readers performing a human equivalent of text-to-speech conversion may rely to a considerable extent on formal properties of the text for the generation of prosody. Secondly, we have not looked at deterministic relations but much more at associations between the characteristics of text and intonation. If we assume that the several subsystems are not completely orthogonal, but that they are to some extent related, because speakers aiming to express a certain message tune the choices within different subsystems onto each other, certain associations would be the rule rather than the exception.

Appendix:
Transcription symbols for intonation contours

Transcription	IPO notation	Description
$\overset{*}{R}$	1	prominence-lending rise (early in syllable)
$\overset{*}{F}$	A	prominence-lending fall (early in syllable)
$\overset{*}{R}\ \overset{*}{F}$	1 A	sequence of $\overset{*}{R}$ and $\overset{*}{F}$ associated with two successive accented syllables
$R\overset{*}{\&}F$	1&A	combination of prominence-lending rise and fall on the same syllable
$\overset{*}{R}\ FF$	1 D	prominence-lending rise (early in the syllable) followed by gradual falling pitch until onset of next $\overset{*}{R}$
LR%	0 2	non-prominence-lending rise (late in the syllable), starting from the baseline
$\overset{*}{R}H\%$	1 ∅	$\overset{*}{R}$ followed by level high pitch until the end of the phrase

Notes:
— *R* represents pitch rise; F represents pitch fall; FF represents gradual pitch fall, usually extending over several syllables; *L* represents low level pitch; *H* represents high level pitch.
— '&' indicates that both pitch movements are associated with the same syllable.
— '*' indicates that a pitch movement is associated with an accented syllable.
— '%' indicates that the movement or level tone is associated with a boundary.
— IPO notation conforms to 't Hart—Collier—Cohen (1990).

For movements associated with single syllables, the precise timing is specified by the rules for phonetic realization.

Sandhi processes in natural and synthetic speech

Willy Jongenburger—Vincent J. van Heuven

Abstract

Starting from the naive principle that a text-to-speech system should imitate natural speech as closely as possible, the main concern of this project is to make a stock-taking of sandhi phenomena in the natural speech of the model speaker. Next, diphone speech of the model speaker is evaluated in order to decide which sandhi phenomena are and which are not already implicitly present in the diphones. Those that are not implicitly present have to be (explicitly) accounted for by rule in the transcription module MORPHON.

1. Introduction

Let us assume, as a first approximation, that a text-to-speech system should imitate natural speech as closely as possible. Our text-to-speech system should then imitate the human sound adjustments (sandhi processes). We investigated which sandhi rules do apply in the speech of our designated talker PB, and which rules do not. For this purpose we made an inventory of the sandhi processes known to be applicable to Dutch (section 2). Next, we decided, on the basis of informal listening, to what extent each of these processes is actually manifest in the speech of our model speaker (section 3). A pragmatic criterion based on frequency of occurrence was used to decide whether a sandhi process is compulsory or not (section 4). In section 5 the distribution of the glottal stop is discussed. Section 6 deals with the question to what degree the sound adjustments are implicitly present in our diphone inventory. Finally, in section 7 we shall present our recommendations for the transcription module.

2. Sandhi processes

We shall now discuss the different types of sandhi processes. An exhaustive list of sandhi rules plus examples is included in appendix 1; Table 1 presents a summary of the rules investigated. Our primary source is Trommelen—Zonneveld (1979).

We have subdivided the various sandhi rules into the following four classes:

I. Morpheme modification rules related to "syllable structure" modify sequences of consonants and vowels. They eliminate awkward sequences of only consonants or only vowels by insertion or elision of vowels and consonants, respectively, and generate regularly alternating CV-syllables.

II. There are several sandhi processes that concern vowels; these are called "vowel-adjustments". For this category of adjustments, stress is an important factor. Unstressed vowels are weak and often lose a part of their articulation (vowel shortening, vowel reduction); they can even disappear completely.

III. In the case of "assimilation" spreading of features takes place. When assimilation takes place a phonological feature of a segment changes under the influence of its phonetic context and that segment loses its identity. For instance, an unvoiced [f] can change to a voiced [v]: *afdak* [ɑfdɑk] 'shed' becomes [ɑvdɑk]. Assimilation is not inevitable; the speaker can prevent assimilation by making pauses. Clearly, assimilation processes will apply sooner as speaking rate increases.

IV. Finally, we also want to investigate the language-specific allophonic rule that turns a light [l] into a dark [ɫ] in certain environments.

3. Sound adjustments in the speech of PB, procedure and results

If we want to imitate the speech of our model speaker PB, we have to know which sandhi rules apply in his speech. For our analysis of the speech of PB we have chosen four texts (approximately 1,500 words). These texts are radio comments and news reports of which we have recordings by PB. Potential cases of sandhi rule application were marked in the texts automatically rather than by hand. For this purpose the above set of sandhi rules was incorporated into an existing letter-to-sound conversion program (Berendsen—Langeweg—van Leeuwen 1986) using the phonological rule compiler TooLip developed by van Leeuwen (1989a).

The first author then listened to the corresponding speech, and indicated for each position where a sandhi rule could apply, whether or not it did.

Before we go on to the results section some remarks are in order:

— Sandhi rules that apply across words, such as assimilation and degemination, are ignored when a prosodic pause is present between the words. Such applications of sandhi rules are left out of the statistics.
— When two sandhi rules can (theoretically) apply at the time to one segment, one of the rules will apply and the other will be blocked. In a sequence as *openkluis* [o:pəŋklʌys] 'open safe-deposit' the rule "n-elision after ə" is said to be blocked by the assimilation rule "n ⇒ ŋ/ — k".
— When two different, independent sandhi rules can lead to the same spoken realization of a word, we cannot tell which sandhi rule has applied. In these cases we say rather arbitrarily that the rule with the less specific context did apply and the rule with the more specific context is blocked. We suppose, for instance, that *miljoenen mensen* [mɪlju·nə mɛnsə] 'millions of people' is the result of assimilation and degemination and not of n-elision. This means that we treat the rule "n-elision" as blocked.

In Table 1 the results are presented. By means of the acquired overview we can determine how often a sandhi rule has applied in the speech of PB, how often the rule has not applied, and how often the rule is blocked by another rule.

Table 1. Frequency of application of 32 sandhi rules in text corpus (further see text)

	applied	not applied	blocked	N	p	c/o
degemination	95.9	4.1	-	73	<.01	c+
t-elision	22.6	48.4	29.0	31	.13	c
χ-elision	-	-	-	0	-	o
n-elision *vɔlgəs*	11.1	88.9	-	9	.04	o-
schwa-insertion	11.1	88.9	-	18	<.01	-
j-insertion	25.9	74.1	-	27	.02	o
w-insertion	10.0	90.0	-	10	.02	o-
n-elision after ə	26.5	64.2	9.3	162	<.01	
glottal stop	56.2	43.8	-	397	.02	
e:-shortening	70.6	29.4	-	17	.14	c
a:-shortening	31.0	69.0	-	29	.06	o
o:-shortening	14.3	85.7	-	21	<.01	o-
i·-shortening	9.4	90.6	-	32	<.01	o-

Table 1—Continued

	applied	not applied	blocked	N	p	c/o
vowel reduction	8.0	84.0	8.0	50	<.01	o-
vowel raising	-	100.0	-	1	-	o
i-gliding *pja:no:*	-	-	-	0	-	o
i-gliding *so:sja:l*	100.0	-	-	6	.03	c+
car.ov. ass. *ɔp sak*	79.7	20.3	-	59	<.01	c+
antic.ass. *azbak*	90.8	9.2	-	77	<.01	c+
antic.ass. *batpak*	100.0	-	-	2	.50	c
final devoicing	100.0	-	-	77	<.01	c+
n ⇒ ŋ / _ ɣ,χ,k	89.5	10.5	-	19	<.01	c+
n ⇒ m / _ p,b,m	91.4	2.9	5.7	35	<.01	c+
n ⇒ ɲ / _ j	100.0	-	-	1	-	c
n ⇒ ɱ / _ f,v,w	84.2	10.5	5.3	57	<.01	c+
s,j ⇒ ʃ	100.0	-	-	5	.06	c
t,j ⇒ c	-	-	-	0	-	c
t-j ⇒ c	100.0	-	-	6	.03	c+
p,j ⇒ pj	-	-	-	0	-	c
d,j ⇒ ɟ	-	-	-	0	-	c
d-weakening	50.0	50.0	-	8	1.00	o
dark ɫ	45.3	54.7	-	95	.41	o

Note: In the first column the relative frequency of the cases in which the sandhi rules do apply is indicated, in the second column the relative frequency of the cases in which the sandhi rules do not apply is and in the third column the relative frequency of the cases in which the sandhi rules are blocked. The fourth column lists the number of cases for each sandhi rule, the fifth column for each sandhi rule the value of p for the proportion applied/not applied by means of a binomial test (50 percent-50 percent), and finally the sixth column specifies whether a sandhi rule is compulsory (c) or optional (o); c+ means incontestably compulsory, o- means incontestably optional.

4. Interpretation of the results

In order to decide whether or not a sandhi rule is compulsory in PB speech, we apply two criteria:

— $p < .05$, the proportion applied/not applied should significantly deviate from the 50 percent-50 percent proportion
— one of the categories "applied" or "not applied" should contain at least 75 percent of all cases (75/25-test).

The results for 15 out of the 33 sandhi rules satisfy both conditions. This means that we have a strong cue in the decision whether or not these rules are compulsory. Rules that have been applied in at least 75 percent of all cases we call compulsory (these cases are marked in Table 1 with c+), rules that have not been applied in at least 75 percent of all cases we call optional (marked by o−).

For the remaining rules that satisfy neither condition, we will base our decision whether or not the sound adjustments are compulsory, on the consideration that PB has a rather formal speaking style. Therefore, informal sandhi rules are optional.[1] Further, we assume that, on the analogy of compulsory assimilation processes of voice and place, the sandhi rules of palatalization are compulsory as well in the speech of PB.

The rule of "t-elision in consonant clusters" does not apply in 48.4 percent, applies in 22.6 percent and is blocked in 29.0 percent of all potential cases. Research in order to find sub-regularities in the application of this rule failed. Therefore, the assumption that the articulation of [t] in consonant clusters demands rather difficult, acrobatic movements of the organs of speech must settle the matter. We expect that t-elision will apply in order to increase speech comfort.

Research in order to detect subregularities in the application of the rule "n-elision after schwa" has shown that this sandhi rule respects the ideal structure of a word, i.e., a regular alternation of consonants and vowels. When a syllable or word final /n/ is followed by another consonant, elision of /n/ will change the undesirable sequence of consonants to a more favorable sequence, for instance *kijken door* [kɛɪkən do:r] 'look through' becomes [kɛɪkə do:r]. This is exactly what happens in PB speech: the /n/ is elided within a phonological phrase before a consonant; /n/ is not elided when followed by a vowel. This means that n-elision respects the ideal structure -CVCVC-.

In order to find subregularities in the application of the rule "l ⟹ ɫ" we have taken into consideration the transcriptions of the Speech Database project (van Zanten—Damen—van Houten, this volume). These data show that an "in-between" form of [l] appears in word final position and that in non-word-final position the light [l] appears. This means that a truly dark [ɫ] hardly ever appears in PB speech. This fact is probably due to the cultivated speaking style of PB.

Glottal stop insertion is a rather special case. Although the proportion 56.2 percent applied / 43.8 percent not applied (with $N=397$ and $p= .02$) significantly deviates from a 50/50 proportion, this ratio is hardly satisfactory.

In order to discover subregularities in the insertion of the glottal stop we shall examine our database more closely in section 5.

5. Distribution of the glottal stop

Several factors prove to be of importance for glottal stop insertion. We have investigated the influence of the following factors on glottal stop insertion:

— *prosodic pause*: it appears that when a prosodic pause precedes the (morpheme-)initial vowel, a glottal stop is always inserted; within a phonological phrase no regularity is found;
— *feature voice of the preceding phoneme*: it appears that when a (by definition voiced) vowel precedes the (morpheme-)initial vowel, a glottal stop is generally inserted; when the preceding phoneme is an unvoiced consonant in general no glottal stop is inserted; when the preceding phoneme is a voiced consonant no regularity is found;
— *length of the target word and its left neighbor*: it appears that, independently of the length of the left neighbor, a glottal stop is inserted when the target word is polysyllabic; when the target word is monosyllabic no glottal stop is inserted;
— *prominence* of the syllable where the glottal stop is to be inserted: a prominent syllable is more likely to undergo glottal stop insertion than a non-prominent syllable.

The effects of the different factors on the glottal stop insertion seem to be interwoven with each other. Intricate interactions between the factors determine whether a glottal stop is or is not inserted. When we take into consideration all possible combinations of the three most important conditioning factors (prosodic pause, prominence and length of the target word), we end up with Table 2.

With the help of this table we can predict glottal stop insertion for each combination of the conditioning factors. When we predict, for instance, that a glottal stop is inserted when the target word is polysyllabic with lexical stress on the initial syllable in a phonological phrase, this prediction will be true in 61 cases and false in 15 cases. This means that in this specific condition we make a wrong prediction in 20 percent of the cases. In the table, "*" marks the correctly predicted cases and the underlined cases are the incorrectly predicted. Out of the total of 397 cases of potential glottal stop insertion we make 95 wrong predictions, i.e., 24 percent. This means that we can predict correctly whether a glottal stop will or will not be inserted in 76 percent of all potential glottal stop positions in the corpus. For a more elaborate treatment of glottal stop insertion based on the PB-corpus, the reader is referred to Jongenburger—van Heuven (1991). For a discussion of acoustic correlates of glottal stops on a more general level, see Krech (1968) for German and Malécot (1975) for French.

Table 2. Glottal stop distribution as a function of three dichotomous linguistic variables

pause	prominence	polysyllabic	+[ʔ]	-[ʔ]	%error
+	+	+	7	0	0
+	+	-	6	0	0
+	-	+	4	0	0
+	-	-	64	0	0
-	+	+	61	*15**	20
-	+	-	*17**	19	47
-	-	+	15	*14**	48
-	-	-	*49**	126	28

Note: The first column indicates whether a pause does (+) or does not (-) precede the initial vowel; the second column whether the initial syllable is prominent (+) or not (-); the third column whether the word is polysyllabic (+) or monosyllabic (-): the fourth column indicates how often a glottal stop is inserted in the specific condition; the fifth column how often no glottal stop is inserted in the specific condition; the sixth column lists the percentage of errors that will be made by the prediction. Incorrect decisions are marked by an asterisk

6. Sound adjustments in diphones

In this stage of the project we know which sandhi rules apply in the speech of PB. Our text-to-speech converter which is based on diphone concatenation, should imitate these sounds adjustments. Since diphones contain the transitions between two sounds, we expect that sound adjustments (such as assimilation) will already be present to a certain degree in some, if not all, diphones of the PB inventory. We will have to decide for each sandhi rule whether the adjustments that are implicitly present in the diphones satisfy the listener, that is are strong enough, or whether the adjustments in the diphones are not strong enough and will have to be accounted for by explicit rules in the transcription module. We will illustrate this issue as follows. For a word such as *tentzeil* [tɛntsɛɪl] 'canvas' we do not know whether in the diphone concatenation the diphone /tz/ with implicit assimilation of voice should be used or the diphone /ts/ with explicit assimilation as brought about by the rule system MORPHON (see Nunn—van Heuven, this volume). A listening test is needed to decide this matter. For this purpose we prepared a set of stimulus words, which we shall describe in section 6.1. In section 6.2 we will present and discuss the results of the listening test and relate the results to our earlier findings on the sandhi phenomena in PB's speech.

6.1. Stimuli and set-up of the listening test

The set of stimuli we use will have to satisfy several demands that we will discuss now.

In the first place we want to compare two versions of one and the same word: one version with implicit adjustment in the diphones, for instance *tentzeil* by means of concatenation of the diphones: /tɛ ɛn nt tz zɛɪ ɛɪ ɫ/ and the other version with explicit adjustment by rule (/z/ ⇒ [s] / — t) which in our example is obtained by concatenation of the diphones: /tɛ ɛn nt ts sɛɪ ɛɪ ɫ/. Other examples: the word *zeeën* /ze:ən/ 'seas' is presented in the versions /ze: e:ə ən/ and /ze: e:j jə ən/, the word *aanpak* /a:npɑk/ 'approach' is presented in the versions /a:n np pɑ ɑk/ and /a:m mp pɑ ɑk/.

Secondly, the stimulus words have to be presented to the listener in a carrier sentence in order to give the listener an indication of speech rate. We assume that speech rate will influence sandhi processes such that in fast, sloppy speech more sandhi phenomena will occur than in slow, carefully articulated speech. Therefore, the listener needs cues to speech rate in order to properly evaluate the stimuli in terms of pleasantness. We have chosen the carrier sentence *En toen zei ze ... tegen me* /ɛn tu·n zɛɪ zə ... te:ɣən mə/ 'and then she said ... to me'. The target words are embedded in the middle of the utterance.

In the third place the diphones that are used for the stimuli should be taken from the set of diphones with the highest intelligibility. That is why we have chosen the set of PB diphones with 30 reflection coefficients, which are normalized with respect to duration in order to ensure that specific vowels and consonants have the same length in all the diphones in which they occur (van Bezooijen 1990; van Bezooijen—Pols, this volume). We want to note here that no integrally articulated complex consonant clusters are present in our selection of PB diphones. This means that sound adjustments such as insertions and elisions in consonant clusters such as in *melk* [mɛlək] 'milk' and *postbode* [pɔsbo:də] 'post man' cannot be implicitly present in the diphones and thus will always have to be accounted for by rules. For these sandhi processes we cannot make a distinction between implicit and explicit adjustments. Still we can make two versions of each stimulus word, for example /mɛ ɛl lk/ versus /mɛ ɛl lə ək/ and /pɔ ɔs st tb bo: o:d də/ versus /pɔ ɔs sb bo: o:d də/. When the listeners give a negative judgment for both versions, that is if both versions sound unpleasant, this might mean that we need integrally articulated complex consonant clusters after all.

In the case of vowel adjustments we can often make sets of stimulus words that consists of more than two versions. For example the word *minuut* 'minute' can be realized in three versions: /mi· i·n ny· y·t/, /mɪ ɪn ny· y·t/, /mə ən ny· y·t/. Note that these adjustments, too, cannot be implicitly present in the diphones.

In some cases the diphones needed for a version do not exist. For example the word *afdak* 'shelter' can only be made with implicit adjustment in the diphones: /ɑf fd dɑ ɑk/. Because the diphone /vd/ is not contained in the diphones set, we cannot concatenate the diphones /ɑv vd dɑ ɑk/ for the version with explicit adjustment by rule.

A further possible imperfection of the diphone set is that there are no geminates. This means that we cannot generate the word *stamppot* 'hutch potch' in the version [stɑmppɔt] without degemination, but can only create the version with degemination [stɑmpɔt]. For the complete set of stimulus words we refer to Jongenburger (1991).

Subjects of the rather informal listening test were the two authors and a colleague at Leiden University. For each set of stimulus words, subjects were asked to note their preference for one word of the set. Where a set is larger than two stimulus words, they had to rank the alternatives in terms of acceptability. In the case where there is only one stimulus word, they were asked if the realization of the word was acceptable or not.

6.2. Results of the listening test

We want to compare the results of the present experiment with our earlier findings on the sandhi phenomena in PB speech. For this purpose we present the data of the listening test and information on sandhi in the speech of our designated talker in Table 3.

Table 3. Subjects' preferences for each sandhi rule and application of sandhi rules in natural PB speech

sandhi rule	subjects' preference in diphone speech	natural PB speech
degemination	+/*	+
t-elision	+	+
χ-elision	+!	–
n-elision before s	+!	–

Table 3—Continued

sandhi rule	subjects' preference in diphone speech	natural PB speech
schwa-insertion	–	–
homorganic glide insertion:		
j-insertion after iˑ	–	–
j-insertion after eː	+!	
w-insertion after yˑ	–	–
w-insertion after oː	+!	–
n-elision after schwa	+	+
aː-shortening	+!	–
oː-shortening	–	–
eː-shortening	+	+
iˑ-shortening	–	–
vowel reduction to schwa	–	–
schwa-elision	–	–
vowel raising	+!	–
i-gliding [pjaːnoː]	–	–
i-gliding [soːʃaːlə]	*	+
assimilation of voice:		
v ⇒ f in a [1 stress] syll.	+	+
v ⇒ f in a [≥ 2 stress] syll.	+	+
z ⇒ s in a [1 stress] syll.	+	+
z ⇒ s in a [≥ 2 stress] syll.	+	+
f ⇒ v	–	+
s ⇒ z	–	+
p ⇒ b	–	+
χ ⇒ ɣ	–	+
k ⇒ g	–	+
t ⇒ d	–	+
homorganic nasal adjustment:		
n ⇒ ŋ / _ χ	+	+
n ⇒ ŋ / _ k in a [1 stress] syll.	–	+
n ⇒ ŋ / _ k in a [≥ 2 stress] syll.	+	+
n ⇒ m / _ p	–	+
n ⇒ m / _ b	+	+
n ⇒ m / _ m	–	+
n ⇒ ɱ / _ f	–	+
n ⇒ ɱ / _ v	–	+
n ⇒ ɱ / _ w	–	+

Table 3—Continued

sandhi rule	subjects preference in diphone speech	natural PB speech
homorganic nasal adjustment:		
n ⇒ ɲ / _ j	+	+
palatalization:		
t - j ⇒ c	+	+
p - j ⇒ pj	–	+
d - j ⇒ ɟ	*	+
s - j ⇒ ʃ	*	+
d-weakening	–	–

Note: The left column identifies the sandhi processes. The column in the middle gives the preferences of the subjects for each sandhi process; the symbol '+' means that the subjects prefer the adjustment to be explicit (by rule), '–' means that they prefer the adjustment to be implicit, '*' means that required diphones are lacking, '!' means discrepancy between natural and diphone speech. The right column indicates for each sandhi rule whether in PB speech the rule does or does not apply.

It appears from Table 3 that sound adjustments by assimilation of voice implicitly present in the diphones are strong enough when these processes are anticipatory. In case of carryover assimilation, however, the adjustments need to be explicitly accounted for by rule; here the adjustments implicit in the diphones are not strong enough.

The homorganic nasal adjustments implicitly present in the diphones are satisfactory with the exception of the processes:

n ⇒ ŋ / _ χ
n ⇒ ŋ / _ k before a [1 stress] syllable
n ⇒ m / _ b
n ⇒ ɲ / _ j

Subjects prefer these adjustments to be explicitly accounted for by rule. Observe that such anticipatory homorganic nasal adaptation is sufficiently reflected in the diphones when the nasal occurs in a syllable with primary stress with the conditioning segment following in a secondarily stressed syllable (e.g. *ˈinˌkoop* ⇒ [ˈɪnko:p] 'purchase'). However when the nasal occurs in a syllable with secondary stress followed by the conditioning phoneme in a syllable bearing primary stress, the strength of the assimilation is considered insufficient, (e.g., [ˌɔnˈkʌys] *onkuis* 'without chastity'). Clearly, a precise, stressed, articulation of a speech sound makes it resistant to the assimilation process. When we assume that listeners are aware of this fact, they expect less or weaker adjustment in primary stressed than in secondary stressed syllables. This explains why the relatively weak implicit adjustment in primary stressed syllables does satisfy the subjects whereas the implicit adjustment in secondary stressed syllables is insufficient.[2] While selecting the stimulus material for this experiment little attention was paid to this matter but it is interesting to investigate this matter in greater detail in the future.

For the processes of palatalization we note that two types of adjustments cannot be accounted for by the present diphone set. Stimulus words which contain palatalization phenomena of the type dj ⇒ ɟ and sj ⇒ ʃ are judged unsatisfactory by the subjects. In both cases only the versions with adjustment by rule are presented to the subjects; the versions with implicit adjustment in the diphones cannot be made because the diphones /dj/ and /sj/ are absent from the set of diphones. This also means that i-gliding of the type [so:ʃa:lə] cannot be realized with the current diphone set. It seems that the diphone set should be expanded with the diphones /sj/ and /dj/.

It appears from Table 3 that the subjects prefer the elision processes to apply with the exception of schwa elision. The process of weakening should not be applied. Further, we see that shortening of /a:/ and /e:/ are evaluated as acceptable, whereas shortening of o: and i· are evaluated as unacceptable. For the other vowel adjustments we see that schwa insertion, vowel reduction to schwa, and i-gliding should not apply in order to get acceptable speech but that vowel raising should apply.

Looking at the results for the homorganic glide insertion we find that explicit insertions are required only after [−high] vowels (e:, o:) and not after a [+high] vowel (i·, y·).

We mentioned in section 6.1 the absence of integrally articulated complex consonant clusters in our diphone set. From our data in Table 3 we conclude that processes such as insertions and elisions in consonant clusters (t-elision, χ-elision, n-elision before s, schwa insertion and schwa elision) can be accurately accounted for by the diphone set. Target words where degemination has taken place, seem to be less acceptable with respect to temporal organization. A duration rule that doubles the duration of the plosive might solve the problem. So we draw the conclusion that there is no great need for integrally articulated complex consonant clusters.

Now let us compare these results with what actually happens in PB speech (articulation rate of the diphone speech is comparable to the articulation rate of PB "live": (5.7 syll/s versus 5.4 syll/s, respectively). We see that some sandhi rules do not apply in the speech of PB while application of these very rules is preferred by the subjects (marked in Table 3 by "!").

Apparently, we cannot just copy speech characteristics from our model speaker to less than optimal quality speech such as diphone speech. The recordings of the speech of PB were made under favorable conditions so that the speaker knew that the intelligibility of his speech is optimal. Diphone speech, however, is not optimally intelligible and therefore requires different speech features. This has implications for the acceptability of synthetic speech based on the sandhi phenomena such as they appear in PB's speech. This observation leads us to the decision to make two different sets of sandhi rules so that the user of the text-to-speech system can choose which set to use. One set includes all the sandhi rules in the way that PB applies them, leading to a close imitation of PB, the other set of rules leads to more acceptable diphone speech, at last as far as sandhi is concerned, and is not necessarily based on what PB does. This set of rules includes the former set extended with the rules preferred by the subjects.

7. Recommendations for the transcription module

In order to obtain synthetic speech that imitates natural PB speech as closely as possible, the following set of sandhi rules should be used:

— t-elision in consonant clusters
— n-elision after schwa before a consonant (within a phonological phrase)
— e:-shortening
— carryover assimilation of voice
— homorganic nasal adjustment:

$n \Rightarrow ŋ$ / _ χ
$n \Rightarrow ŋ$ / _ k before a [1 stress] syllable
$n \Rightarrow ŋ$ / _ b
$n \Rightarrow ɲ$ / _ j

— palatalization:

t-j ⇒ c

— final devoicing
— glottal stop under specific conditions (see section 4).

This set can be extended by the following rules to obtain more acceptable diphone speech:

— χ-elision
— n-elision before s
— j-insertion after e:
— w-insertion after o:
— a:-shortening
— vowel raising

Appendix: Survey of sandhi rules

Modification rules related to syllable structure

— Degemination
reduction of two identical consonants to one occurs in Dutch whenever two identical consonants are adjacent.
stampot /stamppɔt/ ⇒ [stampɔt] 'hotchpot', *misstap* /mɪsstap/ ⇒ [mɪstap] 'misstep'

— t-Elision in consonant clusters
postbode /pɔstbo:də/ ⇒ [pɔsbo:də] 'postman', *kastje* /kastjə/ ⇒ [kasjə] 'cupboard'

— χ-Elision
schrijven /sχrɛɪvən/ ⇒ [srɛɪvən] 'write'
schroeven /sχru·vən/ ⇒ [sru·vən] 'screws'

— n-Elision before s
every n after schwa and before s can be elided.
volgens /vɔlɣəns/⇒ [vɔlɣəs] 'according to', *wegens* /we:'ɣəns/⇒ [we:ɣəs] 'because of'

— Schwa-insertion after /l/ and /r/ and before another tautosyllabic consonant
arm /arm/ [arəm] 'arm', *lantaarn* /lanta:rn/ ⇒ [lanta:rən] 'lantern', but *armen* / armən/ *[arəmən] 'arms'

— Homorganic glide insertion
between a stem-final vowel (not schwa or /a:/) and a following suffix that begins with a vowel, a glide (/w/ after a back vowel and /j/ after a front vowel) is inserted in order to prevent a succession of vowels.
drieën /dri·ən/ ⇒ [dri·jən] 'threes', *kanoën* /ka:no:ən/ ⇒ [ka:no:wən] 'to canoe'

— n-Elision after schwa
particularly in western dialects of Dutch syllable-final /n/ after schwa can disappear, except when the context of /n/ is /ə _ də/.
ramen /ra:mən/ ⇒ [ra:mə] 'windows', *eigendom* /ɛɪɣədɔm/ ⇒ [ɛɪɣədɔm] 'property', but *volgende* /vɔlɣəndə/⇒ *[vɔlɣədə] 'next'

— Glottal stop
a glottal stop is inserted when a vowel is in hiatus position, for instance at the beginning of a word, in the sequence [schwa - unreduced vowel]

or in the sequence of two identical vowels. Rules are unclear in the literature.
aap /#a:p/ ⇒ [ʔa:p] 'monkeys', *beamen* /bəa:mən/ ⇒ [bəʔa:mən] 'to assent', *moe oefent* /mu· u·fənt/ ⇒ [mu·ʔu·fənt] 'mum is practising'

Vowel adjustments

— a:-, o:-, e:-, i·-shortening
these are the optional processes that lead to a shortening of vowels in non primary stressed initial syllables. Shortening only applies to long vowels in open syllables, followed by a consonant in the next syllable.
banaan /ba:na:n/ ⇒ [bɑna:n 'banana', *politie* /po:li·tsi·/ ⇒ [pɔli·tsi·] 'police', *melaats* /me:la:ts/ ⇒ [mɪla:ts] 'leprous', *minuut* /mi·ny·t/ ⇒ [mɪny·t] 'minute'

— Vowel reduction to schwa
this rather informal rule applies to unstressed vowels.
Canada /ka:na:da:/ ⇒ [ka:nəda:] 'Canada', *economie* /e:ko:no:mi·/ ⇒ [e:kəno:mi·] 'economics', *salaris* /sa:la:rəs/ ⇒ [səla:rəs] 'salary'

— Vowel raising
if the vowel /e:/ is followed by another vowel or by by a glide (as a result of homorganic glide insertion), then /e:/ is raised to /i·/. This rule only applies to unstressed non-initial syllables.
ideaal /i·de:a:l/ ⇒ [i·di·a:l] 'ideal', *Koreaan* /ko:re:a:n/ ⇒ [ko:ri·a:n] 'Korean'

— i-Gliding
a non-initial, unstressed [i·] looses its syllabic properties between an obstruent and a vowel.
kopieer /ko:pi·e:r/ ⇒ [ko:pje:r] 'copy', *Aziaat* /a:zi·a:t/ ⇒ [a:zja:t] 'Asian', *sociaal* /so:si·a:l/ ⇒ [so:sja:l] 'social'

Assimilation processes

— Carryover assimilation of voice
fricatives are unvoiced if preceded by an obstruent.
op zak /ɔp#zɑk/ ⇒ [ɔpsɑk] 'in ones pocket', *zegt veel* /zɛχt#ve:l/ ⇒ [zɛχt fe:l] 'says a lot', *afzien* /ɑf#zi·n/ ⇒ [ɑfsi·n] 'give up'

— Anticipatory assimilation of voice: [−voice] ⇒ [+voice]
obstruents are voiced if followed by a voiced plosive.
opdienen /ɔpdi·nən/ ⇒ [ɔbdi·nən] 'serve', *asbak* /ɑsbɑk/ ⇒ [ɑzbɑk] 'ash tray'

— Anticipatory assimilation and final devoicing
all syllable final obstruents are unvoiced.
broodplank /bro:dplaŋk/ ⇒ [bro:tplaŋk] 'bread-board', *bed* /bɛd/ ⇒ [bɛt] 'bed'

— Homorganic nasal adjustment
the place of articulation of the nasal becomes identical to the place of articulation of the following consonant.
bilabial:
/n/ ⇒ /m/ / _ p,m,b *onbewust* /ɔnbəwœst/ ⇒ [ɔmbəwœst] 'unconscious'
velar:
/n/ ⇒ /ŋ/ / _ k,χ,g *inclusief* /ɪnkly·zi·f/ ⇒ [ɪŋkly·zi·f] 'inclusive'
labiodental:
/n/ ⇒ /ɱ/ / _ f,v,w *onwel* /ɔnwɛl/ ⇒ [ɔɱwɛl] 'ill'
palatal:
/n/ ⇒ /ɲ/ / _ j *onjuist* /ɔnjʌyst/ ⇒ [ɔɲjʌyst] 'incorrect'

— Palatalization
the place of articulation of plosives, fricatives and nasals becomes identical to the place of articulation of [j] (palatal).
/t/ dental ⇒ palatal [c] in *weet je* /we·t jə/ [we:cə] 'do you know'
/p/ bilabial ⇒ palatal [pʲ] in *heb je* /hɛp jə/ [hɛpʲə] 'do you have'
/d/ alveolar ⇒ palatal [ɟ] in *djatie* /djati·/ [ɟati] 'teak'
/s/ dental ⇒ palatal [ʃ] in *was je* /wɑs jə/ [wɑʃə] 'were you'

— d-Weakening
the obstruent [d] becomes sonorant after a long vowel or a diphtong and before a schwa.
rode /ro:də/ ⇒ [ro:jə] 'red', *houden* /haʊdə/ ⇒ [haʊwə] 'keep'

— l ⇒ ɫ
a word initial "light" [l] sounds different from a word final "dark" [ɫ]
leren [le:rə] 'learn', *dal* [daɫ] 'valley'

Notes

1. It appears from Table 1 that seven sandhi processes hardly occur in the text: for these rules no p-value is given. We assume that the informal sound adjustments are optional in PB's speech.
2. Note that no such discrepancy is found for carryover assimilation of voice.

Part VI

Signal analysis

Speech quality and speaker characteristics

Berry Eggen—Sieb G. Nooteboom

Abstract

One of the applications of speech-coding algorithms is the generation of the output speech of text-to-speech systems. Linear predictive coding (LPC) is still one of the most powerful algorithms used for this purpose. This chapter describes some experiments which evaluate the quality of LPC speech. In particular, intelligibility and naturalness of LPC speech are studied. Ways are indicated to improve existing LPC speech-coding schemes. One alternative, the glottal-excited LPC synthesizer, is described in more detail.

1. Introduction

Linear predictive coding (LPC) is one of the most frequently used speech-coding algorithms in the SPIN/ASSP program. It is used as an analysis tool to derive basic speech parameters, and it is also used as a synthesis tool to generate the speech output of the SPIN/ASSP text-to-speech system.

Despite its many advantages such as the capability to resynthesize highly intelligible speech, the possibility to manipulate perceived aspects of speech, and the power to provide accurate estimates of speech parameters, LPC also has its shortcomings. LPC speech lacks naturalness, and speaker characteristics are degraded. The research reported on in this chapter aimed for two things. One was the assessment of some limitations of LPC as a scheme for speech analysis, manipulation and synthesis, the other was the exploration of ways to remove some of the drawbacks of LPC.

Intelligibility is an important attribute of speech quality. In general, LPC-based speech-coding schemes are capable of synthesizing highly intelligible speech which cannot easily be discriminated from natural speech by existing articulation tests. We tried to increase the sensitivity of such a test by measuring the intelligibility in the presence of interfering speech. Our main goal was to see if, in the case of synthetic speech, small differences in intelligibility can be magnified into large differences by adding interfering speech.

Intelligibility of synthetic speech is just one attribute of speech quality. Other factors, such as naturalness, also play an important role. As LPC lacks naturalness, we tried to determine what requirements are needed for the generation of natural-sounding speech. We did so by investigating the LPC residue, i.e. the error signal defined as the difference between the actual speech samples and the linearly predicted ones. In particular, we determined the relative importance of amplitude and phase information of the residue for the synthesis of natural-sounding male and female speech.

Besides intelligibility and naturalness, preservation of speaker characteristics may also be an important feature of a high quality speech-coding scheme. We found that the proper reproduction of the prosodic structure of natural speech by means of LPC resynthesis is not sufficient to reliably preserve the identity of different speakers (Eggen—Vogten 1990). We decided to concentrate our efforts on the improvement of the LPC speech coding scheme. We implemented a glottal-excited (GE) LPC speech synthesizer which incorporates a more detailed model of the human voicing source.

This chapter gives an overview of our attempts to formulate some limitations of LPC and it discusses possible ways to improve LPC. Section one describes a study on the intelligibility of various speech-coding schemes in the presence of interfering speech. Section two discusses the experiments on the synthesis of natural-sounding speech. The GE-LPC synthesizer is described in section three, and some general conclusions are presented at the end of this chapter.

2. Intelligibility of synthetic speech in the presence of interfering speech

Traditional articulation tests are not always sensitive enough to distinguish between various sorts of highly intelligible speech. Therefore, the need for more sensitive tests is apparent. It has been suggested by Nakatani—Dukes (1973) that small differences in intelligibility can be turned into large differences by adding noise to the test speech. We used interfering speech as a masker, since speech is frequently a source of interference in everyday listening situations. Both a traditional articulation test without noise and a newly developed "Monosyllabic Adaptive Speech Interference Test (MASIT)" were used to evaluate the intelligibility of nine different speech-coding schemes (Eggen 1989a).

MASIT estimates the speech interference threshold (SIT) of a list of 50 CVC words. The SIT is defined as the signal-to-noise (S/N) ratio of the test speech and the interfering speech where 50 percent of the stimuli are correctly identified. The CVCs are embedded in neutral carrier phrases and presented at S/N levels which are determined by a simple up-and-down adaptive procedure.

All speech material was spoken by the same male speaker. The speech-coding algorithms can be roughly categorized into four groups of different bit-rates. 120 kbit/s pulse code modulated speech was used as reference (PCM). The 20 kbit/s group contained an LPC version with 18 coefficients (LPC18) and a multipulse version with 12 pulses and 10 LPC coefficients (MPE). The third group comprised three 12 kbit/s LPC versions. Two of them used different formant-coding algorithms (LPC10F1, LPC10F2), the third one used the 10 LPC coefficients directly (LPC10). The fourth group of 4 kbit/s contained a software simulation of a hardware synthesizer (MEA), quantized reflection coefficients (RFC), and speech coded by means of temporal decomposition (TDC).

The carrier phrases also served as a basis for constructing the interference speech. Five tracks of interfering speech were mixed and played backwards. Before mixing, the interference speech was processed with the same nine speech-coding algorithms used for the test sentences. In this way, test and interfering speech were of the same quality.

The results of the articulation test and MASIT are presented in Figures 1a and 1b, respectively. The averages for eight subjects are shown. The Q measure shown in Figure 1b is defined as the difference between the SIT of the test speech and that of the PCM reference speech. A one-way analysis of variance was performed on the data. Both the articulation test and MASIT showed significant differences between the nine speech-coding types. According to post-hoc comparisons, the speech types can be categorized into different groups as indicated by the dashed lines in Figures 1a and 1b.

The articulation test shows no difference between speech types of the 4 and 12 kbit/s groups. MASIT does a much better job in distinguishing between these speech types. It can also be seen from these figures that MASIT not always magnifies differences in articulation scores. For instance, the difference between MPE and the 12 kbit/s group has disappeared in the case of MASIT. This means that, in the case of synthetic speech, differences in intelligibility are not always magnified by adding interfering speech; they may even disappear. Therefore, Nakatani's suggestion is apparently not generally valid. Furthermore, it can be concluded that the effect of the interfering speech on the test speech strongly depends on the particular speech-coding scheme used. Different speech-coding schemes code different acoustic-phonetic properties of the speech signal, some of which are more liable to be affected by interfering speech than others. We must conclude that, at least for synthetic speech, MASIT cannot replace traditional articulation tests. However, MASIT can be a valuable tool to assess the performance of speech-coding algorithms in noisy environments.

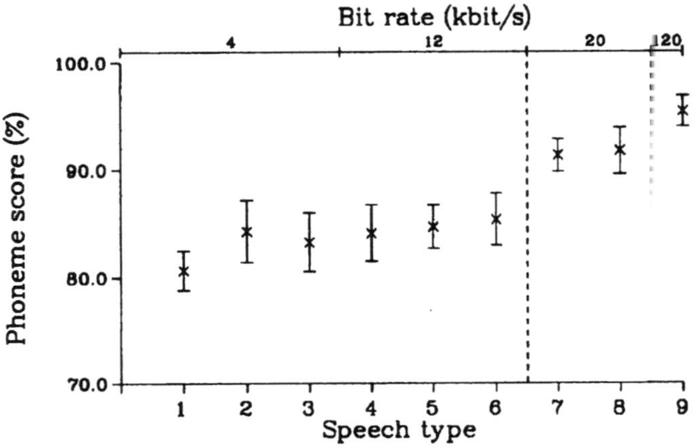

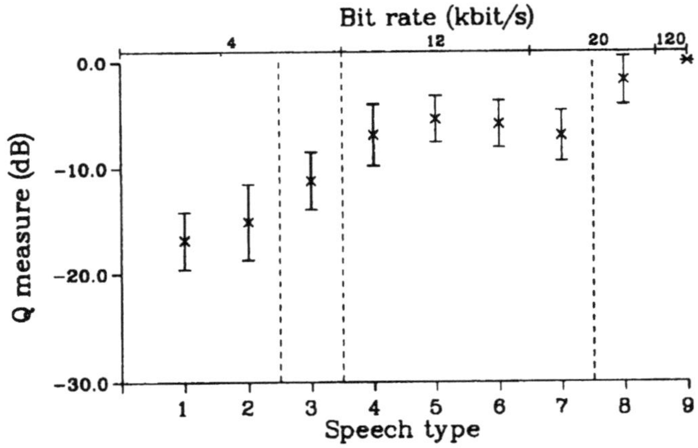

Figure 1. 1a. Results articulation test (without noise): mean percentage of phonemes correctly identified

1b. Results MASIT: Q measure in dB. The averages for 8 subjects are shown. The vertical bars represent the 95 percent confidence intervals. The parameter bit-rate is indicated at the top of the figure. The sub-divisions of the speech-coding algorithms are indicated by dashed lines. (Speech types: 1 = TDC, 2 = MEA, 3 = RFC, 4 = LPC10, 5 = LPC10F1, 6 = LPC10F2, 7 = MPE, 8 = LPC18, 9 = PCM)

3. The relative importance of amplitude and phase of the LPC residue for the synthesis of natural-sounding speech

The residue seems the obvious choice to study in more detail if we want to improve naturalness of LPC speech. It is defined as the difference between the actual speech samples and the linearly predicted ones. Theoretically, this means that the residue contains all the information necessary to give LPC speech a natural-sounding quality. The importance of the LPC residue also becomes apparent when we listen to it. In many cases, large parts of the LPC residue are intelligible, and the speaker of the original utterance can be identified.

Inspired by Atal—David (1978), we used a short-time Fourier representation of the LPC residue to study the relative importance of amplitude and phase information for the synthesis of male and female voices (Verhelst—Eggen 1990). As we wanted to interpret our experimental findings in terms of a speech synthesis filter, we chose a time-frequency representation based on the simplified speech production model of Figure 2.

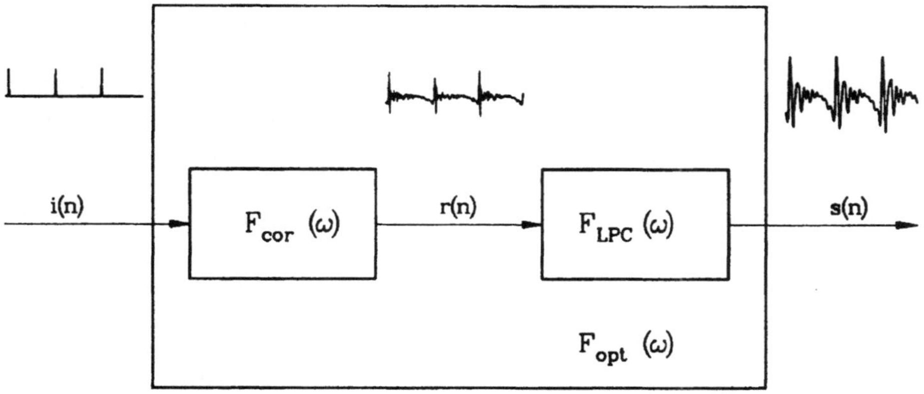

Figure 2. Simplified speech-production model. The optimal synthesis filter is formed by a cascade of a correction filter F_{cor} and an LPC filter F_{LPC}. i(n) = deltapulse, r(n) = LPC residue, s(n) = speech signal

According to this model, speech is considered as the output of an optimal synthesis filter F_{opt} which is excited by a deltapulse. As the impulse responses of F_{opt} overlap in time, it is difficult to determine F_{opt} directly from the speech wave. We can circumvent this problem by rewriting F_{opt} as a cascade of a correction filter F_{cor} and an LPC synthesis filter F_{LPC}. As the spectral characteristics of the residue, which forms the output of F_{cor}, are expected to be globally flat, the effective duration of the impulse response of F_{cor} is expected to be short, so that it can be approximated by a pitch-synchronous segmentation of the LPC residue.

Amplitude and phase spectra of the impulse response of F_{cor} were calculated using a fast Fourier transform (FFT) algorithm. After selected spectral modifications (see below), the inverse FFT was computed, and the modified LPC residue was constructed by overlap-adding the manipulated impulse responses. Next, the modified residue was used to drive the LPC filters which resulted in four different speech versions. The following spectral manipulations were performed: the phase spectrum was set to zero or left original, and the amplitude spectrum was given a constant value or remained unchanged.

Twenty short sentences, produced by 10 male and 10 by female speakers, were processed with the analysis-resynthesis system. The four versions of each sentence were presented to 12 subjects in a balanced paired-comparison experiment. Subjects had to indicate on a 5-point scale which one of the two stimuli of a pair they preferred. The stimuli were presented through headphones.

The inherent qualities of the four versions were determined by applying an analysis of variance on the preference scores. The data show the following over-all quality ranking for the four versions: version 1 (original amplitude/original phase), version 3 (original amplitude/zero phase), version 2 (constant amplitude/original phase), version 4 (constant amplitude/zero phase), where the versions are ordered in decreasing quality. Figures 3a and 3b show the quality factors of the utterances produced by the males and females, respectively.

The results show that amplitude information of the LPC residue is more important than phase information with respect to speech quality. For male voices the original amplitude information alone is almost sufficient to make the synthetic speech indistinguishable from natural speech. However, for female voices phase information also significantly increases speech quality. In general, we can conclude that coding of amplitude and phase information of the LPC residue can improve speech quality. The next section describes a possible way to code this information.

4. Implementation of a glottal-excited LPC synthesizer

Various reasons made us decide to implement a Glottal Excited (GE-) LPC synthesizer. Firstly, the study described in section 3 showed that both

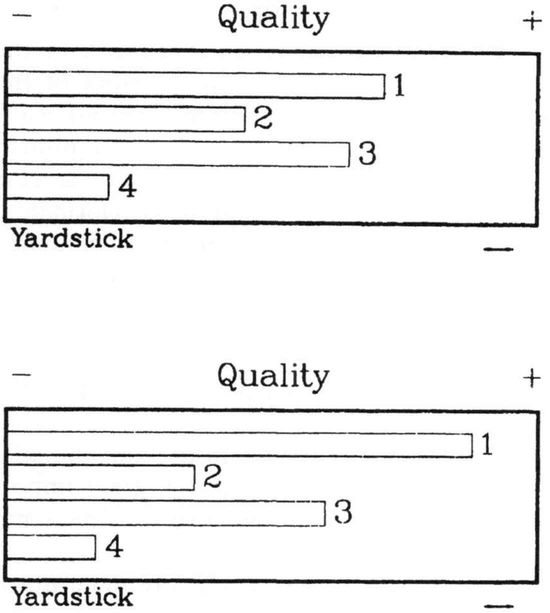

Figure 3. Quality judgments of the four speech versions
3a. Male utterances
3b. Female utterances
Version 1 = original amplitude/original phase, version 2 = constant amplitude/original phase, version 3 = original amplitude/zero phase, version 4 = constant amplitude/zero phase. Quality differences are significant at the 5 percent level if they differ by more than the yardstick

amplitude and phase information of the LPC residue can improve naturalness of synthetic speech. One way to code this information could be the use of a model of the human voicing source. Secondly, pilot experiments on the identification of individuals by their LPC resynthesized speech, showed that prosodic information alone is not sufficient to code speaker identity (Eggen—Vogten 1990). This implies that the LPC model of human speech production should also be improved in order not to degrade speaker characteristics. Thirdly, it was felt that speech research needs more sophisticated tools for manipulating complex aspects of speech like, for instance, speaker characteristics. A GE-LPC analysis-resynthesis system could be such a tool. In this section we describe the implementation of the GE-LPC analysis-resynthesis system in more detail (see also Eggen 1989b).

In the case of the LPC model, the characteristics of glottal excitation, vocal-tract filtering, and lip radiation are described by one filter which, for voiced speech, is excited with deltapulses. Within the framework of the GE-LPC synthesizer, however, we can control the characteristics of the voicing source and the vocal-tract filter independently. The GE-LPC synthesizer also provides the possibility to simulate some nonlinear source-filter interaction phenomena (Klatt—Klatt 1990). The vocal tract is modelled as an all-pole filter consisting of complex pole pairs (formants) only. The combined effect of glottal excitation and lip radiation is modelled with the Liljencrants-Fant (LF) model (Fant—Liljencrants—Lin 1985).

The following steps are involved in the estimation of the parameters of the GE-LPC synthesizer from the speech wave.

I. A high-pass FIR-filter is used to remove noise below 30 Hz from the speech wave.

II. Since the voice-source parameters are estimated in the time domain, a linear phase response of the recording system is of great importance. A first-order all-pass filter is used to remove low-frequency phase distortions.

III. Because the parameters of the GE-LPC synthesizer are determined pitch-synchronously, the moments of glottal closure are estimated from the speech signal. The algorithm that we developed for this purpose first calculates the LPC mean-squared prediction error as a function of time, using a sliding covariance analysis (Wong—Markel—Gray 1979). The error signal is then smoothed with a second-order low-pass filter and is searched for maxima. These maxima indicate moments of glottal closure or opening.

IV. Within the closed-glottis interval, the speech waveform is approximated as a freely decaying oscillation, determined only by the resonances of the vocal tract. Therefore, the vocal-tract filter is estimated with the closed-phase covariance method. Once the vocal-tract filter is known, the source signal is calculated by inverse filtering the phase-corrected speech signal.

V. The LF model is automatically positioned on the measured source signal by means of a least-squares fit in the time-domain. Next, the spectral slope of the stylized signal is optimized by performing a frequency-domain least-squares fit. The LF parameters can also be optimized interactively. At all times, the model and the measured curves can be graphically compared in both the time and frequency domain.

The most difficult part of the analysis is the determination of the inverse filter. Our choice to model the vocal tract by a formant filter is reasonable for a majority of speech sounds. However, nasals and fricatives require both poles (formants) and zeros. At present, methods for estimating poles and zeros simultaneously are not yet available (see further de Veth—van Golsteijn-Brouwers—Boves, this volume).

Through simulation we found that the GE-LPC synthesizer is capable of producing natural-sounding speech. In particular, the low-frequency part of the speech is much better modelled by the GE-LPC synthesizer. It was also found that manipulation of the parameters of the LF voice-source model can cause perceptually strong effects. For instance, by changing the parameter that models the closure of the vocal folds it is possible to manipulate the high-frequency slope. Changes of this parameter are perceived very well. From our findings we conclude that the GE-LPC synthesizer is an important tool to study the acoustic fine-details of speech. In particular, it seems a good tool to study speaker characteristics. This has been confirmed in a listening experiment where subjects had to identify speakers by their voices. It was shown that listeners use both voice source and vocal tract information to perform the identification task (Eggen 1992).

5. Summary and conclusions

This chapter presented research on the quality of LPC speech. We developed a Monosyllabic Adaptive Speech Interference Test (MASIT) which was used to evaluate the intelligibility of different speech-coding schemes. It was shown that, in the case of synthetic speech, differences in intelligibility are not always magnified by adding interfering speech. This means that MASIT provides information which cannot be obtained by traditional articulation tests. In particular, MASIT can be applied to assess the performance of speech-coding schemes in noisy environments.

We implemented a pitch-synchronous analysis-resynthesis system with which we systematically manipulated the amplitude and phase spectra of the LPC residue. These stimuli were judged by subjects in a paired-comparison experiment. For female voices, both amplitude and phase information were necessary to synthesize more natural-sounding speech, whereas for male voices amplitude information alone was sufficient to make the synthetic speech almost indistinguishable from natural speech.

We coded some of the amplitude and phase information of the LPC residue by using a more detailed model of the human voicing source. Through simulation, it was found that this synthesizer is capable of generating more natural-sounding speech. Also, the new synthesizer features some parameters which have been shown to be of importance for the manipulation of speaker characteristics and for the preservation of speaker identity.

Acknowledgments

We would like to thank Werner Verhelst for his contributions to the research reported on in this chapter.

Robust ARMA analysis for speech research

Johan de Veth—Wim van Golstein Brouwers—Louis Boves

Abstract

Aiming at system identification of the human speech production system we have developed a new speech signal analysis technique. In this contribution we first explain the ideas behind and the assumptions underlying the new method. Next, two practical problems are discussed which have always played a role in speech signal analysis, but which are usually neglected. After reviewing the main theoretical and practical considerations, we discuss some of our inverse filter and speech synthesis experiments that were based on the new signal analysis technique.

We shall indicate why, at least for the speech signal analysis techniques investigated in this study, post-processing of the speech parameter estimates should be performed and extra independent information sources of the speech production system (e.g. simultaneously measured physiological signals like electroglottogram signal) should be consulted to facilitate more reliable interpretation of estimated speech signal parameters.

1. Introduction

In this contribution we report on the achievements of the SPIN/ASSP project "Pole-zero analysis of speech". The aims of this project were (1) development of an accurate method for speech signal analysis that allows for system identification of the human speech production system and (2) examination of the possibilities offered by the new technique for speech research in general and for the study of the speech production system in particular.

During the first part of our project we have developed a new analysis technique, which (at least in theory) should meet our first aim. After having implemented the new technique, we have conducted many experiments with synthetic speech-like signals and natural speech signals in order to fine-tune our computer algorithm. In the second part of the project we have performed several inverse filtering and speech synthesis experiments employing the new method (our second aim).

Due to space limitations we will confine our attention in this contribution mainly to (a) the ideas behind and the assumptions underlying the new

method, (b) two important practical problems and (c) some of our speech research experiments.
A comprehensive description of the technique itself can be found in de Veth—van Golstein Brouwers—Boves—van Heugten (1991) and van Golstein Brouwers—de Veth—Boves—van Heugten (1991).

Taking the results of our natural speech signal experiments as a reference we will then discuss the possibilities and limitations of the new technique for speech research (section 6). Finally, we close the paper with the conclusions (section 7).

2. Robust ARMA analysis: ideas and assumptions

2.1. System identification

As already stated in the introduction, we aim in this research for system identification of the human speech production system. This means that we want to calculate the true parameter values of the speech production system from the speech signal. Thus merely modeling the speech spectral envelope as closely as possible with some well-chosen parametric (or non-parametric) description (i.e. spectral estimation) is not enough. In addition to accurately matching the spectrum we want the calculated values to correspond closely to the actual parameter values of the system which produced the speech signal. System identification of the human speech production system enables one to correctly interpret estimated parameters. By contrast, correct interpretation of the estimated speech parameters is not guaranteed for spectral estimation methods. This can be understood as follows. For some speech sounds it is well known that the human speech production system may contain zeros (anti-formants) in addition to poles (formants) (for example liquids and nasal consonants). In those cases, approximating the spectrum using an all-pole analysis technique may yield results which cannot be safely interpreted as the actual parameter values of the vocal tract, despite a close spectral correspondence between the actual speech spectrum and the estimated all-pole spectrum. The reason for this is that the zeros may obscure the actual spectral characteristics of the poles (and vice versa) (see Figure 1). As a consequence incorrect values for the poles may be calculated. This is an undesirable state of affairs, for example when rule extraction for allophone synthesis is being performed. This is the reason why we aimed to develop a pole-zero system identification technique.

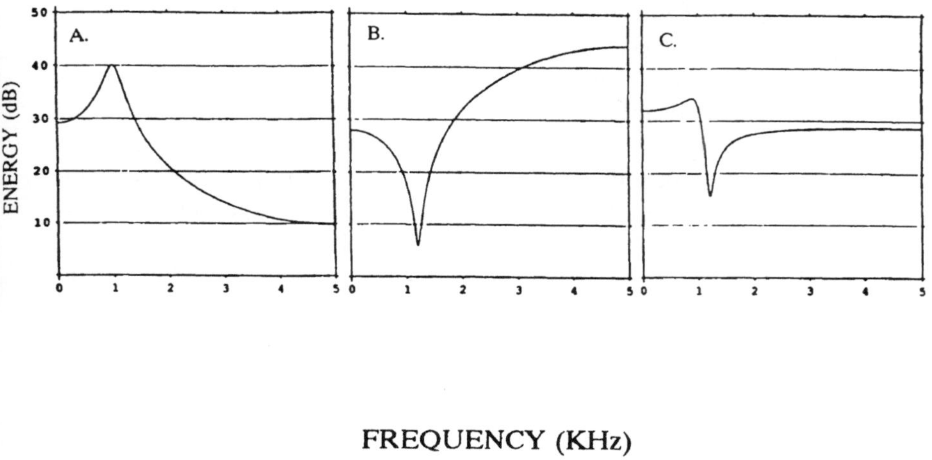

Figure 1. Poles and zeros may mask each other's spectral characteristics
(A) Spectrum of a pole with centerfrequency/bandwidth equal to 1000/300 (Hz)
(B) Spectrum of a zero with centerfrequency/bandwidth equal to 1200/100 (Hz)
(C) Combined spectrum of the pole and zero shown in (A) and (B)

2.2. Assumptions RARMA technique

We started with a classical auto-regressive moving-average (ARMA) technique to estimate the poles and zeros for voiced speech segments (Boves—van Golstein Brouwers—Hendriks—de Veth 1987). Classical ARMA should ideally be the optimal pole-zero analysis technique, because the poles and zeros are simultaneously estimated. We quickly found, however, that estimates of the poles and zeros obtained with a classical ARMA-analysis needed major improvement to be suited for system identification (Boves et al. 1987). Classical ARMA techniques are based on the idea that the poles and zeros may be calculated by adjusting the parameter values of a pole-zero model such that the spectrum of the residual signal is equal to a constant. The residual signal is defined as the signal one obtains after filtering the speech signal under analysis with the inverse of the calculated pole-zero model. In other words, in a classical ARMA technique it is assumed that the speech production system consists of a pole-zero model excited by a signal whose spectrum is a constant. This means that the excitation signal is either Gaussian white noise (GWN) or one (and only one) Dirac delta pulse.

As already pointed out by Mathews et al. (1963) when they introduced pitch synchronous analysis, in case of voiced speech signals the periodic pulse-shaped character of the excitation (with a new pulse at the beginning of each pitch period) is not adequately modeled by assuming the excitation signal to be spectrally flat. It is well known that the spectrum of a periodic sequence of Dirac delta pulses is a line-spectrum: every line has the same amplitude, with a constant distance between neighboring spectral lines that is equal to the repetition frequency of the Dirac delta pulses. Between every two spectral lines the spectrum is essentially equal to zero. Thus, a line spectrum is certainly not equal to a constant.

Following a suggestion by Lee (1988) we replaced the assumption of a spectrally flat excitation by the assumption of a mixed excitation consisting of GWN and some outliers which represent the periodic pulse excitation by the glottal pulses (see Figure 2). As the statistical mixed excitation assumption is based on the mathematical robustness theory, the new pole-zero estimation algorithm is called Robust ARMA (RARMA) analysis (or Robust LPC-analysis in case of all-pole models). For all-pole techniques Lee (1988) has convincingly shown that with this robustness assumption very accurate estimates of the system parameters of an all-pole system can be obtained: relative to conventional all-pole analysis the accuracy of the estimated parameters is improved by an order of magnitude.

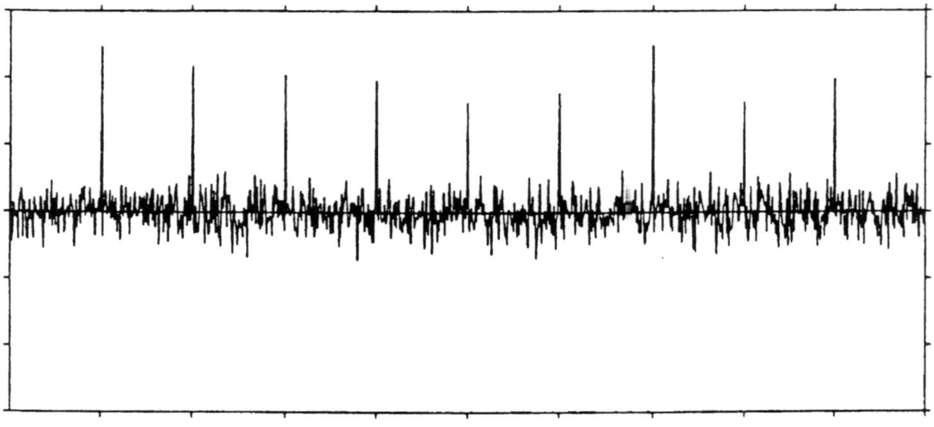

Figure 2. According to the robustness assumption the excitation signal is a statistical mixture of GWN and some outliers

At this point the reader is able to fully understand why we have chosen a robust pole-zero analysis technique: (1) for system identification of the speech production system a pole-zero analysis technique is needed and (2) due to the periodic pulse excitation in voiced speech segments the assumption of a spectrally flat excitation needs to be replaced by the robustness assumption of a mixed excitation consisting of GWN and some outliers. We can now formulate the basic assumptions underlying our method with more mathematical rigor. Our Robust ARMA analysis technique is based on the following five assumptions about the human speech production system (Fant 1960; Lee 1988; de Veth et al. 1988):

I. for short time intervals (say about 25 ms) the speech production system is time invariant,
II. the speech production system is linear,
III. the voice-source can be modeled as a pole-zero system that is excited by a mixture of Gaussian white noise and a number of outliers which conform to an unknown distribution (robustness assumption),
IV. the vocal tract can be modeled as a pole-zero system, and
V. the radiation from the lips can be modeled as a first order differentiator.

It is known that these assumption only approximately describe the real properties of the speech production system. Consider for example the first assumption. It has been known for a long time that the acoustic impedance of the glottis varies continuously as function of time during the open phase of every glottal period (for a discussion see Cranen 1987). Thus, at least during part of each glottal period the speech production system is inherently time variant. Despite this and other approximations (Fant 1960; Flanagan 1972), the five assumptions mentioned above can be integrated into a pole-zero estimation technique with powerful capabilities for speech research as we shall see below (sections 4 and 5).

The performance of the Robust ARMA analysis technique which we have implemented has been extensively tested for synthetic speech-like signals (Boves et al. 1987; de Veth et al. 1991). The synthetic signals in these experiments were obtained by exciting a pole-zero model with a periodic pulse-train. These experiments clearly showed that our implementation of the Robust ARMA analysis technique performed much better than the classical ARMA algorithm we started with (Boves et al. 1987). Based on these experiments we have concluded that Robust ARMA analysis suits our purposes better than classical ARMA analysis.

2.3. Comparison with conventional LP-techniques

There are two important differences between the assumptions underlying RARMA and the assumptions which (often only implicitly and sometimes even unconsciously) are employed when a conventional Linear Prediction (LP) technique (for example LPC) is used. First, conventional LP-analysis is essentially an all-pole analysis: zeros are completely left out of consideration. We have already explained above (in section 2.1) why a pole-zero estimation algorithm is needed to perform system identification. All-pole techniques are not suited for this aim.

The second difference is the assumption about the excitation signal: conventional LP-techniques (like classical ARMA techniques) assume spectrally flat excitation, instead of a statistical mix of GWN and some outliers. Again, we have already discussed above (in section 2.2) why the robustness assumption is preferred.

For the sake of clarity, four different families of analysis techniques are shown in Table 1 as a function of the assumptions regarding model structure and excitation signal.

Table 1. Of the four different families of techniques for speech signal analysis we need Robust ARMA analysis techniques to be able to perform system identification of the speech production system

	all-pole model	pole-zero model
conventional techniques	conventional LP	classical ARMA
Robust techniques	Robust LP	Robust ARMA

Because we aim at system identification of the speech production system a pole-zero model is required. Due to the inadequacy of classical ARMA techniques the robustness assumption is adopted. Thus, we have chosen the Robust ARMA analysis technique to estimate poles and zeros from (natural) speech signals.

3. Practical problems

3.1. Model order selection

The physical and the physiological characteristics of the speech production system, and consequently the appropriate model order for the analysis, may change during the course of an utterance. It is expected that the number of poles and zeros changes less often than pole and zero frequency. Therefore, it is probably sufficient to select the model order for groups of analysis frames associated with a single speech sound.

First we have tried to estimate the optimal model order using only statistical criteria. To that end several methods proposed in the literature were implemented and compared. An extensive simulation study (van Golstein Brouwers et al. 1988) showed that: (a) Sometimes the order selection was hampered by inaccurate RARMA estimates. The most important cause for such inaccuracies is the fact that sometimes the estimation process (which is essentially non-linear minimization of the (Robust) energy of the residual signal (de Veth et al. 1991)) finds a local minimum instead of the desired absolute minimum. (b) A weak pole can be replaced by one or more weak zeros or a weak zero can be replaced by one or more weak poles, without any influence on the spectrum of the residual signal. As a consequence, statistical procedures may prefer a model with a zero where a pole is expected on acoustic-phonetic grounds. (c) When physically meaningful poles and zeros are close to each other, they mask each other's spectral characteristics. As a consequence too low a model order may be preferred and close spectral events are not resolved.

These observations led to the use of an alternative approach (van Golstein Brouwers 1989) in which a first estimate of the model order is made on acoustic-phonetic grounds. Then an analysis is made using a model order which is slightly higher than this first estimate. When interpreting the results it must be realized that some poles and zeros may be physically meaningless. These non-physical poles and zeros can assume several shapes: There can be extra poles and zeros with a large bandwidth; also, extra poles and zeros can have almost identical parameters, so that they cancel each other. Thus, unlike what one would hope and expect a priori, the spurious poles and zeros do not always lie close to the origin of the z-plane. Spurious poles and zeros should be removed.

3.2. Additional assumption for source-filter separation

When we recall the assumptions underlying the RARMA algorithm (section 2.2), we see that both the voice source and the vocal tract may contain poles and zeros. The RARMA technique, however, yields poles and zeros without making any distinction between the subsystems which may have produced them. Therefore, during the interpretation of pole-zero estimates for either inverse filtering or rule development one important additional hypothesis is used: the estimated poles and zeros can be uniquely assigned to either the voice-source or the vocal tract. It is known that this is not always possible (Gobl 1988; Fant—Lin 1988). Sometimes a pole (or zero) can be allocated to the vocal tract and therefore inserted in the inverse filter and the estimated glottal flow signal looks acceptable; however, if the same pole (or zero) is allocated to the voice source, the estimated glottal flow signal looks different but seems equally acceptable. It appears that these problems can only be solved when independent criteria for the accuracy of inversefiltered signals are available (for example in the form of independent, simultaneously measured physiological signals, such as electroglottogram signal (EGG), photoglottogram signal, etc.).

Apart from the intrinsic ambiguity just mentioned, we can discern three more reasons why source-filter separation can be hindered in practice: the model order selection strategy described in section 3.1, the technical conditions during which the speech signals were recorded and the spectral shape of the speech signals. In every case the source-filter separation problem relates to the lack of accuracy of parameter estimates.

3.2.1. Source-filter separation and model order selection strategy

The choice of the model order may contribute in the following way to the complexity of source-filter separation. For applications in speech synthesis the spectral balance of the vocal tract filter as well as the spectral balance of the voice source are constrained. The vocal tract filter parameters may not deviate too much from the ideal values, or else synthesis would yield the wrong phoneme. The estimated voice source signal should ideally be easily modeled by the synthetic source generator. However, it may occur that extra poles and zeros chosen according to our model order selection strategy contribute significantly to the general spectral balance. This is the case when such poles (zeros) are not close to the origin in the z-plane or when such a pole or zero is not canceled by a nearby zero or pole. Should such poles or zeros be left out in such a case (because they can be allocated neither to the source nor to the filter) then a spectral balance may be created in the inverse filtered signal which deviates too much from the spectral range which may be modeled by the synthetic source generator. When this occurs analyzing the speech wave with a slightly reduced model order may probably help.

3.2.2. Source-filter separation and recording conditions

During recording some background noise will always be present. With such a noise floor present it can occur for some sounds that part of the recorded frequency spectrum is only filled with noise. This can occur particularly for speech sounds that have an intrinsically low energy or an exceptionally large spectral dynamic range. In those cases estimated poles and zeros will be positioned during analysis in such a way that not only the spectral structure of the speech signal but also the noise floor itself will be modeled.

During the interpretation of the analysis results it is important that the poles and zeros associated with the presence of the noise are not interpreted as source- or vocal tract parameters. Probably the best way of dealing with such estimates is determining the frequency where the noise floor becomes predominant over the speech spectrum and disregard any pole and zero estimated above this frequency. Acceptable inverse filter results may then be obtained by low-pass filtering the speech signal and choosing only poles and zeros in the inverse filter which lie below the cutoff-frequency of the low-pass filter.

3.2.3. Source-filter separation and spectral shape

Some speech sounds are characterized by a block-shaped spectral structure (for example /u/). Such a spectrum is mainly characterized by the fact that it contains a steep ramp. Poles, zeros or combinations of these lying next to the steep ramp are often not resolved (for a discussion in case of conventional all-pole modeling see Makhoul 1975). Apparently, during the non-linear minimization of the (Robust) energy of the residual signal the reduction in (Robust) residual energy by adjusting the parameters in such a way that the steep ramp is closely modeled is greater than the reduction due to correct modeling of the poles and zeros at either side of the steep ramp. In these situations a sophisticated way of pre-filtering is probably needed to reduce the effect of the steep ramp (i.e. pre-whitening), before the remaining poles and zeros may be successfully resolved.

In summary, we conclude that separation of source and filter parameters for the purpose of inverse filtering or rule development is not always possible in a unique way as a result of intrinsic ambiguity, the model order used during analysis, recording conditions and the spectral shape of the phoneme under analysis.

4. RARMA for voice source signal estimation

4.1. Procedure for voice source signal estimation

In this section we discuss the results of a series of experiments where RARMA estimates have been used to reconstruct the voice source signal.

The procedure used to obtain estimated glottal flow signals consists of the following steps:

I. Record speech- and electroglottogram (EGG-) signal simultaneously.
II. Correct the speech signal for low-frequency phase-distortion in the microphone amplifier.
III. Determine moments of closing of the glottis from moments where a maximum in the differentiated EGG-signal appears.
IV. Choose the model order for analysis.
V. Calculate parameter estimates using either two pitch periods or the closed glottis interval (using the timing information taken from the differentiated EGG-signal) or using a fixed window length and shift.
VI. Interpret estimated poles and zeros and attribute them to either voice source, vocal tract filter or otherwise act according to the suggestions in section 3.
VII. Filter the speech signal with the inverse of the vocal tract-poles and zeros to obtain an estimate of the differentiated flow-signal.
VIII. Integrate the differentiated flow-signal (using a factor 0.99) to obtain an estimate of the flow-signal.
IX. Judge the estimated signal quality with regard to wave shape and timing.

In this chapter we will not go into the details of these steps, because we have discussed these elsewhere (de Veth et al. 1988, 1989, 1990). We will focus here on a comparison of Robust ARMA results with other techniques for obtaining the parameters of the optimal inverse filter.

4.2. Comparison of Robust ARMA with other inverse filtering techniques

We have compared inverse filter results obtained with the RARMA technique with those of other analysis methods in order to assess the reliability of the RARMA technique for estimation of the glottal flow. To this end we have analyzed VCV utterances with four different analysis techniques. The vowels used in these experiments were chosen as one of /aː,eː,iˑ,oː,uˑ/ and the consonants as one of /j,w,r,l,m,n/. The analysis techniques used were: RARMA over two complete glottal periods (pitch-locked RARMA), RARMA confined to the closed glottis interval (CGI-RARMA), CGI-Robust LPC and CGI-Covariance LPC.

In case of the pitch-locked analyses continuous tracks of zeros were found in addition to continuous pole tracks. However, the inverse filter results in this case were much worse than with the other three techniques:

During the closed glottis interval a large residual ripple was observed. In addition, the estimated flow pulses showed more period-to-period variability and irregularities during the open glottis interval.

It appears that by using an analysis window as long as two complete glottal cycles some average is being estimated of the parameters in the closed phase and those in the open phase, instead of the "true" system parameters. For this reason we preferred CGI-analyses.

For CGI-RARMA no continuous zero tracks were found. Probably for these short window lengths the number of parameters of the estimated poles and zeros is too large in comparison to the small number of signal samples to base the estimation?

A second reason for the lack of zero tracks in case of CGI-RARMA may be a low Q-factor of the zeros. This would also explain why the poles found by CGI-RARMA and CGI-Covariance LPC were virtually identical. Should this be true, however, then there is little reason for any pole-zero estimation algorithm to be employed. In general we preferred the inverse filter results of CGI-Covariance LPC over those of CGI-RPLC, because the residual ripple in the closed glottis interval showed the lowest amplitude (see Figure 3).

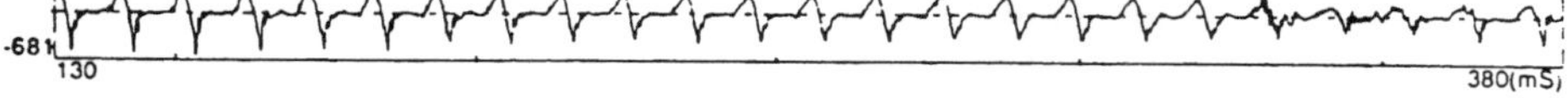

Figure 3. Inverse filter results for
(A) the 12th order CGI-covariance LPC technique,
(B) the 12th order CGI-robust LPC technique and
(C) the (14,8)-order CGI-robust ARMA technique in case of the utterance /e:le:/ spoken by a male native speaker of Dutch

It appears that the loss of accuracy of the parameter estimates in case of CGI-Covariance LPC (as a consequence of the zeros present) is smaller than the loss of accuracy in case of pitch-locked RARMA (as a consequence of the inherent non-stationarity of the speech production system). Thus, we see that the choice of the analysis method and the choice of the analysis window are closely related to each other. To conclude, one could say that the best combination of analysis window and analysis technique for inverse filtering (CGI-Covariance LPC) is the one that restricts the loss of reliability to the minimum possible.

5. RARMA for speech synthesis

We have employed the RARMA technique for analysis-resynthesis and for rule development for (Dutch) allophone synthesis. The analysis-resynthesis experiments were used as a first step towards a new rule-developing environment.

The analysis-resynthesis method is described in section 5.1. How we used the experience gained from these experiments for allophone rule development is discussed in section 5.2.

5.1. Analysis-resynthesis

For our analysis-resynthesis experiments we started with an adapted version of the method proposed by Vogten (1983):

1. The speech signal is analyzed by Robust ARMA analysis, which yields parameters for poles and zeros.
2. The amplitude of the excitation signal is calculated using the residual signal.
3. The fundamental frequency and the voiced/unvoiced decision are calculated using a pitch extractor (Vogten 1985). If necessary, the results are corrected by hand.
4. The excitation signal, which is composed of either a pulse train or Gaussian white noise, is generated using the amplitude, pitch and voiced/unvoiced parameters.
5. This excitation signal is filtered using the poles and zeros calculated in step 1 resulting in the resynthesized wave form.

Visual inspection of the resynthesized waveforms and informal listening tests revealed that the resynthesized speech signals contained occasional "clicks" and "under water sounds". It is well known that clicks are transient perturbations which occur frequently in straightforward LPC resynthesis methods (Vogten 1983). These transient perturbations are introduced at frame boundaries whenever parameter values exhibit a large frame-to-frame variation (Verhelst—Nilens 1986). Various solutions have been proposed in the literature to avoid these clicks.

For example, Vogten (1983) proposed an excitation synchronous update of the frame parameters and Verhelst—Nilens (1986) proposed a superposition method for the resynthesized speech-frames. The occasional "under water" impression of the resynthesized speech is caused by the fact that sometimes poles (and zeros) are estimated with extremely small bandwidths. In resynthesis such poles cause sine-like signals which die out very slowly and result in the impression of extraneous sound that are reminiscent of under water sounds. Therefore, it appears that the best way to handle this problem is to eliminate small bandwidth poles.

Based on these findings we concluded that in order to obtain improved resynthesis results the estimated vocal tract pole- and zero-parameters needed additional post-processing. Furthermore, we found it necessary for voiced speech segments to use the more sophisticated voice source synthesis model proposed by Klatt—Klatt (1989). This lead us to replace steps 4 and 5 of the analysis-resynthesis scheme described above by the following steps:

4′. For the first analysis frame determine by hand which estimated poles and zeros should be assigned to the vocal tract.
5′. For all subsequent analysis frames of the same phoneme, track the vocal tract poles and zeros using a dynamic programming parameter tracker (Ney 1983).
6. The parameter tracks are inspected manually. If deemed necessary, the center frequency of a pole (or zero) which deviates too much from the mean of its neighboring pole frequencies is replaced by this mean. In case a track misses a pole (or zero) parameter, this hole is filled by adding a pole (or zero) whose center frequency is equal to the mean of its neighboring pole (zero) frequencies. If one or more parameters in an analysis frame have been changed or added, the original shape of the estimated spectrum is restored as much as possible by adjusting the bandwidths of the poles and zeros.
7. The Klatt voice source parameters 'open quotient' (OQ) and 'source formant bandwidth' are estimated by minimizing the difference between the log-amplitude spectrum of the estimated RARMA-parameters and the resynthesized speech. The source formant center frequency was kept fixed at 100 Hz.
8. The excitation signal for the vocal tract is calculated.
9. The resynthesized speech signal is calculated by filtering the synthetic source signal with the vocal tract parameters.

During informal listening tests for this analysis-resynthesis scheme, we judged the resynthesized speech quality to be similar to LPC-16 results. It appears, however, that still better results may be obtained when: (a) the source formant center frequency is estimated, instead of kept fixed at one single value, and (b) all voice source parameters are smoothly varying quantities as a function of analysis frame number.

5.2. Allophone rule extraction

The development of allophone rules is based upon the phonetic interpretation of speech analysis results, i.e. assignment of estimated poles (and zeros) to either the vocal tract or the voice source. This process may be facilitated if the phonetician rule-developer does not have to depend solely on raw RARMA parameter estimates. It would be a great help if he would have access to an intelligent proposal for the vocal tract parameters. As we have seen in the previous section, our analysis-resynthesis scheme provides such a proposal, namely the pole-zero parameters obtained after steps 4′–6.

We have applied this new approach to rule development for Dutch voiced consonants (de Veth et al. 1990; Loman et al. 1991). This process of rule development is illustrated in Figure 4 for the Dutch voiced consonant /l/. We analyzed CVC syllables where the first consonant is /l/ and the second consonant is /k/. The vowel was any of the 12 monophthongs of Dutch. The speaker to be modeled by our text-to-speech system produced all the CVC utterances twice.

For Dutch /l/ it appeared that four poles and one zero are essential; also, it appeared that the frequencies of F_3 and F_4 of the /l/ depend very much on the feature [round] of the following vowel. These findings are summarized in Figure 4.

Data like those in Figure 4 result in basic acoustic specifications of sound elements, and in rules that specify context dependency. The rules are formulated in an SPE-like formalism, e.g.

initial values F3 = 2500 Hz, F4 = 3300 Hz for /l/

1 ⇒ 2 SET F3 = F2
F3 +:= 200 / --- [+vow, +round]

1 ⇒ 1 F4 := 2500 / --- [+vow, +round] {a:/ɑ}

(Kerkhoff et al. 1986; see also ten Bosch, this volume).

Informal listening tests revealed that application of these two rules in our allophone synthesizer yields highly intelligible and natural sounding /l/-sounds (de Veth et al. 1990). Therefore, we conclude that the combination of the Robust ARMA analysis technique and the post-processing steps 4′–6 provides a powerful tool for the phonetician/rule-developer.

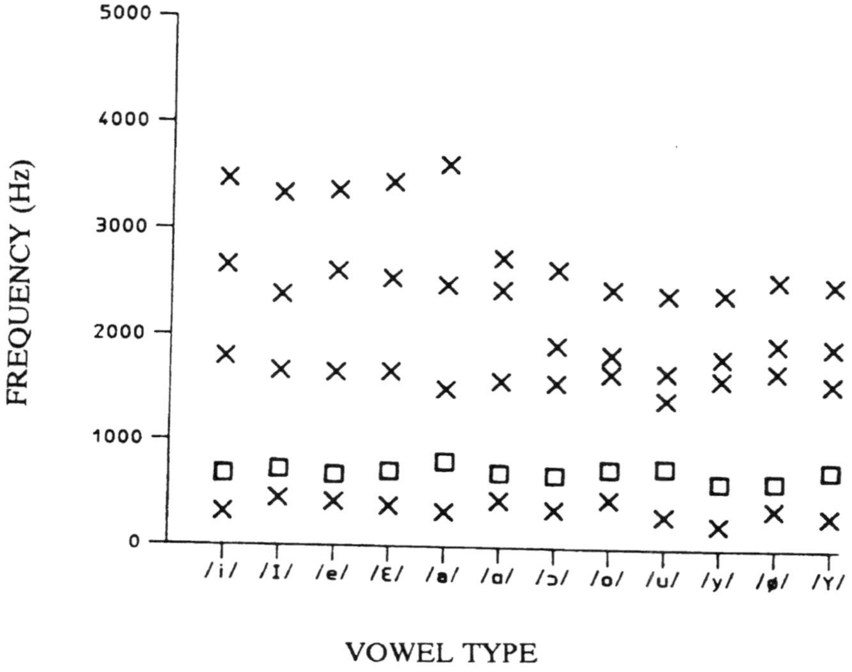

Figure 4. Estimated frequency of pole 1, 2, 3 and 4 and zero 1 for /l/, followed by one of 12 Dutch vowels

6. Discussion

Comparison of the results obtained from the Robust ARMA technique for natural speech with results for synthetic signals gives rise to a number of remarks. The analysis results from natural speech signals show misestimates, poles and zeros that are difficult to interpret and gaps in parameter tracks much more often than one would be led to expect by the results for synthetic signals. As a consequence of these difficulties we concluded that a conventional LP-technique like CGI-Covariance LPC is to be preferred over CGI-RARMA or pitch-locked RARMA for inverse filtering. Also we found it necessary to post-process Robust ARMA results with smoothing techniques before resynthesis and rule-development could be successfully carried out. The conclusion is inevitable that despite of the features we have built into the RARMA method in order to overcome the limitations of conventional LP-methods, there are still important differences between the speech production system and the way it is modeled during Robust ARMA analysis. In this section we shall discuss these discrepancies, which cause (and explain) the limitations of the RARMA technique.

We can discern two kinds of limitations: "ill-posed problem" limitations and "ill-conditioned problem" limitations. A problem is called ill-posed when the assumptions underlying the method used to solve it deviate too much from the true conditions of the process under study. In addition, a problem is called ill-posed when we have to rely too heavily on assumptions because of lack of information (more parameters than data).

The second kind of limitations mentioned (ill-conditioning) have to do with practical problems like measuring conditions, numerical properties of the algorithms employed and so forth. We will concentrate here on the "ill-posed problem" limitations, because we feel that these are at the heart of the matter when applying RARMA analysis (or any other analysis technique, for that matter) to natural speech signals. We think that it is not relevant to try to alleviate the ill-conditioning problems before a successful attempt has been made to try and solve the ill-posed problem limitations first.

It is wellknown that speech signals are the product of a number of different physical processes, which are not entirely independent:

I. The spectrum of the voice source exhibits a fine-structure of small valleys and peaks superimposed upon the overall decline of -12 dB/octave (see for example Cranen 1987).
II. The voice source characteristics may vary from glottal period to glottal period.
III. The vocal tract system has either an all-pole or a pole-zero structure depending on several details of the articulation (Fant 1960).
IV. The acoustic impedance of the glottis is not equal to infinity. Therefore, source-filter interaction occurs. Feng (1986) has shown that source-filter interaction can be interpreted in the time domain as a window over the impulse response of the source-filter system without interaction. As a consequence of this windowing effect, the bandwidth of any pole in the system is enlarged and additional side bands appear in the spectrum. This results in an effective masking of zeros and pole-zero pairs of the source-filter system without interaction.
V. With nasalization present the speech signal measured at some point in front of the speaker is an interference signal: at the position of the microphone an acoustic interference pattern exists, due to the sound waves radiated from the lips and those originating from the nose. Therefore, the measured speech signal contains poles and zeros belonging to the speech production system as well as pole-zero pairs which are essentially the result of the interference patterns.

In short, speech is the result of a number of complex physical processes, some of which are still not very well understood (Feng 1986). Separating the different physical processes underlying the measured speech signal (or in fact any measured signal) requires that the underlying processes exhibit more or less different spectral and/or temporal characteristics, which do not overlap and/or compensate each other. When this is not the case, it becomes impossible to separate the different processes if one has only access to the eventual signal. One then needs additional and independent information or one has to rely on additional assumptions about the individual processes. This is one of the main problems while trying to separate contributions of voice source and vocal tract using the speech signal only.

For analysis of speech signals we can point out two additional features that make every analysis technique based on minimization of a residual error essentially an ill-posed problem. Analysis of speech signals characterized by a block-shaped spectrum (for example /u·/ and nasal vowels) with any parametric spectral estimation technique based on whitening of the residual spectrum is bound to yield inaccurate parameters of the underlying system. It appears that minimization of the residual energy profits more from adjusting the parameters such that the steep edge in the signal spectrum is modeled accurately than by parameter adjustment such that the fine-structure on both sides of the steep edge in the signal spectrum is resolved.

As a second feature we point out that it is always assumed by parametric spectral estimators that the spectrum of the excitation signal fills the complete frequency band from zero to half sample frequency. Whenever the excitation is severely band-limited (like for many voiced consonants) the speech signal will only carry the characteristics of the vocal tract within the excited band. Vocal tract poles and zeros outside this band cannot be established from the output signal.

We conclude that there are significant discrepancies between the speech production system and the way it is modeled during Robust ARMA analysis. The physical processes underlying the speech signal are complex, not mutually independent and some only in part understood.

7. Conclusions

For system identification of the human speech production system a pole-zero analysis technique is to be preferred over any all-pole analysis method (like LPC) because the characteristics of poles can be masked when zeros are present in the speech signal (and vice versa). We have developed our

ARMA technique based on the robustness assumption for voiced speech signals in order to repair the inadequate classical assumption of a spectrally flat excitation function. As a consequence of the robustness assumption, the quality of the estimated parameters is greatly enhanced.

We found that it is still necessary to post-process RARMA parameters before acceptable inverse filtering results and satisfactory resynthesis can be obtained. Therefore, we conclude that there are significant differences between the human speech production system and the way it is modeled during Robust ARMA analysis. As a consequence of significant discrepancies between the speech production system and the way it is modelled adaptation of any analysis technique to better meet the speech production system during analysis is not a straightforward task. For these reasons one cannot hope to be able to successfully separate source and filter by analysis of the measured speech signal alone with any of the techniques we have studied in the course of this project. The only phonemes which may possibly be an exception to this rule, are sustained vowels. For these phonemes the speech production system is relatively well understood and simple: (a) the vocal tract can be regarded as an all-pole filter and (b) if the poles and zeros of the source spectrum are weak, the source may be modeled as an all-pole filter. Assuming that no source-filter interaction or nasalization is present, the system is then essentially all-pole. System identification and source-filter separation may then be performed using a (robust) all-pole analysis technique: under those circumstances there is no reason to employ a pole-zero estimator.

For all speech sounds other than sustained vowels, system identification and separation of source and filter parameters should be based on a (robust) pole-zero analysis of the speech signal in combination with analysis results of independent information sources relating to the speech production system (for example physiological signals like the EGG-signal).

Part VII

Implementations and evaluation

A stand-alone text-to-speech system

René J. H. Deliege

Abstract

A prototype of a general-purpose stand-alone text-to-speech system has been built that converts text in normal Dutch orthography into speech. This paper describes the development and features of this system. It uses a rule-based grapheme-phoneme conversion and speech synthesis based on diphone concatenation and a formant synthesizer chip. The hardware is built around an 68000 microprocessor.

1. Introduction

In many places, research is going on in the field of text-to-speech conversion, either to tackle a fundamental research topic or to develop a potential product. The present project is in the latter category and aims to realize a stand-alone text-to-speech system. The goal of the project is to combine various sources of expertise into a working demonstrator. For the system described here, the grapheme-to-phoneme conversion and the accentuation rules have been provided by Nijmegen University (Kerkhoff—Wester—Boves 1984). The speech synthesis and intonation rules were supplied by the Institute for Perception Research IPO, Eindhoven (Elsendoorn—'t Hart 1982; 't Hart—Collier 1975; 't Hart—Collier—Cohen 1990).

2. Project strategy

The working method used in this project is a top-down approach and can be divided into three main parts:

I. software development
II. software implementation on a commercially available microprocessor system
III. customized hardware development

Although this approach may at first sight seem somewhat laborious, it was the optimal (fastest) way to work in practice, considering the development equipment at hand. These three steps will now be described in more detail.

1. All hardware-independent software was developed on a VAX computer (under VMS). The reasons for doing so were the fast turnaround time and the availability of a high-level language debugger. The main software development had to do with the integration of the Nijmegen and IPO software parts. The resulting combination was realized as a new feature in DS. Diphone Speech (DS) is a multilingual text-to-speech system (van Rijnsoever 1988a, b) that runs on a VAX computer. In this way the whole text-to-speech process could be tested without bothering about the VAX speech output. As a result of this, the combination of the Nijmegen grapheme-to-phoneme conversion and the IPO diphone speech is also available now for public use in the VAX environment at the sites of all SPIN/ASSP partners.
2. For the implementation of the software on an 68000 microprocessor system, standard hardware was used first. This hardware consists of a 68000 processor board, two 256 kbyte RAM boards and a self built speech board, all connected via a VME bus. The reason for using this kind of hardware twofold. First of all it allowed us to gain experience about the exact hardware requirements. Secondly the presence of a large amount of RAM made it possible to download the software instead of programming it into EPROM, thus giving a faster turnaround time.
3. Finally, the hardware was designed and built. This hardware consists of a 68000 microprocessor, 512 kbyte EPROM, 64 kbyte RAM, a double RS232 interface, a PCF8200 speech synthesizer and an audio amplifier. After testing this customized hardware a printed-circuit board was developed.

3. Functional description

The system is a general purpose text-to-speech board and can be used everywhere where text in ASCII form is available. Four possible kinds of applications are shown in Figure 1.

The first possibility is human entered text through a terminal. This serves mainly demonstration purposes. It can also be used as an educational tool, because in this setup feedback can be given on the various steps involved in text-to-speech conversion. To make the system really stand-alone, a keyboard and an LCD display can be connected instead of the terminal. A possible application for this complete stand-alone system is as a speech communication aid for the speech impaired.

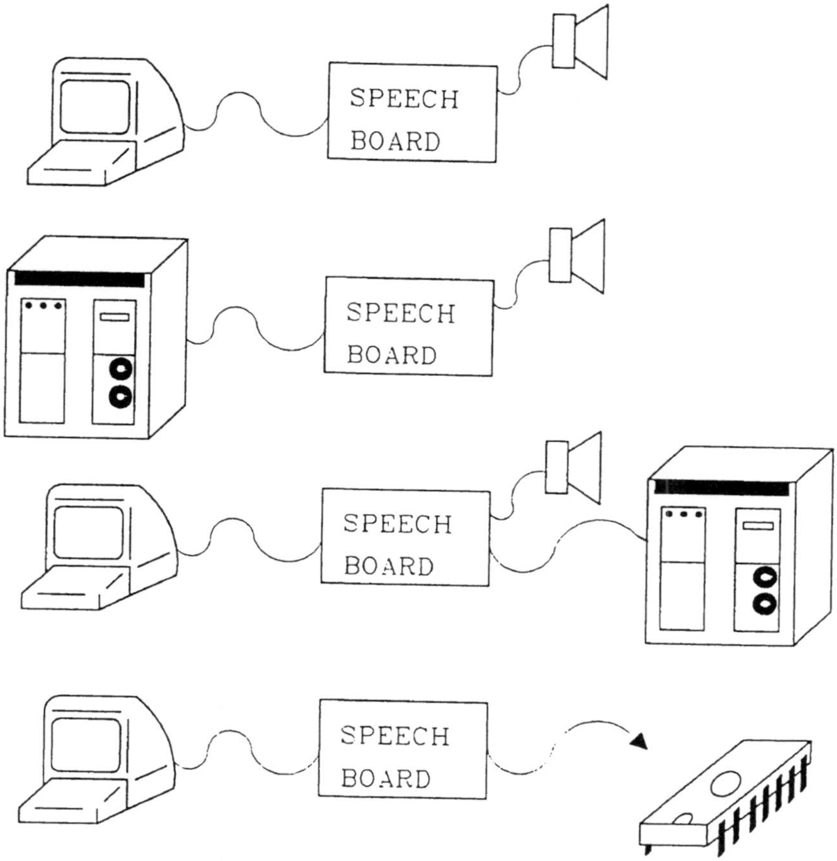

Figure 1. Possible applications

The second possibility will probably be used most often: the input stems from some other device, for instance a computer, a modem or teletext service. The system is then used as a speech generating back-end. The difference with the previous application is that another user interface is available for this application.

The third possibility is to place the system within an existing computer-terminal link to speak texts from and to the computer. This creates a speaking terminal.

The last possibility is to use the system as a speech programming device. Instead of analyzing and coding human speech, text can be entered and the resulting speech codes can be stored in the final application.

The system converts Dutch orthographic or phonetic input into speech. The conversion proceeds in a number of steps (Figure 2):

— the conversion of conventional spelling into a pronunciation representation (phonetic alphabet);
— the assignment of word stress and sentence accents;
— the conversion of phonetic spelling into a sequence of prerecorded, LPC-coded speech segments called diphones;
— the computation of appropriate durations for the concatenated diphones;
— the computation of an appropriate intonation contour for the utterance;
— speech synthesis by means of a hardware formant synthesizer.

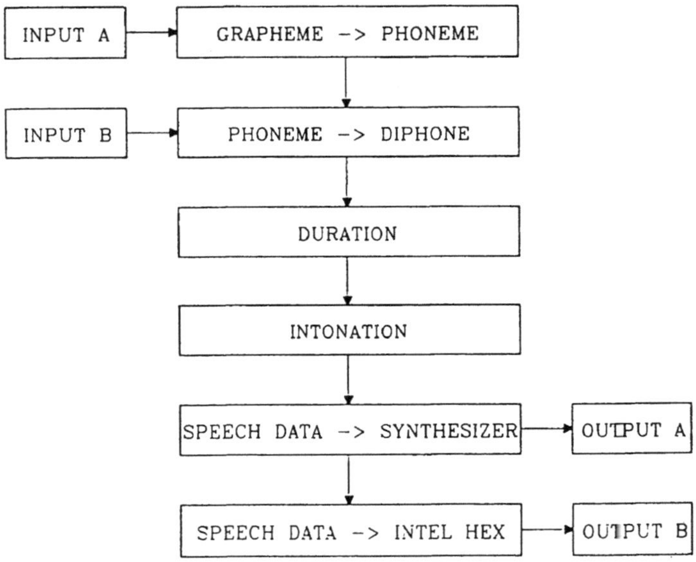

Figure 2. Text-to-speech conversion

The input can consist of either text or commands. Commands are preceded by the special symbol '/'. The input text can be interpreted in two ways, viz. as orthographic or as phonetic spelling. This interpretation can be selected by means of appropriate commands. Thanks to the phonetic-input option, it is possible to use the system in combination with other grapheme-to-phoneme converters than the one incorporated into the system.

The orthographic input can be enriched by user-supplied accentuation markers, the symbol ''. In the absence of such markers, the system itself provides accentuation. Sentence melody (intonation) is entirely computed by rule. A few duration rules are included, e.g., the lengthening of clause final syllables. The system has an exceptions lexicon that can contain the correct pronunciation of irregular forms, e.g., foreign names.

The following facilities are currently available to the user:

— a memory for the last nine sentences
— a permanent memory for nine sentences
— a screen editor
— an editor for the exceptions lexicon
— upload and download facilities for the exceptions lexicon
— a software-adjustable audio volume
— adjustable talking speed
— the simulation of both a male and a female voice

4. Grapheme-to-phoneme conversion

For some time research has been going on at various institutes to come up with (among other things) a grapheme-to-phoneme conversion system for Dutch. At least one of these systems has reached the point where its performance is good enough for practical use and which can easily be implemented in a microprocessor system. This system (Kerkhoff et al. 1984) has been developed at the Institute of Phonetics of Nijmegen University. The system is rule-based, i.e., the grapheme-to-phoneme correspondences are formulated as a set of linguistic rules. This set of rules can be compiled into a Pascal program by means of a rule-compiler program that was developed for this purpose (called FONPARS). In order to use this grapheme-to-phoneme conversion together with the diphone-based speech synthesis, some modifications had to be made, for the following reasons:

— The phonetic output of this conversion had to be translated to the notation as used with the diphones. Because there is no one-to-one correspondence between these two notations a simple table conversion is not possible. In addition there are some ambiguities, as for instance *e*, *i* and *ei* all represent valid phonemes. Therefore some kind of interface software is necessary. The rule format already used for the grapheme-to-phoneme conversion is perfectly suited to this task, so this translation was written as an additional set of rules.
— Some rules have to be added after this translation because a number of phonetic variations used by the diphone synthesis are not provided by the phonetic output of the original system. These variations are the silence phoneme, glottal stop, dark [l] and some complex vowel seqences. In addition, some rules of the existing set had to be modified. These rules take care of effects that are already incorporated in the diphones (e.g., glide insertion).
— The accent information that the original system generates is not in the format that is needed by the intonation module, which stems from IPO.

— The original system uses no exceptions lexicon. For practical applications this is a serious omission. However good the grapheme-to-phoneme rules will be, there will always be irregularities not covered by these rules in a practical application (e.g., jargon, proper names). These irregularities can be covered by putting them together with their correct phonetic translation in a lexicon. In order to obtain maximum benefit from this lexicon, the user should preferably be able to change it. In this case he can tune the lexicon to his own application-specific vocabulary.

5. Intonation

The intonation contour (sentence melody) for a sentence is influenced by the structure of the sentence as a whole. Because this sentence is generated by the system, a suitable intonation contour has also to be generated in each case. Basic elements for this contour are rises and falls of the fundamental frequency. Specifications of these rises and falls have been found through an analysis of natural speech, which had already been performed at IPO ('t Hart et al. 1990). In this analysis the natural pitch contours are replaced by stylized contours that are perceptually equivalent to the original ones. To generate such stylized contours an "intonation grammar" was formulated: an inventory of discrete pitch movements plus a set of rules combining these movements to complete pitch contours, thus generating acceptable Dutch sentence melodies. The rises and falls of the fundamental frequency are superimposed on a declination line, i.e., a gradually falling frequency throughout an utterance. All rises and falls occur between the declination baseline and a parallel line 6 semitones above it.

6. Speech synthesis

Speech synthesis is performed using stored speech fragments and a hardware formant synthesizer. As speech fragments diphones were used that were available at IPO (Elsendoorn—'t Hart 1982). These diphones are then coded into parameters for the speech synthesizer used, the Philips PCF8200 (ten Have—den Ouden 1985). The bit-rate is thereby reduced to 3 kbit/s. The actual memory requirements are 120 kbyte for the diphone data and 30 kbyte for an addressing table.

7. Hardware

The hardware of the system consists of a 68000 microprocessor, 512 (maximal 640) kbyte EPROM, 64 kbyte RAM, a double RS232 interface, a PCF8200 speech synthesizer and an audio amplifier. Figure 3 gives a block diagram of the system.

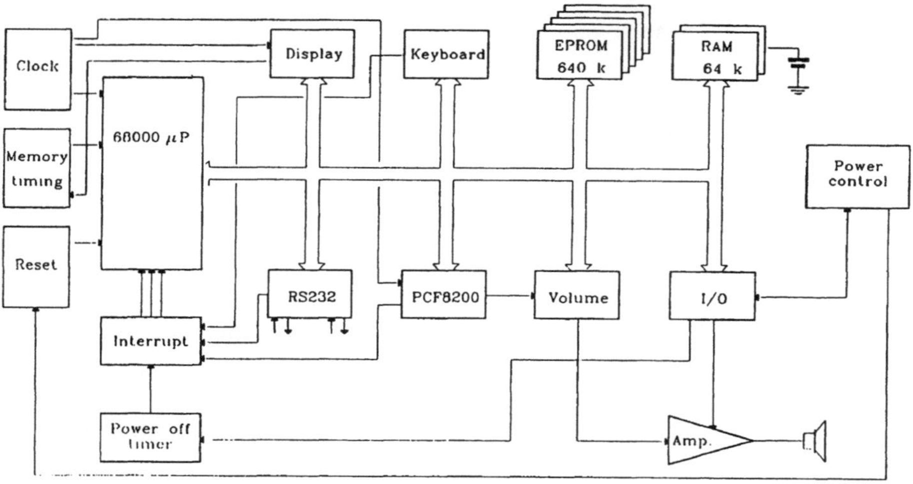

Figure 3. Hardware block diagram

For all components CMOS types are used, thereby drastically reducing the power consumption of the board (80 mA when not speaking). This makes battery powered applications possible. The 68000 was chosen as the central processor because it is one of the most powerful microprocessors available in CMOS. It runs at 12 MHz. The computing power is needed for the grapheme-to-phoneme conversion routine because of its size, and the intonation routine, which uses floating point operations. The on-board audio amplifier delivers a maximum output power of 1.5 Watts. To reduce power consumption, the amplifier is switched on only when a message is being spoken. An on-board lithium battery (10 years' lifetime) ensures the retention of the RAM data. In this way all settings, text memories and the exceptions lexicon are saved even if the board is switched off.

A printed-circuit board has been developed for this system (Figure 4). It has been constructed as a Personal Computer expansion board, so in applications involving a PC, the board can be fitted inside the PC. The board uses only the power supply from the PC connector, text input has to be done via an RS232 link.

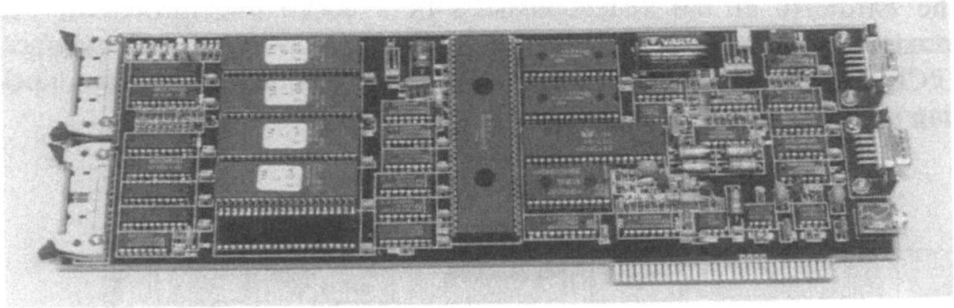

Figure 4. The text-to-speech board

8. Conclusion

This project has resulted in a general purpose, versatile text-to-speech board for Dutch. To turn it into a commercial product it has been transferred to an industrial partner. Applications planned or realized include: a speech communication aid for the speech impaired, a spoken newspaper for the blind, database access via the telephone and car information systems.

Speech Maker: A flexible framework for constructing text-to-speech systems

*Hugo C. van Leeuwen—Enrico te Lindert**

Abstract

Spraakmaker is a text-to-speech system with a flexible underlying framework, Speech Maker. The kernel of this framework is a multi-level, synchronized data structure, called the *grid*, in which almost all linguistic data obtained in the process of deriving speech from text are stored. This data structure has been implemented to improve both the transparency and the flexibility of the text-to-speech system. Around the grid a user interface is built, which enables the user to control the system and to inspect and manipulate the grid at strategic points during the derivation.

Spraakmaker is a specific implementation for the Dutch language which comprises eight major linguistic modules, most of were developed in the ASSP program. Most of the derivational history can be retraced, in the way these modules operate on the grid.

1. Introduction

One of the aims of the ASSP program was the "design and construction of a laboratory system for automatic text-to-speech conversion as an intermediate between research and applications". To serve this purpose, a project was launched in 1989 with as its main objective the development of a flexible text-to-speech system for Dutch. On the one hand, the system had to be able to produce intelligible speech from unrestricted text, and on the other hand it was to provide an environment for linguistic researchers to implement their knowledge concerning the text-to-speech process.

The task of converting text to speech can be subdivided into several more or less independent subtasks, such as grapheme-to-phoneme conversion, text normalizing, pitch control, etc. As is the case in many other systems (Hertz 1982; Kulas—Rühl 1985; Allen—Hunnicutt—Klatt 1987; McAllister 1987; van Rijnsoever 1988a; Hertz 1990), this subdivision has also been made in Spraakmaker. Each subtask is implemented as a linguistic module, and roughly each module of the Spraakmaker system has been devised by a different researcher. The majority of the modules incorporated in Spraakmaker result from other ASSP projects.

The linguistic modules, however, are not altogether independent of each other: they often build on information which has been derived by other modules. In other words, the modules "communicate", they expect certain data to be present and derive new information which is needed by subsequent modules.

In its design, the system aims to make the flow of information explicit. A language-independent framework forms the core of the system. It consists of a specialized data structure, devised to contain the linguistic data produced by the linguistic modules. Furthermore, a user interface is available to inspect the data structure and to control the system. This language-independent framework will be referred to as *Speech Maker*. Linguistic modules can be attached to this framework. If the aim is to implement a text-to-speech conversion system, these modules will often be language-specific.

In the ASSP program, Speech Maker serves as the basis of a text-to-speech system for Dutch. A number of the modules attached to Speech Maker result from other ASSP projects: LABEL (van Holsteijn, this volume), EXPAND (van Holsteijn—van Heuven, this volume), MORPA (Heemskerk—van Heuven, this volume), HIGH-FREQ, PROS-1 (Quené—Kager, this volume), PROS-2 (Dirksen—Quené, this volume), MORPHON (Nunn—Drullman—Collier, this volume) and INTONATION (Terken, this volume). In the speech synthesis module several diphone sets (Drullman—Collier, this volume) have been incorporated. The specific implementation for the Dutch language will be referred to as *Spraakmaker*.

In the following, Speech Maker will be discussed first, and this section addresses the question why we chose to develop the architecture as we did. Then Spraakmaker will be discussed. This section explains which linguistic modules have been attached to the system, and which type of linguistic information is derived during the process of producing speech from an arbitrary input text. Finally, we will discuss the Speech Maker Formalism (SMF). This is a rule-based formalism which enables a linguist developer to express his/her knowledge in a manner which closely corresponds to the way it is represented in the central data structure, and with which new Speech Maker modules can be built.

2. Speech Maker: a framework for text-to-speech systems

Most text-to-speech (TTS) systems consist of a sequential processing structure and a linear data representation (Carlson—Granström 1976; Kerkhoff—Wester—Boves 1984; Kulas—Rühl 1985; Allen et al. 1987; van Rijnsoever 1988a). A sequential processing structure means that the various modules (such as the grapheme-to-phoneme-conversion unit or the pitch-control unit) are called upon in a certain temporal order and do not interact. A linear data representation means that the information which is transferred from one module to the other is coded in a linear way, often by a string of characters. Such a string may contain different pieces of information. For instance, a character string presented for grapheme-to-phoneme conversion may contain information on sentence accent, morphological structure and orthography. The Dutch word *partijvoorzitterschap* 'party chairmanship' can be represented for instance as *part'ij#voor%zitt%er%schap*, where ''' denotes word stress, '#' a morphological boundary between compounds and '%' a morphological boundary between affixes or between a stem and an affix.

In Speech Maker the sequential processing structure is maintained, but the linear data representation is replaced by a multi-level, synchronized data structure. Such a structure was first introduced by Hertz—Kadin—Karplus (1985). In this structure, different types of information (e.g., morphology, orthography, pronunciation, etc.) are represented on different levels. The information on the different levels is synchronized by synchronization markers, which are placed between the data items on each level. For instance, *partijvoorzitterschap* can be represented in Speech Maker as depicted in Figure 1.

morpheme	stem						prefix				stem				suffix		suffix				
grapheme	p	a	r	t	i	j	v	o	u	r	z	i	t	t	e	r	s	c	h	a	p
syllable	0			1			0				0			0			0				

Figure 1. An example of how the word *partijvoorzitterschap* is represented in Speech Maker

Note: Between each data item (e.g. letter, morphological type), a sync mark (vertical bar) is placed. If sync marks are displayed exactly beneath one another, levels are synchronized at that point. Morpheme types are coded directly (instead of indirectly by different morphological boundary types), and word stress (as an attribute of syllable structure) is indicated by a more mnemonic code ('1' and '0' for primary and no stress instead of '''). Since syllable structure and morphological structure do not have a strictly hierarchical relation, they are displayed here beneath and above the grapheme level, so that both structures are clearly visible.

This somewhat more elaborate manner of data representation is chosen mainly for two reasons.

I. We believe that this representation is more transparent. Each level represents a different type of information. The symbols used at a certain level need not necessarily be different from those used at the other levels, simply because the level itself disambiguates. Moreover, text-to-speech systems are still to be improved, and many aspects of text-to-speech conversion may have to be changed. More information of a linguistic nature will become available to the system, which will be increasingly difficult to code transparently in a linear string. For instance, word-class determination is closely related to morphological analysis. Word class is needed for syntactic analysis, which in turn is needed for determination of sentence accent and pause position. Explicitly separating the different types of information will considerably enhance its transparency to the user. And we believe a transparent data representation increases comprehension of the system's internal state. This in turn will increase the speed with which a developer can make new modules or improve existing ones, given the correct tools to interact with such a structure.

II. Separate modules in the TTS system become more independent of each other. A certain module is developed at a certain time. It is designed to deal with a certain kind of input. When a new module is added to a TTS system in which a linear output string from one module serves as the input to another module, it is quite possible that the latter will be confronted with input it cannot deal with. For instance, suppose that word class determination is added to the system. Then, the word class of a certain word, say a *noun*, should be represented in some way, for instance by adding the code *n* preceding the orthographic representation of the word. The grapheme-to-phoneme conversion module, however, will probably not be able to recognize this as information which is not to be pronounced, unless the module is also altered once word-class information is added to the system. This is undesirable, since it means that every module in the entire TTS system may need to be adjusted when the system is expanded. In the case of a multi-level, synchronized data structure, new types of information can simply be ignored.

2.1. The grid: a multi-level, synchronized data structure

The multi-level, synchronized data structure is the heart of Speech Maker. All data transferred between modules pass through this structure. The (linguistic) data in the structure are the only data directly accessible to the user. Owing to its two-dimensional aspects, this multi-level, synchronized data structure has been called *grid*.

The abstraction supported by the grid is that of a finite set of *streams* (in this we follow the terminology introduced by Hertz et al. 1985). A stream is a data structure in which one level of information is represented. The number and nature of streams can be chosen freely, so long as each stream is identified by a unique name. In Figure 1 a grid with three streams is depicted, viz. the morpheme, the grapheme and the syllable stream. In Figure 2, which will be explained in more detail in section 3.1, a larger grid with eight streams is depicted: sentence, int-phrase, word, morpheme, syllable, grapheme, phoneme and pitch.

<table>
<tr><td>sentence</td><td colspan="22">declarative</td></tr>
<tr><td>int-phrase</td><td colspan="22"></td></tr>
<tr><td>word.type</td><td colspan="2">lex</td><td colspan="3">lex</td><td colspan="4">lex</td><td colspan="5">lex</td><td colspan="2">lex</td><td colspan="6">lex</td></tr>
<tr><td>.class</td><td colspan="2">det</td><td colspan="3">noun</td><td colspan="4">verb</td><td colspan="5">prep</td><td colspan="2">det</td><td colspan="6">noun</td></tr>
<tr><td>.accent</td><td colspan="2">-</td><td colspan="3">+</td><td colspan="4">-</td><td colspan="5">-</td><td colspan="2">-</td><td colspan="6">+</td></tr>
<tr><td>morpheme</td><td colspan="2">stem</td><td colspan="3">stem</td><td colspan="4">stem</td><td colspan="5">stem</td><td colspan="2">stem</td><td colspan="4">stem</td><td colspan="2">suffix</td></tr>
<tr><td>syllable</td><td colspan="2">1</td><td colspan="3">1</td><td colspan="4">1</td><td colspan="2">1</td><td colspan="3">0</td><td colspan="2">1</td><td colspan="3">1</td><td colspan="3">0</td></tr>
<tr><td>grapheme</td><td>d</td><td>e</td><td>b</td><td>a</td><td>l</td><td>v</td><td>l</td><td>o|o</td><td>g</td><td></td><td>o</td><td>v</td><td>e</td><td>r</td><td>d</td><td>e</td><td>s</td><td>c|h</td><td>u</td><td>t|t</td><td>i</td><td>n|g</td></tr>
<tr><td>phon.segm</td><td>d</td><td>@</td><td>b</td><td>A</td><td>L</td><td>v</td><td>l</td><td>o</td><td>x</td><td>?</td><td>o</td><td>v</td><td>@</td><td>r</td><td>d</td><td>@</td><td>s</td><td>x</td><td>U</td><td>t</td><td>I</td><td>N</td></tr>
<tr><td>.dur</td><td>46</td><td>69</td><td>39</td><td>54</td><td>100</td><td>154</td><td>46</td><td>123</td><td>69</td><td>15</td><td>123</td><td>62</td><td>54</td><td>46</td><td>46</td><td>54</td><td>77</td><td>77</td><td>63</td><td>54</td><td>63</td><td>126</td></tr>
<tr><td>pitch.type</td><td colspan="3">0</td><td>1</td><td colspan="14">Ø</td><td>A</td><td colspan="3">0</td></tr>
<tr><td>.anchor</td><td colspan="3">-</td><td>v.o.</td><td colspan="14">-</td><td>v.o.</td><td colspan="3">-</td></tr>
<tr><td>.timing</td><td colspan="3">-</td><td>-70</td><td colspan="14">-</td><td>-20</td><td colspan="3">-</td></tr>
<tr><td>.dur</td><td colspan="3">-</td><td>120</td><td colspan="14">-</td><td>120</td><td colspan="3">-</td></tr>
<tr><td>.exc</td><td colspan="3">-</td><td>6.0</td><td colspan="14">-</td><td>-6.0</td><td colspan="3">-</td></tr>
</table>

Figure 2. An example of the most important streams in the grid when all analysis modules have operated

Note: The sentence *De bal vloog over de schutting* has been analyzed. In the grid the following information has been stored: scope and type of sentence (sentence stream), scope of intonation phrase (int-phrase), labels which characterize type of word (word.type), part of speech per word (word.class), accent in sentence (word.accent), morphological structure per word (morpheme), syllable structure and stress pattern per word (syllable), phonemes (phon.segm), segmental duration in ms (phon.dur) and relevant pitch movement parameters (pitch). In the phoneme stream, capitals denote short vowels or allophonic variants, lower-case vowels are long. '@' denotes schwa and '?' denotes glottal stop. In the pitch stream '0' denotes low declination, '1' pitch-lending rise, 'Ø' high declination and 'A' pitch-lending fall. The pitch-lending rise is anchored at the vowel onset (v.o.), starts 70 ms before vowel onset, has a duration of 120 ms., and an excursion of 6.0 semitones.

With each stream, one or more attributes can be associated. Attributes serve to specify different aspects of a certain level of information. For instance, the word level may contain information on parts of speech (noun/verb/...) and on whether or not the word is to receive accentuation. These aspects both concern the word level and are therefore coded as different attributes of the word stream. In Figure 2 the word stream has three attributes, type, class and accent,[1] in which the lexical types (number/abbreviation/lexical/...), In our system, a word carries the position of an accent in a sentence, whereas a syllable carries the position of word internal stress., the parts of speech and sentence accents are stored, respectively. The number and nature of attributes can also be chosen freely, the names of which must be unique within the stream. If there is only one attribute associated with a stream, the identification of the attribute may be omitted since, in that case, the stream identification is sufficient.

A stream is a sequence of *tokens* separated by so-called *sync marks*. A token contains one or more fields, one field for each attribute that has been defined for the stream. For example, in Figure 2 each token of the pitch stream consists of five elements, the second having the value: [1, v.o., -70, 120, 6.0]; the meaning of these values are explained in the caption). When the grid is displayed, the fields of a token are printed above one another. On each line, the fields of a specific attribute are printed. Such lines are called *substreams*, as they represent part of a level.

A sync mark serves both to separate tokens from each other in an individual stream, and to synchronize tokens in one stream with those in other streams. Two (sequences of) tokens in different streams are synchronized if the sync marks in which they are enclosed are printed above each other. So, for instance, in Figure 2 the graphemes *c h* are synchronized with the phoneme *x*, as the sync marks enclosing these items are printed above each other (they are even connected). However, the sync marks need not be connected, as this is not always possible. Thus, the token sequence *s c h u t t* in the grapheme stream is synchronized with the token sequence *stem* in the morpheme stream, despite the fact that the sync marks are not connected.

The general architecture of Speech Maker is as follows: centrally, the grid contains all data relevant to the derivation of speech from text. On the one hand, all linguistic modules operate on the grid, that is, all modules collect their input data from the grid (except for the first, which reads the text from some input device) and write their results back into the grid (except for the last, which produces speech). On the other hand, a user interface is available to the linguist developer to control Speech Maker, with which, among other things, one can inspect and change the contents of the grid at strategic points in the derivation. The general architecture of Speech Maker is depicted in Figure 3, where a specific implementation of linguistic modules is already shown.

2.2. Control of Speech Maker

A linguist developing linguistic modules can control Speech Maker by means of the user interface. This encompasses three main functions which will be discussed in the following order: inspection of the data in the grid, manipulation of these data and control of the data flow within Speech Maker.

Inspection: After application of each linguistic module the linguist can inspect the grid to see whether the module has produced the desired results. Since, in a large text, the grid contains too much information to be grasped by a user in one glance, one can select specific portions of the grid, for instance one sentence at a time, or specific streams. Moreover, the user can not only inspect the results of the linguistic modules, but also the derivation process inside such a module, if the module supports such an option. Of course, this facility must be provided by the constructor of the module, but once such a provision has been made, it is also included in Speech Maker.

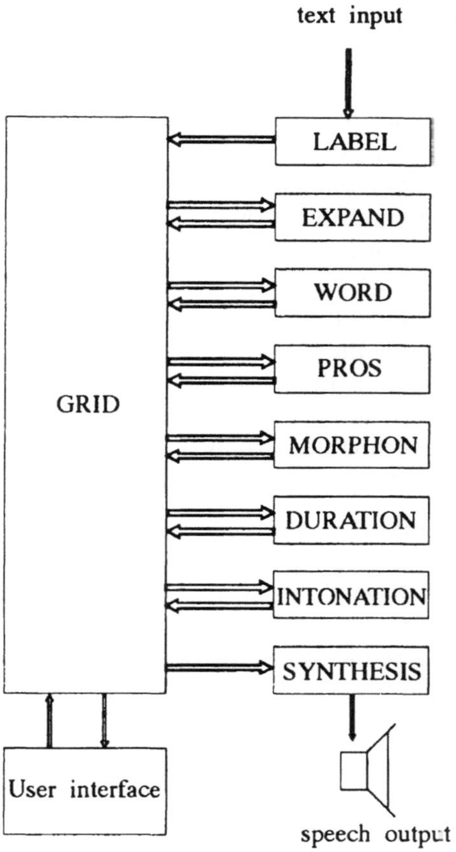

Figure 3. General architecture of Spraakmaker. The eight linguistic modules are called from top to bottom and communicate via the multi-level, synchronized data structure, called *grid*.

Manipulation: Besides inspecting the momentary status of the grid, one can also manipulate the information in the grid. In fact, when inspecting the grid, one invokes a specialized "grid editor". With this tool, one can insert, delete or modify tokens, and modify the synchronization relations between the streams. The grid editor can be an important tool in the development of linguistic modules, since one can prepare (and store) a desired input status of the grid independently of whether previous linguistic modules have operated satisfactorily. On the other hand, Speech Maker can be used as a stimulus generator for all kinds of perceptual experiments involving artificial speech, since it is very easy to modify parameters and store produced utterances.

Control of flow: In normal operation, Speech Maker's input is obtained from a terminal or file, and its output is either audible speech or a waveform written to a file. However, for development and testing purposes one can select a portion of the normal processing trajectory. For instance, to test a specific module, one can instruct the system to stop processing after this module, to display the grid information for inspection, and to simultaneously write it to a file. If the results of this module are satisfactory, these stored grids can serve as input for a testing session of the next module.

A second facility is the possibility of interchanging linguistic modules. When two alternative modules have been developed, it is possible to exchange one module for the other, run a new session with the same input and compare the results of the two sessions. This facility operates on the condition that all input that the alternative modules require is present in the grid, and that the modules produce similar types of output, so that subsequent modules can operate without adjustment.

These three types of interaction provide a linguist with the most important facilities for manipulating Speech Maker's behavior. The user interface has been implemented in X-windows, so that the user has a graphics-oriented tool to control the system in an interactive session. However, all functions can also be invoked by typed-in commands. Thus, also in non-interactive sessions, such as batch jobs, the system can be instructed to operate as desired.

3. Spraakmaker: a text-to-speech system for Dutch

To build a text-to-speech system with Speech Maker, two things must be defined: a specific implementation of the grid, i.e., the number and nature of the streams, and the linguistic modules. In this section we describe how this has been done in the ASSP program for Spraakmaker. First, we discuss which streams are distinguished. Then, we describe how the linguistic analysis modules transfer their data to one another via this grid.

3.1. Spraakmaker's grid

As stated in the previous section, the number and the nature of the streams can be chosen freely. For reasons of efficiency and transparency, we chose to include only one stream per type of information in Spraakmaker. This implies that the full derivational history of an utterance cannot always be retraced. For example, the orthography is represented in the grapheme stream. If an indication of an amount of money, such as "*ƒ* 2,50", is encountered in the text, this will be stored in the grapheme stream. During the derivation, however, this may be altered to the normalized string *twee gulden vijftig* 'two guilders fifty' which overwrites the original information in the grapheme stream, and hence, the original input of this part cannot be retraced from the grid. Most of the linguistic analysis modules, however, produce different types of information, which are stored in different streams. Thus, relatively little information is overwritten during the process of text-to-speech conversion, and hence, most of the derivational history will be retraceable from the grid.

The most important streams included in Spraakmaker are listed below. For reference, the modules which fill these streams are mentioned. These modules are discussed in more detail in the next section.

I. Sentence: indicates the beginning and end of the sentence and its type (declarative/interrogative). Filled by LABEL.

II. Intonation: indicates the onset and offset boundaries of an intonation phrase. Determined by PROS.

III. Word: indicates the beginning and end of a word and contains all information concerning words. Several substreams have been introduced to represent the different aspects of a word. The most important substreams are:
   - word.type: indicates whether a word is lexical (the "normal" words, to be dealt with by the morphological analyzer), a numerical expression, or an acronym (to be dealt with by specialized rule-based expansion modules). Filled by LABEL and altered by EXPAND;
   - word.class: gives the word class (noun/verb/...) of the word. Filled by WORD;
   - word.accent: indicates whether or not the word is to receive sentence accent. Filled by PROS.

IV. Morpheme: indicates the morphological structure of a word and the types (prefix/stem/suffix) of the morphemes. Filled by MORPA, which is part of WORD.

V. Syllable: gives the syllable structure of a word and indicates whether or not the syllable bears stress. Filled by WORD and altered by MORPHON.

VI. Grapheme: gives the orthography of the input. Initialized by LABEL and possibly altered by EXPAND.

VII. Phoneme: gives the phonemic representation associated with the input. Attached to each phoneme is an indication of its duration. The phonemes are determined by WORD and altered by MORPHON. The segmental durations are determined by DURATION.

VIII. Pitch: gives the type of pitch movement according to the Dutch intonation grammar of 't Hart—Collier—Cohen (1990). There are four additional substreams which specify the movement parameters. All information is provided by INTONATION:
- pitch.anchor: gives the timing anchor of the pitch movement (vowel onset/end of voicing);
- pitch.timing: gives the onset relative to the timing anchor;
- pitch.duration: gives the duration of the pitch movement;
- pitch.excursion: gives the excursion of the pitch movement (for instance in semitones).

When all of the linguistic analysis modules have been applied, the grid will roughly resemble Figure 2 for the input sentence *De bal vloog over de schutting* 'The ball flew over the fence'.

3.2. Spraakmaker's linguistic modules

The second aspect of the Spraakmaker implementation is the succession of modules which operate on the grid. The internal structure and performance of the individual modules do not really affect Speech Maker; only their interaction with the grid is important from Speech Maker's point of view. Therefore, in this section we concentrate on this aspect, since most of the modules are described in detail in other contributions to this book. We make an exception, however, for the module WORD, as this is not a module like the others, but more a conglomerate of modules.

Figure 3 shows the configuration of Spraakmaker. The majority of the modules add information to the grid; only two of them (EXPAND and MORPHON) overwrite existing information. In deriving speech from text, the modules are called in the order in which they are depicted. They are discussed below in the same order.

LABEL

The first module, LABEL (van Holsteijn, this volume), reads the input text from a file or from the terminal. It determines the sentence and word boundaries and provides (groups of) words with a label. This label is used in other modules to determine how to arrive at a phonemic transcription. A wide range of labels is used (lexical items, numbers, abbreviations, telephone numbers, amounts of money, etc.) to be able to distinguish different types of input effectively. The grapheme, word.type and sentence streams in the grid are initialized by this module.

EXPAND

The second module is EXPAND (van Holsteijn, this volume), which expands those (groups of) words that have received a special label into a normalized form. This encompasses the majority of the labels distributed by LABEL, e.g., abbreviations, telephone numbers, etc. Five types are not dealt with by EXPAND, viz. lexical, numeral, proper noun, acronym, and punctuation. Lexical items are "normal" words, consisting of alphabetic characters only, numerical items consist of numbers only, proper nouns are for instance names of persons, which cannot be expected to be analyzed properly by the morphologic component, acronyms are capitalized "words" which often denote system or company names (e.g., EXPAND, SMF) and punctuation denotes the punctuation characters in the text. These are the "basic" types which can be expected in a text and are dealt with by WORD. All words with other labels are expanded or transcribed to this basic form and thus receive a new label, being one of the above five labels.

As an example, when the input string *tel. 050-123456* is typed in, after the application of module LABEL this is represented in the grid as in (1):

(1)

word.type:	abbr				tel-nr									
grapheme:	t	e	l	.	0	5	0	-	1	2	3	4	5	6

The module EXPAND will alter the grid into (2):

(2)

word.type:	lex								d	d		p	d		d		d	
grapheme:	t	e	l	e	f	o	o	n	0	5	0	,	1	2	3	4	5	6

where 'd' (from "digits") denotes a numerical expression and 'p' punctuation.

WORD

After the application of EXPAND each word is labelled as one of the five basic types. This label determines the path which is chosen in this module to arrive at the phonemic transcription, since different pronunciation rules apply to each type. The logical structure of the module WORD is classified in Figure 4.

The task of WORD is to cover most (but not all) aspects of grapheme-to-phoneme conversion on the word level. Naturally, this comprises the determination of phonemic representation of the words (including wordstress and syllable structure), but also the determination of their morphological structure and word class. The phonetic representation is needed for speech synthesis. The word classes are needed for prosodic analysis (the next module) and morphological boundaries are needed in MORPHON. Note that these attributes relate to different streams in the grid.

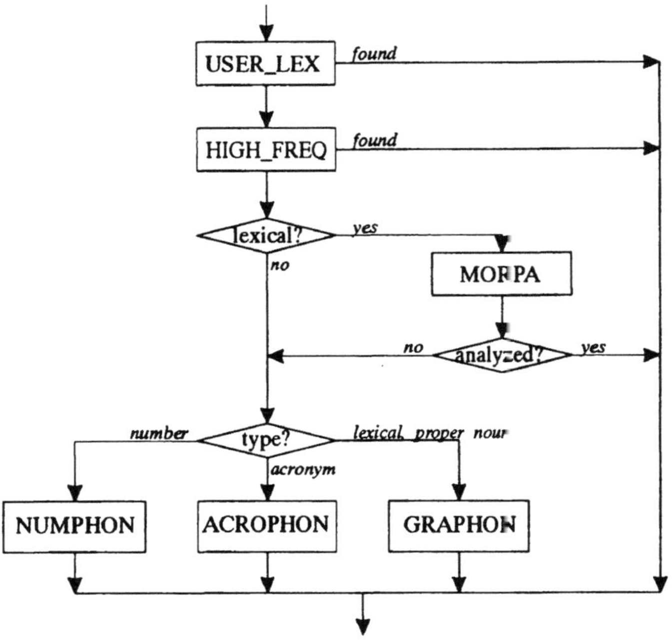

Figure 4. Simplified flow chart of module WORD. Rectangles denote submodules of WORD; diamonds denote branches in the derivational flow

These different types of output are included in one module mainly for reasons of efficiency as it is relatively easy to determine them at the same time. This is due to the fact that WORD is built around MORPA (Heemskerk—van Heuven, this volume), which performs a morphological analysis for the words marked as lexical.

Morphological analysis is needed to enhance the performance of the grapheme-to-phoneme conversion. If a word lexicon is used, in which the phonemic transcription for each word is stored, a very large one is needed to cover a reasonable portion of a language. The whole language can never covered, nor can new words be dealt with. A rule-based approach will be able to deal with all kinds of input, but will make a relatively large number of mistakes (Nunn—van Heuven, this volume), which in part can be attributed to insufficient morphological parsing capabilities. Thus, morphological analysis can help to enhance grapheme-to-phoneme conversion. Most of the new words which arise in a language do not concern new morphemes but concern new combinations of morphemes, which are combined in a regular way. By storing the phonemic transcription for each entry in a morpheme lexicon, the lexicon and the rule-based approach can be combined neatly (Nunn—van Heuven, this volume).

The most basic form of morphological analysis yields the morphological composition of a word. For instance, the word *vergadering* 'meeting' can be parsed as the succession of the prefix *ver-*, the stem *gader* and the suffix *-ing*. In MORPA, the morphological structure of the word is also determined, viz. apart from the individual components, their relation is given in a tree structure. To be able to build this tree, word-class information on the individual components is needed, which is found in a morpheme lexicon, as discussed in Heemskerk—van Heuven (this volume). The word class of the whole tree structure (the word being analyzed) is automatically determined as a result of building the tree.

Thus, in the basic form, MORPA yields word class and morphological structure. However, since a (morpheme) lexicon is used to derive this information, one can also add the phonemic representation (including word stress and syllable structure) to each entry. As a result of the morphological analysis, a broad underlying phonemic representation is more or less delivered for free, and for the purpose of text-to-speech conversion, only the underlying phonemic representation has to be altered into the surface structure (the phonemes to be uttered). This is a fairly regular process which can be well described by means of rules with an error rate much lower than the alternative, deriving the phonemic surface structure directly from graphemes by means of rules (Nunn—van Heuven, this volume).

In Spraakmaker, the following strategy is pursued: irregular and frequent words are stored in a lexicon (Lammens, this volume), which is consulted first. If a word is not present in the lexicon, it is presented to MORPA, which can handle the great majority of the words not present in the lexicon. The few words which remain are sent to the rule-based grapheme-to-phoneme converter (Berendsen—Langeweg—van Leeuwen 1986).

In Figure 4 the actual implementation in Spraakmaker is depicted. The module USER-LEX is a lexicon which can be modified by a user interactively and HIGH-FREQ is a lexicon which is to be filled with a large number of the most frequently occurring words in the near future. Retrieving a word from either of these lexicons supplies the word's grammatical category, its morphological structure, its syllable structure, its stress pattern and, of course, its phonemic transcription.

If a word occurs in neither of these two lexicons, its label determines the submodule to analyze it. Lexical items are first analyzed by MORPA. The few words which cannot be analyzed, are sent to GRAPHON, which also deals with proper nouns. Numbers are dealt with by NUMPHON, acronyms by ACROPHON. Punctuation is not dealt with by WORD; punctuation may affect the pitch contour or the duration of silence between two utterances, but generally no active sound is involved, and hence, no phonemes have to be derived.

However, not all words in Dutch can be characterized by a simple label. Sometimes intricate compounds occur. Special provisions had to be made to handle these cases. For example, the word *65+-kaart* 'senior citizen's card' is composed of a number, two punctuation marks, and a lexical part, respectively. In Spraakmaker's grid, a special stream "subword" was introduced to contain such "sublabels". The derivation of *65+-kaart* in the first three modules then proceeds in the following way. After application of LABEL, the grid will be filled as in (3):

(3)
```
word.type:      | alnum      | p |        l          |
   .class:      |
subword.type:   |  d    | p  |   |
morpheme:       |
syllable:       |
grapheme:       | 6 | 5 | + | - | k | a | a | r | t |
phon.segm:      |
```

Here, *alnum* denotes alphanumeric characters, *l* lexical and *d* digit. Sync marks placed exactly above each other denote points of synchronization, so despite the fact that the MORPHEME and SYLLABLE streams are not yet initialized, *65+* in the GRAPHEME stream is aligned with *alnum* in the WORD.TYPE substream. Next, module EXPAND is applied, as a result of which the grid will be filled as in (4).

(4)
```
word.type:      |                     l                         |
   .class:      |
subword.type:   |  d    |      l       | p |         l          |
morpheme:       |
syllable:       |
grapheme:       | 6 | 5 | p | l | u | s | - | k | a | a | r | t |
phon.segm:      |
```

Thus, EXPAND handles the + and alters the labels such that the structure is ready to be sent to WORD. Inside WORD, MORPA analyzes the lexical part of this construction, *plus* and *kaart*, but the digits *65* are dealt with by NUMPHON. As a result, the grid appears as in (5):

(5)
```
word.type:      |                        l                             |
   .class:      |                       noun                           |
subword.type:   |             d              |   l   | p |     l       |
morpheme:       |  qs   | nsf |     qs       |   s   |   |     s       |
syllable:       |  1    |  0  |  1  |   0    |   1   |   |     1       |
grapheme:       |       6     |      5       |p|l|u|s| - |k|a|a|r|t|
phon.segm:      |v|Y|v|@|n|s|E|s|t|@|x|p|l|U|s|   |k| a |r|t|
```

Here, *qs* denotes quantifier stem, *nsf* native suffix and *s* stem. As can be seen, the stress pattern is not yet correct (the word contains four syllables carrying primary stress). This will be dealt with by MORPHON.

PROS

Module PROS determines which words in a sentence are to be accentuated, and which intonation phrases the sentence can be subdivided in. It takes its input from the word.class substream and writes its output to the word.accent and intonation (sub)streams. In Spraakmaker two alternative prosodic modules are available, PROS1 (Quené—Kager, this volume) and PROS2 (Dirksen—Quené, this volume).

A special function of this module is that it has to disambiguate ambiguous analysis results returned by MORPA. It may happen that one cannot determine the word class of a word by orthography alone. For instance, the word *lopen* can be a verb 'to walk' or a noun in the plural form 'gun barrels'. To resolve this ambiguity one should look at the syntactic context, which is typically not the task of morphological analysis (which works word-internally) but the task of (a form of) syntactic analysis which is performed by PROS. Therefore, the task of disambiguation is assigned to module PROS.

Here, a shortcoming of the grid as presented so far emerges: it is not suited to represent ambiguities, and certainly not those which concern more than one stream at a time. In the case of the word *lopen* the ambiguity only concerns the word class, but with other Dutch words, such as *balletje* 'little ball' or 'little ballet' and *gelig* 'yellowish or lying down', this concerns different aspects (and thus different streams) at the same time. In the first case the ambiguity concerns morphological structure and phonemic representation, in the second all aspects are concerned, viz. word class, morphological and syllable structure, stress pattern, and phonemic representation.

In Spraakmaker, these ambiguities are dealt with in an ad-hoc manner. The information is stored in the grid by means of lists and tree-like structures, but it is hidden from the user's view. At present, this information is accessible but not changeable. Extending the multi-level, synchronized data structure so that it also becomes suitable for these types of ambiguities is a subject for future research.

MORPHON

The module MORPHON (Nunn—van Heuven, this volume) alters the underlying phonemic representation into the surface representation and adjusts the stress pattern where needed. The phon.segm and the syl.stress substreams are therefore both the input and output streams. The module is located after PROS, since some of WORD's output must be disambiguated first by PROS. In contrast to WORD, its scope is the whole sentence.

As a result of WORD, the underlying phonemic form is present in the grid for each morpheme, but the interaction between the morphemes which influence the pronunciation has not been dealt with by WORD. This is left to the rule-based module MORPHON. For instance, the stem *reduc* can be combined with *-eren* to form *reduceren* 'to reduce' or with *-tie* to form *reductie* 'reduction'. Here, the pronunciation of the *c* depends on which suffix it is combined with, just as in English the *c* in 'reduce' and 'reduction' is pronounced differently. Therefore, in the morpheme lexicon its pronunciation is stored as the underlying phoneme /c/, which means: it can either be pronounced as a [k] or an [s]. In MORPHON such transformations, which are largely regular, are applied.

Another phenomenon which has to be dealt with is word-stress assignment to compound words. This must be done for the same reason: a morpheme may or may not be combined with others, and this influences the stress pattern. This, too, is highly regular and is dealt with by MORPHON. For example, when *65+-kaart* has been typed in, grid (5) is the status before MORPHON is applied. All stems have primary stress. After application of MORPHON, the grid status will be as depicted in (6):

(6)

word.type:	l																				
.class:	noun																				
subword.type:	d											l				p	l				
morpheme:	qs			nsf		qs						s					s				
syllable:	2			0		3			0			1					3				
grapheme:	6					5						p	l	u	s	-	k	a	a	r	t
phon.segm:	v	Y	f	@	n	s	E	s	t	@	x	p	l	U	s		k	a		r	t

Note that in this example MORPHON has altered both the stress pattern in the syllable stream and the phonemic representation in the phon.segm substream (the underlying /v/ of /vYv/ has been changed into a /f/).

DURATION

The next module, DURATION, determines the segmental durations of the phonemes. It takes the phonemes, syllable structure, word stress and sentence accent as input. Its output is written to the phon.dur substream. This module is as yet a relatively simple module not resulting from the ASSP program. It only implements a small number of very simple rules. Improvement of this module could be one of the priorities of future research.

INTONATION

The INTONATION (Terken, this volume) module determines the relevant pitch movement parameters. The input is gathered from the sentence, INTONATION, word.accent and syll.stress (sub)streams. Punctuation information is also included. The output is written to the pitch stream and fills all of its substreams. See Figure 2 for an example of what the grid may contain after application of this module.

SYNTHESIS

The last module, SYNTHESIS, calculates the speech waveform. It gathers all the relevant information from the grid, viz. the phonemes, syllable structure, segmental duration, intonation phrase and pitch movement parameters. The output is a sample data buffer which can be written to a file, and/or sent to a digital-to-analog converter which is connected to an amplifier/loudspeaker combination. At present, the synthesis can only be performed using diphones, for the purpose of which several sets of (both standard and reduced) diphones are available (Drullman—Collier, this volume). Allophone synthesis (Loman—Boves, this volume) is expected to be incorporated in Spraakmaker in the near future.

4. Speech Maker formalism

As implemented at present, most of the linguistic analysis modules described above have been developed under stand-alone conditions. The linguistic developers needed to be able to test them stand-alone, and therefore the modules are often devised such that they expect linear input and produce linear output. The modules have now been incorporated in the system in such a way that they do not gather their input directly from the grid and write their results into it, but communicate with it via an interface. Such an interface has been devised for each linguistic module. The implementation of the interface is typically done by a programmer, the "Speech Maker manager", rather than by the linguistic developer.

It may be clear that this is not desirable. Each new module needs a specific interface, and the developer is dependent on the Speech Maker manager to have his/her module incorporated in the system. Moreover, one cannot easily experiment with the Spraakmaker architecture, regarding the linguistic modules which are incorporated and the order in which they are called.

For this purpose, a formalism called "Speech Maker Formalism" (SMF) has been established which enables direct algorithmic manipulation of the contents of the grid, without the need for a specific interface. In fact, SMF itself is the interface.

The idea of a rule formalism is not new. Since many processes in text-to-speech conversion are fairly regular, in many cases rule formalisms have been devised (e.g., Kerkhoff et al. 1984; Holtse—Olsen 1985; van Leeuwen 1989a,b; van Coile 1989) to offer linguists a tool to express their knowledge in a compact, efficient and transparent manner. The data structure on which such rule formalisms operate often is a string, in other words, the formalisms are able to algorithmically manipulate an arbitrary string. However, in Speech Maker we need to manipulate the grid, which can be seen as an arbitrary number of strings which are synchronized at strategic places. The SMF formalism has been devised to serve this purpose, in other words, it is a rule-based formalism which operates on a multi-level, synchronized data structure.

The central idea of this rule formalism is that the developer of a linguistic module, by using SMF, can access and modify the grid in a way that resembles the way in which Speech Maker presents it to the user, viz. in a two-dimensional manner. The linguist formulates two-dimensional rules, which can be seen as stylized "pictures" of the grid, defining how, step by step, the grid should be altered. This differs from the more traditional approach of one-dimensional rule formalisms such as those devised by Kerkhoff et al. (1984) and van Coile (1989) and from specialized programming languages such as Delta (Hertz et al. 1985). Below, a detailed discussion of such an SMF rule follows.

4.1. SMF rules

In SMF, the transformations which should be applied to the grid are expressed by means of rules which consist of a pattern and an action. The pattern specifies a state which should be present in the grid, the action how the grid has to be altered. Both the pattern and the action part can apply to one or more streams in the grid.

As an example, an SMF rule is given below. Its purpose is to attach a certain pitch configuration (indicated by '1 & A') to a syllable with primary stress in an accented word in sentence final position:

```
(7)   sentence:          |
      word.accent:  |<  + |
      syllable:     |   1 |  →  pitch: | 1 & A |
                    ^     ^            ^       ^
```

Here, the arrow '⟶' separates the pattern part (left) from the action part (right). Suppose the grid is in state (8) at the time rule (7) is being tested (the sentence *de man had een geweer* 'the man had a gun' has been analyzed up to the INTONATION module, of which this rule is a part):

(8)

```
sentence:     |            declarative
word.accent:  |  - |  -  |  -  |  -  |  |     +      |
syllable:     |  1 |  1  |  1  |  1  | 0|     1      |
grapheme:     | de | man | had | een |ge|   weer     |
pitch:        |                      x  y           z|
                                                     ↑
```

As will be explained below, the pattern part of (7) matches the grid (8). Therefore the action part will be applied, which results in grid (9):

(9)

```
sentence:     |            declarative
word.accent:  |  - |  -  |  -  |  -  |  |       +        |
syllable:     |  1 |  1  |  1  |  1  | 0|       1        |
grapheme:     | de | man | had | een |ge|     weer       |
pitch:        |                         | 1 |  &  |  A  |
                                        ↑
```

Rule (7) should be interpreted as follows. The pattern part specifies *constraints* on three streams: the sentence stream, the word.accent substream and the syllable stream. The constraints are synchronized by means of the vertical bars, '|'. These denote sync marks which must be present in the specified streams. Bars which are placed exactly beneath each other denote synchronization: the streams must be synchronized at that point in order to have the pattern part match (with respect to the bars). As can be seen, the sync mark, indicated by *z* and the arrow in grid (8), is present in the syllable, word and sentence streams, so this aspect of the pattern part matches.

Continuing to "evaluate" rule (7), preceding this sync mark *z* a '1' must be found in the syllable stream (the bottom line), in other words, the syllable must have primary stress. As can be seen, this, too, is the case in grid (8). Before the '1' yet another sync mark must be found. In the grid, this is the sync mark indicated by *y*. Thus, the bottom line of the pattern part concerning the syllable stream is satisfied.

Now, a special construction of SMF is used at this place in the rule. The sync bar which is mapped to sync mark *y* in the syllable stream is synchronized with the "search left" operator, '|<', in the word stream. Starting from *y* in the syllable stream, one "goes up" one stream to the word stream, and searches for the first sync mark to the left of this point. In grid (8) this is sync mark *x*, but generally this can be the same sync mark (if the original sync mark is also present in the word stream, $x = y$) or it can be another one (the original one is not present, $x < y$, or *x* is in the left context of *y*). Thus, if we had started this process at sync mark *x* in grid (8), the same sync mark, x, would result. The search left operator and its counterpart, the search right operator '>|', are powerful operators for specifying special relations between streams, and it appears that they are often used in the rules.

Finally, rule (7) states in the middle line that between x and y a '+' must be found in the word.accent stream, in other words, the word must be accented. This, too, is the case in grid (8), so the rule can be applied.

The focus marks '^' in the line below the syllable stream constraints serve two purposes. In the first place they serve to relate the sync marks in the action part to the pattern part. Thus, in rule (7) it is specified that '1 & A' in the pitch stream is to be synchronized with the '1' in the syllable stream.

The second function of the focus marks is to determine where the rule should be matched against the grid, and where the matching process should proceed if the rule is applied. The function of the *anchor* (this is the arrow in grids (8) and (9)) is to indicate at which position in the grid a rule should be matched. When the process of matching the rule against the grid is started, the anchor is mapped to one of the focus bars. Which one depends on the matching *direction* this is the direction in which the anchor proceeds through the grid. If this is from left to right, the left focus bar is mapped to the anchor, in right to left matching this is the right focus bar. Then, if the rule matches, the anchor will as a result be mapped to the *other* focus bar, indicating the position where the next matching of a rule (possibly the same one) should occur. In the current example, rule (7), it is assumed that right-to-left matching is applied, and therefore, the right focus bar is mapped to sync mark z, and thus the pattern part matches and the action is applied.

4.2. Other aspects of SMF

It falls outside the scope of this article to discuss all the possibilities of SMF. In general, one can use the pattern part to access data and synchronization information in the grid, and manipulate this information with the action part. An important characteristic that has not yet been mentioned is that the rules are organized in sets of rules, and that it is possible to invoke such a set of rules by means of an *execute statement* in the action part of a rule. When the pattern part of the rule matches the grid, the specified rule set is invoked. In this way one can build hierarchical "programs" to manipulate the grid. One can look upon sets of rules as subroutines, the matching order of rules within the set as a repetition-statement, and rules themselves as complex but compact *if*-statements. One can perform variable instantiation in patterns and use the variables in expressions in the action part. Thus, several important aspects of general-purpose programming languages are available in SMF, not as flexible as in those languages, but more dedicated to the task of manipulating the grid. Rules can be formulated in a two-dimensional manner which corresponds to the mental image one develops of the grid when working with the system. By only having to define information which is directly relevant one can concentrate on the task of manipulating the grid without being bothered or distracted by the syntactical aspects of general-purpose languages (consider, for instance, how one would specify rule (7) in C, Pascal or Prolog). It is our hope that this kind of transparency in the rule formalism improves both the speed of development and the quality of future Speech Maker modules. At present, two minor modules have been implemented in SMF, viz. ACROPHON and NUMPHON.

5. Concluding remarks

Spraakmaker is a text-to-speech system with a flexible underlying framework, Speech Maker. The kernel of this framework is the grid database, in which relations between data are expressed by means of a multi-level, synchronized data structure. At present, the grid is not fully suited to contain ambiguous data, and in Spraakmaker this problem is solved in an ad-hoc manner. Extending the data structure so that it can handle these data elegantly is subject for future research. A user interface enables the user to control the system and to inspect and manipulate the grid at strategic points during the derivation.

Spraakmaker is a specific implementation for the Dutch language which comprises eight major linguistic modules, LABEL, WORD, PROS, MORPHON, DURATION, INTONATION, and SYNTHESIS. Most of the derivational history can be retraced in the way these modules operate on the grid. So, in the event of an error, the module causing this error can be identified easily.

A rule-based formalism called Speech Maker Formalism (SMF) has been devised to enable a linguist to develop new modules. The rules are expressed in a two-dimensional manner which closely corresponds to the way the data are represented in the grid, and the rules operate directly on the grid without the presence of an interface. Two modules have already been implemented in SMF, and we hope to gain more experience with the formalism in the near future.

Acknowledgments

The work on the Spraakmaker project could obviously not have been carried out successfully without the input of the many people working on the ASSP program. Apart from the contributions of the authors of the modules incorporated, Crist Jan Doedens' contribution to the implementation of Spraakmaker deserves special acknowledgement.

Notes

* The authors are listed in alphabetical order.

1. In our system, a word carries the position of an accent in a sentence, whereas a syllable carries the position of word internal stress.
2. '1' denotes a pitch-lending rise, and 'A' a pitch-lending fall. The ampersand expresses that both rise and fall are associated to the same syllable. Since these movements all fall within one syllable, the "pointed hat" pitch contour will be realized (see 't Hart et al. 1990).

Evaluation of text-to-speech conversion for Dutch

Renée van Bezooijen—Louis C. W. Pols

Abstract

Various aspects of text-to-speech conversion for Dutch were evaluated at different linguistic levels and at different stages of development, both with a view of system comparison and diagnosis and with a view of gaining methodological insight. In this contribution an overview will be given of the evaluation studies conducted and the results obtained.

1. Introduction

One of the first research projects to be formulated within the SPIN/ASSP program concerned the evaluation of the quality of the text-to-speech conversion systems to be developed, going from the simplest level, i.e., the segment, to the most complex level, i.e., the text. The aim of the Evaluation of Synthetic Speech project was twofold, namely (1) diagnostic, to assess the flaws of the systems and provide indications as to the direction in which improvement should be sought, and (2) comparative, to establish the relative quality of various systems or different stages of the same system. Moreover, the evaluation project had a major methodological component in that insight into and experience with a variety of evaluation methods was to be gained.

Within the ASSP program, there were two parallel tracks of synthesis development, one diphone-based (at the Institute for Perception Research in Eindhoven) and the other allophone-based (at the Department of Language and Speech, Phonetics section, of the Catholic University of Nijmegen). More information on the two types of synthesis in general can be found in e.g. Holmes (1988). More details on the particular systems at hand are given in Loman—van Bezooijen—Kerkhoff—Boves (1989); van Rijnsoever (1988a); Drullman—Collier (this volume) and Loman—Boves (this volume). Here, only a global description of the diphone and allophone systems will be presented. The synthesis procedures described pertain to the situation in 1990; they deviate in some respects from earlier and later procedures.

As for the diphone synthesis, inventories derived from three different speakers were evaluated in the course of the program. The first and oldest inventory (referred to as BE, the initials of the speaker from whose speech the diphones were derived) was constructed between 1982 and 1986. All BE diphones were produced in stressed syllables. The second inventory, referred to as HZ, differed from the BE inventory, among other things, in the segmentation procedure (semi-automatic versus manual), in the regional background of the speaker (Western Dutch versus Southern Dutch), and in the number of diphones, the HZ inventory being smaller (about 2,000 versus about 2,500 building blocks). Just like the BE diphones, all HZ diphones were produced in stressed syllables. The third and most recent inventory, referred to as PB, was derived from the trained speaker whose speech has formed the basis for many different research activities carried out within the ASSP program. The PB inventory was created in an attempt to improve the existing diphone synthesis quality (1) by raising the sampling frequency from 10 to 20 kHz, (2) by extending the LPC order from 10 (5 formant frequencies and 5 formant bandwidths) to 30 (reflection coefficients), and (3) by adding diphones taken from unstressed syllables to the customary diphones taken from stressed syllables, raising the inventory to about 4000. At a later stage, an LPC-10 version of the PB inventory was also developed (after downsampling to 10 kHz). Input to the diphone program is the text to be synthesized (word, sentence, paragraph) in standard Dutch spelling. This text is converted into a diphone string by means of a set of automatic conversion rules. The relevant diphones are retrieved and concatenated. The form in which the diphones are represented in the resulting speech file depends, among other things, on the LPC order. The LPC-parameter file can be fed into a second program, that provides timing and intonation contours either automatically or under user control.

Research on the allophone synthesis was initiated in 1983. Just as for the diphone synthesis, the input to the program consists of a text in standard Dutch spelling, which is subsequently converted into a phoneme representation by a set of rules, and augmented (semi-manually) with information about word stress, syllable structure, and intonation pattern. The phonetic component of the system interprets the phonological representation in terms of acoustic parameters, executes detailed phonetic adjustments, and drives the actual synthesizer. The formant synthesizer that accepts the input parameters is the one described by Klatt (1980) with some modifications (further see Loman—Boves, this volume). For each phoneme the parameter values that control the synthesizer are defined as initial values in a table. These values are adjusted on the basis of a phoneme's contextual surroundings by means of phonetic rules. The control parameters (formant frequencies and bandwidths, amplitude, fundamental frequency) are calculated for fixed intervals of 5 or 10 ms. The parameter values of two consecutive phonemes are linearly interpolated on the basis of the duration of the transitions.

In addition to the standard allophone and diphone synthesis, in some evaluation tests other types of (synthetic) speech (e.g. stylized diphones, analysis-resynthesis using LPC, "neutrone" synthesis, PCM) were included, for comparative reasons or to assess the effects of certain manipulations. A short explanation of these speech modes will be provided when the relevant tests are presented.

Since the evaluation research, which started in April 1986 and ended in December 1990, has been described in detail elsewhere, both in internal and external publications (see Appendix), this contribution will be confined to a global overview of the main activities deployed, section 2 being devoted to evaluation tests and section 3 to methodological issues. In section 4, some general conclusions will be drawn and suggestions for further research will be presented.

2. Evaluation tests

In this section an overview will be given of the evaluation tests conducted within the Evaluation of Synthetic Speech project. For each test, aim, method, and results will be summarized, with references to the relevant publications. The overview is organized thematically rather than chronologically, section 2.1 pertaining to segmental intelligibility, section 2.2 to consonant cluster quality, section 2.3 to perceived characteristics at the word level, section 2.4 to prosodic adequacy, and section 2.5 to comprehensibility at the text level.

2.1. Segmental intelligibility

Most evaluation tests conducted within the ASSP program were directed at assessing segmental intelligibility, as adequate segmental intelligibility was considered to be the basis for high-quality synthetic output. In addition, some attention was paid to other quality aspects, such as naturalness. A short description will be given of each (type of) segmental test separately: the initial segmental intelligibility test (section 2.1.1), the diphone inventory comparison test (section 2.1.2), the application of diagnostic subtests (section 2.1.3), and the final segmental intelligibility test (section 2.1.4).

2.1.1. Initial segmental intelligibility test

The aim of this test, which was conducted in December 1986, was to assess the segmental state-of-the-art at the start of the ASSP program and to obtain detailed diagnostic information on the intelligibility of all phonemes in all possible phonetic contexts, both allophone and diphone synthesized, to be used for further improvement. Unstressed vowels were excluded. Detailed information can be found in van Bezooijen—Pols (1987) and van Bezooijen (1987a). To construct the stimulus material, the 15 Dutch vowels and 22 Dutch consonants were combined to all phonotactically permissible sequences of CV (word initial and word final), VC (word initial and word final), CC (word medial), and VV (word medial) sequences (C = consonant, V = vowel). These two-phoneme sequences were randomly combined to form — mostly meaningless — CVC, VCV, VCCV, and CVVC words. All stimulus words (N = 787) were synthesized both with the allophone and the BE diphone system. In addition, a reference condition was included, consisting of a subset of the stimulus material spoken by BE and analyzed-resynthesized using tenth order Linear Predictive Coding (LPC-10). Sixteen students from different faculties of the Catholic University of Nijmegen served as subjects. All were naive in the sense that they had no experience in listening to synthetic speech. They were asked to identify all the sounds of the stimuli in an open response task. Use was made of a listening set-up developed by Boxelaar (1986), consisting of a central controller and four personal computers which the subjects used as keyboards to give their responses. The stimuli were presented via a taperecorder.

The responses of the subjects were processed (semi-automatically) in terms of percentages correct (overall and per phoneme in each word position) and in terms of phoneme confusions. The overall percentages correct revealed considerable differences in intelligibility as a function of speech mode, as can be illustrated by the percentages correct CVC word identification: 21 percent for the allophone synthesis, 46 percent for the diphone synthesis and 66 percent for the LPC-10 analysis-resynthesis. The percentages correct phoneme identification in the various word positions showed considerable differences as well, providing information as to which aspects of the synthesis needed improvement. The confusion data suggested what direction efforts at improvement should take. The variance in the scores was rather large, which to a large extent appeared to be due to the varying backgrounds of the subjects in terms of phonetic training. Therefore, unless mentioned otherwise, in the subsequent intelligibility tests only language students (English, German, French, Department of Language and Speech) were enlisted as subjects. However, the condition of no previous experience with synthetic speech was maintained.

2.1.2. Diphone inventory comparison test

In March 1988 an experiment was conducted to assess the relative quality of the BE (first speaker) and HZ (second speaker) diphone inventories (van Bezooijen 1988c). The stimulus material consisted of 450 — mostly meaningless — CVC, VCV, and VCCV words, synthesized with both systems. Eight subjects, four from the South and four from other parts of the Netherlands, took part in the experiment, which comprehended two tasks: an open response identification task, which aimed at assessing intelligibility objectively, and a scaling task, which aimed at measuring subjectively perceived properties of the synthesized words. In the scaling task the subjects were requested to rate five 10-point scales, related to intelligibility, pleasantness, naturalness, broadness of accent, and applicability in a variety of contexts.

The HZ inventory appeared to be significantly more intelligible than the BE inventory, objectively, as shown by the results from the identification task, as well as subjectively, as shown by the ratings on the intelligibility scale. Moreover, all subjects found the HZ synthesis more pleasant, more natural, more standard Dutch, and more applicable in a variety of contexts. So, the HZ inventory proved to be an improvement over the BE inventory in all respects.

2.1.3. Application of diagnostic subtests

On the basis of the results from the initial segmental intelligibility test described in section 2.1.1 a number of changes were introduced to allophone rules pertaining to particular categories of phonemes. Since it would have been inefficient to use a comprehensive test to assess the effects of these "local" changes, four diagnostic subtests (also referred to as "fast diagnostic tests") were developed, related to (1) nasals, (2) fricatives, (3) plosives, and (4) liquids+semivowels+/h/ in initial, medial, and final word positions (van Bezooijen 1988c). The subtests were constructed in such a way that they could be broken down further to be applied to even smaller sets of phonemes (for more details on the construction of the diagnostic subtests, see section 3.1).

The diagnostic subtests were applied three times, the first time (April 1988) to medial plosives (Loman—van Bezooijen—Kerkhoff—Boves 1989; van Bezooijen 1988c); the second time (October 1988) to initial, medial, and final nasals, plosives, and voiceless fricatives (Loman et al. 1989; Loman—van Bezooijen 1988), and the third time (July 1989) to initial, medial, and final voiced fricatives and liquids + semivowels. In the first two tests there were two groups of subjects. One consisted of members of the staff of the Phonetics section of the Department of Language and Speech of the Catholic University of Nijmegen, all of whom had at least some experience with synthesis in general or the allophone system in specific. The other consisted of the customary synthetically naive language students. The subjects participating in the third test were confined to staff members. Results from all three tests showed a — sometimes considerable — increase in intelligibility when compared to the results from the initial segmental intelligibility test. Moreover, the confusions were generally much more systematic, so that it was easier to decide what type of alterations had to be carried out to raise intelligibility further.

2.1.4. Final segmental intelligibility test

In April 1990 a segmental intelligibility test was conducted (chapter 2 in van Bezooijen 1990), comparable to the initial test carried out in December 1986 in the sense that all phonemes were tested in all phoneme positions. The stimulus material consisted of 100 CVC and 100 VCCV words per system. The (mostly meaningless) stimuli were constructed in such a way that the stimulus material for the different systems was maximally comparable without being identical. Eleven subjects participated in the experiment.

Seven different types of synthesis were tested: allophone synthesis, five variants of diphone synthesis, and "neutrone" synthesis. The allophone synthesis represented the state-of-the-art of the allophone system at the end of the ASSP program (in practice: the beginning of 1990). It incorporated the rules which were used to produce the stimuli tested in the various diagnostic subtests, in addition to or modified by the rules formulated on the basis of the results from these tests. The five types of diphone synthesis included two versions of LPC-10 HZ (second speaker) diphones, one standard and the other stylized, and three types of PB (third speaker) diphones, one standard LPC-30 version and two LPC-10 versions, one stylized and one non-stylized. Only the unreduced PB-diphones, taken from stressed syllables, were tested. Diphone stylization was carried out as part of a project to use the systematic information on the transitions between speech sounds contained in diphones to improve the quality of allophone synthesis (cf. ten Bosch, this volume). The stylized synthesis variants were included to assess the success of the stylization procedure. The LPC-10 variant of the PB diphones was included to establish the effect of a more or less economic diphone coding. The last system tested was the "neutrone" synthesis system developed at the Department of Linguistics/Phonetics Laboratory of Leiden University. The neutrone system makes use of no more than 80 phoneme-size building blocks, produced in a coarticulatory neutral environment (cf. van Heuven—Hoos 1991). To produce output speech, the building blocks, stylized drastically and coded with LPC-10, are concatenated without applying any context rules. Discontinuities on the phone borders are smoothed. In the present research the neutrone synthesis was considered as a base line for the evaluation of the more complex allophone and diphone synthesis systems.

The aims of the final segmental intelligibility test were manyfold. As mentioned above, we were interested in the perceptual effects of diphone stylization and different LPC orders for diphone coding. Also, we were curious to know the quality of the output of such a simple procedure as neutrone synthesis. And last but not least we wanted to compare the state of affairs for allophone and diphone synthesis at the end of the ASSP program to the situation at earlier stages of development, as established in the 1986 initial segmental intelligibility test (section 2.1.1) and the 1988 diphone inventory comparison test (section 2.1.2). In addition to assessing these global quantitative effects, there were two more specific aims, namely to obtain detailed quantitative information on the seven systems in terms of percentages correct phoneme identification and to obtain detailed qualitative information in terms of phoneme confusions. This information could be of diagnostic use in future synthesis development, taking place outside the framework of the present ASSP program.

The main results of the final segmental intelligibility test can be summarized as follows: Diphone stylization leads to a significant loss of intelligibility, amounting to 9 percent averaged over the CVC and VCCV words, both for the PB and HZ inventories. The neutrone synthesis has a significantly lower intelligibility than all other systems. The difference with the next system in the rank order (stylized LPC-10 PB diphone synthesis) amounted to 15 percent, averaged over the CVC and VCCV words. The results from the final segmental intelligibility test in terms of percentages correct phoneme identification and phoneme confusions are difficult to summarize in a few lines. For detailed information and extended summaries, see van Bezooijen (1990). The main results with respect to the development of allophone and diphone synthesis intelligibility are depicted graphically in Figure 1, where the mean percentages correctly identified CVC and VCCV words are indicated for four different diphone synthesis variants (the first inventory BE coded with LPC-10, the second inventory HZ coded with LPC-10, the third inventory PB coded with LPC-30 and LPC-10) and two allophone synthesis variants, the first representing the state of the art at the beginning of the program and the second representing the most recent state of affairs.

As for the diphone synthesis, no systematic increase in the intelligibility of the three LPC-10 variants appears to have taken place in the course of

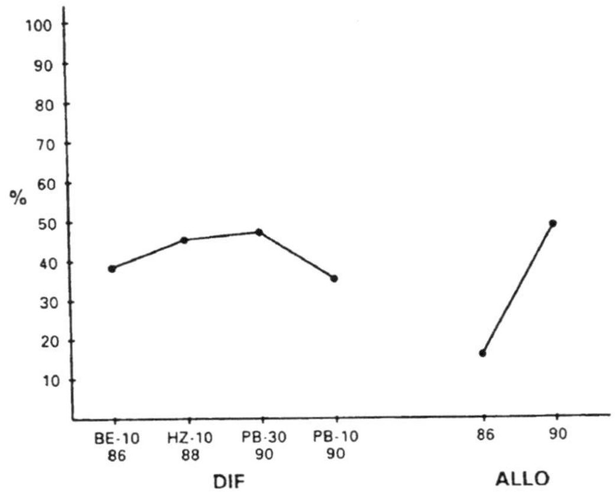

Figure 1. Mean percentages correct word identification (CVC+VCCV) for four versions of diphone synthesis and two versions of allophone synthesis

BE-10 86 = the first diphone inventory BE, coded with LPC-10 and tested in 1986
HZ-10 88 = the second diphone inventory HZ, coded with LPC-10 and tested in 1988
PB-30 90 = the third diphone inventory PB, coded with LPC-30 and tested in 1990
PB-10 90 = the third diphone inventory PB, coded with LPC-10 and tested in 1990
ALLO 86 = allophone synthesis tested in 1986
ALLO 90 = allophone synthesis tested in 1990

the ASSP program: both the (first) BE and the (third) PB inventories have a significantly lower intelligibility (39 percent and 37 percent, respectively) than the (second) HZ inventory (46 percent). The HZ inventory is clearly the best LPC-10 diphone system developed till now. Even the LPC-30 PB inventory (47 percent) is not significantly better. On the other hand, the intelligibility of allophone synthesis can be seen to have increased considerably, from 16 percent in the initial test to 49 percent in the final test, averaged over the CVC and VCCV word scores. Statistically speaking, the intelligibility of the allophone synthesis is now equivalent to that of the HZ-10 and the PB-30 diphone inventories.

What conclusion should be drawn from the differential development in intelligibility of allophone and diphone synthesis? The data suggest that diphone synthesis represents the "easy way". In other words, once a more or less satisfactory (semi-)automatic segmentation procedure has been developed, relatively little time and phonetic knowledge are needed to attain a reasonable level of diphone intelligibility, since the speech phenomena which are most difficult to capture in rules, i.e., the transitions, are contained in the diphone building blocks. However, subsequently raising intelligibility to a higher level appears to be very problematic. In principle there are two possibilities to improve diphone quality, namely (1) by improving the way in which the diphones are "treated", i.e., by improving the way in which they are segmented, represented, and concatenated, and (2) by selecting speakers who are better suited for the diphone synthesis procedure, i.e., by improving the quality of the diphone building blocks at the source. At the IPO, both possibilities have been explored. For example, spectral representation was improved by raising the LPC order (from 10 to 30) and the sample frequency (from 10 kHz to 20 kHz). As one would expect, this does indeed lead to a higher quality, as appears from a comparison of the percentages correct for PB-30 and PB-10. However, the improvement seems to be counteracted by particular aspects of PB's voice and speech, which make him less fit to provide diphone building blocks than for example HZ. In fact, trying to improve diphone quality by selecting a suitable speaker seems to be — at least for the time being — rather a trial-and-error way of tackling the problem. For, although it is common experience that some types of voice and speech react better to LPC treatment than others, knowledge as to what exactly determines suitability and, hence, selection criteria as to what constitutes the best speaker are, unfortunately, lacking at present. The results for the PB inventories seem to indicate that speech training — PB is a highly trained speaker while HZ and BE are not — is a rather poor predictor for the quality of the diphones derived from the speech of the speaker in question.

As for the allophone synthesis, the results clearly show that the beginning is hard, since the synthesis designer has very little to start with. The data in the phonetic literature are fragmented and incomplete, since they have often been obtained for different purposes, with different techniques, in different contexts, from different speakers. This means that a large part of allophone rule development is based on painstakingly observing registrations of sounds in a wide variety of different contexts in an attempt to separate meaningful from meaningless variation, then trying to capture the observed regularities in rules, assessing the perceptual effects trusting one's own ears or using those of others in formal listening tests, and then going back to observing with new questions in mind. This is a very cumbersome and time-consuming procedure. However, as can be seen from Figure 1, it is worth the effort, since the accumulation of knowledge gathered in this way may in the end raise the allophone output to a high degree of intelligibility and also (see section 2.3) to a fair degree of acceptability. Moreover, the value of the phonetic knowledge acquired extends beyond the practical application to speech synthesis: it also deepens our understanding of the properties and mechanisms of human speech at a more theoretical level (see van Bezooijen 1987b, 1988a, 1988b; Pols—van Bezooijen 1991).

2.2. Consonant cluster quality

The aim of this test, which was conducted in August 1987, was to diagnostically evaluate the quality of initial and final consonant clusters, generated by the allophone and the BE diphone systems (van Bezooijen 1987b, 1988a, 1988b). The consonant cluster quality test consisted of two parts, one related to objective intelligibility ("cluster identification test"), the other related to subjectively perceived naturalness, intelligibility, and pleasantness,

The stimulus material in the cluster identification test consisted of 41 two- or three-consonant clusters in initial word position and 102 two-, three-, or four-consonant clusters in final word position. All clusters were embedded in nonsense words, with a fixed non-target consonant /t/. In addition to the two synthetic versions, two reference conditions were included, namely LPC-10 analysis-resynthesis and PCM (Pulse Code Modulation, i.e., digitized natural speech). Both reference conditions were based upon the speech of speaker BE. Eight subjects served as listeners in an open response identification task. The percentages correct initial and final cluster identification were 95 percent and 93 percent for PCM, 75 percent and 85 percent for LPC, 51 percent and 63 percent for diphone-synthesis, and 35 percent and 20 percent for allophone synthesis, fitting the pattern of relative intelligibility found in the initial segmental intelligibility test (section 2.1.1). Many interesting examples of deletions and intrusions were observed, both in production and perception. Moreover, there appeared to be clear differences in listening strategies, in the sense that the relative performance of the subjects varied as a function of stimulus version and cluster.

The stimulus material used to establish perceived naturalness, intelligibility, and pleasantness consisted of 26 clusters, both initial and final, embedded in meaningful Dutch words. The stimuli were judged on three bipolar 10-point scales related to the three characteristics of interest by eight subjects, others than those used in the identification task. The words were also presented in written form, so that the subjects knew which words were intended. Again the same rank orders were found, i.e., increasingly lower scores going from PCM to LPC to diphone synthesis to allophone synthesis. All correlations between pairs of scales were significant, except two in the case of PCM, probably as a result of lack of variance in the scores.

2.3. Perceived characteristics at the word level

In June 1990 a scaling experiment was conducted (1) to obtain information on the way in which different types of synthetic speech were perceived using the method of Categorical Estimation (CE), i.e., subject judgments on n-point scales, and (2) to compare the CE method with two variants of the Magnitude Estimation (ME) method, where the subjects are not restricted by a particular scalar range (see chapter 4 in van Bezooijen 1990). The first aim will be dealt with in the present section. The second, methodological aim will be discussed in section 3.6.

The stimulus material in the CE task consisted of one list of 50 — mostly meaningless — words (25 CVC followed by 25 VCCV) for each of seven types of synthesis, the same as described in section 2.1.4. During the presentation of each list, the subjects were asked to rate eleven 7-point scales: sharp-warm, rough-smooth, low-high, dull-clear, unprecise-precise, slow-fast, halting-fluent, regional accent-standard Dutch, unintelligible-intelligible, unnatural-natural, unpleasant-pleasant. So, each subject gave one rating on each scale for each type of synthesis. Twelve subjects participated in the experiment.

Analyses of variance based on the subject scores revealed a significant system effect for ten of the eleven scales. The only non-significant effect was found for the low-high scale. Subsequent post hoc analyses showed that none of the scales discriminated among the five diphone systems; apparently they were always perceived by the subjects as one block, with similar stimulus characteristics. However, the neutrone system was perceived to differ in a negative sense from (some of) the other systems with respect to warmth, smoothness, clearness, precision, fluency, standard Dutch, intelligibility, naturalness, and pleasantness, whereas the allophone system was perceived to differ in a positive sense from (some of) the other systems with respect to warmth, smoothness, and pleasantness. The latter finding confirms the positive development of allophone synthesis as established in the final segmental intelligibility test described in section 2.1.4. As for the validity of the CE ratings, it could be assessed that the lack of a significant system effect for the low-high scale adequately reflected the (intended) lack of fundamental frequency variation among the systems. Furthermore, the perceived slow-fast differences seemed to correspond with objectively present tempo variations (no fixed duration was imposed). On the other hand, the ratings on the intelligibility scale failed to correlate significantly (be it with a minimal difference) with the more objective percentages correct obtained for the same seven synthesis systems in the segmental intelligibility test described in section 2.1.4.

2.4. Prosodic adequacy

In one of the ASSP projects an algorithm ("PROS") was developed for the automatic assignment of sentence accents in the input text (Quené—Kager 1990). The adequacy of this algorithm was evaluated between November 1988 and February 1989 (van Bezooijen 1989a, 1989d; van Bezooijen—Pols 1989). Subjects were twelve phonetically trained listeners. The stimulus material consisted of four different accent versions of 8 isolated sentences and 24 sentences embedded in texts. The experimental version consisted of the accents assigned automatically to the words in the various sentences by the algorithm (PROS version). A plausible minimum reference was constructed by randomly distributing accents over the content words, the total number of accents being made identical to that yielded by PROS (RANDOM version). Finally, two maximum references were constructed. One consisted of the accents produced by the trained speaker PB (PB version), the other of the accents assigned by the majority of the subjects to the sentences in a paper-and-pencil task (SUBJECTS version). Insight into the adequacy of PROS was gained in three ways. First, we compared the accents assigned by PROS to the accents produced by the majority of the subjects and by PB. Second, a paper-and-pencil evaluation was carried out in which the subjects rated each sentence on a 10-point adequacy scale in two accent versions (accented words capitalized), namely PROS and RANDOM. Third, an auditory evaluation was conducted in which each sentence was rated on adequacy in all four accent versions: PROS, RANDOM, SUBJECTS, and PB. The auditory stimuli were generated by means of diphone synthesis to make sure that the various versions did not differ segmentally. Accents were realized by means of prominence lending F0-movements.

The main finding in this experiment was that the output of PROS was considered "sufficiently" adequate by the subjects, both when presented on paper (mean rating of 6.3) and when presented auditorily (6.0). The advantage of PROS over RANDOM was about 1.5 scale positions. On the other hand, PROS was judged considerably less adequate than the two maximum references SUBJECTS and PB, as appears from the mean adequacy ratings obtained for these versions in the auditory task: 7.7 and 7.4, respectively. It furthermore appeared that the adequacy ratings of the subjects could to a certain extent be predicted by comparing the accents yielded by PROS with those assigned by the majority of the subjects themselves. Two factors seemed to play a role: the number of different accents in relation to the number of identical accents and the nature of the differences. The first factor accounted for 55 percent of the variance in the adequacy scores assigned in the paper-and-pencil task and for 33 percent of the variance in the adequacy scores assigned in the auditory task. A tentative analysis of the second factor revealed nine categories of differences which may have played a role. Those which appeared to be amenable to formalization in terms of rules were later added to PROS. The gain from these improvements was not formally assessed.

2.5. Comprehension at the text level

In recent years, a method has been developed for providing visually handicapped people with an electronic version of newspaper text which can be made audible using speech synthesis. This technique was positively received in Sweden and plans are now being developed to introduce a synthesized daily newspaper in the Netherlands. In June/July 1989 an experiment was conducted to evaluate the suitability of diphone text-to-speech conversion for the realization of a newspaper by presenting a number of diphone synthesized and naturally spoken newspaper texts (weather forecast, sports, etc.) to sixteen visually handicapped people via a taperecorder (van Bezooijen 1989b, 1989e). Half of the subjects received the automatic output of the diphone text-to-speech conversion system; the other half received a manually corrected version, mainly related to word stress and grapheme-to-phoneme conversion errors. The complete PB diphone inventory was used, i.e., both unreduced diphones, segmented from stressed syllables, and reduced diphones, taken from unstressed syllables. Suitability was assessed by means of open questions testing text comprehension ("what will the temperature be today?"), scalar judgments on a number of auditory scales related, among other things, to accuracy of pronunciation, voice, tempo, liveliness, and fluency, and attitudinal questions enquiring after the subjects' opinion on the quality of the synthesized speech and on their interest in gaining access to a synthesized daily newspaper.

Results from the comprehension test showed that the automatic diphone text-to-speech conversion yielded speech which was reasonably comprehensible at the text level. On the average, more than half (62 percent) of the questions were answered correctly. With the manually corrected version of synthetic output almost three quarters of the questions (74 percent) were correct. The difference was significant. The percentage correct answers for the natural version of the newspaper texts was 79 percent, which was significantly different from the automatic synthesis version but not from the manually corrected synthesis version. As for the ratings on the auditory scales, no significant differences were found between the two synthesis versions. In general, the auditory quality of the synthesized texts was judged insufficient or almost sufficient. On the other hand, the natural texts differed significantly from both synthesis versions on all scales; their auditory quality was judged to be largely sufficient or good.

The answers to the attitudinal questions were very similar for the subjects who heard the corrected and those who heard the uncorrected synthesized texts. In both groups it was remarked that listening to synthetic speech requires a lot of concentration and that it cannot compete with natural speech. Opinions on the suitability of synthetic speech for application in a daily newspaper varied, just as the subjects' interest in the introduction of a synthesized daily newspaper. However, responses would very likely have been more positive if the subjects had been able to get used to the characteristics of the synthetic speech and if they had been able to experience the advantages of receiving a daily newspaper in practice.

3. Methodological issues

Within the Evaluation of Synthetic Speech project six studies were conducted which were (predominantly) methodologically oriented. The first concerned the development of diagnostic subtests to be used to assess the effect of changes applied to restricted categories of phonemes (section 3.1). The second pertained to the development of a global intelligibility test, mainly to be employed for comparative rather than diagnostic purposes (section 3.2). The third was related to the intrasubjective consistency of intelligibility scores (section 3.3). The fourth examined the problem of intersubjective consistency of intelligibility scores (section 3.4). The fifth aimed at gaining insight into the relative performance of two segmental intelligibility tests (section 3.5). And finally, the sixth compared three scaling methods to obtain information on subjectively perceived speech characteristics (section 3.6).

3.1. Diagnostic subtests

In section 2.1.1 a comprehensive test for the diagnostic evaluation of segmental intelligibility was described in which all consonants, vowels, and phoneme combinations occurring in Dutch CVC, VCV, VCCV, and CVVC words were included. Together, this fixed set of stimuli totalled 787 words, to be synthesized with each system evaluated. In view of the size of the stimulus material, administration of this test is rather time-consuming. Moreover, since the work on the improvement of a synthesis system — and this holds especially for allophone-based synthesis — is often concentrated on a restricted number of phonemes or phoneme categories at a time, it was thought useful to develop a number of diagnostic subtests that can be used to assess the intelligibility of phonetic subclasses. Four different subtests were devised, related to (1) nasals, (2) fricatives, (3) plosives, (4) liquids+semi-vowels+/h/. As far as is permitted by the phonotactic rules of Dutch, all consonants are tested in three word positions: as the first, prevocalic consonant in CVC words, as the last, postvocalic consonant in CVC words, and as the middle, intervocalic consonant in VCV words. One consonant is tested at a time; the non-relevant consonant in the CVC words always is /*t*/. The point of departure in constructing the diagnostic subtests was that each subtest contains at least one list of 50 words for each of the three word positions. In each word position, each target consonant is presented in five different stimulus words, with five different adjacent vowels. In the remaining stimulus words of each list fillers are placed in the target positions. If for a certain word position the total number of fillers is smaller than the total number of target consonants, one list is added so that the ratio between fillers and target consonants is at least one to one. This procedure results in three or five lists for each subtest. More details on the construction of the stimulus material can be found in van Bezooijen 1988c, section 1.2. Applications of the tests are described in section 2.1.3 of the present chapter.

3.2. Global intelligibility test

The segmental intelligibility test described in section 2.1.1 and the subtests described in section 3.1 both have a primarily diagnostic purpose, which entails that information is collected on each phoneme of interest in a wide variety of phonetic contexts. However, such detailed information is not always necessary. Sometimes, especially when aiming at comparing system performance, it suffices to get an overall idea of the intelligibility of a system, e.g. in terms of mean percentages correct word identification. In those cases, it would be preferable to have a smaller, global test at one's disposition. On the basis of a reanalysis of the results from the initial segmental intelligibility test (section 2.1.1) and the first application of a diagnostic subtest (section 2.1.3) we developed a global intelligibility test, comprehending one CVC list, one VCV list, and one VCCV list. Each list consists of 50 mostly meaningless words, constructed according to the phonotactic rules for Dutch. All phonemes occur in each word position, in principle with equal frequencies of occurrence. If the fixed number of 50 stimulus words in each list resulted in unequal frequencies, the more frequent consonants in Dutch were given the higher values. By combining the phonemes in the various word positions in different ways a virtually limitless number of different stimulus lists can be constructed for each of the three word types. It was assumed that the set-up of fixed distributions of phonemes in each word position would result in stable mean percentages correct CVC, VCV, and VCCV word identification per list. This assumption was checked by means of the results from the diphone inventory comparison test described in section 2.1.2. The stimulus material used in this test consisted of three lists per word type (CVC, VCV, VCCV), constructed according to the guidelines described for the global intelligibility test. All lists were synthesized with two different diphone inventories (BE and HZ). Analyses of variance revealed no significant differences for the CVC lists, so that it can be concluded that this word type did indeed conform to the expected pattern of stable scores over lists. However, the VCV and VCCV lists revealed some significant differences for which no satisfactory explanations could be found. As a consequence instead of a global intelligibility test comprehending one list per word type, a set-up with three lists per word type was recommended (see chapter 4 in van Bezooijen 1988c).

3.3. Intrasubjective consistency of intelligibility scores

The open response cluster identification task described in section 2.2 was replicated with part of the same stimulus material and the same subjects in order to assess intrasubjective consistency over time (van Bezooijen 1988c). The time interval was one month. Results revealed an overall increase in the percentages correct cluster identification of about 5 percent, but the general pattern in terms of differences between the scores for various stimulus lists was identical. This outcome was taken as an indication that group means can be used reliably to measure segmental intelligibility using an open response identification task.

3.4. Intersubjective consistency of intelligibility scores

In various intelligibility tests conducted within the ASSP program non-negligible variation in the subject scores was observed. If a test is to be used as a sensitive instrument to measure intelligibility, differences among subject scores should be reduced as much as possible. To gain insight into the possible sources of intersubjective variation, data from our own evaluation research (initial segmental intelligibility test, cluster identification test, first application of a diagnostic subtest, and the diphone inventory comparison test and replication) were reanalysed, and compared to and supplemented with findings reported in the literature (chapter 5 in van Bezooijen 1988c).

The main conclusions are listed below, separately for the height of the subject scores, the variance of the subject scores, and the correlations between subject scores for different types of synthesis.

— The height of the intelligibility scores is affected by the subjects' educational background: the more practical phonetic knowledge subjects have, the higher the percentages correct they attain. Experience with synthetic speech in general does not seem to guarantee high intelligibility scores, but experience with the specific synthesis system tested does have a positive effect.

— The variance of the scores, especially for diphone and LPC speech, may be affected by the subjects' educational background in the sense that practical phonetic training results in a reduction of the intersubjective differences. The variance of the scores for allophone speech appeared to be high, whatever the characteristics of the subjects employed. However, it should be noted that no data were available for different types of subjects for the later stages of allophone development, when its quality had been improved.

— The data for the correlations between the subject scores for different types of synthesis suggest the existence of speech mode dependent performance on the part of the subjects. In other words, a subject's position in the intelligibility rank order for one speech mode does not necessarily correspond with his/her rank order position for another speech mode. In tests where several speech modes were evaluated with the same subjects, correlations tended to be higher for modes that were similar in quality or type (PCM/LPC, LPC/diphone, diphone/allophone) than for modes that were farther apart.

3.5. Relative performance of two intelligibility tests

In section 3.2 an intelligibility test was described that was developed within the SPIN-ASSP program to obtain a global idea of the intelligibility of a synthesis system, mainly for comparative reasons. With roughly the same purpose, a somewhat similar segmental intelligibility test was developed within the European ESPRIT-SAM program. The main points of agreement are the use of an open response identification task and the use of both meaningful and meaningless words of specified consonant/vowel structures. The main differences between ASSP and SAM pertain to the word types (CVC, VCV, VCCV versus CV, VC, VCV), the number of different vowels (all versus three), the frequency of occurrence of the consonants (between two and five versus three per list), type of sounds to be identified (both vowels and consonants versus only consonants), and the number of sounds to be identified in each stimulus word (all sounds versus one consonant). Moreover, the SAM method aims at language independent evaluation, whereas the ASSP method was developed especially for Dutch. In April 1990 a study was conducted to compare the two tests, both methodologically and with respect to the results they yield (chapter 3 in van Bezooijen 1990). The stimulus material consisted of four CVC lists representing the ASSP method and four CV, four VC, and four VCV lists representing the SAM method. Half of the lists were synthesized with the (by that time high-quality) allophone system and the other half with the intermediate-quality LPC-10 PB diphones (unreduced). Eight subjects participated in the experiment. The SAM guidelines for the set-up of the test were commented on critically (see section 3.3.1 in van Bezooijen 1990). Moreover, the results, necessarily restricted to consonants, yielded by the two methods were compared. The main conclusions can be summarized as follows.

- — The two methods yield similar results in terms of mean percentages consonant intelligibility.
- — There is a tendency for the two methods to yield different results in terms of consonant intelligibility rank orders.
- — The two approaches yield partly different confusions among consonants.

3.6. Comparison of three scaling methods

In section 2.3 the results were presented of a scaling test in which seven synthesis systems, the same as tested in the segmental intelligibility test described in section 2.1.4, were rated on eleven auditory scales using the method of Categorical Estimation (CE). In addition to yielding information on the quality of the systems rated, the scaling test aimed at providing methodological insight into the comparative performance of the Categorical Estimation method and two variants of the Magnitude Estimation (ME) method. In contrast to the CE method, the ratings in the ME method are not limited to a predefined number of values and a predefined range. In the ME method subjects are, in principle, free to choose any — positive — value they wish to express the magnitude of the perceived stimulus attribute. In the present ME task, two stimulus attributes were rated, namely intelligibility and naturalness, one attribute at a time. In the one ME variant (ME+ref) each test series was preceded by a reference series consisting of the same four words as the following test series, synthesized with a fixed synthesis system occupying an intermediate position with respect to the attributes to be rated. To the reference series the more or less arbitrary value of 100 was assigned. This value was supposed to function as a reference point to be used by the subjects when deciding on the value to be assigned to the series of test stimuli. The set-up of the second ME variant (ME-ref) was identical to that of the ME+ref variant, except that there were no reference series. The subjects were instructed not to compare the different test series, to concentrate on each series individually and determine each time which value reflected the stimulus attribute (intelligibility or naturalness) adequately. The stimulus material used in the two ME variants was identical; it consisted of five series of four mostly meaningless words (two CVC and two VCCV) per system. Just as in the CE task the stimulus words were also presented to the subjects on paper.

On the basis of the results yielded by the CE task, the ME+ref task, and the ME-ref task, it was concluded that comparability should be established separately for the two stimulus attributes rated, i.e., naturalness and intelligibility. As far as naturalness is concerned, the three methods appear to be equivalent: completely identical post hoc results, assessing the significance of differences in the ratings for the seven systems, were obtained and all intercorrelations, based on the mean subject scores for the seven systems, were significant. The results for intelligibility are less consistent: partly different post hoc results and both significant and non-significant intercorrelations were found. None of the three methods appears to have much discriminating power. At best three groups of systems were distinguished, a high-quality group consisting of the LPC-30 PB diphone system and the allophone system, an intermediate-quality group consisting of the four LPC-10 diphone systems (two stylized and two non-stylized), and a low-quality group consisting of the neutrone system. However, the Categorical Estimation method has some methodological advantages, especially in terms of efficiency.

4. General conclusions

As stated in section 1 of this chapter, the Evaluation of Synthetic Speech project concerned the evaluation of different aspects of the text-to-speech conversion systems developed within the SPIN-ASSP program, going from the simplest — segmental — level to the most complex — text — level. Two aims of the evaluation were mentioned, namely (1) diagnostic, to assess the flaws of the systems and provide indications as to the direction in which improvement should be sought, and (2) comparative, to establish the relative quality of various systems or different stages of the same system. Moreover, the project was planned to provide methodological insight into and experience with the evaluation of text-to-speech conversion.

As appears from the overview of studies presented in sections 2 and 3, the goals set at the beginning of the program have to a great extent been reached: diagnostic as well as comparative data were gathered at various linguistic levels and methodological know-how was acquired with a variety of evaluation methods. Not all aspects received equal attention, though. Like in most other evaluation research, most effort was put in evaluating segmental intelligibility, in the first place because good segmental intelligibility is considered to be a prerequisite for acceptable synthetic output and in the second place because segmental intelligibility is easiest to quantify, at least with the existing methodology.

As for the diphone synthesis, the segmental evaluation primarily served a comparative function, providing global information e.g. on the relative intelligibility of various diphone inventories, on the relative intelligibility of diphone synthesis as compared to other (re)synthesis procedures (e.g. analysis-resynthesis with LPC and allophone synthesis-by-rule), or on the perceptual effects of manual corrections and different ways of diphone coding and storage. Detailed data on the intelligibility of specific diphone-synthesized phonemes in specific word positions and phonetic contexts were yielded as well, but in the case of diphone synthesis the use of this information for diagnostic purposes is somewhat questionable. There are several reasons for this. In the first place, the whole idea behind diphone synthesis is that the building blocks are self-contained; stored diphones are not very well fit to be modified. Moreover, it should be realized that the building blocks in diphone synthesis do not consist of phonemes but, roughly speaking, of sequences of two phonemes each split in half, which makes it difficult to match them with the subjects' responses to individual sounds as obtained in the intelligibility tests.

The segmental intelligibility tests served a comparative function for the allophone synthesis as well. However, in addition, they proved invaluable for diagnostic purposes, because the phoneme scores and confusions provided detailed information that gave direction to the development of new phonetic rules, the perceptual effects of which were subsequently assessed in a new evaluation (sub)test. This cyclic procedure, in combination with comments on the test results by experienced speech analysts, improvements in the working environment, and new tools for obtaining and examining acoustic data (Loman—van Bezooijen—Kerkhoff—Boves 1989), proved to be successful, as appears from the systematic increase in allophone synthesis intelligibility in the course of the program.

Besides intelligibility at the phoneme level, various other aspects of text-to-speech conversion received attention as well, such as the quality of consonant clusters, the perceived characteristics at the word level, the adequacy of prosody, and text comprehension.

As for the evaluation of consonant clusters, in addition to objective intelligibility in terms of percentages correct identification, subjectively perceived naturalness, intelligibility, and pleasantness were assessed, using the method of scalar judgments. We think separate testing of consonant clusters is necessary, because their quality cannot be deduced directly from the quality of the constituting single consonants. Moreover, we think it is important to evaluate consonant clusters, because they are very frequent, especially in Germanic languages such as English, German, and Dutch.

The perceived characteristics at the word level were established using the method of categorical estimation. Subjects rated bipolar 7-point scales, such as unprecise-precise and halting-fluent, for mostly meaningless words separated by short silent intervals. Seven different synthesis systems were evaluated this way. Of course, the interpretation of the meaning of the scale labels was probably determined to a certain extent by the type of stimuli presented. In our view, the test would have been more interesting if complete phrases had been rated, but it was difficult to solve the methodological problems involved in obtaining prosodically satisfactory and more or less comparable realizations of all systems.

At the prosodic level, evaluation was restricted to the adequacy of automatic sentence accent assignment. Of course, prosody entails much more than the placement of accents, such as the phonetic realization of intonation contours, the distribution of pauses, tempo (variation), and in a certain sense also voice quality. Some of these aspects were investigated and evaluated in other ASSP projects (see for example Terken, this volume; Eefting—Nooteboom, this volume). However, the systematics and interrelationships of various prosodic features should definitely be further looked into, if synthetic speech is ever to compete with natural speech for longer stretches of speech. Unfortunately, it is common experience that it is far from easy to develop algorithms in this area, not only because prosody is a very complex matter where numerous factors interact, but also because the methodology to diagnostically assess the perceptual effects of various (combinations of) prosodic phenomena is lacking to a great extent. In principle, any subject, however phonetically naive, can be requested to break down an auditorily presented stimulus word into individual sounds and label them. The accuracy of the labelling can subsequently be assessed objectively, by matching the response with the intended phoneme. However, to obtain detailed diagnostic information at the prosodic level one will generally have to rely on the perceptual acuity and the linguistic and pragmatic insight of ear-trained subjects. And even then, unlike in the case of intelligibility, it is not quite clear what the reference should be.

One evaluation test was conducted at the text level, within the framework of making a daily newspaper available to people with a visual handicap. The stimulus texts were realized with two variants of diphone synthesis (manually corrected and uncorrected) and natural speech. The test was administered to visually handicapped. Text comprehension was tested by means of open questions and the subjects' general impression by means of scalar judgments for various auditory characteristics. We were satisfied with the method of open questions to test comprehension, but lack confidence in the efficiency and validity of the scalar judgments. Although the two task were administered separately, it cannot be excluded that the subjects, who had no phonetic or linguistic training, found it difficult to separate content and form.

Our general feeling at the end of the Evaluation of Synthetic Speech project is that we would have liked to gain more insight into the contributions of various (combinations of) linguistic and phonetic text-to-speech conversion modules to the quality of speech output at the sentence and text level. It would have been interesting, for example, to assess the adequacy of the pause distribution component in PROS (see Dirksen—Quené, this volume; Quené—Kager, this volume) or the effects of efforts to combine the morphological analysis by means of a lexicon with grapheme-phoneme rules (see Nunn—van Heuven, this volume). Also, in view of the improved quality of allophone synthesis we would have liked to compare subjects' reactions towards allophone synthesized texts with diphone synthesized texts, not only for visually handicapped but also for sighted people. In short, it should be concluded that although much has been done, much remains unknown.

Appendix 1:
Institutes and individuals participating in ASSP

1. Institutes participating in ASSP

Institute of Phonetic Sciences, University of Amsterdam
Herengracht 338, 1016 CG Amsterdam

Institute for Perception Research, Eindhoven
Den Dolech 2, PO Box 513, 5600 MB Eindhoven

Phonetics Laboratory/Department of Linguistics, Leiden University
Cleveringaplaats 1, PO Box 9515, 2300 RA Leiden

Department of Language and Speech, Catholic University of Nijmegen
Erasmusplein 1, PO Box 9103, 6500 HD Nijmegen

Research Institute of Language and Speech, Utrecht University
Trans 10, 3512 JK Utrecht

PTT Research, Dr. Neher Laboratory
Sint Paulusstraat 4, PO Box 421, 2260 AK Leidschendam

2. Members of the Industrial Advisory Board

Ir. B. W. L. M. Sessink	OCE van den Grinten, Venlo (chair)
Prof. Dr. W. H. Vieregge	Dept. of Language and Speech, Catholic University of Nijmegen, Linguistics Foundation
Drs. M. G. Carasso	Philips Research Laboratories, Eindhoven
Prof. Dr. H. Bouma	Institute for Perception Research, Eindhoven
L. H. Portheine	Resus Rehabilitation Systems, Hendrik Ido Ambacht
Prof. Ir. M. Antal	PTT Research, Dr. Neher Laboratory, Leidschendam

3. Members of the Steering Committee

Dr. M. P. R. van den Broecke	Utrecht University (1985–1988)
Prof. Dr. L. Boves	Catholic University of Nijmegen/PTT Research
Prof. Dr. R. C. Collier	Institute for Perception Research (1989–1990)
Prof. Dr. A. Cohen	Utrecht University (coordinator 1985–1988)
Dr. V. J. van Heuven	Leiden University
Prof. Dr. S. G. Nooteboom	Utrecht University (coordinator 1989–1990)
Prof. Dr. Ir. L. C. W. Pols	University of Amsterdam
Dr. M. E. H. Schouten	Utrecht University (1989–1990)

4. SPIN-funded researchers and their ASSP-projects

Ing. P. Allain	Overall technical support
Dr. R. A. M. G. van Bezooijen	Evaluation of synthetic speech (project leader: Pols)
Dr. L. F. M. ten Bosch	From allophone synthesis to diphone synthesis by rule (project leader: Collier)
Ir. D. Broeder	Software distribution
Drs. L. Damen, Drs. E. van Houten, Dr. E. A. van Zanten	Creation of a speech database (project leader: van Heuven)
Dr. Ir. R. J. H. Deliège	Development of a stand-alone text-to-speech system for Dutch (project leader: Collier)
Dr. A. Dirksen	Syntactic parsing and syntax-to-prosody mapping (project leader: Quené)
Drs. R. Drullman	Creation of a complete diphone inventory spoken by designated talker PB (project leader: Collier)
Dr. W. Z. F. Eefting	Tempo variation in natural speech (project leader: Nooteboom)
Dr. Ir. J. H. Eggen	Physical correlates of speaker characteristics (project leader: Nooteboom)
Drs. J. S. M. Heemskerk	Automatic morphological decomposition (project leader: van Heuven)
Drs. Y. van Holsteijn	Text-scanning and editing: Pre-processing of texts (project leader: Quené)

Drs. W. Jongenburger	Phonological and allophonic variation (project leader: van Heuven)
Dr. R. Kager, Dr. H. Quené	Prosodic analysis: Rules for the placement of accents and speech pauses (project leader: van den Broecke)
Drs. J. M. G. Lammens	From text-to-speech via the lexicon (project leader: van den Broecke)
Drs. R. te Lindert	SPEECH MAKER: A laboratory system for text-to-speech conversion (project leader: Boves)
Drs. H. Loman	Allophone synthesis (project leader: Boves)
Drs. A. M. Nunn	Rule-based and lexicon-based grapheme-to-phoneme conversion (project leader: van Heuven)
Dr. I. Petric	Text features affecting listening comprehension in one way speech communication (project leader: Nooteboom)
Drs. J. Reizevoort	Morphological decomposition without a lexicon (project leader: van den Broecke)
Drs. R. J. J. H. van Son	Effects of speech rate on spectro-temporal characteristics of speech (project leader: Pols)
Dr. J. M. B. Terken	Intonational rules (project leaders: Nooteboom, Collier)
Drs. J. de Veth	ARMA-analysis of speech (project leader: Boves)

Appendix 2: Publications by SPIN-funded researchers

1. Dissertations

Deliège, R. J. H.

1989 The 'Tiepstem': An experimental Dutch keyboard-to-speech system for the speech impaired. [Unpublished Ph.D. dissertation, Technical University of Eindhoven.] 134 pp.

Eefting, W.

1991 Timing in talking: Tempo variation in production and its role in perception. [Unpublished Ph.D. dissertation, Utrecht University.] 121 pp.

Eggen, J. H.

1992 On the quality of synthetic speech; Evaluation and improvements. [Unpublished Ph.D. dissertation, Technical University of Eindhoven.] 129 pp.

Leeuwen, H. C. van

1989 TooLip: A Development Tool for Linguistic Rules. [Unpublished Ph.D. dissertation, Technical University of Eindhoven.] 181 pp.

Petrič, I.

1992 Here is the news, predicting listening performance for news texts. [Unpublished Ph.D. dissertation, Utrecht University.] 137 pp.

2. Contributions to journals and books

Baart, J. L. G.—V. J. van Heuven

1990 "Review of 'John Allen—M. S. Hunnicutt—D. H. Klatt: From text to speech, the MITalk system' ", *Lingua* 81: 265–270.

Berendsen, E.—J. M. Lammens—H. C. van Leeuwen

1989 "Grapheme-phoneme conversion", *Informatie* 31: 570–636. [in Dutch.]

Bezooijen, R. van
1989 "Speech synthesis in the Netherlands: A state-of-the-art report", *Gramma* 13: 97–112. [in Dutch.]
1989 "Evaluation of an algorithm for the automatic assignment of sentence accents", in: H. Bennis—A. van Kemenade (eds.), *Linguistics in the Netherlands 1989.* Dordrecht: Foris, 21–30.

Bezooijen, R. van—L. C. W. Pols
1990 "Evaluating text-to-speech systems: Some methodological aspects", *Speech Communication* 9: 263–270.

Bosch, L. F. M. ten
1991 "From data to rules", in: G. Bailly—Chr. Benoit (eds.), *Talking machines: Theories, models—applications.* Amsterdam: Elsevier, 13–26.

Boves, L.
1991 "Considerations in the design of a multi-lingual text-to-speech system", *Journal of Phonetics* 19: 25–36.

Collier, R.
1990 "On the perceptual analysis of intonation", *Speech Communication* 9: 443–451.
1991 "Multi-language intonation synthesis", *Journal of Phonetics* 19: 61–73.

Deliège, R. J. H.
1989 "An experimental Dutch keyboard-to-speech system for the speech impaired", *Speech Communication* 8: 81–89.

Deliège, R. J. H.—R. P. Waterham
1989 "The application of synthetic speech in communication aids for speech impaired", *Informatie* 31: 640–645. [in Dutch.]

Deliège, R. J. H.—I. M. A. F. Speth-Lemmens—R. P. Waterham
1988 "Development and evaluation of two communication aids with speech output", *Nederlands Tijdschrift voor Ergotherapie* 16: 37–40. [in Dutch.]
1988 "Development and evaluation of two communication aids with speech output", *Tijdschrift voor Logopedie en Foniatrie* 60: 220–224. [in Dutch.]
1989 "Development and preliminary evaluation of two speech communication aids", *Journal of Medical Engineering and Technology* 13: 18–22.

Drullman, R.—R. C. Collier
1991 "On the combined use of accented and unaccented diphones in speech synthesis", *Journal of the Acoustical Society of America* 90: 1766–1775.

Eefting, W.
1986 "Artificial speech: The problems of a speaking computer", *Onze Taal* 55: 152–154. [in Dutch.]
1986 "Speech synthesis: The computer is speaking", *Informatie* 28: 1046–1049. [in Dutch.]
1987 *Language and speech technology.* [Poly automatisering zakboekje.] Koninklijke PBNA, D2/128–147. [in Dutch.]
1990 "The effect of 'information value' and 'accentuation' on the duration of Dutch words, syllables, and segments", *Journal of the Acoustical Society of America* 89: 412–424.
1991 "The effect of accentuation and word duration on the naturalness of speech", *Journal of the Acoustical Society of America,* 91: 411–420.

Eefting, W.—A. C. M. Rietveld
1989 "Just noticeable differences of articulation rate at sentence level", *Speech Communication* 8: 355–361.

Eggen, J. H.
1989 "Intelligibility of synthetic speech in the presence of interfering speech", *Speech Communication* 8: 319–327.

Heemskerk, J. S. M.
1989 "Morphological parsing and lexical morphology", in: H. Bennis—A. van Kemenade (eds.), *Linguistics in the Netherlands 1989.* Dordrecht: Foris, 61–70.

Heuven, V. J. van
1987 "Stress patterns in Dutch (compound) adjectives: Acoustic measurements and perception data", *Phonetica* 44: 1–12.

Heuven, V. J. van—A. Hoos
1991 "Hiatus deletion, phonological rule or phonetic coarticulation?" in: A. van Kemenade—F. Drijkoningen (eds.), *Linguistics in the Netherlands 1991.* Dordrecht: Foris, 61–70.

Jongenburger, W.—V. J. van Heuven
1991 "The distribution of (word initial) glottal stop in Dutch", in: A. van Kemenade—F. Drijkoningen (eds.), *Linguistics in the Netherlands 1991.* Dordrecht: Foris, 101–110.

Kager, R.
1988 "Location of sentence accents and pauses in speech", in: M. P. R. van den Broecke (ed.), *Ter Sprake: Spraak als betekenisvol geluid in 36 thematische hoofdstukken.* Dordrecht: Foris, 416–426. [in Dutch.]

Kager, R.—H. Quené
1989 "An algorithm for the assignment of sentence accents for a Dutch text-to-speech system", in: H. Bennis—A. van Kemenade (eds.), *Linguistics in the Netherlands 1989.* Dordrecht: Foris, 101–109.

Lammens, J. M. G.
1988 "Speech and the mental lexicon", in: M. P. R. van den Broecke (ed.), *Ter Sprake: Spraak als betekenisvol geluid in 36 thematische hoofdstukken,* Dordrecht: Foris, 104–122. [in Dutch.]

Nooteboom, S. G.
1988 "Speech coding, synthesis and voice quality", in: B. A. G. Elsendoorn—H. Bouma (eds.), *Working models of human perception.* London: Academic Press, 173–181.

Nooteboom, S. G.—W. Eefting
1992 "To what extent is speech production controlled by speech perception?" Some questions and some experimental evidence", in: Y. Tohkura—E. Vatikiotis-Bateson—Y. Sagisaka (eds.), *Speech perception, production and linguistic structure.* Tokyo: Ohmsha, 439–449.

Pols, L. C. W.
1986 "Variation and interaction in speech", in: J. S. Perkell—D. H. Klatt (eds.), *Invariance and variability of speech processes.* Hillsdale: Lawrence Erlbaum, 140–154.
1988 "Speech technology. What is possible at present, and what isn't, and why", in: M. P. R. van den Broecke (ed.), *Ter Sprake: Spraak als betekenisvol geluid in 36 thematische hoofdstukken.* Dordrecht: Foris, 227–237. [in Dutch.]
1988 "The use of speech in man-machine interaction", in: G. C. van der Veer—G. Mulder (eds.), *Human-computer interaction. Psychonomic aspects.* Berlin: Springer, 361–372.
1989 "Assessment of text-to-speech synthesis systems", in: A. Fourcin—G. Harland—W. Barry—V. Hazan (eds.), *Speech input and output assessment. Multilingual methods and standards.* Ellis Horwood, Chichester, 53–81, 251–266.

Pols, L. C. W.
1989 "Book review of 'Aspects of Speech Technology', M. Jack and J. L. Laver (eds.). Edinburgh: Edinburgh University Press, vii+292 pp." *Language Technology* 12: 55.
1990 "Guest editor of special issue on speech input/output assessment and speech databases", *Speech Communication* 9: 263–388. Editorial/Biography, v–vi.
Pols, L. C. W.—R. van Bezooijen
1991 "Gaining phonetic knowledge whilst improving synthetic speech quality?" *Journal of Phonetics* 19: 139–146.
Quené, H.
1989 "Speaking computers", *Toegepaste Taalwetenschap in Artikelen* 33: 89–94. [in Dutch.]
Quené, H.—R. Kager
1989 "From text to prosody", *Informatie* 31: 570–576. [in Dutch.]
1990 "The derivation of prosody for text-to-speech from prosodic sentence structure", *Computer Speech and Language*, 6: 77–98.
Rietveld, A. C. M.—H. Loman
1986 "/h/, Voiced or Voiceless?" *Glot* 8: 275–285. [in Dutch.]
Son, R. J. J. H. van—L. C. W. Pols
1990 "Formant frequencies of Dutch vowels in a text, read at normal and fast rate", *Journal of the Acoustical Society of America* 88: 1683–1693.
1992 "Formant movements of Dutch vowels in a text, read at normal and fast rate", *Journal of the Acoustical Society of America,* 92: 121–127.
Terken, J. M. B.
1989 "Reaction to 'C. Gussenhoven—A. C. M. Rietveld: Fundamental frequency declination in Dutch: Testing three hypotheses' ", *Journal of Phonetics* 17: 357–364.
1989 "Automatic intonation for text-to-speech conversion", *Informatie* 31: 640–645. [in Dutch.]
1991 "Fundamental frequency and perceived prominence of accented syllables", *Journal of the Acoustical Society of America* 89: 1768–1776.

Terken, J. M. B. —R. Collier
1992 "Syntactic influences on prosody", in: Y. Tohkura—E. Vatikiotis-Bateson—Y. Sagisaka (eds.), *Speech perception, production and linguistic structure*. Tokyo: Ohmsha, 427–438.

Terken, J. M. B.—G. Lemeer
1988 "Effects of segmental quality and intonation on quality judgments for texts and utterances", *Journal of Phonetics* 16: 453–457.

Terken, J. M. B.—S. G. Nooteboom
1988 "Opposite effects of accentuation and deaccentuation on verification latencies for Given and New information", *Language and Cognitive Processes* 2: 145–163.

Veth, J. de—L. Boves—W. G. van Golstein Brouwers
1988 "System identification of the human speech production mechanisms by robust pole-zero analysis of speech", *Signal processing IV: Theories and applications*. Paris, 151–154.

3. Contributions to congress proceedings

Baart, J. L. G.—J. S. M. Heemskerk
1988 "The problem of ambiguity in morphological analysis for a Dutch text-to-speech system", in: W. A. Ainsworth—J. N. Holmes (eds.), *Proceedings SPEECH '88 (7th FASE symposium)*. Edinburgh, Book 3: 959–965.

Bezooijen, R. van
1988 "Evaluation of the quality of consonant clusters in two synthesis systems for Dutch", in: W. A. Ainsworth—J. N. Holmes (eds.), *Proceedings SPEECH '88 (7th FASE symposium)*. Edinburgh, Book 2: 445–452.
1989 "Evaluation of the suitability of Dutch text-to-speech conversion for application in a digital daily newspaper", in: *Proceedings of the Workshop on Speech Input/Output Assessment and Speech Databases*. Noordwijkerhout, 6.3.1.–6.3.4.

Bezooijen, R. van—L. C. W. Pols
1987 "Evaluation of two synthesis-by-rule systems for Dutch", in: *Proceedings of the European Conference on Speech Technology*. Edinburgh, Vol. 1: 183–186.

Bezooijen, R. van—L. C. W. Pols
1989 "Evaluation of a sentence accentuation algorithm for a Dutch text-to-speech system", in: J. B. Tubach—J. J. Mariani (eds.), *Proceedings of EUROSPEECH '89*. Paris, Vol. 1: 218–221.
1989 "Evaluation of text-to-speech conversion for Dutch: from segment to text", in: *Proceedings of the Workshop on Speech Input/Output Assessment and Speech Databases*. Noordwijkerhout, 3.4.1–3.4.4.
1991 "Evaluation of allophone and diphone based text-to-speech conversion at the paragraph level", in: *Proceedings of the Twelfth International Congress of Phonetic Sciences*. Aix-en-Provence, Vol. 3: 498–501.
1991 "Performance of text-to-speech conversion for Dutch: a comparative evaluation of allophone and diphone based synthesis at the level of the segment, the word, and the paragraph", in: *Proceedings of EUROSPEECH '91*. Genova, Vol. 2: 871–874.

Bezooijen, R. van—W. H. Vieregge
1991 "Phonetic Transcription as a means to diagnostically evaluate synthetic speech", in: *Proceedings of the Twelfth International Congress of Phonetic Sciences*. Aix-en-Provence, Vol. 4: 138–141.

Bosch, L. F. M. ten
1990 "Rule extraction for allophone synthesis", in: *Proceedings of the ESCA Workshop on Speech Synthesis*. Autrans, 17–20.
1990 "Rule extraction for allophone synthesis", in: *Reader Colloquium Signaalanalyse en Spraak 1990*. (IPO-report 765.) Eindhoven, Contribution 8.
1991 "Time varying Singular Value Decomposition: An application on speech-like signals", in: *Proceedings ICASSP '91*. Toronto, Vol. 5: 3197–3200.

Bosch, L. F. M. ten—R. C. Collier—L. Boves
1989 "From diphones to allophones: From data to rules", in: J. P. Tubach—J. J. Mariani (eds.), *Proceedings of EUROSPEECH '89*. Paris, Vol. 1: 129–131.

Bosch, L. F. M. ten—H. Loman
1989 "From diphones to allophone rules", in: *Reader Colloquium Signaalanalyse en Spraak 1989*. Utrecht, 29–39.

Boves, L. F. M. ten—J. Kerkhoff—H. Loman
1987 "A new synthesis model for an allophone based text-to-speech system", in: *Proceedings of the European Conference on Speech Technology*. Edinburgh, Vol. 2: 385–388.

Boves, L. F. M. ten—W. van Golstein Brouwers—J. Hendriks—J. de Veth
1987 "From LPC to ARMA (I–II)", in: *Reader Colloquium Signaalanalyse en Spraak 1987*. Amsterdam, 33–38, 111–116. [in Dutch.]

Collier, R. C.—J. M. B. Terken
1987 "Intonation by rule in text-to-speech applications", in: *Proceedings of the European Conference on Speech Technology*. Edinburgh, Vol. 2: 165–168.

Collier, R. C.—A. de Zitter—J. M. B. Terken
1989 "On the perceptual salience of melodical variations and its consequences for intonation synthesis", in: J. P. Tubach—J. J. Mariani (eds.), *Proceedings of EUROSPEECH '89*. Paris, Vol. 2: 108–111.

Deliège, R. J. H.
1986 "Communication aids for speech impaired: Two clear examples of communication aids", in: J. W. Smeets—J. J. Alexander (eds.), *Communication aids for the physically handicapped, Proceedings 'Handicap en Communicatie'*, Technological University Delft, 49–54. [in Dutch.]

Eefting, W.
1988 "Temporal variation in natural speech: Some explorations", in: W. A. Ainsworth—J. N. Holmes (eds.), *Proceedings SPEECH '88 (7th FASE Symposium)*. Edinburgh, Book 2: 503–507.

Eefting, W.—S. G. Nooteboom
1991 "The effect of accentedness and information value on word durations: A production and a perception study", in: *Proceedings of the Twelfth International Congress of Phonetic Sciences*. Aix-en-Provence, Vol. 3: 302–305.

Eggen, J. H.
1987 "Evaluation of synthetic speech by means of a monosyllabic adaptive interference test for speech", in: *Reader Colloquium Signaalanalyse en Spraak 1987*. Amsterdam, 51–54. [in Dutch.]

Eggen, J. H.
1988 "The evaluation of speech quality resulting from differences in speech-coding schemes", in: W. A. Ainsworth—J. N. Holmes (eds.), *Proceedings SPEECH '88 (7th FASE Symposium)*. Edinburgh, Book 4: 1203–1208.
1989 "Determination of the glottal waveform from the speech signal", in: *Reader Colloquium Signaalanalyse en Spraak 1989*. Utrecht, 9–16. [in Dutch.]

Golstein Brouwers, W. G. van—J. de Veth—L. Boves
1988 "Robust ARMA Analysis for estimation of vocal tract parameters", in: W. A. Ainsworth—J. N. Holmes (eds.), *Proceedings SPEECH '88 (7th FASE Symposium)*. Edinburgh, Book 1: 305–312.
1988 "Robust ARMA Analysis for estimation of vocal tract parameters", in: *Reader Colloquium Signaalanalyse en Spraak 1988*. Leidschendam, 43–47.

Heuven, V. J. van
1987 "An unusual effect on the perception of stress", in: *Proceedings of the 11th International Congress of Phonetic Sciences*. Tallinn, USSR, Vol. 3: 306–309.
1988 "Effects of stress and accent on the human recognition of word fragments in spoken context: Gating and shadowing", in: W. A. Ainsworth—J. N. Holmes (eds.), *Proceedings SPEECH '88 (7th FASE Symposium)*. Edinburgh, Book 3: 811–818.
1991 "Stress clash avoidance in Dutch: Inversion of stress pattern in complex nouns", in: *Proceedings of the Twelfth International Congress of Phonetic Sciences*. Aix-en-Provence, Vol. 3: 226–229.

Kager, R.—H. Quené
1987 "Deriving prosodic sentence structure without exhaustive syntactic analysis", in: *Proceedings of the European Conference on Speech Technology*. Edinburgh, Vol. 1: 243–246.

Lammens, J. M. G.
1987 "A lexicon-based grapheme-to-phoneme conversion system", in: *Proceedings of the European Conference on Speech Technology*. Edinburgh, Vol. 1: 281–284.

Leeuwen, H. C. van—E. te Lindert
1991 "Speech Maker: Text-to-speech synthesis based on a multi-level synchronized data structure", in: *Proceedings ICASSP '91*. Toronto, Vol. 2: 781–784.

Loman, H.—R. van Bezooijen—J. Kerkhoff—L. Boves
1989 "A working environment and procedure for the development of speech synthesis rules", in: J. P. Tubach—J. J. Mariani (eds.), *Proceedings of EUROSPEECH '89*. Paris, Vol. 1: 132–135.

Loman, H.—J. de Veth—L. Boves
1991 "The analysis of Dutch nasal consonants using Robust Arma analysis: Consequences for rule development in speech synthesis", in: *Proceedings ICASSP '91*. Toronto, Vol. 2: 773–776.

Nooteboom, S. G.
1991 "Perceptual goals of speech production", in: *Proceedings of the Twelfth International Congress of Phonetic Sciences*, Aix-en-Provence, Vol. 1: 107–110.
1991 "Some observations on the temporal organisation and rhythm of speech", in: *Proceedings of the Twelfth International Congress of Phonetic Sciences*. Aix-en-Provence, Vol. 1: 228–237.

Nooteboom, S. G.—R. van Bezooijen
1991 "Five years of coordinated research on text-to-speech conversion for Dutch — an overview", in: *Proceedings of the Twelfth International Congress of Phonetic Sciences*, Aix-en-Provence, Vol. 3: 470–473.

Petrič, I.
1989 "Are texts meant to be read aloud, suited for the purpose of being listened to?" in: *Proceedings of the 2nd Congress of the Dutch Society of Psychonomy*, Noordwijkerhout. [in Dutch.]

Pols, L. C. W.
1987 "Speech technology research in the Netherlands", in: *Proceedings of the Conference on Speech Technology, Status of Technology and Programmes Worldwide*, Aarhus: Jydsk Telefon, 7.1–7.14.

Pols, L. C. W.

1987 "Speech Technology and corpus linguistics", in: W. Meijs (ed.) *Corpus linguistics and beyond. Proceedings of the Seventh International Conference on English Language Research in Computerized Corpora.* Amsterdam: Rodopi, 285–294.

1988 "Improving synthetic speech quality by systematic evaluation", in: *Proceedings of the Second Symposium on Advanced Man-Machine Interface Through Spoken Language*, Makaha, Oahu, Hawaii, 17/1–17/9. [also in: *Proceedings of the Institute of Phonetic Sciences.* Amsterdam, 12: 19–27.

1989 "Studying speech perception: From simple stationary stimuli to more and more complex speech(-like) signals", in: *Proceedings of the 28th Conference on Acoustics.* Strebské Pleso, High Tatras, Czechoslovakia, 27–34.

1990 "Assessing the speech quality of text-to-speech synthesizers", in: *Proceedings VERBA 90, International Conference on Speech Technology.* Rome, 295–302.

1990 "Does improved performance also contribute to more phonetic knowledge", in: *Proceedings of ESCA Tutorial Day on Speech Synthesis.* Autrans, 49–54.

1990 "How useful are speech databases for rule synthesis development and assessment?" in: *Proceedings of the 1990 International Conference on Spoken Language Processing.* Kobe, Vol. 2: 1289–1292.

1990 " 'Standardized' synthesis evaluation methods", in: *Proceedings International Workshop on International Coordination and Standardization of Speech Database and Assessment Techniques for Speech Input/Output.* Kobe, 53–60.

1991 "Speech perception in the next ten years: Technological solutions vs. acquiring actual speech knowledge", in: *Proceedings of the Twelfth International Congress of Phonetic Sciences.* Aix-en-Provence, Vol. 1: 130–133.

Pols, L. C. W.—L.J. P. van Heugten—F. J. Koopmans-van Beinum—R. van Bezooijen—H. J. M. Steeneken (eds.)

1989 *Proceedings of the ESCA Tutorial Day and Workshop on Speech Input/Output Assessment and Speech Databases.* Noordwijkerhout, 20–23 september 1989.

Quené, H.—R. Kager
1989 "Automatic accentuation and prosodic phrasing for Dutch text-to-speech conversion", in: J. P. Tubach—J. J. Mariani, *Proceedings of EUROSPEECH '89*. Paris, Vol. 1: 214–217.

Quené, H.—A. Dirksen
1990 "A comparison of natural, theoretical and automatically derived accentuations of Dutch texts", in: *Proceedings of the ESCA workshop on Speech Synthesis*. Autrans, 137–140.

Son, R. J. J. H. van
1988 "The automatic segmentation and stylization of parameter curves", in: *Reader Colloquium Signaalanalyse en Spraak 1988*. Leidschendam, 57–60. [in Dutch.]

Son, R. J. J. H. van—L. C.W. Pols
1988 "Differences in formant values of Dutch vowels due to speaking rate", in: W. A. Ainsworth—J. N. Holmes (eds.), *Proceedings of SPEECH '88 (7th FASE Symposium)*. Edinburgh, Book 1: 313–320.
1989 "Comparing formant movements in fast and normal rate speech", in: J. P. Tubach—J. J. Mariani (eds.), *Proceedings of EUROSPEECH '89*. Paris, Vol. 2: 665–668.
1991 "The influence of formant track shape on the perception of synthetic vowels. in: *Proceedings of EUROSPEECH '91*. Genova, Vol. 3: 117–120.

Terken, J. M. B.—R. C. Collier
1989 "Automatic synthesis of natural-sounding intonation for text-to-speech conversion in Dutch", in: J. P. Tubach—J. J. Mariani (eds.), *Proceedings of EUROSPEECH '89*. Paris, Vol. 1: 357–359.
1990 "Designing algorithms for intonation in synthetic speech", in: *Proceedings of the ESCA Workshop on Speech Synthesis*. Autrans, 205–208.

Veth, J. de—L. Boves
1987 "Pole-zero analysis of speech", in: *Proceedings of the Onzième Colloque GRETSI*. Nice.
1987 "Tracking of speech parameters using ARMA analysis techniques", in: *Proceedings of the European Conference on Speech Technology*. Edinburgh, Vol. 1: 37–42.

Veth, J. de—W. G. van Golstein Brouwers—L. Boves
1989 "Robust ARMA analysis for accurate determination of system parameters of the voice source and vocal tract", in: J. P. Tubach—J. J. Mariani (eds.), *Proceedings of EURO-SPEECH '89*. Edinburgh, Vol. 2: 43–46.

Veth, J. de—B. Cranen—H. Strik—L. Boves
1990 "Extraction of control parameters for the voice source in a text-to-speech system", in: *Proceedings ICASSP '90*. Albuquerque, 301–304.

Veth, J. de—W. G. Golstein Brouwers—H. Loman—L. Boves
1990 "Robust ARMA analysis as an aid in developing parameter control-rules for a pole-zero cascade speech synthesizer", in: *Proceedings ICASSP '90*. Albuquerque, 305–308.

4. Interim reports of ASSP

Bezooijen, R. van
1987 "Evaluation of two synthesis-by-rule systems for Dutch: Segmental intelligibility". *SPIN/ASSP-report* 1.
1988 "Evaluation of two synthesis systems for Dutch: Intelligibility and overall quality of initial and final consonant clusters". *SPIN/ASSP-report* 3.
1988 "Evaluation of two synthesis systems for Dutch: Development and applications of intelligibility tests". *SPIN/ASSP-report* 5.
1989 "Evaluation of an algorithm for the automatic assignment of sentence accents in written text". *SPIN/ASSP-report* 9.
1989 "Evaluation of text-to-speech conversion at the text level". *SPIN/ASSP-report* 15.
1990 "Evaluation of Speech Synthesis for Dutch: Comparison of synthesis systems, intelligibility tests, and scaling methods". *SPIN/ASSP-report* 22.

Bringmann, E.
1990 "Philip Bloemendal Corpus". *SPIN/ASSP-report* 21. [in Dutch.]

Broeder, D.
1988 "ADDA-documentation". *SPIN/ASSP-report* 6. [in Dutch.]
1989 "SESAM-documentation". *SPIN/ASSP-report* 14. [in Dutch.]
1990 "CADDA manual". *SPIN/ASSP-report* 23. [in Dutch.]
1990 "SESAM manual". *SPIN/ASSP-report* 24. [in Dutch.]

Dirksen, A.—J. S. M. Heemskerk—A. M. Nunn
1990 "Linguistic analysis in text-to-speech conversion". *SPIN/ASSP-report* 34. [in Dutch.]

Doedens, C. J.—H. C. van Leeuwen—E. te Lindert
1989 "Speechmaker-1". *SPIN/ASSP-report* 11. [in Dutch.]

Eefting, W.
1990 "The effect of 'Information Value' and 'Accentuation' on the duration of Dutch words, syllables and segments". *SPIN/ASSP-report* 20.

Eggen, J. H.
1987 "Start evaluation of available methods for analysis, manipulation and resynthesis of speech". *SPIN/ASSP-report* 2.

Golstein Brouwers, W. G. van—J. M. de Veth—L. Boves—L. J. P. van Heugten
1991 "Manual of the POZAN programme". *SPIN/ASSP-report* 26. [in Dutch.]

Son, R. J. J. H. van
1990 "Formant frequencies of Dutch vowels in a text, read at normal and fast rate". *SPIN/ASSP-report* 16.

5. Final reports of ASSP

Allain, P.
1990 "LVS Programmer's manual". *SPIN/ASSP-report* 32.

Bezooijen, R. van
1990 "Evaluation of synthetic speech". *SPIN/ASSP-report* 28.

Bosch, L. ten
1991 "ALLODIF: Rule extraction for allophone synthesis". *SPIN/ASSP-report* 33.

Broeder, D. G.
1991 "Software-distribution ASSP". *SPIN/ASSP-report* 37. [in Dutch.]

Deliège, R. J. H.
1991 "A stand-alone Dutch text-to-speech system". *SPIN/ASSP-report* 31.

Drullman, R.
1990 "BLOEMDIF: A complete inventory of accented and unaccented diphones". *SPIN/ASSP-report* 27.

Eefting, W.
1990 "Tempo variation in natural speech: An explorative study". *SPIN/ASSP-report* 29.

Eggen, J. H.
1991 "Speech quality and speaker characteristics". *SPIN/ASSP-report* 39.

Holsteijn, Y.
1991 "TEXTSCAN: A preprocessing module for automatic text-to-speech conversion". *SPIN/ASSP-report* 40.

Jongenburger, W.
1991 "Sandhi processes". *SPIN/ASSP-report* 35.

Lammens, J. M. G.
1989 "From text to speech via the lexicon". *SPIN/ASSP-report* 7.

Lindert, E. te
1991 "Spraakmaker-2: A text-to-speech system for the Dutch language". *SPIN/ASSP-report* 43.

Nunn, A. M.
1991 "MORFON: Integration of morphological decomposition and letter-to-sound conversion". *SPIN/ASSP-report* 36.

Quené, H.—R. Kager
1990 "PROS: Automatic sentence analysis, accentuation and phrasing for Dutch text-to-speech conversion". *SPIN/ASSP-report* 17.

Reizevoort, J.
1988 "Morphological decomposition without a lexicon". *SPIN/ASSP-report* 4. [in Dutch.]

Son, R. J. J. H. van
1991 "Aspects of speech rate on spectro-temporal characteristics of speech". *SPIN/ASSP-report* 42.

Terken, J. M. B.
1991 "INTO: Automatic synthesis of intonation for Dutch text-to-speech conversion". *SPIN/ASSP-report* 30.

Veth, J. M. de—W. G. van Golstein-Brouwers—L. Boves—L. J. P. van Heugten
1991 "Research on the human speech production system by means of robust ARMA-analysis". *SPIN/ASSP-report* 38. [in Dutch.]

Zanten, E. van—L. Damen—E. van Houten
1991 "The ASSP Database". *SPIN/ASSP-report* 41.

6. Contributions to working papers

IFA = Institute of Phonetic Sciences, Amsterdam University.
AFN = Institute of Phonetics, Nijmegen University.
IPO = Institute of Perception Research, Eindhoven.
OTS = Research Institute for Language and Speech, Utrecht University.
PRIPU = Progress Report Institute of Phonetics, Utrecht University.

Bezooijen, R. van
1987 "Evaluation of two synthesis systems for Dutch - Phonemes and consonant clusters". *IFA-proceedings* 11: 47–58.

Bosch, L. ten
1989 "From diphones to allophone rules" *AFN-proceedings* 13: 41–49.

Boves L.—J. Kerkhoff—H. Loman—R. J. J. H. van Son
1987 "Automatic text-to-speech synthesis by allophones". *AFN-proceedings* 11: 24–26.

Boves, L.—J. de Veth
1987 "Pole zero analysis of speech". *AFN-Proceedings* 11: 31–32.

Broecke, M. P. R. van den—A. Aerts—J. Reizevoort—T. Veenhof—J. M. G. Lammens—M. Elstrodt
1987 "Type- and token-frequencies of wordclasses, phonemes and phoneme pairs in Dutch". *PRIPU* 12/1: 1–15.

Deliège, R. J. H.—R. P. Waterham
1986 "Application of speech synthesis and resynthesis in two speech communication aids". *IPO Annual Progress Report* 21: 110–115.

Deliège, R. J. H.—I. M. A.F.Speth-Lemmens—R. P. Waterham
1988 "Realization and evaluation of two speech communication aids". *IPO Annual Progress Report* 23: 115–120.

Deliège, R. J. H.
1989 "A stand-alone text-to-speech system". *IPO Annual Progress Report* 24: 43–46.

Drullman, R.
1990 MAKEDIP. A program to create diphones from segmented AP-files. IPO Manual nr. 101.

Eefting, W.
1991 "Production and perception of temporal variation: An explorative study", in: P. Coopmans, M. E. H. Schouten—W. Zonneveld (eds.), *OTS Yearbook 1990,* 13–38.

Eefting, W.—A. C. M. Rietveld
1988 "Just noticeable differences of articulation rate at sentence level". *AFN-proceedings* 12: 17–25.

Eggen, J. H.
1987 "Software for the measurement of speech intelligibility". *IPO Report* 609. [in Dutch.]
1989 "Start evaluation of available methods for analysis, manipulation and resynthesis of speech". *IPO Report* 612.
1989 "A glottal-excited speech synthesizer". *IPO Annual Progress Report* 24: 25–32.

Kerkhoff, J.—H. Loman—L. Boves
1986 "Fonpars2: A compiler for the implementation of phonetic rules". *AFN-proceedings* 10: 75–80.

Lindert, E. te—H. C. van Leeuwen
1990 "Spraakmaker: A text-to-speech system for the Dutch language". *IPO Annual Progress Report* 25, 40–49.

Lammens, J. M. G.
1987 "A lexicon-based grapheme-to-phoneme conversion system for Dutch". *PRIPU* 12/1: 23–31.

Loman, H.—R. J. J. H. van Son—L. Boves—J. Kerkhoff
1987 "Some phonetic rules of the text-to-speech conversion system and naive listeners' judgements about the realization of synthesized CVC-utterances". *AFN-proceedings* 11: 57–79.

Loman, H.—R. van Bezooijen
1988 "Evaluation of Dutch rule synthesis consonants by means of a fast diagnostic test". *AFN-proceedings* 12: 57–72.

Loman, H.—J. Kerkhoff—L. Boves
1989 "A working environment for speech synthesis by rule". *AFN-proceedings* 13: 51–63.

Petrič, I.
1988 "Recall of database texts". *PRIPU* 13/2: 29–36.

Pols, L. C. W.
1986 "Participation in (inter)national projects on speech technology evaluation". *IFA-proceedings* 10: 91–96.
1987 "Distance measures; physical and perceptual aspects". *IFA-proceedings* 11: 59–66.
1988 "A joint Dutch research program for developing a high-quality text-to-speech synthesis system". *IFA-proceedings* 12: 9–17.

Pols, L. C. W.
1989 "Studying speech perception: From simple stationary stimuli to more and more complex speech(-like) signals (revised version)". *IFA-proceedings* 13: 125–131.

Rietveld, A. C. M.—W. Eefting
1987 "Temporal variation in natural speech". *AFN-proceedings* 11: 12–13.

Son, R. J. J. H. van
1987 "Automatic slope measurements on formant track". *IFA-proceedings* 11: 67–78.

Son, R. J. J. H. van—L. C. W. Pols
1991 "The influence of speaking rate on vowel formant track shape as modelled by Legendre polynomials". *IFA-proceedings* 15: 43–59.

References

Abramowitz, M.—I. A. Stegun
1965 *Handbook of mathematical functions*. 9th printing. New York: Dover.

Aerts, A.
1986 Computer hyphenation, a new approach in Dutch. [Unpublished M.A. thesis, Department of Phonetics, Utrecht University.]

Ainsworth, W. A.—J. N. Holmes (eds.)
1988 *Proceedings SPEECH '88 (7th FASE symposium)*. 6 Books. Edinburgh.

Allen, J.—M. S. Hunnicutt—D. Klatt
1987 *From text to speech: The MITalk system*. Cambridge, Mass.: MIT Press.

Atal, B. S.—N. David
1979 "On synthesizing natural-sounding speech by linear prediction", in: *Proceedings ICASSP '79*, 44–47.

Baart, J. L. G.
1987 Focus, syntax, and accent placement: Towards a rule system for the derivation of pitch accent patterns in Dutch as spoken by humans and machines. [Unpublished Ph.D. dissertation, Leiden University.]

Baart, J. L. G.—J. S. M. Heemskerk
1988 "The problem of ambiguity in morphological analysis for a Dutch text-to-speech system", in: W. A. Ainsworth—J. N. Holmes (eds.), Book 3: 959–965.

Bachenko, J.—E. Fitzpatrick
1990 "A computational grammar of discourse-neutral prosodic phrasing in English", *Computational Linguistics* 16: 155–170.

Bailly, G.
1989 "Integration of rhythmic and syntactic constraints in a model of generation of French prosody", *Speech Communication* 8: 137–146.

Bailly, G.—Chr. Benoit (eds.)
1990 *Proceedings of the ESCA Workshop on Speech Synthesis*. Autrans, France.

Benguerel, A-P.
1989 "The effect of coarticulation on the role of transitions in vowel perception", *Phonetica* 46: 880–896.

Bennis, H.—F. Beukema (eds.)
1985 *Linguistics in the Netherlands 1985*. Dordrecht: Foris.

Bennis, H.—A. van Kemenade (eds.)
1989 *Linguistics in the Netherlands 1989*. Dordrecht: Foris.

Bennis, H.—W. U. S. van Lessen Kloecke (eds.)
1984 *Linguistics in the Netherlands 1984*. Dordrecht: Foris.

Berendsen, E.—J. Don
1987 "Morphology and stress in a rule-based grapheme-to-phoneme conversion system for Dutch", in: J. Laver—M. A. Jack (eds.), Vol. 1: 239–242.

Berendsen, E.—J. Lammens—H. C. van Leeuwen
1989 "Van tekst naar foneemrepresentatie" [From text to phonemic representation], *Informatie* 31: 563–569.

Berendsen, E.—S. Langeweg—H. C. van Leeuwen
1986 "Computational phonology: Merged not mixed", in: *Proceedings of the International Conference on Computational Linguistics '86*, 612–614.

Beukema, F.—P. Coopmans (eds.)
1987 *Linguistics in the Netherlands 1987*. Dordrecht: Foris.

Beurden, L. van
1987 "Playing level with Dutch morphology", in: F. Beukema—P. Coopmans (eds.), 21–30.

Bezooijen, R. van
1987a "Evaluation of two synthesis-by-rule systems for Dutch: Segmental intelligibility", *SPIN/ASSP Report* 1. Utrecht: Foundation for Speech Technology.

1987b "Evaluation of two synthesis systems for Dutch: Phonemes and consonant clusters", *Proceedings of the Institute Phonetic Sciences*, University of Amsterdam 11, 47–58.

1988a "Evaluation of the quality of consonant clusters in two synthesis systems for Dutch", in W. A. Ainsworth—J. N. Holmes (eds.), Book 2: 445–452.

1988b "Evaluation of two synthesis systems for Dutch: Intelligibility and overall quality of initial and final consonant clusters". *SPIN/ASSP Report* 3. Utrecht: Foundation for Speech Technology.

Bezooijen, R. van
1988c "Evaluation of two synthesis systems for Dutch: Development and applications of intelligibility tests", *SPIN/ASSP Report* 5. Utrecht: Foundation for Speech Technology.
1989a "Evaluation of an algorithm for the automatic assignment of sentence accents", in: H. Bennis—A. van Kemenade (eds.), 21–30.
1989b "Evaluation of the suitability of Dutch text-to-speech conversion for application in a digital daily newspaper", in: L. C. W. Pols et al. (eds.), 6.3.1–6.3.4.
1989c "Spraaksynthese in Nederland: Een momentopname", [The state-of-the-art of speech synthesis in the Netherlands], *Gramma* 13: 97–112.
1989d "Evaluation of an algorithm for the automatic assignment of sentence accents in written text", *SPIN/ASSP Report* 9. Utrecht: Foundation for Speech Technology.
1989e "Evaluation of text-to-speech conversion at the text level", *SPIN/ASSP Report* 15. Utrecht: Foundation for Speech Technology.
1990 "Evaluation of speech synthesis for Dutch: Comparison of synthesis systems, intelligibility tests, and scaling methods", *SPIN/ASSP Report* 22. Utrecht: Foundation for Speech Technology.

Bezooijen, R. van—L. C. W. Pols
1987 "Evaluation of two synthesis-by-rule systems for Dutch", in J. Laver—M. A. Jack (eds.), Vol. 1: 183–186.
1989 "Evaluation of a sentence accentuation algorithm for a Dutch text-to-speech system". in: J. B. Tubach—J. J. Mariani (eds.), Vol. 1: 218–221.

Boef, H. J.
1989 *Afkortingenlijst van de Nederlandse Taal* [Dutch abbreviation dictionary]. Apeldoorn: Auctor.

Bok-Bennema, R.—R. van Hout (eds.)
1992 *Linguistics in the Netherlands 1992.* Amsterdam: Benjamins.

Bolinger, D. L.
1972 "Accent is predictable (if you're a mind reader)", *Language* 48: 83–96.

Booij, G. E.
1979 *Morfologie van het Nederlands* [Morphology of Dutch]. Amsterdam: Huis aan de drie grachten.
1981 *Generatieve fonologie van het Nederlands* [Generative phonology of Dutch]. Utrecht: Het Spectrum.

Bosch, L. F. M. ten
1989 "From diphones to allophone rules", *AFN-Proceedings* 13: 41–49.
1990 "Rule extraction for allophone synthesis", in: G. Bailly—Chr. Benoit (eds.), 17–20.
1991 "ALLODIF: Rule extraction for allophone synthesis". *SPIN/ASSP Report* 33. Utrecht: Foundation for Speech Technology.
1992 On the application of rule sets on linear symbol strings. [Unpublished MS., Catholic University of Nijmegen.]

Bosch, L. F. M. ten—D. J. M. Weenink (eds.).
1987 *Reader colloquium signaalanalyse en spraak* [Reader colloquium signal analysis and speech]. Amsterdam.

Bouma, H,—D. G. Bouwhuis (eds.)
1984 *Control of language processes* (Attention and Performance 10). London: Lawrence Erlbaum.

Boves, L.
1991 "Considerations in the design of a multi-lingual text-to-speech system", *Journal of Phonetics* 19: 25–36.

Boves, L.—W. van Golstein Brouwers—J. P. M. Hendriks—J. M. de Veth
1987 "From LPC to ARMA (I–II)", in: L. F. M. ten Bosch—D. J. M. Weenink (eds.), 33–37, 111–116.

Boxelaar, G. W.
1986 Manual for program EVAL and additional programs. [Internal Report of the Institute of Phonetic Sciences, University of Amsterdam.]

Bringmann, E.
1990a Documentatie prosodische transcriptie [Documentation of prosodic transcription, unpublished MS., Utrecht University].
1990b "Philip Bloemendal corpus", *ASSP/SPIN report* 21. Utrecht: Foundation for Speech Technology.
1991 The distribution of Dutch reading pauses; the influence of prosodic phrasing—punctuation on pause location and duration. [Unpublished M.A. thesis, Utrecht University].

Broad, D. J.—F. Clermont

1987 "A methodology for modelling vowel formant contours in CVC context", *Journal of the Acoustical Society of America* 81: 155–165.

Broad, D. J.—R. H. Fertig

1970 "Formant-frequency trajectories in selected CVC-syllable nuclei", *Journal of the Acoustical Society of America* 47: 1572–1582.

Broecke, M. P. R. van den—M. Elstrodt—A. Aerts

1986 "Letter- en woordfrequenties in Nederlandse krantentekst" [Letter and word frequencies in Dutch newspaper text], *De Nieuwe Taalgids* 80: 251–256.

Broecke, M. P. R. van den—V. J. van Heuven

1983 "Effect and artifact in the auditory discrimination of rise and decay time", *Perception and Psychophysics* 33: 305–313.

Broeder, D. G.

1991 *Sesam gebruikershandleiding* [Sesam user manual]. *SPIN/ASSP Report* 24. Utrecht: Foundation for Speech Technology.

Carlson, R.—B. Granström

1976 "A text-to-speech system based entirely on rules", in: *Proceedings ICASSP '76,* 686–688.

1986 "Linguistic processing in the KTH multi-lingual Text-to-speech System", in: *Proceedings ICASSP '86.* Tokyo, 2403–2406.

Carlson, R.—B. Granström—S. Hunnicutt

1989 Multilingual text-to-speech development and applications. [Internal report of the Department of Speech Communication and Music Acoustics, Royal Institute of Technology (KTH), Stockholm.]

Charpentier, F—E. Moulines

1989 "Pitch-synchronous waveform processing techniques for text-to-speech synthesis using diphones", in: J. B. Tubach—J. J. Mariani (eds.), Vol. 2: 13–19.

Chomsky, N.—M. Halle

1968 *The Sound Pattern of English.* New York: Harper & Row.

Clark, J.—C. Yallop

1990 *An introduction to phonetics and phonology*. Oxford: Basil Blackwell.

Cohen, A.—R. Collier—J. 't Hart

1982 "Declination: Construct or intrinsic feature of speech pitch?" *Phonetica* 39: 254–273.

Cohen, A.—S. G. Nooteboom (eds.)

1975 *Structure and process in speech perception*. (Communication and Cybernetics 11.) Berlin: Springer.

Cohen, P.—J. Morgan—M. Pollock (eds.)

1990 *Intentions in communication*. Cambridge, Mass.: MIT Press.

Coile, B. M. J. van

1987 "A model of phoneme durations based on the analysis of a read Dutch text", in: J. Laver—M. A. Jack (eds.), Vol. 2: 233–236.

1989 "The Depes development system for text-to-speech synthesis", in: *Proceedings ICASSP '89*, 250–253.

Collier, R.—H. 't Hart

1975 "The role of intonation in speech perception", in: A. Cohen—S. G. Nooteboom (eds.), 107–121.

Collier, R.—J. M. B. Terken

1987 "Intonation by rule in text-to-speech applications", in J. Laver—M. A. Jack (eds.), Vol. 2: 165–168.

Collier, R.—A. L. J. de Zitter—J. M. B. Terken

1989 "On the perceptual salience of melodical variations and its consequences for intonation synthesis". In J. P. Tubach, J. J. Mariani (eds.), Vol. 2: 108–111.

Cooper, W. E.—J. Paccia-Cooper

1980 *Syntax and Speech*. Cambridge, Mass.: Harvard University Press.

Cooper, W. E.—J. M. Sorensen

1977 "Fundamental frequency contours at syntactic boundaries", *Journal of the Acoustical Society of America* 62: 683–692.

Cooper, W. E.—E. C. T. Walker (eds.)

1979 *Sentence processing: Psycholinguistic studies presented to Merrill Garrett*. Hillsdale, N.J.: Lawrence Erlbaum.

Cranen, L. I. J.

1987 The acoustic impedance of the glottis, measurements and modeling. [Unpublished Ph.D. dissertation, Catholic University of Nijmegen.]

Cutler, A.
1982 "Prosody and sentence perception in English", in: J. Mehler—E. C. T. Walker—M. Garrett (eds.), 201–216.

Cutler, A.—C. Clifton
1984 "The use of prosodic information in word recognition", in: H. Bouma—D. G. Bouwhuis (eds.), 183–196.

Cutler, A.—D. Norris
1979 "Monitoring sentence comprehension", in: W. E. Cooper—E. C. T. Walker (eds.).

Daelemans, W.
1987 Studies in language technology: An object-oriented computer model of morphophonological aspects of Dutch. [Unpublished Ph.D. dissertation, Catholic University of Leuven.]

De Mori, R.—C. Y. Suen (eds.)
New systems and architectures for automatic speech recognition and synthesis. Berlin: Springer.

Delattre, P.
1969 "An acoustic and articulatory study of vowel reduction in four languages", *International Review of Applied Linguistics and Language Teaching* 8: 295–325.

Deliège, R. J. H.—I. M. A. F. Speth-Lemmens—R. P. Waterham
1989 "Development and preliminary evaluation of two speech communication aids", *Journal of Medical Engineering and Technology* 13: 18–22.

Di Benedetto, M. G.
1989 "Vowel representation: Some observations on temporal and spectral properties of the first formant frequency", *Journal of the Acoustical Society of America* 86: 55–66.

Dijk, T. A. van
1988 *News as discourse.* Hillsdale, N.J.: Lawrence Erlbaum.

Droste, F. G. (ed.)
1987 *Mainstreams in Linguistics.* Amsterdam: Benjamins.

Drullman, R.—R. Collier
1991 "On the combined use of accented and unaccented diphones in speech synthesis", *Journal of the Acoustical Society of America* 90: 1766–1775.

Duez, D.
1989 "Second formant locus-nucleus patterns in spontaneous speech: Some preliminary results on French", *Phonetic Experimental Research Institute of Linguistics University of Stockholm (PERILUS)* 10: 109–114.

Eggen, J. H.
1989a "Intelligibility of synthetic speech in the presence of interfering speech", *Speech Communication* 8: 319–327.
1989b "A glottal-excited speech synthesizer", *IPO Annual Progress Report* 24: 25–32.

Eggen, J. H—L. L. M. Vogten
1990 "Degradation of speaker identification for LPC formant-coded speech", *Journal of the Acoustical Society of America* 87: S109.

Elsendoorn, B. A. G.
1984 "Heading for a speech synthesis system for Dutch", *IPO Annual Progress Report* 19: 32–35.

Elsendoorn, B. A. G.—H. Bouma (eds.)
1989 *Working Models of Human Perception*. London: Academic Press.

Elsendoorn, B. A. G.—J. 't Hart
1982 "Exploring the possibilities of speech synthesis with Dutch diphones", *IPO Annual Progress Report* 17: 63–65.

Engstrand, O. (ed.)
1987 *Papers from the Swedish Phonetics Conference*. Uppsala: Department of Linguistics, University of Uppsala.

Engstrand, O.
1988 "Articulatory correlates of stress and speaking rate in Swedish VCV utterances", *Journal of the Acoustical Society of America* 85, 1863–1875.

Erp, A. J. M. van
1988 Computerleesbare fonetische transcripties; een beschrijving van de syntax die in de module CONVERSIE.PAS als uitgangspunt is genomen [Computer readable phonetic transcriptions; a description of the syntax which was used as a starting point in the CONVERSIE.PAS module]. Dr. Neher Laboratorium intern rapport 87 DNL/012. 2nd edition.

Fant, G.
1960 *Acoustic theory of speech production.* 's Gravenhage: Mouton.

Fant, G.—J. Liljencrants—Q. Lin
1985 "A four-parameter model of glottal flow", *Speech Transmission Laboratory —Quarterly Progress and Status Report* 4: 1–13.

Fant, G.—Q. Lin
1988 "Frequency domain interpretation and derivation of glottal flow parameters", *Speech Transmission Laboratory — Quarterly Progress and Status Report* 2: 1–21.

Feng, G.
1986 Modelisation acoustique et traitement du signal de parole. Le cas des voyelles nasales. [Unpublished Ph.D. dissertation, Laboratoire de Phonetique, Université de Stendhal, Grenoble.]

Ferguson, G. A.
1981 *Statistical analysis in psychology and education.* International student edition, 2nd printing, 381–406. New York: McGraw-Hill.

Flanagan, J. L.
1972 *Speech analysis, synthesis and perception.* (2nd edition.) Berlin: Springer.

Foss, D. L.
1969 "Decision processes during sentence comprehension: Effects of lexical item difficulty and poistion upon decision times". *Journal of Verbal Learning and Verbal Behavior* 8: 457–462.

Foss, D. J.—M. Gernsbacher
1983 "Cracking the dual code: Toward a unitary model of phoneme identification". *Journal of Verbal Learning and Verbal Behavior* 22: 609–632.

Fowler, C. A.—J. Housum
1987 "Talkers' signaling of 'new' and 'old' words in speech and listeners' perception and use of the distinction", *Journal of Memory and Language* 26: 489–504.

Fuchs, A.
1984 " 'Deaccenting' and 'default accent' ", in: D. Gibbon—H. Richter (eds.), 134–164.

Gay, T.
1978 "Effect of speaking rate on vowel formant movements", *Journal of the Acoustical Society of America* 63: 223–230.
1981 "Mechanisms in the control of speech rate", *Phonetica* 38: 148–158.

Gay, T.—T. Ushijima—H. Hirose—F. S. Cooper
1974 "Effect of speaking rate on labial consonant-vowel articulation", *Journal of Phonetics* 2: 47–63.

Gazdar, G.—C. Mellish
1989 *Natural language processing in Prolog: An introduction to computational linguistics.* Workingham: Addison-Wesley.

Gee, J. P.—F. Grosjean
1983 "Performance structures: A psycholinguistic and linguistic appraisal", *Cognitive psychology* 15: 411–458.

Gibbon, D.—H. Richter, (eds.)
1984 *Intonation, accent and rhythm.* Berlin: Walter de Gruyter.

Gobl, C.
1988 "Voice source dynamics in connected speech", *Speech Transmission Laboratory —Quarterly Progress and Status Report* 1: 123–159.

Goldman-Eisler, F.
1972 "Pauses, clauses, sentences", *Language and Speech* 15: 114–121.

Golstein Brouwers, W. G. van
1989 "How to select the model order for Robust ARMA analysis of speech", *Proceedings of the Speech Research Group of the PTT Research Neher Laboratories* 4: 3–10.

Golstein Brouwers, W. G. van—J. M. de Veth—L. Boves
1988 "Robust ARMA analysis for estimation of vocal tract parameters", in: W. A. Ainsworth—J. N. Holmes (eds.), Book 1: 305–312.

Golub, G. H.—C. F. van Loan
1983 *Matrix computations.* Oxford: North Oxford Academic.

Gopal, H. S.—A. K. Syrdal
1988 "Effects of speaking rate on temporal and spectral characteristics of American English vowels", *Research Laboratory of Electronics MIT Speech Communications Group Working Papers* 6: 162–180.

Gunter, B.
1988 *Poor reception: Misunderstanding and forgetting broadcast news*. Hillsdale, N.J.: Lawrence Erlbaum.

Gussenhoven, C.
1984 *On the grammar and semantics of sentence accents*. Dordrecht: Foris.
1988 Review of Baart (1987), *Linguistics* 26: 882–886.

Haggard, G.
1986 "Finding minimal perfect hash functions", *ACM SIGCSE Bulletin* (Special issue 17th SIGCSE technical symposium.) 18: 191–193.

Hart J. 't —A. Cohen
1973 "Intonation by rule: A perceptual quest", *Journal of Phonetics* 1: 309–327.

Hart, J. 't—R. Collier
1975 "Integrating different levels of intonation analysis", *Journal of Phonetics* 3: 235–255.

Hart, J. 't—R. Collier—A. Cohen
1990 *A perceptual study in intonation: An experimental-phonetic approach to speech melody*. Cambridge: Cambridge University Press.

Hauwermeiren, P. van
1975 *Het leesbaarheidsonderzoek* [The readability research]. Groningen: Tjeenk Willink.

Have, M. ten—J. den Ouden
1985 "A new CMOS formant speech synthesizer for high quality speech", in *The official proceedings of Speech Tech '85, New York, 22–24 April 1985*. New York: Media Dimensions, 253–256.

Heemskerk, J. S. M.
1989 "Morphological parsing and lexical morphology", in: H. Bennis—A. van Kemenade (eds.), 61–70.

Hemert, J. P. van
1985 "Automatic diphone preparation", *IPO Annual Progress Report* 20: 23–32.

Hendriks, J. P. M.—L. Boves
1988 "Definition of relations in an acoustic phonetic database", in: *Proceedings ICASSP '88*, New York, 643–646.

Hendriks, J. P. M.—L. Boves—A. H. A. Swagten—M. Lagendijk—H. van der Griendt

1990 SPEX-news. Speech Processing Expertise Centre, Leidschendam.

Hendriks, J. P. M.—C. G. J. Houben

1988 "Structure of and retrieval from an acoustic phonetic database", in: W. A. Ainsworth—J. N. Holmes (eds.), Book 6: 1139–46.

Hermes, D. J.

1988 "Measurements of pitch by subharmonic summation", *Journal of the Acoustical Society of America* 83: 257–264.

Hermes, D. J.—J. C. van Gestel

1991 The frequency scale of speech intonation, *Journal of the Acoustical Society of America* 90: 97–102.

Hermes, D. J.—J. 't Hart

1987 "Visual feedback of intonation for the deaf by means of automatically stylized contours", *Research News – International Journal of Rehabilitation Research* 10: 457–458.

Hertz S. R.

1982 "From text to speech with SRS", *Journal of the Acoustical Society of America* 72: 1155–1170.

1990 "A modular approach to multi-dialect and multi-language speech synthesis using the Delta system", in: G. Bailly—Chr. Benoit (eds.), 225–228

Hertz, S. R.—J. Kadin—K. Karplus

1985 "The Delta rule development system for speech synthesis from text", *Proceedings of the IEEE* 73: 1589–1601.

Heuven, V. J. van—A. Hoos

1991 "Hiatus deletion, phonological rule or phonetic coarticulation?" in: A. van Kemenade—F. Drijkoningen (eds.), 61–70.

Hirschberg, J.

1990 "Accent and discourse context: Assigning pitch accent in synthetic speech", in *Proceedings of the seventh national conference*, Boston: American Association for Artificial Intelligence, 952–957.

Holmes, J. N.

1988 *Speech synthesis and recognition*. Berkshire: van Nostrand Reinold.

Holtse, P.—A. Olsen
1985 SPL: A speech synthesis programming language. *Annual Report Institute of Phonetics University of Copenhagen* 19: 1–42.

Horowitz, E.—S. Sahni
1976 *Fundamentals of data structures*. Maryland: Computer Science Press.

Horst, P. J. van der
1990 "Leestekenwijzer" [Punctuation guide], 's-Gravenhage: SDU.

Hulst, H. van der—N. Smith (eds.)
1982 *The structure of phonological representations*. Vols. 1–2. Dordrecht: Foris.

Hunnicutt, S.
1985 "Intelligibility versus redundancy — conditions of dependency", *Language and Speech* 28: 45–56.

Jongenburger, W.
1991 "Sandhi processes". *SPIN/ASSP Report* 35. Utrecht: Foundation for Speech Technology.

Jongenburger, W.—V. J. van Heuven
1991 "The distribution of (word initial) glottal stop in Dutch", in: A. van Kemenade—F. Drijkoningen (eds.), 101–110.

Kager, R.—H. Quené
1987 "Deriving prosodic sentence structure without exhaustive syntactic analysis", in: Laver, J.—M. A. Jack (eds.), Vol. 1: 243–246.

Kager, R.
1989 *Stress and destressing in English and Dutch*. Dordrecht: Foris.

Kager, R.—E. Visch
1988 "Metrical constituency and rhythmic adjustment", *Phonology* 5: 21—71.

Keijsper, C. E.
1989 "Over het automatisch zetten van zinsaccenten" [On the automatic placement of sentence accents], *Forum der Letteren* 30: 255–266.

Kemenade, A. van—F. Drijkoningen (eds.)
1991 *Linguistics in the Netherlands 1991*. Dordrecht: Foris.

Kerkhoff, J.—H. Loman—L. Boves
1986 "FONPARS2: A compiler for the implementation of phonetic rules", *AFN-proceedings* 10: 75–80.

Kerkhoff, J.—J. Wester—L. Boves
1984 "A compiler for implementing the linguistic phase of a text-to-speech conversion system", in: H. Bennis—W. U. S. van Lessen Kloecke, 111–119.

Kintsch, W.—T. A. van Dijk
1978 "Toward a model of text comprehension and production", *Psychological Review* 85: 363–394.

Klatt, D. H.
1975 "Vowel lengthening is syntactically determined in a connected discourse", *Journal of Phonetics* 3: 129–140.
1976 "Linguistic uses of segmental duration in English: Acoustic and perceptual evidence", *Journal of the Acoustical Society of America* 59: 1208–1221.
1980 "Software for a cascade/parallel formant synthesizer", *Journal of the Acoustical Society of America*, 67: 971–995.

Klatt, D. H.—L. C. Klatt
1990 "Analysis, synthesis and perception of voice quality variations among female and male speakers", *Journal of the Acoustical Society of America* 87: 820–857.

Knuth, D.
1973 "Sorting and searching". Chapter 3 of *The art of computer programming*. Reading, Mass.: Addison-Wesley.

Koopmans-van Beinum, F. J.
1980 Vowel contrast reduction: An acoustic and perceptual study of Dutch vowels in various speech conditions. [Unpublished Ph.D. dissertation, University of Amsterdam.]
1992 "The role of focus words in natural and synthetic continuous speech: Acoustic aspects", *Speech Communication* 11: 439–452.

Koskenniemi, K.
1983 Two-level morphology: A general computational model for word-form recognition and production. [Unpublished MS., Department of General Linguistics, Helsinki.]

Krech, E. A.
1968 *Sprechwissenschaftlich-phonetisch Untersuchungen zum Gebrauch des Glottisschlageinsatzes in der allgemeinen deutschen Hochlautung*. Basel: Karger.

Krull, D.
1989 "Second formant locus patterns and consonant-vowel coarticulation in spontaneous speech", *Phonetic Experimental Research Institute of Linguistics University of Stockholm (PERILUS)* 10: 87–108.

Kruyt, J. G.
1985 Accents from speakers to listeners: An experimental study of the production and perception of accent patterns in Dutch. [Unpublished Ph.D. dissertation, Leiden University.]

Kuehn, D. P.—K. L. Moll
1976 "A cineradiographic study of VC and CV articulatory velocities", *Journal of Phonetics* 4: 303–320.

Kulas, W.—H. W. Rühl
1985 "Syntex – Unrestricted conversion of text to speech for German", in: R. De Mori—C. Y. Suen (eds.), 517–535.

Lacoume, J. L.—A. Chehikian—N. Martin—J. Malbos (eds.)
1988 *Signal Processing*. Vol. 4, *Theories and applications*. Amsterdam: Elsevier.

Ladd, R.
1980 *The structure of intonational meaning: Evidence from English*. Bloomington: Indiana University Press.
1987 "A model of intonational phonology for use in speech synthesis by rule", in: J. Laver—M. A. Jack (eds.), Vol. 1: 21–24.

Lammens, J. M. G.
1987 "A lexicon-based grapheme-to-phoneme conversion system", in: J. Laver—M. A. Jack (eds.), Vol. 1: 281–284.
1989 "From text to speech via the lexicon", *SPIN/ASSP Report* 7. Utrecht: Foundation for Speech Technology.

Langeweg, S.
1988 The stress system of Dutch. [Unpublished Ph.D. dissertation, Leiden University.]

Laver, J.—M. A. Jack (eds.)
Proceedings of the European Conference on Speech Technology. Vols. 1–2. Edinburgh: CEP Consultants.

Laver, J.—J. McAllister—M. McAllister—M. Jack

1988 "A prolog-based text-to-phoneme conversion system for British English", in: *Proceedings of the second symposium on Advanced Man-Machine Interface Through Spoken Language*. Hawaii 12: 1–11.

Laver, J.—M. McAllister—J. McAllister

1989 "Pre-processing of anomalous text-strings in an automatic text-to-speech system", in: S. Ramsaran (eds.).

Lee, C. H.

1988 "On robust linear prediction of speech", *IEEE Transactions on Acoustics, Speech and Signal Processing* 36: 642–650.

Leeuwen, H. C. van

1988 GRAFON (versie 17.8), [GRAFON (version 17.8), IPO Manual nr. 89, Eindhoven: Institute for Perception Research.]

1989a TooLip: A development tool for linguistic rules. [Unpublished Ph.D. dissertation, Eindhoven University of Technology.]

1989b "A development tool for linguistic rules", *Computer, Speech and Language* 3: 83–104.

Lehiste, I.

1970 *Suprasegmentals*. Cambridge, Mass.: MIT Press.

Levelt, W. J. M.—G. B. Flores d'Arcais (eds.)

1978 *Studies in the perception of language*. Chichester: John Wiley.

Liang, F. M.

1983 Word hy-phen-a-tion by computer. [Unpublished Ph.D. dissertation, Stanford University.]

Liberman, M.

1978 The intonational system of English. [Distributed by Indiana University Linguistics Club, Bloomington.]

Liberman, M.—A. Prince

1977 "On stress and linguistic rhythm", *Linguistic Inquiry* 8: 249–336.

Lieberman, Ph.

1963 "Some effects of semantic and grammatical context on the production and perception of speech", *Language and Speech* 6: 172–187.

Lindblom, B. E. F.
1963 "Spectrographic study of vowel reduction", *Journal of the Acoustical Society of America* 35: 1773–1781.
1983 "Economy of speech gestures", in: P. F. MacNeilage (ed.), 217–246.
1989 "Phonetic invariance and the adaptive nature of speech", in: B. A. G. Elsendoorn and H. Bouma (eds.), 139–173.

Lindblom, B. E. F.—B. Lyberg—K. Holmgren
1981 Durational patterns of Swedish phonology: Do they reflect short-term motor processes? [Distributed by the Indiana University Linguistics Club, Bloomington.]

Lindblom, B.—S. J. Moon
1988 "Formant undershoot in clear and citation-form speech", *Phonetic Experimental Research Institute of Linguistics University of Stockholm (PERILUS)* 8: 21–33.

Lindert, E. te—C. J. Doedens—H. van Leeuwen
1989 "Spraakmaker-1", *SPIN/ASSP Report* 11. Utrecht: Foundation for Speech Technology.

Lisker, L.
1987 "On reconciling monophthongal vowel percepts and continuously varying F patterns", *Haskins Laboratories: Status Report on Speech Research* SR–79/80: 167–174.

Loman, H.—R. van Bezooijen
1988 "Evaluation of Dutch rule synthesis consonants by means of a fast diagnostic test". *AFN-proceedings* 12: 57–72.

Loman, H.—R. van Bezooijen—J. Kerkhoff—L. Boves
1989 "A working environment and procedure for the development of speech synthesis rules", in: J. B. Tubach—J. J. Mariani (eds.), Vol. 1: 132–135.

Loman, H.—J. Kerkhoff—L. Boves
1989 "A working environment for speech synthesis by rule" *AFN-proceedings* 13: 51–63.

MacNeilage, P. F. (ed.)
1983 *The production of speech*. New York: Springer.

Makhoul, J.
1975 "Linear prediction: A tutorial review", *Proceedings of the IEEE* 63: 561–580.

Malécot, A.
1975 "The glottal stop in French", *Phonetica* 31: 51—63.

Mallant, M. E.

1992 "Een bolhoed of een platte hoed?" [A bowler hat or a flat hat, Internal Report no. 854, Eindhoven: Institute for Perception Research].

Martin, J. G.

1970 "On judging pauses in spontaneous speech", *Journal of Verbal Learning and Verbal Behavior* 9: 75–78.

McAllister, M.

1987 "The structural design of the CSTR text-to-speech system", in: *Proceedings of the European Conference on Speech Technology '87*, 59–62.

Mehler, J. —E. C. T. Walker—M. Garrett (eds.)

Perspectives on mental representation: Experimental and theoretical studies of cognitive processes and capacities. Hillsdale, N.J.: Lawrence Erlbaum.

Michon, J. A.—J. L. Jackson (eds.)

Time, mind, and behavior. Berlin: Springer.

Monaghan, A. I. C.

1989 "Using anomalies for intonation: Some proposals", *Work in Progress* 22. Department of Linguistics, University of Edinburgh.

1990a "Rhythm and stress-shift in speech synthesis", *Computer Speech and Language* 4: 71–78.

1990b "A multi-phase parsing strategy for unrestricted text", in: G. Bailly—Chr. Benoit (eds.), 109–112.

1990c "Treating anaphora in the CSTR text-to-speech system", in: G. Bailly—Chr. Benoit (eds.), 113–116.

Moortgat, M.

1987 "Generalized Categorial Grammar", in: F. G. Droste (ed.).

Nakatani, L. H.—K. D. Dukes

1973 "A sensitive test of speech communication quality", *Journal of the Acoustical Society of America* 53: 1083–1092.

Neijt, A. H.—V. J. van Heuven

1992 "Rules and exceptions in Dutch stress", in: R. Bok-Bennema—R. van Hout (eds.), 185–196.

Nespor, M.—I. Vogel

1982 "Prosodic domains of external sandhi rules", in: H. van der Hulst—N. Smith (eds.), Vol. 1: 225–255. Dordrecht: Foris.

1986 *Prosodic phonology.* Dordrecht: Foris.

Ney H.
1983 "Dynamic programming algorithm for optimal estimation of speech parameter contours", *IEEE Transactions on Systems, Man and Cybernetics* 13: 208–214.

Nooteboom, S. G.
1972 Production and perception of vowel duration. [Unpublished Ph.D. dissertation, Utrecht University.]
1985 "A functional view of prosodic timing in speech", in: J. A. Michon—J. L. Jackson (eds.), 242-252.

Nooteboom, S. G.—J. P. L. Brokx—J. J. Rooij
1978 "Contributions of prosody to speech perception", in: W. J. M. Levelt—G. B. Flores d'Arcais (eds.), 75–107.

Nooteboom, S. G—J. G. Kruyt
1987 "Accents, focus distribution, and the perceived distribution of given and new information: An experiment", *Journal of the Acoustical Society of America* 82: 1512–1524.

Nord, L.
1987 "Vowel reduction in Swedish", in: O. Engstrand (ed.), 16–21.

Nunn, A. M.
1991 "MORFON: Integration of morphological decomposition and letter-to-sound conversion". *SPIN/ASSP Report* 36. Utrecht: Foundation for Speech Technology.

Os, E. A. den
1988 Rhythm and tempo of Dutch and Italian; a contrastive study. [Unpublished Ph.D. dissertation, Utrecht University.]

O'Shaughnessy, D. D.
1987 *Speech communication.* Reading, Mass.: Addison-Wesley.
1989 "Parsing with a small dictionary for applications such as text to speech", *Computational Linguistics* 15: 97–106.
1990 "Relationships between syntax and prosody for speech synthesis", in: G. Bailly—Chr. Benoit (eds.), 109–112.

Olaszy, G.—G. Gordos—G. Nemeth
1990 "Phonetic aspects of the Multivox text-to-speech system", in: G. Bailly—Chr. Benoit (eds.), 277–280.

Olive, J.
1990 "A new algorithm for a concatenative speech synthesis system using an augmented acoustic inventory of speech sounds", in: G. Bailly—Chr. Benoit (eds.), 25–29.

Papoulis, A.
1962 *The Fourier integral and its applications*. New York: McGraw-Hill.

Petrič, I.
1991 Text features affecting listening performance in one way speech communication. [Unpublished MS., Utrecht University.]
1992 Here is the news: Predicting listening performance for news texts. [Unpublished Ph.D. dissertation, Utrecht University.]

Pierrehumbert, J.—J. Hirschberg
1990 "The meaning of intonational contours in the interpretation of discourse", in: P. Cohen—J. Morgan—M. Pollock (eds.), 271–312.

Plomp, R.—A. M. Mimpen
1979 "Improving the reliability of testing the speech reception threshold for sentences", *Audiology* 18: 43–52.

Pols, L. C. W.
1977 Spectral analysis and identification of Dutch vowels in monosyllabic words. [Unpublished Ph.D. dissertation, Free University, Amsterdam.]

Pols, L. C. W.—R. van Bezooijen
1991 "Gaining phonetic knowledge whilst improving synthetic speech quality?" *Journal of Phonetics* 19: 139–146.

Pols, L. C. W.—L. J. P. van Heugten—F. J. Koopmans-van Beinum—R. van Bezooijen—H. J. M. Steeneken (eds.)
1989 *Proceedings Workshop Speech Input/Output Assessment and Speech Databases*. Noordwijkerhout.

Quazza, S.—G. Varese—E. Vivalda
1989 "Syntactic pre-processing for high quality text-to-speech", in: J. P. Tubach—J. J. Mariani (eds.). Vol. 1: 506–509.

Quené, H.—A. Dirksen
1990 "A comparison of natural, theoretical and automatically derived accentuations of Dutch texts", in: G. Bailly—Chr. Benoit (eds.), 137–140.

Quené, H.—R. Kager
1990 "PROS — automatic prosodic sentence analysis, accentuation, and phrasing for Dutch text-to-speech conversion". *SPIN/ASSP Report* 17. Utrecht: Foundation for Speech Technology.
1992 "The derivation of prosody for text-to-speech from prosodic sentence structure", *Computer Speech and Language* 6: 77–98

Ramsaran, S.
1989 *Studies in the Pronunciation of English.*

Reizevoort, J.
1988 "Morfologische decompositie zonder lexicon" [Morphological decomposition without a lexicon], *SPIN/ASSP Report* 4. Utrecht: Foundation for Speech Technology.

Renkema, J.
1987 *Schrijfwijzer* [Writing guide]. 's-Gravenhage: SDU.

Rijnsoever, P. A.
1988a From text to speech — user manual for Diphone Speech program DS. [IPO Manual nr. 88, Eindhoven: Institute for Perception Research.]
1988b A multilingual text-to-speech system. *IPO Annual Progress Report* 23: 34–40.

Riley, M. D.
1990 "Tree-based modelling for speech synthesis", in G. Bailly—Chr. Benoit (eds.), 229–232.

Santen, J. van—J. Olive
1990 "The analysis of contextual effects on segmental duration", *Computer, Speech and Language* 4: 359–390.

Scharpff, P. J.—V. J. van Heuven
1988 "Effects of pause insertion on the intelligibility of low quality speech", in: W. A. Ainsworth—J. N. Holmes (eds.), Book 1: 261–68.

Scheffé, H.
1952 "An analysis of variance for paired comparisons", *Journal of the Statistical Society of America* 47: 381–400.

Schulman, R.
1989 "Articulatory dynamics of loud and normal speech", *Journal of the Acoustical Society of America* 85: 295–312.

Selkirk, E. O.
1984 *Phonology and syntax: The relation between sound and structure.* Cambridge, Mass.: MIT Press.
1986 "On derived domains in sentence prosody", *Phonology Yearbook* 3: 371–405.

Siegel, D. C.
1974 *Topics in English morphology*. Cambridge, Mass.: The MIT press.

Silverman, K.
1987 The structure and processing of fundamental frequency contours. [Unpublished Ph.D. dissertation, Cambridge University.]

Snader, J.C.
1987 "Look it up faster with hashing", *Byte,* January: 129–144.

Son, R. J. J. H. van—L. C. W. Pols
1989 "Comparing formant movements in fast and normal rate speech", in: J. P. Tubach—J. J. Mariani (eds.), Vol. 2: 665–668.
1990 "Formant frequencies of Dutch in a text, read at fast and normal rate", *Journal of the Acoustical Society of America* 88: 1683–1693.

Strange, W.
1989a "Evolving theories of vowel perception", *Journal of the Acoustical Society of America* 85: 2081–2087.
1989b "Dynamic specification of coarticulated vowels spoken in sentence context", *Journal of the Acoustical Society of America* 85: 2135–2153.

Terken, J. M. B. —R. Collier
1989 "Automatic synthesis of natural-sounding intonation for text-to-speech conversion in Dutch", in: J. P. Tubach—J. J. Mariani, Vol. 1: 357–359.
1991 "Syntactic influences on prosody", in: Y. Tohkura—E. Vatikiotis-Bateson—Y. Sagisaka (eds.), 427–438.

Tohkura, Y.—E. Vatikiotis-Bateson—Y. Sagisaka (eds.)
1991 *Speech perception, production and linguistic structure.* Tokyo: Ohmsha.

Traunmüller, H.
1988 "Paralinguistic variation and invariance in the characteristic frequencies of vowels", *Phonetica* 45: 1–29.

Trommelen, M.—W. Zonneveld
1979 *Inleiding in de generatieve fonologie* [Introduction to generative phonology]. Muiderberg: Coutinho.
1986 "Dutch morphology, evidence for the right-hand head rule", *Linguistic Inquiry* 17: 147–169.
1989 *Klemtoon en metrische fonologie* [Stress and metrical phonology]. Muiderberg: Coutinho.

Tubach, J. P.—J. J. Mariani (eds.)
1989 *Proceedings of EUROSPEECH '89.* Vols. 1–2. Edinburgh: CEP Consultants.

Vaissière, J.
1987 "The use of allophonic variations of /a/ in automatic continuous speech recognition in French", *Research Laboratory of Electronics MIT Speech Communications Group Working Papers* 5: 15–25.

Verhelst, W. D. E.—J. H. Eggen
1990 "On the role of amplitude and phase in the synthesis of male and female voices", *Journal of the Acoustical Society of America* 87: S109.

Verhelst, W.—P. Nilens
1986 "A modified-superposition speech synthesizer and its applications", in: *Proceedings ICASSP '86*. New York, 2007–2010.

Veth, J. de—L. Boves—W. van Golstein Brouwers
1988 "System identification of the human speech production mechanism by robust pole- zero analysis of speech", in J. L. Lacoume—A. Chehikian—N. Martin—J. Malbos (eds.), 151–154.
1989 "Robust ARMA analysis for accurate determination of system parameters of voice source and vocal tract", in: J. P. Tubach—J. J. Mariani (eds.), 43–46.

Veth, J. de—B. Cranen—H. Strik—L. Boves
1990 "Extraction of control parameters for the voice source in a text-to-speech system", in: *Proceedings ICASSP '90*. Albuquerque, 300–304.

Veth, J. de—W. van Golstein Brouwers—H. Loman—L. Boves
1990 "Robust ARMA analysis as an aid in developing parameter control rules for a pole-zero cascade speech synthesizer", in: *Proceedings ICASSP '90*. Albuquerque, 305–308.

Visch, E. A. M.
1990 *A metrical theory of rhythmic stress phenomena*. Dordrecht: Foris.

Vogten, L. L. M.
1983 Analyse, zuinige codering en resynthese van spraakgeluid. [Analysis, economical coding and resynthesis of speech, unpublished Ph.D. dissertation, Eindhoven University of Technology.]
1985 "LVS-routines available for Pascal and Fortran programs for the IPO VAX 11/780", *IPO report* 68, Eindhoven: Institute for Perception Research.

Wagenaar, W. A.—R. Schreuder—G. J. Wijlhuizen
1987 "Readability of instructional text, written for the general public", *Applied Cognitive Psychology* 1: 155–167.

Wester, J.
1985 "Language technology as linguistics: A phonological case study of Dutch spelling", in: H. Bennis—F. Beukema (eds.), 205–212.

Wijk, C. van—T. J. M. Sanders
1987 "Linguïstische criteria voor tekstkwaliteit" [Linguistic criteria for text quality], *Toegepaste Taalwetenschap* 426: 691–697.

Willems, L. F.
1986 "Robust formant analysis", *IPO Annual Progress Report* 21: 34–40.
1987 "Robust formant analysis for speech synthesis applications", in: J. Laver—M. A. Jack (eds.), Vol. 2: 250–253.

Wingfield, A.
1975 "The intonation-syntax interaction: Prosodic features in perceptual processing of sentences", in: A. Cohen—S. G. Nooteboom (eds.), 146–56.

Witten, I. H.
1982 *Principles of computer speech.* New York: McGraw-Hill.

Wong, D. Y.—J. D. Markel—A. H. Gray
1979 "Least squares glottal inverse filtering from the acoustic speech waveform", *IEEE Transactions on Acoustics, Speech, and Signal Processing* 27: 350–355.

Wouden, T. van der
1988 "CELEX: Building a multifunctional polytheoretical lexical database", in: *Proceedings Budalex.*

Name Index

Abramowitz, M. 182,183,*383*
Aerts, A. 51,107,111,*380,383,387*
Ainsworth, W. A. 370,372,373,376,*383, 384,392,394,403*
Allain, P. 362,378
Allen, J. 27,48,49,64,76,88,117,194,317, 318,365,*383*
Atal, B. S. 283,*383*
Baart, J. L. G. 83,84,116,122,133,135, 136,138,143,144,365,370,*383,393*
Bachenko, J. 117,141,*383*
Bailly, G. 117,366,*383,386,394,400–402*
Benguerel, A.-P. 182,*384*
Bennis, H. 366–368,*384,385,393,396,406*
Benoit, Chr. 366,*383,386,394,400–402*
Berendsen, E. 46–50,62–64,88,93,97,103, 262,329,365,*384*
Bergem, D. R. van 191
Bergh, H. van den v,ix,xiii,5,13,36
Beukema, F. *384,406*
Beurden, L. 49,75,93,109,110,*384*
Bezooijen, R. van vii,xi,8,127,148,156, 158,165,168,195,198,268,339,342–345,347–351,353,354,356,358,362, 366,369,370,371,374,375,377,378, *380,381,384,385,399,402*
Bloemendal, Ph. 377,*386*
Boef, H. J. 31,*385*
Bok-Bennema, R. *385,400*
Bolinger, D. L. 135,*385*
Booij, G. E. 150,*386*
Bosch, L. F. M. ten vi,x,xiv,3,84,193,197, 199–201,203,204,302,344,362,366, 371,378,*380,386*
Bouma, H. 361, 368, *386, 389, 390, 399*
Bouwhuis, D. G. *386,389*
Boves, L. vi,xi,xiii,xv,3,97,147,157,158, 160,161,165,166,194,207,208,287, 289–291,293,309,318,333,339,340, 343,358,362,363,366,370–374,376–381,*386,392–394,396,399,405*
Boxelaar, G. W. 342,*386*
Bringmann, E. 83,143,209,210,219,377, *386*
Broad, D. J. 172,181,182,211,216,329, *387*
Broecke, M. P. R. van den 51,221,362,363, 368,*380,387*
Broeder, D. G. 212,222,362,377,378,*387*
Brokx, J. P. L. 115,*401*
Carasso, M. G. 361
Carlson, R. 46,48,64,117,318,*387*
Charpentier, F. 237,*387*
Chehikian, A. *397,405*
Chomsky, N. 93,94,108,131,135,166,195, *387*
Clark, J. 172,*388*
Clermont, F. 172,181,182,*387*
Clifton, C. 115,*389*
Cohen, A. v,xvii,1,243,245,248,259,309, 326,362,*388,393,406*
Cohen, P. *388,402*
Coile, B. M. J. van 152,334,*388*
Collier, R. vi,x,xiii,3,115–117,147,150, 152,155,242,243,245,248,259,309, 318,326,333,339,362,363,366,369, 371,372,376,*388,389,393,404*

Cooper, W. E. 116,172,*388,389,392*
Coopmans, P. 380,*384*
Cranen, L. I. J. 293,304,377,*389,405*
Cutler, A. 115,238,*389*
Daelemans, W. 48,49,64,76,*389*
Damen, L. vi,x,xiv,207,265,362,379
David, N. 283,*383*
Davis, C. 84
De Mori, R. *389,397*
Delattre, P. 175,*389*
Deliège, R. J. H. vii,xi,6,9,309,362,365, 366,372,378,*380*
Di Benedetto, M. G. 181,*389*
Dijk, T. A. van 17,26,*389,396*
Dirksen, A. v,ix,69,88,97,127,131,132, 143,243,318,331,360,362,376,378, *402*
Doedens, C. J. 117,338,378,*399*
Doetjes, J. 84
Don, J. 48,49,97,103,*384*
Drijkoningen, F. 367,*394,395*
Droste, F. G. *389,400*
Drullman, R. vi,x,xiii,3,147,150,155,318, 333,339,362,366,378,380,*389*
Duez, D. 181,*390*
Dukes, K. D. 280,*400*
Eefting, W. vi,x,xiv,10,191,209,225,359, 362,365,367,368,372,378–382
Eggen, J. H. vi,xi,279,280,283,285,287, 362,365,367,372,373,378,379,*381, 390,405*
Elsendoorn, B. A. G. 148,193,195,309, 314,368,*390,399*
Elstrodt, M. 51,*380,387*
Engstrand, O. 172,175,*390,401*
Erp, A. J. M. van 211,212,*390*
Fant, G. 150,160,286,293,296,304,*391*
Feng, G. 304,305,*391*
Ferguson, G. A. *391*
Fertig, R. H. 172,181,182,*387*
Fitzpatrick, E. 117,141,*383*
Flanagan, J. L. 293,*391*
Flores d'Arcais, G. B. *398,401*
Foss, D. L. 238, *391*
Fowler, C. A. 229,*391*
Fuchs, A. 122,*391*
Garrett, M. *388,389,400*
Gay, T. 172,173,175,*392*
Gazdar, G. 142,*392*
Gee, J. P. 116,121,141,258,*392*
Gernsbacher, M. 238,*391*
Gestel, C. J. van 247,*394*
Gibbon, D. *391 392*
Gobl, C. 296,*392*
Goldman-Eisler, F. 116,*392*
Golstein Brouwers, W. G. van vi,xv,161, 289,290,295,370,372,373,377,378, *386,392,405*
Golub, G. H. 2[illegible]2,*392*
Gopal, H. S. 172,175,*392*
Gordos, G. 194,*401*
Granström, B. 46,48,64,117,318,*387*
Gray, A. H. 16[illegible],286,*406*
Griendt, H. van der 208,*394*
Grootveld, M. 84
Grosjean, F. 116,121,141,258,*392*
Gunter, B. 15,17,23,*393*
Gussenhoven, C. 116,122,135,138,144, 369,*393*
Haggard, G. 57,*393*
Halle, M. 93,94,108,131,135,166,195,*387*
Hart, J. 't 115,116,148,152,194,195,243, 245,248,259,309,314,326,338,*388, 390,393,394*
Hauwermeiren, P. van 17,*393*
Have, M. ten 314,*393*
Heemskerk, J. S. M. v,ix,6,45,49,50,53, 67,75,83,89,90,94,99,101,104,108, 110,123,144,210,222,318,328,329, 362,367,370,378,*383,393*
Hemert, J. P. van 148,*393*
Hendriks, J. P. M. 207–210,291,372,*386, 393,394*
Hermes, D. J. 152,247,*394*
Hertz, S. R. 131,317,319,320,334,*394*
Heugten, L. J. P. van 290,375,378,379,*402*
Heuven, V. J. van v,vi,ix,x,xiii,xv,xxii,6, 45,49,50,53,61,67,69,71,80,84,87, 89,90,92,94,95,99,101,104,108– 110,115,123,144,210,211,215–218, 220–222,261,266,267,318,328,329, 331,345,360,362,363,365,367,373, *387,394,395,400,403*
Hijzelendoorn, M. 84,222
Hirose, H. 172,*392*
Hirschberg, J. 117,129,141,242,*394,402*

Holmes, J. N. 147,339,370,372,373,376, *383,384,392,394,403*
Holmgren, K. 229,*399*
Holsteijn, Y. van v,xiii,27,79,97,318,326, 327,363,379
Holtse, P. 334,*395*
Horowitz, E. 56,*395*
Horst, P. J. van der 35,*395*
Houben, C. G. J. 208–210,*394*
Housum, J. 229,*391*
Hout, R. van *385,400*
Houten, E. van vi,x,xiv,207,265,362,379
Hoven, P. van den 25
Hulst, H. van der *395,400*
Hunnicutt, S. 27,48,76,88,117,194,229, 317,365,*383,387,395*
Jack, M. A. 27,369,*384,385,388,395,397, 398,406*
Jackson, J. L. *400,401*
Jongenburger, W. vi,x,xv,92,95,215–218, 220,221,261,266,269,363,367,379, *395*
Kadin, J. 131,319,*394*
Kager, R. v,ix,47,48,89,94,97,109,115, 121,123,128,132,243,318,331,350, 360,363,368,369,373,376,379,*395, 402*
Karplus, K. 131,319,*394*
Keijsper, C. E. 258,*395*
Kemenade, A. van 366–368,*384,385,393–395*
Kerkhoff, J. 97,158,160,165,166,194,302, 309,313,318,334,339,343,358,372, 374,*380,381,396,399*
Kintsch, W. 26,*396*
Klatt, D. H. 27,48,76,88,116,117,160,193, 194,286,301,317,340,365,368,*383, 396*
Klatt, L. 160,286,301,*396*
Knuth, D. 56,*396*
Koopmans-van Beinum, F. J. 116,149,150, 155,175,375,*396,402*
Koskenniemi, K. 72,*396*
Krech, E. A. 266,*396*
Krull, D. 181,*397*
Kruyt, J. G. 115,242,252,253,*397,401*
Kuehn, D. P. 172,*397*
Kulas, W. 117,317,318,*397*
Lacoume, J. L. *397,405*
Ladd, R. 116,117,135,*397*
Lagendijk, M. 208,*394*
Lammens, J. M. G. v,ix,xiii,45,46,49,58, 62,98,101,329,363,365,368,373, 379–381,*384,397*
Langeweg, S. 50,88,89,93,95–97,110, 262,329,*384,397*
Laver, J. 27,29,369,*384,385,388,395,397, 398,406*
Lee, C. H. 292,293,*398*
Leeuwen, H. C. van vii,xi,8,28,40,46,50, 51,80,88,90,93,94,97,117,131,262, 317,329,334,365,374,*381,384,398, 399*
Lehiste, I. 116,*398*
Lessen Kloecke, W. U. S. van *384,396*
Levelt, W. J. M. *398,401*
Liang, F. M. 104,105,107,108,*398*
Liberman, M. 135,*398*
Lieberman, Ph. 229,*398*
Liljencrants, J. 160,286,*391*
Lin, Q. 89,160,286,296,*391*
Lindblom, B. E. F. 155,171,172,175,181, 229,240,*399*
Lindert, E. te vii,xi,8,28,51,80,90,94,117, 131,317,363,374,378,379,*381,399*
Lisker, L. 175,*399*
Loan, C. F. 202,*392*
Loman, H. vi,xiii,3,147,157,158,160,165, 166,194,302,333,339,340,343,358, 363,369,371,372,374,377,*380,381, 396,399,405*
Lyberg, B. 229,*399*
MacNeilage, P. F. *399*
Makhoul, J. 297,*399*
Malbos, J. *397,405*
Malécot, A. 266,*399*
Mallant, M. E. 254,*400*
Mariani, J. J. 371,372,374,376,377,*385, 387,388,399,402,404,405*
Markel, J. D. 161,286,*406*
Martin, J. G. 219,*397,400,405*
McAllister, J. 27,*398*
McAllister, M. 27,317,*398,400*
Mehler, J. *389,400*
Mellish, C. 142,*392*
Michon, J. A. *400,401*

Mimpen, A. M. 152,*402*
Moll, K. L. 172,*397*
Monaghan, A. I. C. 40,41,117,129,*400*
Moon, S. J. 172,*399*
Moortgat, M. 74,*400*
Morgan, J. *388,402*
Moulines, E. 237,*387*
Nakatani, L. H. 280,281,*400*
Neijt, A. H. 109,*400*
Nemeth, G. 194,*401*
Nespor, M. 116,118,125,129,140,141,*400*
Ney, H. 301,*401*
Nilens, P. 300,301,*405*
Nooteboom, S. G. v,vi,x,xi,xiv,xvii,1,25, 115,150,209,225,228,242,279,359, 362,363,368,370,372,374,*388,401, 406*
Nord, L. 172,*401*
Norris, D. 238,*389*
Nunn, A. M. v,ix,xiii,69,71,80,84,87,88, 211,267,318,328,329,331,360,363, 378,379,*401*
O'Shaughnessy, D. D. 40,117,121,172, *401*
Olaszy, G. 194,*401*
Olive, J. 194,201,*401,403*
Olsen, A. 334,*395*
Ooijen, B. A. van 84
Os, E. A. den 172,175,*401*
Ouden, J. den 314,*393*
Paccia-Cooper, J. 116,*388*
Pacilly, J. 84,222
Papoulis, A. *402*
Petrič, I. v,ix,xiii,5,13,26,36,363,365, 374,*381,402*
Pierrehumbert, J. 242,*402*
Plomp, R. 152,*402*
Pollock, M. *388,402*
Pols, L. C. W. vi,vii,x,xi,xiii,xxii,8,127, 155,156,158,165,168,171,176,180, 183,195,198,208,209,268,339,342, 347,350,362,363,366,368–371,374–376,*381,382,385,402,404*
Portheine, L. H. 361
Prince, A. 135, *398*
Quazza, S. 117,*402*
Quené, H. v,ix,47,48,69,88,97,115,121, 127,128,131,132,243,318,331,350, 360,362,363,368,369,373,376,379, *395,402*
Ramsaran, S. *398,403*
Renkema, J. 35,*403*
Reizevoort, J. v,6,45,49,50,61,101,363, 379,*380,403*
Richter, H. *391,392*
Rietveld, A. C. M. 191
Rijnsoever, P. A. van 244,310,317,318, 339,*403*
Riley, M. D. 30
Rooij, J. J. de 115,*401*
Rühl, H. W. 117,317,318,*397*
Sagisaka, Y. 31,368,370,*404*
Sahni, S. 56,*395*
Sanders, T. J. M. 26,*406*
Santen, J. van 201,*403*
Scharpff, P. J. 115,*403*
Scheffé, H. 151,*403*
Schouten, M. E. H. 143,362,*380*
Schreuder, R. 17,*405*
Schulman, R. 181,*403*
Selkirk, E. O. 116,118,140,*403*
Sessink, B. W. L. M. 361
Siegel, D. C. 49,109,*403*
Silverman, K. 129,*403*
Smith, N. *395,400*
Snader, J. C. 56,*404*
Son, R. J. J. H. van vi,x,xiii,93,155,171, 176,183,208,209,363,369,376,378–382,*404*
Sorensen, J. M. 116,*388*
Speth-Lemmens, I. M. A. F. 6,366,380,*389*
Stam, M. 191
Steeneken, H. J. M. 375,*402*
Stegun, I. A. 182,183,*383*
Strange, W. 181,*404*
Strik, H. 377,*405*
Struch, P. 10
Suen, C. Y. *389,397*
Swagten, A. H. A. *394*
Syrdal, A. K. 172,175,*392*
Terken, J. M. B. vi,xiv,117,152,191,208, 209,241,242,318,333,359,363,369, 370,372,376,379,*388,404*
Tohkura, Y. 358,370,*404*
Toussaint, P. 84
Traunmüller, H. 181, *404*

Trommelen, M. 85,93,95,103,261,*404*
Tubach, J. P. 371,372,374,376,377,*385*, *387*, *388*, *399*, *402*, *404*, *405*
Ushijima, T. 172,*392*
Vaissière, J. 175,*404*
Varese, G. 117,*402*
Vasbinder, J.-W. 10
Vatikiotis-Bateson, E. 368,370,*404*
Verhelst, W. D. E. 283,288,300,301,*405*
Veth, J. de vi,xi,xv,161,287,289,290,293, 295,298,302,363,370,372–374,376–380,*386*, *392*, *405*
Vieregge, W. H. 361,371
Visch, E. A. M. 96,123,*395*, *405*
Vivalda, E. 117,*402*
Vogel, I. 116,118,125,129,140,141,*400*
Vogten, L. L. M. 149,152,174,280,285, 300,301,*390*, *405*
Wagenaar, W. A. 17,*405*
Walker, E. C. T. 73,*388*, *389*, *400*
Waterham, R. P. 6,366,380,*389*
Weenink, D. J. M. *386*
Wester, J. 88,97,309,318,*396*, *406*
Wijk, C. van 26,*406*
Wijlhuizen, G. J. 17,*405*
Willems, L. F. 153,174,*406*
Wingfield, A. 115,*406*
Witten, I. H. 148,*406*
Wong, D. Y. 286,*406*
Wouden, T. van der 79,*406*
Yallop, C. 172,*388*
Zanten, E. A. van vi,x,xiv,207,265,362, 379
Zitter, A. L. J. de 242,254,372,*388*
Zonneveld, W. 85,93,95,103,261,*380*, *404*

Subject Index

accent 141
  rule 137
accented
  diphones 159
  syllables 159
accentuation 116,122,128
  of units 230
adaptation principle 226
affixation (in Dutch) 110
  adjective derivations 110
  noun derivations 110
  Romance derivations 110
  verb derivations 110
affix(es)
  native vs. non-native 102
aid for the speech impaired 310
Algemeen Beschaafd Nederlands (ABN) 159
allophone
  rule development 301
  rule set 195
  synthesis 194,300
  voiced consonants 301
all-pole analysis technique 290
ambiguity 67
analysis-resynthesis 299
applications of text-to-speech systems 13
  presenting information from database 13
  presenting spoken instructions 13
  presenting spoken newspapers 14
appreciation 163
architecture
  of rule-based TTS 160
  of Spraakmaker 323
argument 136
ARMA 291
  classical 291
  robust (RARMA) 291
articulation tests 280
assimilation, see Sandhi rules
ASSP-speech database
  morphological analysis 210
  paragraph boundary assignment 210
  phonemic transcription 210
  stress assignment 210
  syllabification 210
attribute 321
average chain length 57

boundary tone 254
boundary marker 254

caching 64
categorical grammar 74
  reduction laws 74
CELEX, CEntre for LEXical data 51,112
chart parsing 142
closed-glottis interval (CGI) 298
closed-phase covariance method 286
clusters (of consonants) 159
coarticulation 171,146
compositional semantics 135
comprehension of sentence 115
concatenation (of diphones) 159
complexity
  time complexity 57
    for hashed chains 58
    for morphological decomposition 58

complexity (*continued*)
for tries 58
space complexity 58
for hashed chains 58
for tries 59
comprehension 18,19,350
computer phonetic alphabet (CPA) 210
consistency
of intelligibility scores 353
intersubjective 354
intrasubjective 353
consonant clusters 159
context word (CW) 118,125
context feature 31
COST 210
CPA, computer phonetic alphabet 210

database
diphones 146
environment for speech data (DEMSI) 208
high-frequency word forms 49
newspaper text 36
normal vs. fast speech 173
short sentences 162
texts for extraction of duration rules 208
training data for morphological decomposition 112
data structure
chain 55
grid 320
stream 320
substream 322
sync mark 321
token 321
multi-level, synchronized 320
trie 56
deaccenting 133
declination 246
resets 246
decomposition and recomposition 49
default table 204
degemination 274
DEMSI, speech database environment 208
designated talker 159,173,207,231,244, 265
dictionary of Dutch function words 120
Diphone Speech (DS) 310
diphone 159
accented 159
concatenation 159
set 194
stylization 198
synthesis 193
unaccented 159
Dirac delta pulse 291
disambiguation 30
of punctuation characters 30
distance measure 164
duration
of segments 161,235
of syllables 235
of vowels 160,176
as a function of rate 176
intrinsic 160
of words 230
appropriate 239
inappropriate 239
d-weakening 276
Dynamic Time Warping (DTW) 164

electroglottogram (EGG) 297
electronic newspaper 350
elision
of n before s 274
of n after schwa 274
of t in consonant clusters 274
of χ 274
error(s) 37
avoidable 37
unavoidable 37
evaluation 36
of accented vs. unaccented diphones 163
of allophone synthesis 340
of allophone rules 166
of diphone inventories 340
formal, of text-to-speech systems 339
diagnostic 339
diagnostic subtests 352
comparative 339
informal, of text-to-speech systems 132
of grapheme-phoneme conversion 107

evaluation (*continued*)
of lexical access 107
using hashing 61
using trie data structure 61
of morphological decomposition (MORPA) 82
of neutrone synthesis 344
of pattern-based decomposition (PADMAN) 112
of prosodic adequacy 349
assignment of pitch accents 349
of RARMA 298,301
of segmental intelligibility 341
of consonant clusters 347
diagnostic subtests 343
global intelligibility tests 353
of segmental rules 146
of speech database labelling 214
of speed of different lexical access modes 58
of sentence prosody (PROS1) 126,349
of text comprehension 350
of TextScan 36
expansion 28,34
rule-based 34
lexicon-based 34
experimental tasks
appreciation 163
comprehension 18,19,350
identification
of phonemes 343
of speakers 287
naturalness judgment, scaling 237
phoneme monitoring 238
rating (scaling) 18,20,237,343
categorical estimation (CE) 348
magnitude estimation (ME) 348
recall 18
measured in number of logical propositions 19
expression 28

features
syntactic 142
FFT spectrum 163
files
label file 212
sampled data file 209
flow signal 297
differentiated 297
fluency 159
focus
focus-accent theory 133,135
markers 135
rule 137
formant
analysis
of accented vs. unaccented diphones 163
bandwidths 161
dynamics 161,181
effect of duration 188
effects of rate 188
Legendre polynomials 182
point-to-point-analysis 183
frequencies 161
target frequencies 175
as a function of context 180
as a function of rate 178
as a function of stress 179
tracking 161
transitions, see also formant dynamics 161
frame, as used in DEMSI 210
frequency of occurrence, of morphemes 72
function word (FW) 118,125
functor 136

Gaussian White Noise (GWN) 291
GE-LPC synthesizer 283
control of voicing source 285
Generative Phonology 166
given vs. new information 122,126,128, 229
Glottal Excited, see GE-
glottal stop 12,16,17,215,266
distribution of 266
insertion rule 274
grammar
independence 57
rules 132
sophistication of 142
grapheme-to-phoneme conversion 313
rule compiler (FONPARS) 313
grid 320

GWN, see Gaussian White Noise

hash function 56,57
hiatus position 215
Hifreq, high-frequency word form lexicon 49
homorganic
  glide insertion 274
  nasal adjustment 275
hyphenation (by computer) 105
  in Dutch 107
  in English 107

i-gliding 275
inflection 71
information
  structure 229
  value 229
    given words 229
    new words 229
    old words 229
insertion
  of glottal stop 274
  of homorganic glide 274
  of schwa 274
Int domain (intonational phrase) 118,124, 140
intelligibility (see also experimental tasks) 146,165,279
  of logatoms 165
  of sentences 165
interference speech 281
intonation 241
  contour 314
  human 241
  synthetic 241
inventory (of diphones, see database) 146
inverse filtering 286
I-phrase (intonational phrase) 140
isochrony (at word level) 229

knowledge 161
  acoustic phonetic 145

LA, see lexical access
labeling 32
  by hand 159
label file 212
l-darkening 276
Legendre polynomial functions 182
lexical access 47
  modes of lexical access 49
Lexical Morphology 49,75
lexical phonology and morphology 103
lexicalized phrase 106
lexicon(s) 34,43
  application-specific 314
  exceptions 314
  lemma lexicon 52
  main lexicon 48,51,55
  morpheme lexicon 52,70
  user lexicon 47,51
  word form lexicon 52
LF model (Liljencrants-Fant) 286
liaison 140
Liljencrants-Fant model 286
limitations
  ill-posed problem 302
  ill-conditioned problem 302
Linear Predictive Coding, see LPC
linguistic modules, as used in Spraakmaker
  DURATION 332
  EXPAND 327
  INTONATION 333
  LABEL 326
  MORPHON 331
  PROS 331
    PROS1 331
    PROS2 331
  SYNTHESIS 333
  WORD 327
    ACROPHON 329
    GRAPHON 329
    HIGH_FREQ 329
    MORPA 329
    NUMPHON 329
    USER_LEX 329
listenability 15
listening performance 16
low-frequency phase-distortions 285
LPC (Linear Predictive Coding) 11,280, 293
  analysis 161
  Glottal Excited (GE-) LPC synthesizer 283
    pitch synchronous determination of parameters 286
  limitations of LPC 280

LPC (*continued*)
LPC-residue 283
amplitude information 283
phase information 283
MASIT (Monosyllabic Adaptive Speech Interference Test) 280
melodic configuration (see pitch movement)
metric labeling rule 137
metrical tree 135,140
model
Liljencrants-Fant (LF model) 286
order 293
speaker, see designated talker
target undershoot 171
Monosyllabic Adaptive Speech Interference test 280
morpheme 71
boundaries 98,104,111
lexicon 70,97
morphological classification 71
morphological decomposition 103
lexicon-based 104
pattern-based 105
implementation 111
performance 112
training lexicon 112
rule-based 103
morpho-phonological peculiarities 72
morpho-syntactic properties 71,105
morpho-syntactic well-formedness 74
multiple regression 22
naturalness 159,165,235
n-deletion, see n-elision
n-elision 101,274
newspaper text 36
orthographic island 29
orthographic form 71
orthography
correspondence with pronunciation 67
palatalization 276
parameter extraction 161
particle 125
pauses 219
planned pauses 219
silent pauses 219
Phi domain (phonological phrase) 118, 124,140
Phi-phrase, see Phi domain
phoneme monitoring 238
phonological form 71
phonological restrictions on word analysis 72
phonological rule(s) 68,98
phrase
intonational (Int domain, I-phrase) 118,124,140,248
realization of 246
phonological (Phi domain, Phi-phrase) 118,124,140
prosodic 139
structure (rules) 133,136
phrasing 116,122,128
rule 140
pitch
movement 252
peak 250
size 250
pitch-synchronous analysis 291
poles (formants) 290
pole-zero
structure 160
system 290
polysyllabic words 160
predicate 121,122,125
preprocessing module 28
primary table 55
Prolog 72
pronunciation
correspondence with orthography 67
of words 67
prosodic
phrase 139
sentence structure 116,118
transcription 127
PSOLA (Pitch Synchronous Overlay and Add) 237,238
punctuation characters 29
textual 29
metatextual 29
disambiguation of 30
RARMA (robust ARMA) 291
closed-glottis interval 297

RARMA (*continued*)
  pitch-locked 297
  post-processing 299
rating, see experimental tasks
reaction time 238
recall 18
  measured in number of logical propositions 19
reduction
  of vowels 171,275
  law (in categorical grammar) 74
redundancy
  contextual 229
  lexical 227
rule-based synthesis 194
rule(s) 34
  accent 137
  assignment 196
  condition-free 199
  context 166
  convergence of 204
  development for /l/ 166
  extraction 198,203
  file 195
  focus 137
  format 194
  grammar 132
  metric labelling 137
  numerical 196,199
  perceptual relevance of 194
  phonetic 166
  phonological 68,98,199
  phrase structure 133,136
  phrasing 140
  Righthand Head Rule (RHR) 74,102
  Sandhi, see Sandhi rules
  segmental 146
  sequence 203
  sets 203
  transformational (PROS2) 131
  update 165
rule compiler (for text-to-speech systems)
  FONPARS 313
  TooLip 262
sampled data file (SDF) 209
Sandhi rules 262
  assimilation 262,275
    of voicing (anticipatory) 101,275
    of voicing (carryover) 101,275
    d-weakening 276
    final devoicing 275
    homorganic nasal adjustment 275
    palatalization 276
  blocking of rules 263
  compulsory rule 264
  implicit Sandhi effects in diphones 267
  language specific allophonic rule 262, 276
    l-darkening 276
  morpheme modification rules 262,274
    degemination 274
    glottal stop insertion 274
    homorganic glide insertion 274
    n-elision 274
    schwa insertion 274
    t-elision in consonant clusters 274
    χ-elision 274
  vowel adjustment rules 262,275
    i-gliding 275
    reduction to schwa 275
    vowel raising 275
    vowel shortening 275
scaling, see experimental tasks
schwa
  insertion 274
  reduction to schwa 275
search operator 189
segmentation
  criteria for speech waveforms 212
  as module in TextScan 27,29
  as module in MORPA 69
semantic restrictions on word analysis 73
sentence melody (see intonation)
SESAM, waveform editor 211
SIT (Speech Interference Test) 280
SMF (Speech Maker Formalism) 333
  rules 334
sonagram display 164
source-filter separation 295
space complexity 58
    for hashed chains 58
    for tries 58
speaker characteristics 280
speaking rate 173

speaking terminal 311
spectrum 290
Speech Interference Test (SIT) 280
Speech Maker 318
  Formalism (see SMF) 333
speech
  production system 290
  synthesizer 314
  transients 193
speed
  of articulation 227
  of perceptual processing 238
spelling changes 72
SPEX, Speech Processing EXpertise Centre 208
Spraakmaker 318
  architecture 323
  stream 320
spurious poles and zeros 294
stand-alone text-to-speech 309
  software
    development 310
    implementation 310
  hardware 315
    development 310
    implementation 310
standard speaker, see designated talker
Standard Dutch, see Algemeen Beschaafd Nederlands
stream 132,320
  substream 322
  as used in Spraakmaker 325
stress 69
  assignment 99,109
  compound rule 106
  primary 160
  retraction rule 107
  secondary 160
  shift rule 106
substream 322
suprasegmentals 116
syllabification 69
syllables
  accented 159
  unaccented 159
sync mark 321
syntactic
  categories 71
  clause 124,128
  constituents 124,128
  labeling 123
  parsing 119
  structure 68,124,128,134
synthesis (of speech)
  allophone-based (see allophone synthesis) 145
  diphone-based (see diphone synthesis) 145

target undershoot model 171
t-elision, in consonant clusters 274
time complexity 58
  for hashed chains 58
  for morphological decomposition 58
  for tries 58
tempo variation 225
text analysis 29
text features determining listenability 18
  phrase length 18
  sentence complexity 18
  sentence length 18
  text complexity 18,24,25(note)
  word length 18
TextScan 28
  segmentation 27,29
  expansion 28
text-to-speech conversion (see also stand-alone TTS) 311
  lexicon-based 98,101
  rule-based 98,101
textual unit 28,32
  single 32
  compound 32
  ambiguous 33
token, as used in Speech Maker 321
TooLip, rule compiler for text-to-speech systems 262
transcription
  phonetic 68
  prosodic 127
transients 193
tune-to-text association 241

unaccented
  diphones 159
  syllables 159
unit accentuation 230

utterances 159
natural 164
synthetic 164

VCV utterances 297
verb
group 121,125
phrase 138
voice source signal reconstruction 296
vowel
raising 275
reduction 171
shortening 275

waveform editor (SESAM) 211
word duration 230
word grammar 73
word stress (see stress)
working environment 165

χ-elision 274
X-windows 324

zeros (anti-formants) 290

Bei Fragen zur Produktsicherheit wenden Sie sich bitte an:
If you have any questions regarding product safety,
please contact:

Walter de Gruyter GmbH
Genthiner Straße 13
10785 Berlin
productsafety@degruyterbrill.com